AIM Higher!

ISAT Language Arts Review

Level H

Robert D. Shepherd

Victoria S. Fortune

aim higher!®
Great Source Education Group
Wilmington, MA

Editorial Staff

Dan Carsen
Victoria S. Fortune
Robert D. Shepherd
Barbara R. Stratton

Design & Production Staff

Kazuko Ashizawa
Paige Larkin

Cover Design

Seann Dwyer, Studio Montage, St. Louis

Cover Photo

© Ariel Skelley/CORBIS

Consultant

Jennifer Aldred, Reading Consultant

aim higher! More than just teaching to the test™

Trademarks and trade names are shown in this book strictly for illustrative purposes and are the property of their respective owners. The authors' references herein should not be regarded as affecting their validity.

Copyright © 2003 by Great Source Education Group, a division of Houghton Mifflin Company.
All rights reserved.

Great Source® and AIM Higher® are registered trademarks of Houghton Mifflin Company.

No part of this work may be reproduced or transmitted in any form or by any means, electronic or mechanical, including photocopying and recording, or by any information storage or retrieval system without the prior written permission of Great Source Education Group, a division of Houghton Mifflin Company, unless such copying is expressly permitted by federal copyright law. Address inquiries to: Permissions, Great Source Education Group, 181 Ballardvale Street, Wilmington, MA 01887.

First Edition

Printed in the United States of America

1 2 3 4 5 6 7 8 9 10   DBH   07 06 05 04 03

International Standard Book Number: 1-58171-451-3

Contents

Pretest 1

Part 1: Test-Taking Strategies

1 This Is Only a Test • Test-Taking Strategies 33
   Types of Test 40
   Preparing for Tests 42
   Types of Test Question 44

2 ISAT for Reading/ISAT for Writing • Understanding Your State Exams 47

Part 2: Reading Skills Review

3 Words for the Wise • Developing Your Vocabulary 57
   Using Context Clues 63
   Using Word Parts 66
   Building a Strong Vocabulary 72

4 Picture This! • Notetaking and Graphic Organizers 73
   Tools for Gathering, Organizing, and Presenting Ideas ... 79
   Notes in Rough Outline Form 80
   Types of Graphic Organizer 84

5 Talking Back to Books • Active Reading 95
   Before Reading: Previewing a Selection 104
   During Reading: Using Active Reading Strategies 111
   After Reading: Reflecting and Responding 112

6 I Think I've Got It! • Reading Comprehension .. 115
   Responding to Questions about the Main Idea 123
   Responding to Questions about Supporting Details 125
   Responding to Questions about Sequence 126
   Responding to Questions about Cause and Effect 127
   Responding to Questions That Require Inferences 129

Part 3: Genre-Specific Reading Skills

7 A Tale to Tell • Understanding Fictional Narratives 137
   Elements of Narrative Fiction 144
   Two Approaches to Analyzing a Story 146
   Presenting Evidence: Quotations, Paraphrases, and Summaries 157

8 Real People, Real Events • Understanding Nonfiction Narratives 163
   What Is Nonfiction? 168
   Understanding Nonfiction Narratives 172
   Purpose in Nonfiction Narratives 173
   Elements of Nonfiction Narratives 173
   Actively Reading a Nonfiction Narrative 175

9 Just the Facts • Understanding Informative Nonfiction 183
   Informative Writing in Everyday Life 188
   Accuracy in Informative Writing 189
   Strategies for Informative Writing 192

10 A Matter of Opinion • Understanding Persuasive Nonfiction 203
   Understanding Facts and Opinions 211
   Understanding Persuasion 221

Part 4: Writing Skills Review

11 Step by Step • The Writing Process for Examinations 231
   Stages in the Process of Writing 238
   Variations on the Writing Process 241
   Prewriting 241
   Drafting 264
   Evaluation and Revision 265
   Proofreading Your Work 269

12 Sentence Sense • Constructing and Editing Sentences 275
   Sentence Types 280
   Expanding and Combining Sentences 286
   Editing and Proofreading Sentences 292

13 Perfect Paragraphs • Main Ideas and Supporting Details 299
   What Is a Paragraph? 304
   Ordering and Organizing Ideas in a Paragraph .. 311

14 Excellent Essays • Introduction, Body, and Conclusion 317
   What Is an Essay? 322
   Prewriting: Planning an Essay 325
   Drafting: Writing the Introduction 329
   Drafting: Writing the Body Paragraphs 332
   Writing the Conclusion 338

Part 5: Reading and Writing— Beyond the Basics

15 Stylin' • Voice and Style in Writing 341
   Different Voices for Different Audiences and Purposes .. 349
   Elements of Voice: Level, or Register 350
   Elements of Voice: Word Choice, or Diction 355
   Elements of Voice: Mood and Tone 367
   Elements of Voice: Concreteness versus Abstractness ... 373
   Other Elements of Voice 375

16 Mind Matters • Reading, Writing, and Thinking 377
   Thinking Critically 384
   Thinking Creatively 400

Part 6: Guided Writing Practice

17 Guided Practice: Writing about Literature 409

18 Guided Practice: Writing Narrative Nonfiction .. 415

19 Guided Practice: Expository, or Informative, Writing 419

20 Guided Practice: Persuasive Writing 423

Posttest 427

Glossary 465

Index 474

iv AIM Higher! ISAT Language Arts Review

© Great Source. All rights reserved.

Pretest

ISAT for Reading
ISAT for Writing

Pretest

ISAT for Reading and Writing

This Pretest is like the Illinois Standards Achievement Test (ISAT) for Reading and the Illinois Standards Achievement Test (ISAT) for Writing. The Pretest is organized as follows:

Part 1: ISAT for Reading

Session 1: One reading selection with multiple-choice questions and an extended-response question

Session 2: Two reading selections with multiple-choice questions

Session 3: One reading selection with multiple-choice questions and an extended-response question

Part 2: ISAT for Writing

Session 1: Response to one assigned writing prompt

Session 2: Response to one writing prompt chosen by the student

ISAT for Reading: SESSION 1

Directions This story is about a young boy who learns some valuable lessons about basketball and about life. Read the story. Then answer multiple-choice questions 1 through 20 and the extended-response question.

Knowing the Ledge
by Dan Carsen

"Man, Hector, when Friday's basketball tryout comes, you better hope the team needs a backup backup towel boy! Baaahhh ha ha ha!"

For the third day in a row, Marco was picking on Hector while Tony and Darius laughed. Each recess period that week had been the same: Instead of cracking jokes about one another, as they usually did, Marco, Tony, and Darius had decided that little Hector was an easy new target. Hector had just missed another lay-up on the school's outdoor court. Marco, the tallest of all the boys, was trying to look big and tough by making Hector seem small and weak.

Hector was already nervous. Tryouts for the school basketball team were only two days away. He wanted to make the team badly because some of his buddies would probably be on it, too. For several weeks, Hector had been practicing at lunchtime, at recess, and even at home with his sister, but today he felt as if it had all been a waste of time. As the bell rang and teachers began calling everyone inside, Hector mumbled to himself, "Man, I can't even make a lay-up."

He trailed in behind the group, alone, his head down, walking slowly under the chilly gray October sky.

Later that day, Hector walked home from his bus stop in the same sad way, looking like someone who had found a million dollars but lost it a minute later. He didn't realize that his sister, Maria—or "Kip," as everyone called her—had been watching him from their window. When he came into the apartment, frown and all, she asked, "Hermanito, what on Earth is wrong with you?"

Hector looked at Maria for a second as he tried to hold in his feelings. Now that he was away from his friends, he burst into tears.

"I can't even make a lay-up!" he wailed. "I'll be lucky to be a towel boy. I'm too short and too skinny!"

Maria, who knew all about the pressure of trying out for basketball teams, understood exactly how her little brother felt.

"Hey, hey. Chill out, little brother. I bet that fool Marco was dissin' you again, right? Don't even worry about it. Look at me. I'm captain of the varsity squad, and I'm tiny."

"But you're bigger than me!" wailed Hector.

"Yeah, but the people I play against, and sometimes beat, are even bigger than Dad—way bigger than me. It's not all about size, Hermanito. It's about heart, hustle, and most importantly, brains. Knowledge is power. That's why I do damage on the court and in the classroom. That's why I have a scholarship, not just skills and wins, from playing basketball."

"But how can all that help me?" asked Hector, terrified, tears still streaming down his face. "I have tryouts the day after tomorrow!"

"Let's hit the court, brotherman. I'm gonna show you what you need to do, once and for all."

The air was chilly, but the sun still lit the concrete court around the corner from the apartment. It was a place that Kip knew well. She had practiced and practiced there for hours. On the weekends, she often watched the older guys play. They really knew the game, so she would study their tricks. One of the best players she had ever seen had hair that was going gray around his temples. He didn't run quite as fast or jump quite as high as some of the other players, but his team always seemed to win. It was mainly because he knew how to pass, play smart, and make his teammates better.

"All right, now, listen," said Kip, sounding like a cross between a sister, a coach, and an Army drill sergeant. "You're quick, and I've seen you pass. You're really good at those two things already. When you go to school tomorrow, I want you to remind two of your big friends—but not Marco—about how you can pass. Tell them—and this is really important—that you're going to try to be the point guard, so all you really care about is getting assists. Let them know that all they have to do is get open, and you're going to pass the ball to them so they get to score all day."

Hector nodded his head. He thought Tony and Darius would like that.

Kip went on. "Now I can help you with the two other things I think you need to be a good, smart basketball player. When you take an outside shot, do you have trouble reaching the hoop?"

"Sometimes, yeah."

"OK. This is what you do." Kip held the ball near her stomach. "Shoot from down here—get your whole body into it. Remember, there's a lot more power in your back and legs than in your arms. Make your whole body act like a powerful spring. Go ahead, try it."

They were standing a few feet behind the foul line. Hector grabbed the ball from her and then hunched over the way she had. When he sprang up and let the ball fly, it soared over the top of the backboard!

"Whoa, whoa, lil' brother! You're too strong now."

Hector smiled for the first time since recess. He began to adjust his aim for his new way of shooting the ball. After a while, he started making shots from farther away than he ever had before. He started making so many that Kip had to say something:

"Now don't get greedy. Remember, you're the point guard. It's your job to score only when a chance for a really easy shot comes along, or when no one else can. Your main job is to see the whole court and to get your teammates involved. You need to control the pace of the game, and most of all, to be careful and smart with the ball."

"OK, Hermana," said Hector. "Wasn't there something else that you said I need to know?"

"Ahhh—the most important thing of all. All great basketball players know it, even if they don't put it into words. Let me see if I can explain so a little eighth-grade biscuithead like you will understand." They both smiled at her gentle joke.

"Aha—I've got it!" she continued. "My coach put it to me like this last year. She said, 'You have to know the ledge.' I had no idea what she was talking about until she explained it some more. She said that, to be a great basketball player, especially a point guard, you have to walk a fine line—like a ledge that you don't want to fall over—between fun and discipline, between the great feeling of scoring and keeping a cool head. You have to know where that ledge is between playing smart and staying under control or getting carried away in the moment by the crowd's roar or by anger or by wanting to show off. You have to have emotion, be creative, and play hard, but you also have to remember to be intelligent and do what's best for the team at all times. You have to walk right along that thin edge for the whole game. I think that's the best way I can explain it. You understand?"

"I think so," said Hector, as he swished a twenty-five-footer through the hoop for the first time in his life. He smiled, but not too much.

The next day at lunch, Hector told Tony and Darius about his strategy.

"Hey, guys," Hector said. "If I make the team, I wanna be the point guard. I'll pass to you big guys. I'll get all the assists, and you two will get to score all day!"

Unfortunately, Marco overheard and chimed in: "You gonna pass towels to the forwards? Baaahhh ha ha ha!!"

This time, no one laughed at Marco's joke. The lunch table grew quiet. Hector turned his head from the awkward silence and looked out the cafeteria window at the school basketball court. He had a plan. He had something to give him hope. Tony and Darius seemed to be daydreaming. Maybe they were thinking about getting their names in the local newspaper by scoring so many points, with Hector's help.

After finishing their pizza, the boys had about fifteen minutes to play outside. Hector started practicing his new shot technique. Just as the net went swish, Darius came over and said, "With a shot like that, I don't know why you only want to pass, but let's practice."

Hector, Darius, and Tony began sprinting up and down the court. Hector delivered some perfectly placed passes so the two bigger boys could make lay-ups in stride, without even slowing down. Hector even practiced looking one way while passing another. He thought that that might work well against tough defenders. Darius and Tony began to enjoy playing with Hector. Being on the receiving end of such good passes was fun and good practice for games, too. The three started to communicate with each other using only their eyes and body language. It was as if they knew in advance what the others were going to do, where they were going to run, where a pass would be thrown.

They were disappointed when the bell rang and they had to go inside.

The next day was rainy and cold, so the boys couldn't practice at lunch, but Hector still had to hear Marco's taunts:

"Rain's good for your new position, towel boy. You can wash the towels just by going outside! Baaahhh ha ha ha!"

Hector ignored him, but he felt nervous. He wasn't going to get a chance to practice again, and the tryouts were going to be held on the new indoor court. Hector hadn't played on that court since his gym class had switched from basketball to other sports months earlier. After lunch, Hector managed to take his mind off the tryouts only because his science class was super-exciting: The teacher played a video about the physics and math involved in sports. Hector hoped that that was a good sign.

School was over, and the tryouts were about to start. About twenty-five students waited together in the gym. There were only twelve spots on the team. Most of the students were bigger than Hector.

The school's one gym teacher, Mr. Stitt, was also the basketball coach. In a loud, deep voice that echoed off the gym walls, he began: "OK, everyone. Let's get started. Just play your best. We're going to start with three-on-three scrimmages."

Hector, Tony, and Darius stayed close to each other to make sure they'd be on the same team for tryouts. It worked, and they were a team.

PART 1: ISAT for Reading
SESSION 1

"Know the ledge. Know the ledge," Hector repeated to himself to calm his nerves and focus his mind. The whistle blew. Hector's team started with the ball. Hector took it and started dribbling it up the court. Darius and Tony fanned out, just as they had the day before at lunchtime. Hector had an open shot at the basket, but he decided that he was too far away. He looked left but passed right, delivering a perfect bullet to Tony, who was streaking for the basket. Tony caught it in stride, leapt through the air, and kissed the ball gently off the backboard. Two points, easy as could be!

Next, a player from the other team began to run the ball down the court the other way. Hector pretended not to be looking, but quick as a cat, he pounced on the ball and stole it. The baffled player, who was a foot taller than Hector, stood between him and the basket. Hector couldn't shoot over him, but Darius came to the rescue. Just as Darius darted around the two boys toward the basket, Hector bounced a pass under the arms of the player who was guarding him. Darius scooped up the ball and scored an easy lay-up. Easy points for Darius, and another assist for Hector!

Meanwhile, Mr. Stitt was talking with a custodian who was taking a break to watch the action. Mr. Stitt said, "Did you see that? He makes it look easy for the other players. That kid's smart. How'd an eighth grader get so much court-sense? Someone must have coached him. We need a kid like that."

Hector, Darius, and Tony kept up the passing and the scoring, just as they had practiced. They won the scrimmage ten to six.

In the next scrimmage, Marco the hotshot was scoring baskets left and right, but no one else on his team even got the ball, so Marco's team was outscored ten to seven.

The tryouts continued late into the afternoon. Everyone had to shoot some foul shots. Next, Mr. Stitt ran lay-up, dribbling, and passing drills. Hector especially loved the passing drills. Marco didn't like anything unless he got to score points, and Mr. Stitt noticed the bored look on Marco's face during the drills.

At the end of the afternoon, Mr. Stitt said, "Thank you all for trying out. You're all good players, and I have some hard thinking to do this weekend. When you come to school on Monday, a list of who made the team will be posted outside the gym. Our first practice is Tuesday, so make sure to bring your basketball shoes that day. And remember, if you didn't make it, there's always the youth basketball league."

Hector was nervous all weekend. When Monday came, he ran without stopping from the bus to the gym. Only three boys from his lunchtime crew had made the team. There they were, at the top of the list—Hector, Darius, and Tony.

GO ON

Pretest

Directions *For each question, choose the best answer. You may look back at the selection as often as necessary.*

"Knowing the Ledge," by Dan Carsen

1. What role does Marco predict that Hector will end up playing on the basketball team?
    - Ⓐ point guard
    - Ⓑ guard
    - Ⓒ forward
    - Ⓓ towel boy

2. Which of the following events happens first?
    - Ⓐ Hector's sister teaches him about basketball.
    - Ⓑ Tryouts for the basketball team are announced.
    - Ⓒ Marco teases Hector cruelly.
    - Ⓓ Kip (Hector's sister) learns to play basketball.

3. Which of the following kids is the tallest?
    - Ⓐ Hector
    - Ⓑ Darius
    - Ⓒ Tony
    - Ⓓ Marco

4. How does Kip help Hector to improve his outside shot?
    - Ⓐ by teaching him to pass the ball to others
    - Ⓑ by teaching him to walk the ledge
    - Ⓒ by teaching him to keep his cool
    - Ⓓ by teaching him to use his whole body

5. Which of the following is true?
    - Ⓐ Kip is good at basketball but not good at her schoolwork.
    - Ⓑ Kip is bad at basketball but good at her schoolwork.
    - Ⓒ Kip is bad at basketball and at her schoolwork.
    - Ⓓ Kip is good at basketball and good at her schoolwork.

PART 1: ISAT for Reading
SESSION 1

6. What would Kip argue is the most important characteristic of a good basketball player?
    Ⓐ height
    Ⓑ overall size
    Ⓒ brains
    Ⓓ shooting ability

7. Why does Hector throw the ball over the backboard when he is taking the lesson from his sister?
    Ⓐ because he is too strong for his own good
    Ⓑ because the new technique he has learned gives him extra power
    Ⓒ because he is mad at his sister and disgusted with practicing basketball
    Ⓓ because the basket is set lower than on a regulation court like the one at school

8. Hector's sister's nickname is Kip. Which of these phrases, starting with the letters K, I, and P, clearly describes Kip's beliefs?
    Ⓐ Keep It Physical
    Ⓑ Kicking Is Prohibited
    Ⓒ Knowledge Is Power
    Ⓓ Kindness Is (for) Pussycats

9. The "ledge" is a symbol for what?
    Ⓐ maintaining a balance between having fun and being disciplined
    Ⓑ giving up conscious control, like someone who is free falling
    Ⓒ the wall that an athlete sometimes runs into when he or she hits a slump
    Ⓓ taking risks (that is, standing at the edge, where things are dangerous)

10. With which of the following ideas about basketball would Hector's sister agree?
    Ⓐ A good player is someone who shoots every chance he gets.
    Ⓑ A good player is someone who makes his or her teammates look good.
    Ⓒ A good player is someone who racks up a lot of points.
    Ⓓ A good player is someone who is taller and faster than other players.

GO ON

ISAT Reading and Writing Pretest 9

Pretest

11. Why does Hector's sister call him a "biscuithead"?
    - Ⓐ because she thinks that he is stupid
    - Ⓑ because she is kidding around in a friendly way
    - Ⓒ because he hasn't been listening to what she has been saying
    - Ⓓ because he has a flat-top haircut

12. Why do Darius and Tony begin to like, very much, playing with Hector?
    - Ⓐ because Hector compliments them on their shots
    - Ⓑ because Hector passes the ball to them
    - Ⓒ because Hector drops out to give them a chance to join the team
    - Ⓓ because Hector teaches them his famous "twirling on the finger" trick

13. What is the most likely reason why Marco wasn't chosen for the team?
    - Ⓐ He hogged the ball and wasn't a team player.
    - Ⓑ He used inappropriate language.
    - Ⓒ He made fun of other kids.
    - Ⓓ The coach just didn't like him, personally.

14. Why does Marco say that rain will be good for Hector's new position?
    - Ⓐ Hector will be able to run between the raindrops.
    - Ⓑ Hector will be able to use the rain to wash the team's towels.
    - Ⓒ the rain will keep Hector off the courts, so he won't embarrass himself.
    - Ⓓ Hector will amuse everyone by slipping and falling down.

15. What does the coach see in Hector?
    - Ⓐ that Hector is aggressive
    - Ⓑ that Hector is fast
    - Ⓒ that Hector is taller than other kids
    - Ⓓ that Hector is smart

PART 1: ISAT for Reading
SESSION 1

16. Hector baffles the other player by pretending not to be looking and then stealing the ball. What does *baffled* mean?
    - Ⓐ confused and surprised
    - Ⓑ happy and carefree
    - Ⓒ hopeful and encouraging
    - Ⓓ jolly and silly

17. Which character is referred to as "Hermanito" and "brotherman"?
    - Ⓐ Darius
    - Ⓑ Marco
    - Ⓒ Tony
    - Ⓓ Hector

18. Which of the following does Kip teach her brother?
    - Ⓐ Basketball is both physical and mental.
    - Ⓑ Basketball is physical, but not mental.
    - Ⓒ Basketball is mental, but not physical.
    - Ⓓ Basketball is neither physical nor mental.

19. At the beginning of the story, what is Hector very worried about?
    - Ⓐ practicing basketball with his sister, who is a great player
    - Ⓑ having mean friends who no longer want to play ball with him
    - Ⓒ trying out for the team when he doesn't feel ready for it
    - Ⓓ being disqualified from sports because his grades are so low

20. Hector tells his friends that he wants to be point guard. "I'll get all the assists," he says, "and you two will get to score all day!" In basketball, when do you get credit for an *assist*?
    - Ⓐ when you pass the ball to another player who makes a shot
    - Ⓑ when you get into position so that another player can throw the ball to you and you can take a shot
    - Ⓒ when you pass the ball under the arm of a player on the opposing team
    - Ⓓ when you make a shot over the top of the head of another player

GO ON

ISAT Reading and Writing Pretest 11

Pretest

Extended-Response Question

21. Hector's sister tells him that whether a person is playing basketball or doing schoolwork, knowledge is power. What evidence from the story supports Kip's opinion?

_____

_____

_____

_____

_____

_____

_____

_____

_____

_____

_____

_____

_____

_____

End of PART 1: SESSION 1

STOP

Note to Students: Your written response will be scored using a rubric like the one on page 50.

PART 1: ISAT for Reading
SESSION 2

ISAT for Reading: SESSION 2

Directions *This article is about the possibility of life on Mars. Read the article. Then answer multiple-choice questions 22 through 35.*

How to Become a Martian
by Gary Leavitt

Back in 1877, an astronomer in Italy named Giovanni Schiaparelli turned his telescope toward Mars and observed *canali* on the planet's surface. *Canali* is the Italian word for channels, or grooves in the surface of something. In 1894, an American businessman named Percival Lowell built an observatory near Flagstaff, Arizona, to study these channels. Lowell hypothesized that the channels on Mars were actually canals—artificial waterways built by intelligent creatures who lived on the red planet. Later research, however, including space probes sent to Mars by the United States and the Soviet Union, proved that there were no canals on Mars. The findings on these space missions dashed hopes of discovering the canal-building, intelligent Martians Lowell had envisioned.

In 1976, when NASA probes sent back pictures of the so-called "face" on Mars, some people on Earth wanted to believe that the face was a monumental carved portrait, created by a race of ancient Martians. For twenty years, the debate raged about what the face was and how it got there. In 1997, NASA's Mars Global Surveyor arrived on Mars and was able to take a photograph of the face that was ten times sharper than the original picture taken by the Viking spacecraft. Alas, the face turned out to be a rock formation, much like the mesas found in the American West. Again, dreams of finding evidence of intelligent life on Mars were dashed.

Interestingly, recent evidence shows that life might have existed on Mars at one time.

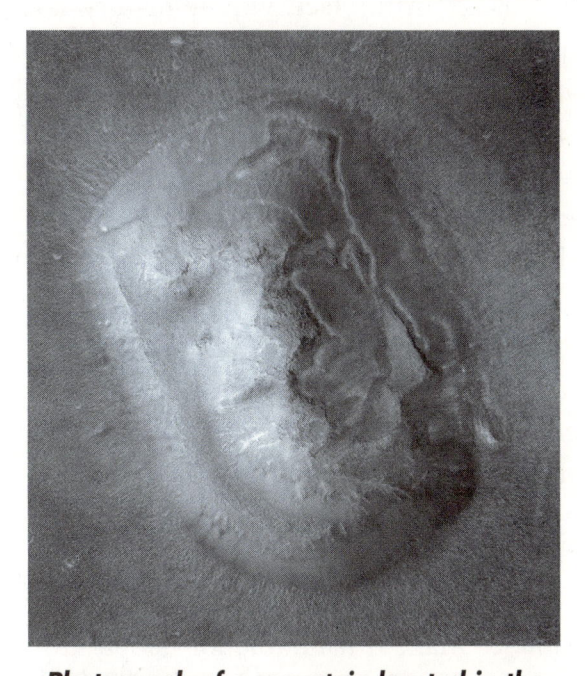

Photograph of a mountain located in the Cydonia Mensae region of the planet Mars. The photograph is of a natural landform and is not, as some people have claimed, a carving by ancient, intelligent Martians. Photo courtesy of the National Aeronautics and Space Administration (NASA/JPL/Malin Space Science Systems).

Pretest

On August 6, 1996, researchers at NASA's Johnson Space Center in Houston announced that a meteorite from Mars contains within it what might be fossils of tiny bacteria that lived on Mars 3.6 billion years ago. The fossils, which were discovered after the meteorite landed in Antarctica, are less than 1/100th the width of a human hair, hardly the highly evolved alien life forms portrayed in the movies. Nevertheless, evidence of past biological activity on Mars was a very exciting discovery.

Today, Mars is a cold, barren rock with a very thin atmosphere. Evidence suggests, however, that billions of years ago, Mars had a much denser atmosphere and lots of running water. It may be that primitive life once existed on Mars but died out. Scientists at NASA are planning future missions to Mars in order to investigate this theory further. Still, most scientists would agree that there is no evidence of intelligent life on Mars now or at any time in the past.

If Christopher McKay of the NASA Ames Research Center has his way, this scientific "fact" will be history. McKay supports the theory that it may be possible to turn Mars into a planet with an environment like that of Earth. The process of transforming Mars or any other planet to make it more like Earth is known as terraforming.

To terraform Mars, we would first have to build factories on Mars to create greenhouse gases that would help to make the atmosphere denser and more hospitable to life as we know it. As these gases raised the temperature near the surface of Mars, they would vaporize the carbon dioxide now trapped as ice in polar ice caps on Mars. This process would further increase the temperature and cause ice to melt, thereby providing the necessary water to support life. The next step would be to plant trees and other plants that would take up carbon dioxide in the atmosphere and create oxygen for people to breathe.

Eventually, by terraforming Mars, we might be able to make it habitable for people from Earth. Large colonies could be established on our neighbor in the solar system, and then there really would be intelligent life on Mars—our own descendants.

PART 1: ISAT for Reading
SESSION 2

Directions *For each question, choose the best answer. You may look back at the selection as often as necessary.*

"How to Become a Martian," by Gary Leavitt

22. What is this selection mostly about?
    - Ⓐ exploring the climate and terrain of Mars
    - Ⓑ mistakes space researchers have made
    - Ⓒ the possibility of past or future life on Mars
    - Ⓓ people who wish to live on other planets

23. Who was the first person known to have observed channels on Mars?
    - Ⓐ Percival Lowell
    - Ⓑ Giovanni Schiaparelli
    - Ⓒ Gary Leavitt
    - Ⓓ Christopher McKay

24. What was Percival Lowell's theory about how the channels on Mars got there?
    - Ⓐ They were created by rivers and streams.
    - Ⓑ They were created by melting polar ice caps.
    - Ⓒ They were canals built by Martians.
    - Ⓓ They were cracks in the planet's surface created by tectonic shifts.

25. With which statement would Giovanni Schiaparelli and Christopher McKay most likely agree?
    - Ⓐ Before researchers explore other planets, they should work to solve problems on Earth.
    - Ⓑ There are no further significant discoveries to be made about Mars.
    - Ⓒ Researchers must be certain of their findings before telling others about them.
    - Ⓓ Investigating theories that others find outlandish sometimes leads to exciting developments.

GO ON

Pretest

26. A discovery within a meteorite from Mars supports which of the following ideas?
    - Ⓐ that Antarctica and Mars have very similar climates
    - Ⓑ that Mars is currently capable of supporting life
    - Ⓒ that Mars was once capable of supporting life
    - Ⓓ that there are miniature life forms on Mars

27. What does the word *terraform* mean?
    - Ⓐ to level a natural landform, such as a mesa or hill
    - Ⓑ to describe natural landforms in terms of human characteristics
    - Ⓒ to transform another planet to make it Earthlike
    - Ⓓ to create a topographical map of the landscape of another planet

28. What does this selection imply about research theories that are later shown to be incorrect?
    - Ⓐ that those who first came up with these theories were foolish
    - Ⓑ that even incorrect theories can eventually lead to valuable discoveries
    - Ⓒ that misguided research can be costly and waste valuable resources
    - Ⓓ that those who later disprove these theories are smarter than those who proposed them

29. Which of the following is not mentioned in the article as one of the things that would need to happen before Mars could be suitable for human habitation?
    - Ⓐ Greenhouse gases would need to be produced to make the atmosphere denser.
    - Ⓑ Polar ice caps would need to melt to provide water on the planet's surface.
    - Ⓒ Plants and trees would have to be planted to create oxygen in the atmosphere.
    - Ⓓ Factories would have to be built to produce food for the people who would colonize Mars.

PART 1: ISAT for Reading
SESSION 2

30. What does Christopher McKay's research reveal about him?
    Ⓐ that he wants NASA to send him on an expedition to Mars
    Ⓑ that he is an innovative thinker who isn't afraid to take risks
    Ⓒ that he believes people will be able to live on Mars within the next decade
    Ⓓ that he finds earlier theories about the possibility of intelligent life on Mars to be ridiculous

31. According to the article, if there is life on Mars in the future, it will probably come from where?
    Ⓐ from the fossils found in the Martian meteorites
    Ⓑ from Earthlings who have colonized the planet
    Ⓒ from a planet outside our solar system
    Ⓓ from life carried to Mars aboard an asteroid or a comet

32. What does the Italian word *canali* mean?
    Ⓐ canals   Ⓑ rivers   Ⓒ channels   Ⓓ roads

33. What did the "face" on Mars turn out to be?
    Ⓐ a natural rock formation like a mesa
    Ⓑ a monumental sculpture built by ancient Martians
    Ⓒ lines left by creatures that once lived on Mars but died out
    Ⓓ a basin, or hole, formed in ancient times by a spring, or water source

34. Which of the following statements about Mars is true?
    Ⓐ It is covered with canals built by intelligent creatures.
    Ⓑ It features a monumental sculpture of a face.
    Ⓒ It contains fossils of what look like ancient bacteria.
    Ⓓ It is too far away for us to explore it.

35. The facts that Mars once had running water and a denser atmosphere support which of the following ideas?
    Ⓐ Mars was always too hot to have life on it.
    Ⓑ Mars was always too cold to have life on it.
    Ⓒ Mars could have had life on it at one time.
    Ⓓ Mars never, at any time, had life on it.

GO ON

ISAT Reading and Writing Pretest 17

Pretest

ISAT for Reading: SESSION 2, continued

Directions *This selection is about a family making a big change. Read the selection. Then answer multiple-choice questions 36 through 49.*

Leaving Taiwan
by Lucy Lee

In the living room of an apartment in Tienhsiang, Taiwan, a family anxiously awaited the return of Father. Six-year-old Jung danced around the room. Mother sat reading on a mat on the floor. Twelve-year-old Chiang was slumped in a corner, looking glum. He sighed heavily and then asked, "Mother, when do you think Father will return?"

"When, Mother, when?" cried out Jung.

"He will be home as soon as he finds out," answered their mother.

"Finds out," Chiang echoed. "Finds out whether we can go to the United States. Finds out whether we can move to America."

"Aren't you excited about moving to America?" said Jung.

"I think it would be more exciting to stay here in our own home. Wouldn't you miss living in Taiwan? Wouldn't you miss playing with your friends?" asked Chiang.

"I don't know," said Jung, suddenly confused. She stopped dancing and stood motionless for the first time all afternoon.

"Moving to the United States could be a wonderful opportunity," said Mother. "We would be lucky if we could get visas so we could move there."

"Lucky?" said Chiang. "How can it be lucky to leave our friends and family, to move so far away from home?"

"America offers more opportunities, especially for you and Jung," said Mother. "In America, you can be anything you want when you grow up."

"Can I go to ballet class and be a ballerina?" asked Jung, jumping up on her toes and twirling around.

"If that is what you want," laughed Mother.

"What I want," Chiang announced, "is for things to stay just the way they are now."

Mother put down her book and looked a long time at Chiang, as if she were studying him. Then she said, "I know how you feel, son. But that is impossible, even if we do not go to America."

Chiang sat silently for a while, thinking about what Mother had said. Suddenly, the family heard the front door of the apartment swing open.

"Father!" cried Jung, running down the hallway to greet him.

Moments later, Father was standing in the living room with Jung in his arms and a huge smile on his face.

"We got the visas!" he announced. "In a few months we will move to America."

"Oh, Father!" shouted Jung, throwing her arms around his neck.

Mother stood up and went to embrace Father and Jung. Chiang saw happiness shining in Mother's eyes.

He sat in the corner, watching his family uncertainly. "Mother, Father," he said, "do you really think life will be better for us in America?"

"Chiang," Father answered, "if your mother and I were not completely convinced this was the best thing for you and your sister, we would never take you away from your home here."

"It will be a challenge at first," added Mother. "New roads can be frightening because you don't know what to expect, but they can be exciting, too. It will be well worth the change."

Chiang began to think about America—what he had read about or seen in the movies and heard from friends.

"Will life be very different in America?" he asked.

"Chiang, I would not tell you something that is not true," said Father. "America *is* very different from Taiwan; we will all have to adjust. You will have to learn to speak a new language and meet new people from many countries around the world. Their ways and customs may seem strange at first, but think of all you will learn. You will make new friends with American boys and girls. You will learn to play their games, and you can teach them yours. You will even find that some of your games are the same. You can look forward to many exciting times."

Chiang remained quiet for a few moments while his parents watched him anxiously. Slowly, a thin smile spread across his face. "I think I might be able to learn a lot about America by going to baseball games!" he exclaimed.

Amid the laughter, Chiang joined his family's circle as they celebrated the new direction their life would take in America.

Pretest

Directions For each question, choose the best answer. You may look back at the selection as often as necessary.

from "Leaving Taiwan," by Lucy Lee

36. Where is the family in this selection considering moving?
    - Ⓐ to Taiwan
    - Ⓑ to Hong Kong
    - Ⓒ to mainland China
    - Ⓓ to the United States

37. At the beginning of the selection, why are the family members who are gathered in the living room anxious?
    - Ⓐ They all agree that they do not want to leave Taiwan.
    - Ⓑ They are waiting to find out if Father has gotten visas.
    - Ⓒ They are waiting to find out if Father has lost his job.
    - Ⓓ They all agree that they do want to leave Taiwan.

38. At the beginning of the selection, why is Chiang glum?
    - Ⓐ He wants to go to the United States, but his sister doesn't.
    - Ⓑ He does not want to go to the United States.
    - Ⓒ His best friend has just moved to the United States.
    - Ⓓ His father has told him that he cannot watch baseball on television.

39. What is one major theme of this selection?
    - Ⓐ Nothing really changes; in other words, all change is an illusion.
    - Ⓑ Change can be really negative, so learn to appreciate what you have.
    - Ⓒ By working hard at it, a person can keep change from occurring.
    - Ⓓ Change is inevitable, so people should learn to embrace change.

40. When does Chiang show his personality?
    - Ⓐ when he expresses his wish not to leave friends and family
    - Ⓑ when he listens to what his mother has to say
    - Ⓒ when he asks if the other family members would miss living in Taiwan
    - Ⓓ when he changes his mind about moving because of baseball games

**PART 1: ISAT for Reading
SESSION 2**

41. What does Jung dream of becoming in America?
  Ⓐ a teacher of English
  Ⓑ a baseball player
  Ⓒ a soap opera star
  Ⓓ a ballet dancer

42. What will Chiang probably miss most about Taiwan when his family moves?
  Ⓐ his teachers
  Ⓑ his friends
  Ⓒ the food
  Ⓓ his relatives

43. Chiang's mother assures her children of which of the following?
  Ⓐ They can look forward to many exciting times in America.
  Ⓑ America is really not very different from Taiwan.
  Ⓒ Any American can grow up to be a ballet or baseball star.
  Ⓓ They will be able to speak their own language in America.

44. What motivates Chiang's mother to want to move her family to America?
  Ⓐ the luxuries that she will be able to enjoy there
  Ⓑ the fact that in the United States, she will earn more money
  Ⓒ the increased opportunities that her children will have in the United States
  Ⓓ the fact that moving to the United States will not mean much change for her family

45. At the beginning of this story, Father is away, attempting to get visas for the family. What is a *visa*?
  Ⓐ a portrait photograph to be used on a license
  Ⓑ a document that allows a person to travel to a particular country
  Ⓒ a license that a person needs in order to drive a car
  Ⓓ a card that allows a person to take a job

GO ON

Pretest

46. Which description of the United States best fits Chiang's mother's idea of that country?
- Ⓐ the land of the free
- Ⓑ the land of the brave
- Ⓒ America the beautiful
- Ⓓ the land of opportunity

47. At the beginning of the selection, Mother is reading. Where is she sitting as she reads?
- Ⓐ in a beanbag chair
- Ⓑ on the front stoop
- Ⓒ in a collapsible lawn chair
- Ⓓ on a mat on the floor

48. Chiang sees happiness shining in his mother's eyes. What makes Mother so happy?
- Ⓐ Her daughter is going to be a famous ballet star.
- Ⓑ Father has gotten visas for the family.
- Ⓒ Her son has returned from a long journey.
- Ⓓ Father has gotten a new job in America.

49. Why does Father want the family to move?
- Ⓐ The children are sick and need medical attention in another country.
- Ⓑ They will be able to attend lots of baseball games in the other country.
- Ⓒ He and his wife are convinced that moving to the United States is the best thing for the children.
- Ⓓ He and his wife are convinced that moving to the United States will mean being able to get good jobs.

End of PART 1: SESSION 2

STOP

ISAT for Reading: SESSION 3

Directions This selection is about a man who used his imagination to solve real problems creatively. Read the selection. Then answer multiple-choice questions 50 through 69 and the extended-response question.

Rising to the Challenge
by Victoria Fortune

In late August of 1929, John J. Raskob, a wealthy businessman, and Al Smith, former governor of New York, announced that they were going to build the tallest building in the world. When the Empire State Building was completed in March of 1931, the men had indeed accomplished their task. The Empire State Building was the tallest, and many believed, the most magnificent building in the world. It no longer holds the title as the world's tallest building, but there is one record that has not been surpassed since the day the mooring mast was erected on top of this architectural icon. Never before or since has a skyscraper been built so quickly. It took only eleven months to construct the 1,252-foot structure, which towers 102 stories above the sidewalks of New York. The speed with which it was built is a testament to the imagination and efficiency of the architects and builders, particularly the head builder, Paul Starret.

Starret knew that if he could win the bid to build the Empire State Building, one of the greatest architectural feats ever undertaken, its construction would be his crowning achievement. Starret and his brother William, of the firm Starret Brothers & Eken, had the advantage of being the last builders that Raskob and Smith interviewed for the job. All the other builders who bid on the project before the Starrets touted their extensive experience and the vast amount of equipment they had on hand for the job. When the owners asked the Starrets what equipment their firm had available, Paul Starret said none. He pointed out that this building was going to be unlike any building ever constructed; they were going to have to invent new equipment. Raskob and Smith were impressed by Starret's sense of the unknowns that would be involved in the job, and Starret Brothers & Eken won the bid.

The adage "time is money" is especially true in the construction business. Each day that workmen toil on the site of a commercial building is more money spent, while none is made. With the issue of speed in mind, the architectural firm Shreve, Lamb & Harmon created an ingenious design that allowed the Empire State Building to be pieced together like a gigantic jigsaw puzzle. There was very little on-site handwork required in the design. All the pieces of the building—the massive steel girders, the 10 million bricks, the limestone façade, the aluminum spandrels and windows—were mass-produced at factories, so that they were ready to be installed as soon as they arrived at the construction site. According to the historian John Tauranac, Richard Shreve described the construction site as "a great assembly line—only the assembly line did the moving; the finished product stayed in place." That assembly line had to be kept moving at all costs, and Paul Starret came up with numerous innovations to ensure that there were no delays.

One of the builders' great concerns was the need to have plenty of materials on hand while minimizing the danger and inconvenience to nearby pedestrians and drivers. Materials were usually placed in large piles around a site, taking up valuable space in the street and often causing traffic delays and creating hazardous conditions. To resolve this problem, Starret created an unloading area in the basement of the new Empire State Building. Trucks drove right into the building to unload their materials. This delivery system was run on such a tight schedule that if a truck was late or missed its place in line, it had to wait until the next day to get back in line. The only materials that were unloaded from the street were the massive steel girders that created the frame of the building. Traffic was never stopped during the construction of the Empire State Building.

With each floor that was added, the time that it took to deliver materials up to the workmen grew longer. The traditional method of delivery was via wheelbarrow. Workmen on the upper floors often wasted valuable time waiting for the bricks, concrete, hardware, or whatever they needed to complete their tasks. To speed up the assembly line, Starret had an innovative miniature railway system installed. A set of tracks ran around each floor, and a manual lift could raise the cars all the way up to the top floor. Each cart carried the equivalent of eight wheelbarrows' worth of materials. The carts were loaded in the basement and then rolled by hand up to the workmen, who now had a constant supply of materials.

Another factor that often slowed progress was lunchtime. With thousands of workmen on site each day, it was no easy task to get them down to the ground to eat lunch and then back up to their places within half an hour. Starret again came up with a completely novel idea. He thought, if we can't get the men to lunch, we'll bring lunch to the men. He arranged with a local restaurateur to set up a cafeteria in the building. As the building rose higher, more cafeterias were added, so that the workmen never had to go more than about twenty floors to get lunch. This solution saved yet more valuable time.

The skyscraper rose almost a floor a day, or four and a half stories a week, so that it seemed to materialize almost out of nowhere, to the great astonishment of New Yorkers looking on. The architects' efficient design, along with Paul Starret's ability to think beyond the obvious and invent creative solutions to problems, were the major factors contributing to the speed with which the monumental building was erected. Tauranac compares the feat to the momentous achievements of the builders of the Gothic period, who built stone structures higher than ever before: "The builders of the Empire State Building threw steel into the sky not just higher, but faster than anybody had ever dreamed possible."

PART 1: ISAT for Reading
SESSION 3

Directions For each question, choose the best answer. You may look back at the selection as often as necessary.

"Rising to the Challenge," by Victoria Fortune

50. What is this article mostly about?
    - Ⓐ the men who owned the Empire State Building
    - Ⓑ the use of miniature railway systems on construction sites
    - Ⓒ the way skyscrapers are built
    - Ⓓ the innovations that made it possible for the Empire State Building to be built so quickly

51. Which of the following sentences states the main idea of the article?
    - Ⓐ "The adage 'time is money' is especially true in the construction business."
    - Ⓑ "The Empire State Building was the tallest, and many believed, the most magnificent building in the world."
    - Ⓒ "The speed with which it was built is a testament to the imagination and efficiency of the architects and builders, particularly the head builder, Paul Starret."
    - Ⓓ "The delivery system was run on such a tight schedule that if a truck was late or missed its place in line, it had to wait until the next day to get back in line."

52. What advantage did the Starret brothers have over the other builders who were being interviewed for the job of building the Empire State Building?
    - Ⓐ They were related to one of the owners.
    - Ⓑ They were the last builders to be interviewed.
    - Ⓒ They had the best reputation for getting a job completed on time.
    - Ⓓ None of the other builders could start the job right away.

53. What was it about Paul Starret that most impressed the owners who wanted to build the Empire State Building?
    - Ⓐ He had more experience than any of the other builders.
    - Ⓑ He understood that the job would require an innovative approach and new equipment.
    - Ⓒ He had all the necessary equipment for the job, so they would not have to buy any.
    - Ⓓ He promised to finish the building faster and more cheaply than any of the other builders.

GO ON

ISAT Reading and Writing Pretest 25

Pretest

54. Which of the following is not mentioned as one of the materials used in the construction of the Empire State Building?
- Ⓐ bronze
- Ⓑ steel
- Ⓒ limestone
- Ⓓ aluminum

55. How long did it take to build the Empire State Building?
- Ⓐ 11 months
- Ⓑ 12 months
- Ⓒ 18 months
- Ⓓ 19 months

56. In addition to Paul Starret, whom does the writer credit for the speed with which the Empire State Building was constructed?
- Ⓐ John J. Raskob
- Ⓑ Shreve, Lamb & Harmon
- Ⓒ William Starret
- Ⓓ Al Smith

57. Why was it important that the building be constructed so quickly?
- Ⓐ Renters were anxious to have access to their space.
- Ⓑ Neighbors complained about the noise and inconvenience of the construction.
- Ⓒ The builders had another big job awaiting them as soon as they finished the Empire State Building.
- Ⓓ The longer it took to construct the building, the more money it would cost.

58. How did the architects contribute to the speed with which the Empire State Building was erected?
- Ⓐ They finished the designs for the building in record time.
- Ⓑ They hired a large team of architects to work on the design.
- Ⓒ They designed the building so that it could be pieced together like a puzzle.
- Ⓓ They designed new equipment that helped speed up the construction process.

PART 1: ISAT for Reading
SESSION 3

59. Richard Shreve described the construction site as "a great assembly line—only the assembly line did the moving; the finished product stayed in place." What did he mean by this?
    A All the building materials were made at the construction site.
    B Constructing the building was tedious and repetitive work.
    C The workers moved up the building as they assembled it, rather than floors of the building moving past the workers.
    D The workers were building a "product" that would be there for many generations to come.

60. According to the article, which of the following happened first in the process of construction?
    A Materials were unloaded from trucks in the basement of the building.
    B Materials were installed by workmen.
    C Materials were manufactured at factories off-site.
    D Materials were loaded onto carts for delivery.

61. Which of the following words most accurately describes Paul Starret?
    A rigid
    B inventive
    C artistic
    D callous

62. What evidence from the selection shows that Starret was concerned about the convenience and safety of citizens who passed by the worksite?
    A He posted a lot of signs warning passersby to stay clear of the worksite.
    B He had workers hand out hard hats to people passing by the worksite.
    C He used the basement of the worksite for unloading materials, rather than using the sidewalks.
    D He hired guards to patrol the worksite and keep passersby a safe distance away.

GO ON

Pretest

63. What invention did Starret create to make sure that workmen received their materials as quickly as possible?
    - Ⓐ an elevator
    - Ⓑ a wheelbarrow
    - Ⓒ an escalator
    - Ⓓ a miniature railway system

64. Why did Starret build cafeterias inside the Empire State Building as it was being erected?
    - Ⓐ to make sure that the workers got enough to eat
    - Ⓑ to attract visitors to the Empire State Building
    - Ⓒ to make some extra money and help keep costs down
    - Ⓓ to make sure that workers ate lunch and got back to work quickly

65. The author of the article says that building a cafeteria in a worksite was "a completely novel idea." What does this mean?
    - Ⓐ It had never been done before.
    - Ⓑ It was an idea worth writing a book about.
    - Ⓒ It was a good moneymaking idea.
    - Ⓓ It was a brilliant idea.

PART 1: ISAT for Reading
SESSION 3

66. Based on information in the article, which of the following can you conclude?

- Ⓐ The Empire State Building eventually collapsed due to poor design and construction.
- Ⓑ The Empire State Building was voted the "Most Beautiful Building in the World" in 1931.
- Ⓒ The owners went bankrupt because they could not find enough renters to fill the building.
- Ⓓ Since 1931, buildings have been built that are taller than the Empire State Building.

67. Which of the following statements is true?

- Ⓐ Since the completion of the Empire State Building in 1931, more floors have been added.
- Ⓑ Five million bricks were used in the construction of the Empire State Building.
- Ⓒ To this day, no other skyscraper has been built as quickly as the Empire State Building was.
- Ⓓ Traffic around the worksite was stopped at least once a week during the construction of the Empire State Building.

68. What do the builders of the Gothic period have in common with the builders of the Empire State Building?

- Ⓐ They also built structures higher than anyone had before.
- Ⓑ They created many innovations in the building process.
- Ⓒ They built structures more quickly than anyone had before.
- Ⓓ They also built their structures out of stone.

69. Which of the following best describes the theme of this article?

- Ⓐ Constructing a skyscraper is the ultimate achievement for a builder.
- Ⓑ Do not dwell too long on your accomplishments, for they will soon be overshadowed.
- Ⓒ With great foresight and creativity, the height of humankind's imagination can become reality.
- Ⓓ Slow and steady usually wins the race.

GO ON

Pretest

Extended-Response Question

70. There is an old saying that necessity is the mother of invention. A famous American inventor, Henry Beulah, added, "If necessity is the mother of invention, then resourcefulness is the father." (Resourcefulness is the ability to use one's imagination to come up with solutions to problems.) How does this saying relate to the way that Paul Starret went about building the Empire State Building?

_____
_____
_____
_____
_____
_____
_____
_____
_____
_____
_____
_____
_____

End of PART 1: SESSION 3   STOP

Note to Students: Your written response will be scored using a rubric like the one on page 50.

PART 2: ISAT for Writing
SESSION 1

ISAT for Writing: SESSION 1

You will have forty minutes to write your essay. Use your own paper.

Narrative Prompt

Many of us have been lost or been in an unfamiliar place. Think about a time when you got lost or were in a new place for the first time.

Write a narrative essay about your experience. Describe what happened to you and how you reacted.

End of PART 2: SESSION 1

Note to Students: Your written response will be scored using a rubric like the one on pages 51–53.

Pretest

ISAT for Writing: SESSION 2

Write **one** essay. Choose between the persuasive and the expository prompt. You will have forty minutes to write your essay. Use your own paper.

Persuasive Prompt

Your school is involved in a mentorship program to help fourth graders from the local elementary school become interested in reading. Your teacher has asked everyone in your class to write a letter to a fourth grader to encourage him or her to read more.

Write a persuasive letter to a fourth grader to encourage him or her to read widely and regularly. In your letter, discuss the importance and benefits of reading. Use examples from your own experience to support your arguments.

OR

Expository Prompt

Most people have a favorite pastime that they enjoy. Whether it is art, music, sports, games, animals, collecting, or creating something, there are hundreds of ways to pass the time and enjoy oneself.

Write an expository essay providing information about one of your favorite pastimes. Explain the reasons why it is important to you and what you have learned from participating in this activity.

End of PART 2: SESSION 2

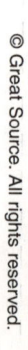

Note to Students: Your written response will be scored using a rubric like the one on pages 54–56.

Chapter 1
This Is Only a Test

Test-Taking Strategies for Language Arts Students

First Encounter

Read this short story. Then try your hand at the exercises that follow. You will not be graded on the exercises at this time. At the end of the chapter, you will be directed to return to these exercises to revise and proofread your work.

The Toughest Test in the Galaxy

by Drew Johnson

When my neighbor Ragnar first told me his secret, I was a little distracted by the fact that his face had just fallen into my sink. After all, you don't see something like that every day, do you? Now that I know his family is from a big red planet orbiting the star Proxima Centauri, the whole business of the fake face doesn't seem as weird to me. Don't get me wrong, though; having an alien as a best friend is still a little peculiar.

Maybe I should back up and explain the whole story. My family and I just moved into town a couple of weeks ago. Last Saturday afternoon, I heard a knock at the front door. Ragnar was standing outside. He introduced himself as one of my neighbors and gave me a "Welcome to the Neighborhood" fruit basket. It did strike me as odd that the fruit was all plastic, especially since one piece had a bite out of it. Still, a gift is a gift, so I accepted it gratefully and invited him inside to chat. He agreed but warned me that he had a bit of a cold.

We chatted in the living room for a while, and it turned out we had a lot in common. Ragnar told me he enjoyed playing football and soccer and that he collected bubble gum cards of famous opera singers. I didn't really understand that last part, but I love playing soccer and football as much as the next person does.

We talked for so long that our throats were getting dry, so I asked Ragnar if he would like a drink.

"Do you have any trichloromethylcarbonate solution?" he asked.

"Uh, no. I don't think so," I replied. "We do have milk, juice, and water."

"Water sounds good."

I handed Ragnar a glass and motioned him toward the kitchen sink. As he hovered over the faucet, his nose started to twitch, and his head began shaking.

"Ah, ah, ah, CHOO!" It was one of the loudest sneezes I had ever heard. I guess he sneezed so hard that he knocked his face loose, because it was lying in the sink when he finished.

I found myself staring at a lightly scaled, three-eyed being from another planet—sort of like *E.T.* meets *The Creature from the Black Lagoon.*

Talk about your new experiences!

Many people might have run screaming into the street, calling for the police. Not me, though. You see, I had a great sixth-grade social studies teacher, and she taught my class about cultural diversity. I knew that if you treat others with dignity and respect, they usually treat you the same way. I figured this was a universal truth, not just an Earthly one. Either way, I was about to find out.

"Ragnar, your face has fallen off," I said in the same sort of calm, polite voice you might use to tell someone that his shoes are untied. "Can I get you some—I don't know—some glue or something?"

"Uh, thanks, Kyle, but I don't need glue. This thing," he pointed to his face, "hooks right onto my primary ears." He put his human face back on. "Nifty, huh?" My calmness must have degenerated into something like panic, because he quickly

First Encounter

added, "I guess I have some explaining to do."

I agreed that an explanation would be a big help toward letting me sleep at night, so Ragnar told his story. It turns out that his family had recently moved to Earth so that he could get a decent education. On his home planet, Wenerehwon, the opportunity to go to high school was granted to only a handful of students from a population of many millions.

"You have to pass a test to get into high school," Ragnar explained.

"Hey, we have tests like that here on Earth," I told him. "We have these state tests. You have to pass them to get a high-school diploma."

"You do? Oh, no!" Ragnar looked so upset that I was worried that his face might fall off again.

"Hey, Rags, take it easy. State tests aren't so difficult."

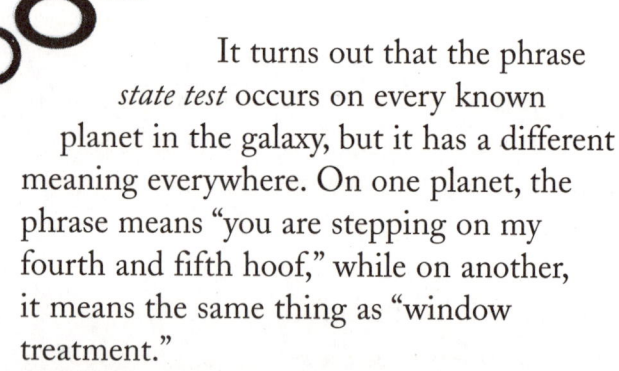

It turns out that the phrase *state test* occurs on every known planet in the galaxy, but it has a different meaning everywhere. On one planet, the phrase means "you are stepping on my fourth and fifth hoof," while on another, it means the same thing as "window treatment."

"On my planet," explained Ragnar, "there is only one state, and the state test consists of only one question. The instructor asks, 'What am I thinking of?' and if you answer incorrectly, you don't get to go to high school. I answered, 'You are

36 AIM Higher! ISAT Language Arts Review

thinking of a spotted monkey snowboarding down a diamond mountain,' but it turns out the instructor was thinking about having a tuna sandwich for lunch."

I was wondering how they came to have tuna sandwiches on the planet Wenerehwon, but I said, "Your planet's state test seems pretty unfair. I mean, there's no way to prepare for a test like that, and it tests nothing except how lucky you are. On Earth, our state tests are easier than yours. You can prepare for our tests by studying the skills and concepts described in the state standards and by learning about how to take tests well."

"Are you saying that more than 0.000001% of the population can pass your tests?" he asked.

"Sure. If you combine knowledge of the strategies with a positive approach to the test, you can get a passing score. It takes a little bit of work, but everyone—human or alien—can have a good chance of passing."

Ragnar paused for a moment and then asked, "This state test—Kyle, will you help me prepare for it?"

We made a bargain. I would help Ragnar learn the skills and strategies needed to pass the state language arts test, and Ragnar would take me to visit Europa (one of the moons of Jupiter) for my fourteenth birthday. It was a good deal for both of us.

We shook hands to seal the deal. "I actually have a chance to pass a state test," Ragnar mused. "I can definitely say that it would be a new experience for me."

"OK, then, Spaceman," I said, "Let's get started."

Test-Taking Strategies

Your Turn

Exercise A Recalling and Interpreting Answer the questions in complete sentences.

1. **A. Recalling Details**

   What gift did Ragnar bring to his new neighbor? What does Ragnar like to collect? To drink?

   _____
   _____
   _____

   B. Interpreting Details

   Even before the "face-off" incident, there were some indications that Ragnar might be an alien. What were these signs, and what was unusual about them?

   _____
   _____
   _____

2. **A. Recalling Details**

   What does Kyle offer to Ragnar to help the alien fix his face?

   _____
   _____
   _____

   B. Interpreting Details

   What do you think Kyle is feeling when he sees Ragnar's face fall off, and why doesn't he run screaming into the street?

   _____
   _____
   _____

3. A. Recalling Details

On the planet Wenerehwon, what is the sole question on the state test?

_____

_____

B. Interpreting Details

How does Ragnar feel about the state test on his planet, and how do you know?

_____

_____

_____

4. A. Recalling Details

What does Kyle tell Ragnar about state tests on planet Earth?

_____

_____

_____

B. Interpreting Details

In what ways are state tests on Earth different from state tests on Wenerehwon?

_____

_____

_____

_____

Meets ISAT Standards
1.A.3b
1.B.3c
1.B.3d
1.C.3a
1.C.3d
2.B.3c
3.A.3
3.B.3a
3.C.3a
5.C.3c

Throughout this text, standards will appear in a box like this one. The standards listed in the box cover the concepts and skills explained on the page or two-page spread where the box appears.

Exercise B Synthesizing In the short story you read at the beginning of this chapter, the main character offers to help an alien to do well on a state examination. Imagine that an alien from another planet has asked you for advice on how to do well on this kind of exam. What advice would you give the alien? On your own paper, write a letter that offers tips and suggestions that might help an alien to succeed when taking a state test on Earth. Make notes before you begin to write.

Test-Taking Strategies 39

Test-Taking Strategies

This Is Only a Test

Tests exist everywhere in our society, not just in school. In fact, newborn babies are given a test, called the APGAR, at one minute and again at five minutes after they are born, to find out how responsive they are. (In case you are interested, APGAR is a test of Activity, Pulse, the Grimace reflex, Appearance, and Respiration.) As you can see, the testing process begins early!

APGAR is just the first of hundreds of tests that the average person encounters in a lifetime. Pie-eating contests, three-legged races, and other such events are all kinds of tests. Just to get a driver's license, a person has to pass a test on traffic laws and regulations. Even a generally mind-numbing activity like watching television can include testing. After all, game shows test knowledge of everything from history and geography to movies, sports, and current events.

The simple truth is that you will encounter tests in one form or another throughout your entire life. Clearly, therefore, the more test-taking skills you can learn, the better off you will be. The rest of this chapter will describe some of the most important school-related tests you will encounter and provide some suggestions about how to prepare for them.

Types of Test

Imagine that a group of ten students is asked to draw a picture of a dog. Each of the drawings will probably contain similar elements, since everybody will draw an animal with two eyes and four legs. Yet the word *dog* is not very specific, so any two people would create different pictures. One might draw a realistic Doberman pinscher, while the other might draw a cartoon Chihuahua.

Just like dogs, most tests share some basic characteristics, but there is also a great deal of variation among them. Learning about the different types of tests can help you to understand and prepare for them better. You do not want to prepare for a little Chihuahua-like test, only to find yourself confronted by an exam that is more like a snarling Doberman pinscher.

40 AIM Higher! ISAT Language Arts Review

Here is a list of the types of test you will encounter throughout your academic career:

> Meets ISAT Standards
> 1.A.3b
> 1.B.3c
> 1.B.3d
> 1.C.3a

There are two major types of test, achievement tests and aptitude tests.

Aptitude Test. An **aptitude test** attempts to measure an individual's underlying ability, or potential. IQ tests are a well-known type of aptitude test. An aptitude test for typing would measure not whether a person already knew how to type but rather such skills as manual dexterity, hand-eye coordination, and so on—the underlying abilities that a person needs in order to become a really good typist.

Achievement Tests. An **achievement test** measures what a student has learned. Suppose that an employer asks a potential employee to take a typing test. The test requires the job applicant to retype a passage, typing as many words as he or she can in five minute's time. That would be an achievement test. The test measures how well the applicant has learned the skill of typing.

Three types of achievement test are the classroom test; the standardized, norm-referenced test; and the criterion-referenced test.

- **Classroom Tests.** Most of the tests that you will take during your school years will be **classroom tests.** These are given by individual teachers and are designed to find out whether you have learned certain skills and concepts from your classwork.

- **Standardized, Norm-Referenced Tests.** A standardized test, also known as a norm-referenced test, is one that is used to compare the skills of individuals and groups. Examples of standardized, norm-referenced tests include the Iowa Test of Basic Skills (ITBS), the Comprehensive Test of Basic Skills (CTBS), the Metropolitan Achievement Test (MAT), and the National Assessment of Educational Progress (NAEP) tests. When you take such a test, you can find out how your scores compare to those of other students of your age, background, and region.

- **Criterion-Referenced Tests.** These exams assess a student's ability to meet a set of standards for achievement. In simple terms, **standards** are lists of skills and concepts that students are supposed to master. Each state has its own set of academic standards. State standards are often broken down into **benchmarks** that tell what a student is supposed to know or be able to do at a certain age or grade level. (Throughout this book, when part of a lesson deals with a goal or benchmark from your state's standards, that standard is listed in a box like the one on this page.) This book has been prepared to help you to meet or exceed the standards tested by the **ISAT Reading and Writing exams.**

Test-Taking Strategies

Test-Taking Strategies

Preparing for Tests

Many of the later chapters in this book will provide specific strategies and guidelines for succeeding on the eighth-grade ISAT reading and writing exams. Before diving into the specifics, however, you should think about some general strategies for taking any kind of test. These are described in the chart below. Since you will encounter tests throughout your life, these skills will come in handy often.

Approaching Tests with Confidence

1. **Practice.** One of the best ways to improve your test scores is to take a practice test like the actual test that you will be taking. The Pretest and Posttest in this book are both practice tests for the ISAT exams. They are modeled closely on your actual state exams, and taking them will help you to become familiar with the types of question contained on those exams. Knowing beforehand the types of question and format for directions that will appear on the exams will help you to spend more time actually answering questions when you take the real exams.

2. **Believe in yourself.** Research shows that when students believe they are going to do well on an exam, their scores go up. Believe in yourself and in your abilities.

3. **Practice some more.** Study the lessons and exercises in this book. These are the best possible practice for the exams!

4. **Build your vocabulary.** Chances are very, very, very good that most tests you take in the future will have some form of writing on them. Even math tests, these days, contain word problems that require written responses. Having a large vocabulary increases your chances of succeeding on most tests. The simple reason for this is that it is hard to answer a question if you do not even understand what the question is asking. When you encounter a new word, write it down. Later, transfer the new word to a list that you keep in your journal and write down its meaning. Then, try to work the word into your own writing and speech. You'll be amazed at how much your vocabulary grows in a short time!

5. **Think positively.** Negative thoughts can cause you to fail, but positive thoughts can cause you to succeed. If you start to have negative thoughts, recall something positive about yourself. Think, "I am doing all I can to prepare for this exam." Remind yourself of times when you succeeded at difficult tasks.

6. **Simulate test conditions.** Normally, when you are taking an important exam, answering the phone and talking to your friends is not allowed. Teachers

More ▶

tend to frown on this behavior, and rightly so. With this in mind, try to study in an environment that is similar to a real test-taking situation. For example, use a desk or table, not your bed, and try to limit interruptions. Again, few teachers allow you to watch television while taking a midterm. (One way to work is to set goals for your study and then to reward yourself for accomplishing them.)

Meets ISAT Standards
1.A.3b
1.B.3c
1.B.3d
1.C.3a

7. **Sleep and eat well before the tests.** Get plenty of sleep the night before the test. Eat nutritious meals the night and morning before the tests. Do not skip breakfast. Resting and eating well will help you do your best during the exams.

8. **Do not be thrown by something you do not understand.** Remember, no one is expected to get a perfect score, and there will be a few items on every test that most people will not understand. When you come across something that you do not understand, remain calm, reread that part of the test, and try to figure out what is being said. Use the strategies described in this book to make your best guess. Then go on to the items that you do understand.

9. **Practice relaxation techniques.** Some people are helped by such techniques as breathing slowly and deeply or by closing their eyes and imagining pleasant, quiet scenes.

10. **Exercise your skills over a period of time.** One of the best things that you can do to get ready for a test is to find out what skills will be tested and then to practice those skills over a long period of time. Since your state exams are tests of reading and writing skills, begin now to practice your reading and writing regularly. For example, every week, try to read one or two magazine articles between 400 and 1,000 words long. (Try getting a subscription to a magazine about a subject that really interests you, or check out the magazine sections in your school and community libraries.) Start keeping a journal now. Write in it every day. Here are some possibilities for types of entry that you could make a regular part of your journal:

Journal Ideas

Dear Diary. Simply tell what happened in your day.

Feelings First. Describe your changing feelings about people, places, things, and events around you.

Great Expectations. Describe your goals, dreams, wishes, and hopes for the future.

Imaginings. Let yourself go. Describe daydreams and wild imaginings that answer *What if?* questions, like *What if dogs could read minds?* or *What if kids ran schools?*

News Views. Be a pundit! Give your reactions to and opinions about current events.

Critically Speaking. Write your own mini-reviews of movies, television shows, sporting events, CDs, and computer games.

More ▶

Test-Taking Strategies 43

Test-Taking Strategies

Personal Portraits. Create character sketches of people you know. (Be kind!)

The Fame Game. Create character sketches of famous people (celebrities, historical figures, etc.).

Learning Log. Tell about the new things that you've learned in school and in life.

On the Agenda. Make to-do lists for tomorrow, next week, ten years from now, or fifty years from now.

Dream Team. Record your dreams. (You'll remember them more easily if you lie awake in bed in the morning for a bit, thinking about what they were.)

Credos. Tell what you believe in strongly and why.

Kudos. If you were handing out prizes, to whom would you give them and why? Explain.

Suggestion Box. Describe ways to make the world a better place.

Eye Catching. Describe the marvelous or weird things that you notice around you during the day—especially those unusual things that people might overlook, like a sandwich sitting on a mailbox or a big, burly weight-lifter type buying a home-and-garden magazine.

Types of Test Question

There are many different question types, but two of the most common are multiple-choice questions and extended-response questions. **Multiple-choice questions** ask a question and then provide possible answer choices. Your goal is to pick the best possible response. **Extended-response questions** ask a question but provide nothing else. It is up to you to generate your own response and write it in the space provided.

In general, extended-response questions are harder to answer than multiple-choice questions. This can be illustrated by looking at the two problems below.

1. Where can the largest of all rodents be found, what is this rodent called, and what parts of its habitat are most important for its existence? Explain in a brief essay. *(extended-response question)*

2. What is the largest rodent in South America? *(multiple-choice question)*
   - Ⓐ the blue whale
   - Ⓑ the common mouse
   - Ⓒ the capybara
   - Ⓓ the beaver

Most multiple-choice questions can be separated into two parts, a leader line and answers. The leader line asks you a question. In this case, the **leader line** is "What is the scientific name of the largest..." **Answers** are simply the choices from which you have to pick the best answer. Of these answers, all but one, in most cases, are **distractors**—answers that are incorrect. Make sure that you understand the leader line before you proceed to look at the answers. This prevents mistakes caused by rushing and not reading the question properly. Eliminating distractors is another good strategy for approaching multiple-choice questions.

Both questions deal with the capybara, but the second one is obviously easier. If you do not know the answer to Question 1, your chances of guessing correctly are very slim. With Question 2, your goal is to pick the correct answer choice, so you have a one-in-four chance of guessing correctly.

These are already better odds than you had with Question 1, but with a little work, you can increase your chances even more. Look at the four choices and eliminate any choices you know are incorrect. Choice A can be eliminated, since the blue whale is not a rodent, and it does not live in South America. It travels in the oceans around South America, but it almost never goes ashore (thankfully). This leaves you with three choices.

A capybara

Choice B, *the mouse*, might appeal to many students because they have heard the words *mouse* and *rodent* together. In other words, this answer is the only one they recognize, so they pick it. Ask yourself, however, "How big is a mouse? Is there a chance that it is the *largest* rodent in South America?" Obviously, you are much better off choosing between Choices C and D. Which is it? The answer is C, but more importantly, you had a fifty-fifty chance of getting Question 2 correct. Compare these odds with your odds of guessing correctly the answer to Question 1!

A good approach to writing for state tests will be covered in later chapters. For now, look over these tips for handling multiple-choice questions:

Meets ISAT
Standards
1.A.3b
1.B.3c
1.B.3d
1.C.3a

How to Approach Multiple-Choice Questions

1. If you do not immediately know the answer to a question, go on to the other questions and come back later to the one you could not answer.

2. Pay particular attention to negative words, such as *not* or *except*, in directions or leader lines.

3. Eliminate answers that are obviously wrong first. Then choose the one that seems most likely from the ones that remain. (This was a technique used to answer the sample multiple-choice question above.)

4. Remember that on multiple-choice tests, you are supposed to choose the *best* answer to the question. If one answer is partly right but another is completely right, choose the one that is completely right.

5. For some tests, wrong answers and answers left blank are given the same score. If there is no additional penalty for a wrong answer, always make your best guess when you are not sure of an answer. Eliminate any answers you know to be wrong, and choose from those that remain. You will have at least some chance of choosing the correct answer.

Test-Taking Strategies

Your Turn

Meets ISAT Standards
1.A.3b
1.B.3c
1.B.3d
1.C.3a

Exercise Fill in the circle next to the correct answer to each multiple-choice question.

1. Your state reading and writing tests are examples of _____ tests.
   - Ⓐ classroom
   - Ⓑ criterion-referenced
   - Ⓒ standardized, norm-referenced
   - Ⓓ aptitude

2. If the principal in a private school wanted to find out how well her students scored compared to students in other private schools, what kind of test might she use?
   - Ⓐ aptitude
   - Ⓑ criterion-referenced
   - Ⓒ norm-referenced
   - Ⓓ achievement

3. A(n) _____ question is one that requires a student to create an answer on his or her own.
   - Ⓐ multiple-choice
   - Ⓑ standardized
   - Ⓒ extended-response
   - Ⓓ none of the above

4. Each of the following can help you prepare for a test EXCEPT
   - Ⓐ building your vocabulary.
   - Ⓑ having a positive attitude.
   - Ⓒ keeping a journal of new words.
   - Ⓓ getting anxious or uptight about taking it.

5. Imagine that you are taking a multiple-choice test that does NOT deduct a penalty for incorrect answers. If this is the case, you should
   - Ⓐ answer every question.
   - Ⓑ answer all the questions you know.
   - Ⓒ skip the tough questions.
   - Ⓓ try to eliminate incorrect answers to questions that are difficult. If you cannot eliminate any choices, leave the question blank.

Return to the exercises at the beginning of the chapter, revise your work as necessary, and submit the exercises to your teacher for grading.

Chapter 2
ISAT for Reading
ISAT for Writing
Understanding Your State Exams

Understanding Your State Exams

To assess how well students in Illinois have met the state's standards in reading and writing, the State Department of Education created these tests:

- The Illinois Standards Achievement Test in Reading
- The Illinois Standards Achievement Test in Writing

These tests are commonly referred to as **ISAT for Reading** and **ISAT for Writing.** The Pretest and Posttest in this book are very similar to the ISAT Reading and Writing exams. The following is a description of the parts of these exams:

ISAT for Reading

At Grade 8, the ISAT Reading exam has three 40-minute sessions.

In **Session 1,** you will be given a single passage to read. Next, you will answer seventeen to twenty multiple-choice questions about the passage. Finally, you will answer, in writing, one extended-response question about the passage. An **extended-response question** is one that requires you to come up with your own answer and to state that answer at some length. In your answer to the extended-response question, you will have to use evidence from the reading passage.

In **Session 2,** you will be given two passages to read. You will answer fourteen multiple-choice questions about each of the passages.

Session 3 will be just like Session 1, except, of course, that the reading passage will be different.

The reading passages will be literary works or informational articles. The **literary works** will include both fiction and nonfiction passages taken from such sources as novels, short stories, and magazines. Biographies, autobiographies, personal essays, and speeches may appear in the ISAT Reading exam as either literary or informational texts. The **informational texts** used as reading passages include articles from magazines, newspapers, and trade journals and may include profiles of people or discussions of scientific or social phenomena. The questions on the ISAT Reading exam will test your ability to comprehend, or make meaning from, these literary and informational texts. Chapters 7 through 10 are devoted to teaching you how to make sense of literary and informational texts.

The multiple-choice questions on the ISAT Reading exam may ask you about vocabulary in the reading passages; about information that is **explicitly,** or directly, provided in the reading passages; or about information that is **implicitly,** or indirectly, suggested

More ▶

48 AIM Higher! ISAT Language Arts Review

by the reading passages. To answer vocabulary questions, you will have to draw upon your own knowledge of vocabulary; on **context clues,** or hints, in the readings; and on your ability to analyze words by looking at their parts (that is, their prefixes, suffixes, base words, and roots). You will learn more about the vocabulary skills in Chapter 3. To answer questions about explicit ideas, you will have to identify specific information provided in the texts. To answer questions about implicit ideas, you will have to make inferences, or draw conclusions. An **inference** is a logical conclusion based upon information that you are given. For example, suppose that you read that a character turns red, stomps his feet, and pounds a table. From these facts you might infer that the character is angry.

Meets ISAT Standards
1.A.3a
1.A.3b
1.B.3c
1.B.3d
1.C.3d
2.B.3a

ISAT for Writing

At Grade 8, the ISAT Writing exam has two 40-minute sessions.

In **Session 1,** you will be given a single writing prompt (set of directions for writing). You will spend the entire time writing in response to that prompt.

In **Session 2,** you will be given two writing prompts. You will choose one of the two prompts and spend the entire time writing in response to that prompt.

Each ISAT Writing exam contains a mixture of persuasive, expository, and narrative writing prompts. When you respond to a **persuasive** writing prompt, you take a position and develop one side of an argument. When you respond to an **expository** prompt, you explain, interpret, or describe something based upon background material or information provided in the prompt. When you respond to a **narrative** prompt, you do one of two things:

1. You recount and reflect upon a significant experience. If the prompt asks you to recount an experience, you are expected to describe the action and your own reactions.

2. You report and record reactions to an observed event. If the prompt asks you to report on an event, you are expected to tell the story of the event and describe the reactions of the participants.

Chapters 11 through 20 of this text are devoted to teaching you writing skills and preparing you for the ISAT Writing exam.

Look back over the Pretest on pages 1 through 32. Familiarize yourself with the test format and question types on the reading and writing exams.

Understanding Your State Exams 49

Understanding Your State Exams

A rubric is a list of criteria or standards used to evaluate a piece of writing. Your written responses on the ISAT for Reading and the ISAT for Writing will be scored using rubrics like the ones that appear below and on the following pages. Study these rubrics, and use them to evaluate the writing that you do for the Pretest and Posttest in this book. This will help you to understand how your written responses on the state tests will be scored. The rubric below is like the one that will be used to score your written responses to the extended-response questions in the ISAT for Reading. A 4 is the highest score.

Extended-Response Reading Rubric

4
- I demonstrate understanding by explaining the key ideas from the text, both stated and unstated.
- I use information from the text to interpret or connect the text to other situations or texts through analysis, evaluation, inference, and comparison.
- I include specific text examples and important details to support fully my explanation.
- I effectively weave text examples into my interpretation.

3
- I demonstrate understanding by explaining some key ideas from the text, both stated and unstated.
- I use information from the text to interpret or connect the text to other situations or texts, but there are some gaps in my analysis, evaluation, inference, or comparison.
- I include some examples and important details to support my explanation, but they may not be specific.
- I partially weave text examples into my interpretation.

2
- I demonstrate understanding by explaining only the stated or the unstated key ideas from the text.
- I use information from the text with little or no interpretation (a summary).
- I include only limited text examples to support my explanation.
- I use mostly the author's ideas or mostly my own ideas (unbalanced).

1
- I explain little or nothing from the text.
- I use inaccurate, unimportant, or no text examples.
- I write too little to show understanding of the text.

0
- I write nothing.
- I write nothing related to the text.
- I write about something other than the assignment.

This rubric is like the one that will be used to score your response to the narrative writing prompt in the ISAT for Writing. A 6 is the highest score.

Rubric for Narrative Writing

Score: 6

Focus
- I stayed on one subject.
- I used an engaging introduction that lets my readers know what the subject is.
- My reactions are related to the story.
- I commented on the subject by the end of the story.
- I used an effective closing that ends my story and ties the whole narrative together.

Elaboration
- I developed all major episodes equally with specific detail.
- I used many different ways to develop the details (such as points of view, dialogue, others' reactions).
- I developed most of the episodes in depth so that my readers can clearly imagine them.
- My word choice is sophisticated and adds to the detail.

Organization
- I wrote in chronological order with a beginning, middle, and end and no time gaps.
- My story flows because I tied my sentences and paragraphs together in different ways.
- All episodes and reactions are interrelated.
- All paragraphing is purposeful.
- My word choice and varied sentence structure help tie my story together.

Integration
- I wrote a fully developed narrative on the subject (focus) and included many details for all episodes (elaboration).
- I wrote the sequence of episodes in chronological order (organization), and my sentences and paragraphs fit smoothly together throughout (coherence and cohesion).

Score: 5

Focus
- I stayed on one subject.
- My audience knows what I am talking about from the beginning because I used a clear introduction.
- My reactions are related to my story.
- I commented on the subject by the end of the story.
- I used an effective closing that ends the story and ties the whole narrative together.

Elaboration
- I developed all major episodes with specific detail.
- I developed most episodes with an even amount of detail.
- I used different ways to develop the details (such as points of view, dialogue, others' reactions).
- My word choice may add to the detail.

Organization
- I wrote a developed narrative, but some parts of my paper are better than others.
- I stayed on the subject (focus), I included details for all of my episodes (elaboration), I wrote the sequence of episodes in chronological order (organization), and my sentences and paragraphs fit smoothly together in most parts of my story (coherence and cohesion).

Integration
- I wrote a developed narrative, but some parts of my paper are better than others.
- I stayed on the subject (focus), I included details for all of my episodes (elaboration), I wrote the sequence of episodes in chronological order (organization), and my sentences and paragraphs fit smoothly together in most parts of my story (coherence and cohesion).

More ▶

Understanding Your State Exams

Understanding Your State Exams

Narrative Writing Rubric, continued

Score: 4

Focus
- I stayed on one subject.
- My audience knows what I am talking about because I introduced the subject in the opening of the story.
- I included appropriate reactions.
- I commented on my subject by the end of the story.
- I used a closing.

Elaboration
- I developed many major episodes with specific detail, but some are not developed enough.
- I developed the episodes with some depth, but my readers may have questions and may not be able to imagine clearly all of the episodes.
- My word choice may add to the detail.

Organization
- I wrote in chronological order with a beginning, middle, and end, but there are some time gaps.
- Most sentences and paragraphs fit together because I used devices to make my story flow.
- I may have drifted off subject, but most episodes are in logical order.
- Most paragraphing is appropriate.
- I use some good word choice and varied sentence structure to tie my story together.

Integration
- My narrative is simple yet clear.
- I stayed on the subject (focus), gave enough details (elaboration), and used chronological order (organization).
- I could have explained my episodes in more depth.

Score: 3

Focus
- My subject is clear, but my readers may need to read the prompt to understand the story.
- I may have drifted off subject.
- I included my reactions.
- I may not have included a closing.

Elaboration
- I developed some of my major episodes with specific details, but some are not detailed enough.
- I may have repeated the same details.
- I may have listed only some episodes and reactions.
- The story may not have enough depth for my readers to imagine the episodes.

Organization
- I wrote a story in chronological order with a beginning, middle, and end, but it has many time gaps.
- The transitions I used may confuse my readers or interfere with their ability to understand my story.
- Some of my paragraphing is appropriate.
- I may have drifted way off subject.

Integration
- I stayed on the subject most of the time (focus), gave some details (elaboration), and wrote the story mostly in chronological order (organization).
- My readers must figure out what I am writing about because at least one of the episodes is incomplete.

More ▶

52 AIM Higher! ISAT Language Arts Review

Narrative Writing Rubric, continued

Score: 2

Focus
- My subject may be unclear.
- I repeated the same details over and over.
- I included ideas that do not relate to my subject.
- I did not tell the story in chronological order.
- I wrote about many events without tying them together.
- I did not include my reactions.
- I have not written enough to demonstrate my skill at focusing.

Elaboration
- I listed <u>only</u> episodes or reactions without including details.
- I have written only general details, or I have merely repeated information over and over.
- I have not written enough to demonstrate my skill at elaborating my ideas.

Organization
- I tried to write a story, but my readers must figure out what I mean.
- I started with reasons or examples instead of telling a story.
- I didn't paragraph my writing appropriately.
- I drifted way off subject.
- I did not write enough to demonstrate my skill at organizing my ideas.

Integration
- I tried to write a narrative, but I didn't stay on the subject (focus), give enough details (elaboration), or write in chronological order (organization).
- My readers may be confused.
- I did not write enough to demonstrate my skill at combining focus, elaboration, and organization.

Score: 1

Focus
- My subject is unclear.
- I did not include any reactions.
- I have not written enough to demonstrate my skill at focusing.

Elaboration
- My subject is unclear.
- I have not written enough to demonstrate my skill at elaborating my ideas.

Organization
- I did not use chronological order or paragraphing to tell my story.
- I did not write enough to demonstrate my skill at organizing my ideas.

Integration
- I did not write about the topic or I did not complete the assignment.
- I did not write enough to demonstrate my skill at combining focus, elaboration, and organization.

Conventions   Score: 2
- I have mastered correct use of sentence construction.
- I use pronouns correctly.
- I have few run-ons or fragments in proportion to the amount I have written.
- I have mastered basic use of punctuation and capitalization.
- I have mastered correct use of verb tense and subject-verb agreement.
- I have few minor and very few major errors in my writing.

Conventions   Score: 1
- The number of errors in my paper interferes with my readers' understanding of what I have written.

Understanding Your State Exams

This rubric is like the one that will be used to score your response to the persuasive or expository writing prompt on the ISAT for Writing. A 6 is the highest score.

Rubric for Persuasive or Expository Writing

Score: 6

Focus
- My subject or position is clear.
- I have an engaging opening.
- I commented on my subject.
- I have an effective closing that ends the paper and ties the whole paper together.

Support
- I used many ways to develop details and support, such as evidence, explanations, and examples.
- All of my major points are developed in specific detail.
- I used interesting words throughout.
- I used details evenly.

Organization
- I used appropriate paragraphing.
- My writing flows easily from one idea to the next.
- I varied my sentence structure and word choice.
- All of my paragraphing is purposeful and appropriate.
- I tied my sentences and paragraphs together in different ways, such as parallel structure, pronouns, transitions that indicate time, to make my story flow (coherence and cohesion).

Integration
- I have a fully developed paper for my grade level.
- I have a clear and developed focus.
- I included balanced, specific details.
- My sentences and paragraphs fit smoothly together.

Score: 5

Focus
- I wrote an introduction that makes my subject and position clear.
- My closing does more than restate what is in my introduction.

Support
- I used details throughout.
- I used several ways to develop details, such as evidence, explanation, and examples.
- I used interesting words to add detail and support.

Organization
- I used appropriate paragraphing.
- My writing flows easily from one idea to the next.
- I varied my sentence structure.
- Most of my points are appropriately paragraphed.
- Some of the word choice and sentence structure I used produces cohesion.
- I tied my sentences and paragraphs together in different ways, such as parallel structure, transitions, pronouns, and repetition.

Integration
- I have a developed paper for my grade level.
- I have a clear and developed focus.
- I included specific details.
- Some parts of my paper are better than others.

More ▶

Persuasive or Expository Writing Rubric, continued

Score: 4

Focus
- My subject or position may be introduced by previewing in the introduction.
- If I previewed, I talked about only those points I previewed.
- My conclusion may be a restatement of the introduction.

Support
- I used many details. I developed most of my main points with specific details.
- All of my key points are supported, but some may have more support than others.
- I may have used some interesting words.

Organization
- Most of my paragraphing is appropriate.
- Most of my writing flows from one idea to the next.
- I tied my sentences and paragraphs together in different ways.

Integration
- My paper is simple, yet clear and appropriate for my grade level.
- I included the essentials but nothing more.

Score: 3

Focus
- My subject or position is identified in a brief opening or at least somewhere in the paper.
- I may have talked about more or fewer points than I stated in my introduction.
- I may not have a closing.
- I may not have written enough.

Support
- Some of the major points in my paper may be developed by specific detail.
- I may have included some details that give information beyond the major point.

Organization
- I may have used transitions in my paragraphs that confuse my readers.
- I used some appropriate paragraphing.
- I may have drifted off the subject.
- My writing does not flow from one idea to the next.

Integration
- My paper is partially developed for my grade level.
- My readers may need to figure out what I am writing about because at least one of the features is not complete.

More ▶

Understanding Your State Exams 55

Understanding Your State Exams

Persuasive or Expository Writing Rubric, continued

Score: 2

Focus
- My subject and event may be unclear.
- I may have been repetitious.
- I may have drifted off the subject.
- I may have written a response that is not persuasive or expository.
- I have written about multiple subjects or positions without tying them together.
- I may not have written enough.

Support
- I used few details.
- I may have used a list of details that have some extensions.
- I have written only general details, or I have merely repeated information over and over.
- I may not have written enough.

Organization
- My writing has few appropriate paragraphs.
- I drifted way off the subject.
- My writing does not flow from one idea to the next.
- The sentences in my paragraphs can be reordered without changing the meaning.
- My paper is not persuasive or expository.
- I may not have written enough.

Integration
- I am beginning to use the features of writing.
- My paper is confusing.
- I may not have written enough.
- I did not write a persuasive or expository paper.

Score: 1

Focus
- My writing is confusing.
- I have not written enough.

Support
- My writing includes no details, or the details I include are confusing.
- I have not written enough.

Organization
- My writing is confusing.
- I may not have written enough.

Integration
- My writing is confusing.
- I did not fulfill the assignment.
- I did not write enough.

Conventions   Score: 2
- I have mastered correct use of sentence construction.
- I use pronouns correctly.
- I have few run-ons or fragments in proportion to the amount I have written.
- I have mastered basic use of punctuation and capitalization.
- I have mastered correct use of verb tense and subject-verb agreement.
- I have few minor and very few major errors in my writing.

Conventions   Score: 1
- The number of errors in my paper interferes with my readers' understanding of what I have written.

Chapter 3

Words for the Wise

Developing Your Vocabulary

First Encounter

Read this short essay. Then try your hand at the exercises that follow the essay. You will not be graded on the exercises at this time. At the end of the chapter, you will be directed to return to these exercises to revise and correct your work.

From the Village to the World

by Andres Jobim

Soccer's biggest tournament, the World Cup, takes place every four years. This tournament is arguably the most popular sporting event in the world. Fans on every continent watch this international soccer meet with a passion that borders on lunacy. Thirty-two national teams vie for first place, competing against each other in ninety-minute matches. In the end, only one nation's team can claim victory. In some countries, when the national team is playing, all business comes to a halt. Buses no longer run. Shops and restaurants are closed. The streets are practically deserted. Everyone watches the game.

The first World Cup tournament was held in 1930; however, soccer (known as "football" in most countries outside the United States) has been played in one form or another for centuries. A Chinese military manual from 200 B.C. describes an exercise in which soldiers had to kick a leather ball into a net. The Romans also had a game called "Harpastum." Two teams played on a rectangular field. Each team attempted to move a ball into the opponent's territory.

Another early version of soccer was played in the villages of Great Britain from around A.D. 700. The game was called "mob football" because it resembled a donnybrook: Each match was a violent struggle, a brawl. Punching, biting, and kicking were a major part of mob football. In fact, the game was so rough that several English kings tried to prevent it from being played at all. King Henry V wanted his subjects to spend their time learning useful military skills such as archery. A game in which Englishmen kept beating each other to a pulp did not help King Henry to create the skilled army he needed. He tried to eradicate the game, but mob football survived.

During the 1800s, mob football changed quite a bit. The introduction of a standard set of rules enforced by referees greatly reduced the violence of the game. Once its former belligerence had been tamed, soccer became appealing to a larger audience. It was around this time that many English public schools (which are like private schools in this country) began to promote soccer. These schools viewed the sport as one way to keep their students healthy and robust. The schools wanted active and industrious students, not passive and indolent ones. This view of soccer as a good form of exercise continues today.

The popularity of soccer increased throughout the twentieth century. The first World Cup tournament was played in Uruguay in 1930. Only thirteen nations competed in this event. As time passed, more and more nations began to field soccer teams. By 2002, more than two hundred nations battled for the thirty-two slots in the World Cup. The tournament itself takes about one month to play. The first half lasts a fortnight. The second half of the World Cup also takes about two weeks.

Countries whose teams traditionally do well in the tournament include Italy, Germany, and Brazil. No matter which countries' teams go to the final, more than a billion people around the world will watch them play. The game has come a long way from the days of rough-and-tumble mob football.

Your Turn

Exercise A Fill in the circle next to the correct answer to each multiple-choice question. Use clues from sentences in the preceding essay to figure out what each word means.

1. Which of the following words is closest to the meaning of *vie*?
   - Ⓐ discuss
   - Ⓑ quarrel
   - Ⓒ compete
   - Ⓓ brawl

2. What does it mean to *eradicate* something?
   - Ⓐ destroy it
   - Ⓑ put it away
   - Ⓒ misplace it
   - Ⓓ sustain it

3. *Indolent* and _____ have similar meanings.
   - Ⓐ energetic
   - Ⓑ young
   - Ⓒ wiry
   - Ⓓ lazy

4. What does *donnybrook* mean?
   - Ⓐ a game of skill
   - Ⓑ a free-for-all
   - Ⓒ a boxing tournament
   - Ⓓ a celebration

5. Which of the following is a *fortnight*?
   - Ⓐ seven days
   - Ⓑ fourteen days
   - Ⓒ three weeks
   - Ⓓ seven weeks

AIM Higher! ISAT Language Arts Review

Exercise B Use a dictionary to complete the following exercise. Choose a word from the list below. (Each of these words appears in the selection you have just read about soccer.) First, write the word you have chosen and its definition. Next, choose another word in the dictionary that has the same word part and a similar meaning. Circle the part of the new word that is the same in both words. An example has been done for you.

Meets ISAT Standards
1.A.3a
1.A.3b
1.B.3c
1.B.3d
2.A.3a
3.A.3
5.B.3a

    arguably   deserted   belligerence

    lunacy   skilled   industrious

EXAMPLE:
WORD AND DEFINITION: enforced. The word enforce means "to compel, or force, observance of or obedience to" a law or a set of rules or a type of behavior.
SIMILAR WORD AND DEFINITION: forceful. The word forceful means "characterized by or full of force." Synonyms include powerful, strong, determined, and effective.

WORD AND DEFINITION: _____

_____

_____

_____

SIMILAR WORD AND DEFINITION: _____

_____

_____

_____

Exercise C On your own paper, write a sentence for each of the words that you chose for Exercise B. In each sentence, use a common type of context clue to show the meaning of the word.

Developing Your Vocabulary

Developing Your Vocabulary

Words for the Wise

Have you ever had the feeling that a newly learned word was following you? You probably never noticed the word before you learned its meaning. Suddenly, once you are familiar with this new word, it seems to appear everywhere. You see it written in huge letters on billboards. You hear it spoken on the radio. Even your parents use the word in conversation. Are they somehow *in* on this conspiracy?

If you have ever had this experience with a new word, you are not alone. It happens quite often when people learn new words. The reason is simple. When you do not know the meaning of a word, your mind often ignores it as if it weren't there. This is especially true if you understand a sentence even though you do not know what one word in it means. That word might be heard and processed by your brain at a subconscious level, but it may not be transferred to consciousness because understanding the unfamiliar word is unnecessary.

Once you learn the meaning of the word, however, you start to recognize it everywhere. Suddenly you hear and see that new word all over the place. The word was always there, but since you did not understand it and could not gain any meaning from it, you simply ignored it.

New words might seem as if they are following you, but the fact is that they have been there all along. They have not changed; you have. You are now more aware of the world around you. You understand a part of the world that you did not comprehend before. This sort of awareness is a very powerful tool to have.

Using Context Clues

Vocabulary questions are very common on state examinations. The chances are good that you can figure out the meaning of an unfamiliar word on an exam by looking at its context. The **context** of a word is simply the words that come before and after it. The hints that these words give you are called **context clues**.

Meets ISAT
Standards
1.A.3b
1.B.3c
1.B.3d

Types of Context Clue

Restatement (direct definition). The meaning of the word is stated directly in the sentence: "Thirty-two national teams *vie* for first place, competing against each other in ninety-minute matches."

Apposition. The definition of the word comes right next to it in the sentence: "The idea of time-travel creates many *paradoxes*, or apparent contradictions."

Comparison. The meaning of the word is revealed by mentioning a similarity to something already known: "Jane thought her mother was *pulchritudinous*, and everyone agreed that indeed, her mother was beautiful."

Contrast. The meaning of the word is revealed by mentioning a difference between the thing or action named by the word and something already known: "The king tried to *eradicate* the game, but somehow mob football survived."

Synonym. Another, more familiar word with a similar meaning is used: "Though the country was small, it was known to be *belligerent*, or warlike."

Antonym. Another, more familiar word with an opposite meaning is used: "The school wanted hard-working students, not *indolent* ones."

Inference. Clues and facts are provided to let you make an informed guess about the meaning of the word: "The *irascible* man screamed at the receptionist. He stamped his feet and threw magazines across the waiting room. He demanded to speak to the person in charge."

Developing Your Vocabulary

Your Turn

Exercise Fill in the circle next to the correct answer to each multiple-choice question.

1. It took four large industrial cranes just to lift the *colossal* statue off the ground.

   What does *colossal* mean?
   Ⓐ tiny
   Ⓑ artistic
   Ⓒ gigantic
   Ⓓ brittle

2. Although the commercials for the film were *tantalizing*, the film itself turned out to be very dull.

   What does *tantalizing* probably mean?
   Ⓐ very short
   Ⓑ exciting
   Ⓒ deep
   Ⓓ boring

3. There are many different *calamities*—hurricanes, earthquakes, and floods—that can cause even the sturdiest house to collapse.

   Based on the examples given, what is a *calamity*?
   Ⓐ a tornado
   Ⓑ a type of insurance
   Ⓒ a disaster
   Ⓓ an everyday event

4. Showing his skill and expertise, the driver *adroitly* steered his car around the track.

   What does *adroitly* mean?
   Ⓐ masterfully
   Ⓑ dangerously
   Ⓒ hurriedly
   Ⓓ loudly

5. College professors spend their *sabbaticals* in various ways. Some use the time to do research on subjects that interest them, some travel, and others just relax.

   Meets ISAT Standards
   1.A.3b
   1.B.3c
   1.B.3d

   What is a *sabbatical*?
   - Ⓐ a college class
   - Ⓑ a kind of currency
   - Ⓒ a leave of absence
   - Ⓓ a new job

6. Interest in the new action figure has *ebbed*. Toy stores are doing everything they can just to sell the figures that they still have in the store.

   What does *ebb* mean?
   - Ⓐ hasten
   - Ⓑ spend
   - Ⓒ increase
   - Ⓓ decline

7. Merrill was such a *narcissist*. His house was filled with mirrors so that he could admire himself at every possible moment.

   What is a *narcissist*?
   - Ⓐ someone who enjoys owning mirrors
   - Ⓑ someone who loves himself or herself excessively
   - Ⓒ someone who constantly watches his or her face for signs of aging
   - Ⓓ someone who hates to go outside

Developing Your Vocabulary

Developing Your Vocabulary

Using Word Parts

As you know, a new outfit does not have to be made up entirely of new clothes. For example, you might buy a new shirt but keep your old pair of blue jeans. The outfit is still new, since you have never worn that particular combination of clothes before, even if the blue jeans, socks, and shoes you wear along with the new shirt are clothes you have had for some time.

In the English language, many words are like new outfits. They contain parts of old words within them. This "re-wearing" of word parts can be used to your advantage. If you learn the meaning of a word part, you might be able to understand an unknown word that has the same word part in it. For example, if you know that *hydrophobia* is "fear of water," then you could guess that *hydropower* means "powered by water." The recycled word part *hydro*—the Greek word for "water"—means the same thing in both words.

The major word parts are **prefixes, suffixes, base words,** and **roots.** Word parts are used to create **derived forms** of words and **compound words.** A group of words containing a common word part is called a **word family.** The chart on the following page lists these word parts and their meanings.

Word Parts

Word Part	Definition	Example
Root	A word part that has a specific meaning and cannot stand alone	**spec** (Greek root meaning "to observe or look at," found in words like **spec**tacle and **spec**tator)
Prefix	A part added to the beginning of a word or root	**pre–, anti–** (as in **pre**view and **anti**dote)
Suffix	A part added to the end of a word or root	**–able, –ment** (as in work**able** and establish**ment**)
Base word	An ordinary word to which a prefix or suffix can be added	**resident + ial = residential** (base word with suffix)
Derived word	A word formed by adding one or more prefixes and/or suffixes to a base word or root	**practical + ity = practicality** (base word with suffix added to create a derived form)
Compound word	A word made up of two base words	**man + made = manmade** (two base words that make a compound word)
Word family	A group of words that share the same base word or root	in**spec**tion, **spec**tacle, **spec**ulate (all share the Greek root **spec**)

Notice that a base word can act as a word on its own, or it can have prefixes and suffixes added to it to create a derived word with a slightly different meaning. Base words are sometimes combined to form compound words. The meaning of a compound word is generally a combination of the meanings of the two base words. A root, however, *must* be combined with one or more other word parts to become a word. Roots alone are not considered words.

Take the time to study the charts on the following pages and become familiar with these common word parts. Learning these parts will help you to analyze unknown words and figure out their meanings. For example, if you know that the root *fungi–* means "any of the organisms in the kingdom Fungi, including mushrooms," and that the suffix *–cide* means "killing," then you can make an informed guess about the meaning of *fungicide*.

Developing Your Vocabulary

Developing Your Vocabulary

Some Common Prefixes and Suffixes

Prefix	Meaning	Example	Definition
anti–	against	*antisocial*	avoiding contact with others
bi–	two, twice	*bicycle*	two-wheeled
co–	with	*cooperate*	work with
inter–	between	*interpersonal*	between people
intra–	within	*intramural*	within the walls (of one place)
mal–	bad	*malpractice*	improper treatment
micro–	small	*microscopic*	very small
mini–	small, short	*miniseries*	small (or short) series
mis–	wrong	*misnomer*	wrong name
multi–	many	*multicultural*	representing many cultures
non–	not	*nonessential*	not essential
post–	after	*postwar*	after the war
pre–	before	*preview*	see before
pro–	forward, ahead	*proactive*	taking initiative, acting first
re–	again	*rewrite*	to write again
semi–	half, partly	*semiconscious*	partly, not fully conscious
sub–	under	*submarine*	under the sea
trans–	across	*transport*	carry across

Suffix	Meaning	Example	Definition
–al	relating to	*transitional*	relating to change
–able, –ible	capable of	*bearable*	capable of being borne
–cide	killing	*insecticide*	substance that kills insects
–fold	multiplied by	*tenfold*	ten times as much
–ful	full of	*spiteful*	full of spite
–ism	doctrine, belief	*patriotism*	belief in one's country
–itis	inflammation	*rhinitis*	inflammation of the nose
–or	one who does something	*inventor* *conductor*	one who invents one who conducts

Some Common Roots and Word Families

Root	Meaning	Examples
anim	living	animation
auto	self	autobiography
bibl, biblio	book	bibliography, bibliophile
capt	take	captive, capture
chron, chrono	time	chronology, geosynchronous
corp	body	corpus, corporeal, corps
cred	know, believe	credulous, creed, incredible
dem, demo	people	democracy, endemic
duc, duct	carry, lead	conduct, deduction, induce
ge, geo	earth	geology, geosynchronous
homo	same	homogeneous, homonym
hydro	water	hydraulic, hydrate, hydrant
junct	join	junction, conjunction
log, logy	word, thought, study of	sociology, neologism, dialogue
mand	command	mandate, reprimand
narc	numbness, stupor	narcotic, narcolepsy
path	sadness, suffering	pathological, sympathetic
phag, phagus	eat, consume	sarcophagus, esophagus, phagocyte
phil	love	philanthropy, philharmonic
phon	sound	phonic, phonograph
ped, pod, pode	foot, footlike	pedestrian, podium, pseudopod
psych	of the mind	psychology, psychosomatic
spec	see	inspection, speculate, spectacle
tange	touch, feel	intangible, tangential
tele	far, across distance	telephone, telegraph
ten	stretch or hold	tenacious, tendon
therm	heat	thermal, thermodynamic, thermometer
vor, vore	swallow, devour	carnivore, voracious

Meets ISAT Standards
1.A.3a
1.B.3c
1.B.3d
1.C.3f

Developing Your Vocabulary

Your Turn

Exercise A On each line in the chart below, you will see a word that is missing one or more of its parts (such as a prefix, root or base word, or suffix) or its definition. Fill in the definition or missing word part for each derived word below. The first one has been done for you.

	Prefix	Root or Base Word	Suffix	Definition
EXAMPLE:	un–	manage	–able	unable to be controlled or managed
1.		venge	_____	full of vengeance
2.	bi–	_____	–ly	once every two weeks
3.	inter–	department	–al	_____
4.	_____	combat	–ant	someone who does not fight in a war
5.	_____	conduct	_____	a compound or element that is partially able to conduct electricity

Exercise B Use the charts of prefixes, suffixes, and roots on the preceding pages to determine the meanings of the italicized words in the following sentences. Write the meaning of each word on the line provided.

1. The director held an *animated* discussion with the actor about showing up on time.

   _____

2. Jared had been thinking about a nature documentary that he saw on television, so when he thought he saw a tiger in the woods, this was probably an example of *autosuggestion*.

   _____

3. On the *Star Trek* television program, the characters were able to beam down from their ship to a planet's surface using *teleportation*.

   _____

70 AIM Higher! ISAT Language Arts Review

4. The divers communicated under the water by means of a *hydrophone*.

_____

Meets ISAT
Standards
1.A.3a
1.A.3b
1.B.3d

5. Scientists have found spectacular living creatures in the deepest oceans, living by means of nutrients that they get from *geothermal* gases released from cracks, or vents, in the sea floor.

_____

6. Few North Americans are *insectivores*.

_____

7. In North Africa lies the Great Sahara Desert; most of the people of the continent, of course, live in *sub-Saharan* Africa.

_____

8. People who practice different religions can learn to *coexist* in peace.

_____

9. Yolanda decided to do her *postgraduate* studies in a remote village in Uruguay.

_____

10. "Welcome, carbon-based *bipeds*," said the alien to its human visitors.

_____

Developing Your Vocabulary 71

Developing Your Vocabulary

Meets ISAT
Standards
1.A.3b
1.B.3c
1.B.3d
5.C.3c

Building a Strong Vocabulary

Learning a new word is not as simple as reading the definition of the word once and remembering it forever. It if were, we would all be enthralling raconteurs with gargantuan lexicons. Unfortunately, it is not that simple, which is why most kids have difficulty with that last sentence (translation: "interesting storytellers with enormous vocabularies").

Understanding how most people learn new words is an important step in building a vocabulary. Typically, word acquisition occurs in three stages. In the first stage, a word is not known. The unknown word is often just skipped or ignored when a person is reading or listening. Actually learning the word is the second stage of word acquisition. A word becomes part of the **passive vocabulary,** meaning that it is understood when encountered, but it is not actively used in the learner's speech and writing. In the final stage, a word becomes part of the **active vocabulary.** This means that the speaker or writer uses the word himself or herself, in addition to being able to interpret what it means when it is used by others.

Moving new words from Stage 1 to Stage 2 is important for comprehension. The key to expanding your vocabulary, however, is to move words from Stage 2 to Stage 3. The reason for this has to do with your brain's short-term memory. **Short-term memory** can be thought of as a section of your brain that has space for only about seven pieces of information at any one time.

Information is constantly moving in and out of short-term memory. This is what makes it easy to learn about a word but then forget about it quickly. What you want to do is to make sure that your brain moves the definition of a new word into your **long-term memory.** This is just what the name implies—a place where the brain stores information that can be accessed again and again over time. Words that you use in your active vocabulary are stored in your long-term memory, which is why bringing an unknown word to Stage 3 is important.

There are several steps you can take to move the definition of an unknown word into your long-term memory. Think of a time, place, or situation in which you might need to use the word. If the word reminds you of something or somebody, tie the definition of the word to your memory of that thing or person. Try to use the word at least once a day for a week. This might be easier to do than you think.

Another way to remember new words is to keep a learning log. A **learning log** is simply a journal in which you keep track of what you have learned in school and in your own life. A learning log is a great place to record new words and their definitions. Record the word, its context, and its meaning. Your learning log can serve as your personalized dictionary.

Return to the exercises at the beginning of the chapter, revise your work as necessary, and submit the exercises to your teacher for grading.

Chapter 4
Picture This!
Notetaking and Graphic Organizers

First Encounter

Below and on the following pages are these materials: an informative essay, the rough outline used to take notes on the essay, and an analysis chart used to organize information from the essay. Read these materials. Then try your hand at the exercises that follow. You will not be graded on the exercises at this time. At the end of the chapter, you will be directed to return to these exercises to revise and correct your work.

Marine Iguanas of the Galápagos

by Elena Ramirez

Iguanas are large, generally harmless lizards with spines from neck to tail. They are typically found in deserts or in tropical forests. Some, however, live much of their lives in or near the ocean. The marine iguanas of the Galápagos Islands off the coast of Ecuador are unique creatures. They differ from their land-lover cousins in their appearance, in their adaptations to both land and water, and in their feeding habits.

Marine iguanas can be readily distinguished from their land-dwelling cousins by their appearance. While most land iguanas are bright green or brown, marine iguanas are mostly black. Some males develop bright green or red splotches during the mating season. The black skin allows marine iguanas to absorb the sun's heat and blend in perfectly with the black lava rocks of the islands.

The dinosaur-like ridges and spikes on their necks and backs make marine iguanas seem ferocious and aggressive. Male iguanas occasionally attack each other, but few predators will attack an adult iguana. The iguanas' long, sharp claws help them to climb rocky cliffs and cling onto slippery rocks at low tide, especially when waves crash against them. Marine iguanas have a rounded snout, or nose, that makes it easier to use their razor-sharp teeth to scrape algae off ocean rocks. The iguanas also use their sharp teeth to chew on the seaweed. Their long tails help them to steer in the water. Their bodies are highly adapted for a dual life in the ocean and on land.

Unlike most land-dwelling iguanas, marine iguanas are able to swim and dive in the ocean. Marine iguanas can dive to depths of five to fifteen feet. Larger males can dive to about fifty feet to feed on algae on the ocean floor. These amazing lizards usually dive for a few minutes at a time, but there are records of iguanas staying underwater for half an hour.

Like land iguanas, marine iguanas are cold-blooded. They cannot regulate their body temperature, so they must rely on heat from the sun to warm their bodies. When marine iguanas swim, their heart rate decreases, and blood moves away from the surface of their skin. This conserves energy and body heat. After being in the cold ocean water, the iguanas rest in the sun to absorb more heat.

Finally, marine iguanas are unique because of their feeding habits. Marine iguanas are mostly vegetarian, dining on algae (seaweed) on rocks in or near the water. Unlike most other reptiles and mammals, marine iguanas are able to swallow seawater as they eat because of small glands between their eyes and nostrils that remove salt from the water. The iguanas store the salt in their nostrils and frequently sneeze to expel the salt. When they sneeze, the whitish salt spray sometimes comes back down on their foreheads.

Marine iguanas have adapted to their environment at the edge of the sea with great success. The marine iguanas of the Galápagos Islands have many surprising features. Their odd appearance, adaptations to both land and water, and unique feeding habits make marine iguanas one of the most interesting species in the animal kingdom.

First Encounter

The following is a rough outline of notes that one student made based on the essay on the preceding pages.

One Student's Rough Outline

Title: Marine Iguanas of the Galápagos
Author: Elena Ramirez

Intro
—Iguanas not just desert/tropical forest-dwellers
—Some live in/near sea
—Marine iguanas of Galápagos Islands near Ecuador
Thesis: Marine iguanas unique because of appearance, adaptations to land & sea, feeding habits

Odd appearance
—Black with green or red spots
    —Color = camouflage, helps lizard absorb heat
—Ridges & spikes on neck/back (like dinosaur) → protection from predators or rival males
—Sharp claws
    → can cling to rocks when waves crash
    → iguanas able to climb cliffs
—Rounded snout & sharp teeth → scrape algae from rocks
    —Eat seaweed (marine algae)
—Long tails
    —Steer in water

Adaptations to land & water
—Good swimmers & divers
    —Dive 5–15 ft.
    —Larger males dive as deep as 50 ft.
    —Hold breath for up to $\frac{1}{2}$ hr.
—Reptile (like other lizards) = cold-blooded
    —Ocean water cools them off
    —Sun warms them up
    —Rest in sun after swim/dive
—Must conserve energy & body heat when swimming
    —By decreasing heart rate
    —By moving blood away from skin

Feeding habits
—Mostly vegetarian—eat algae (seaweed) in tidepools or near shore
—Can swallow seawater—glands remove salt in water
—Store salt in glands above nostrils → sneeze it out

Meets ISAT Standards
1.A.3b
1.B.3b
1.B.3c
1.B.3d
1.C.3a
1.C.3d
1.C.3f
5.C.3c

Here is an analysis chart that the student used to organize information from the essay. It shows the different parts of the marine iguana and their functions:

One Student's Analysis Chart

Marine Iguanas

Part	Function
Black skin	Blends in with color of lava rocks, absorbs sun's heat
Ridges & spikes	Ward off predators, rivals
Sharp claws	Hang on to slippery rocks in surf at low tide, help iguanas climb cliffs
Rounded snout	Easier to scrape algae off rocks
Sharp teeth	Scrape & chew seaweed (algae)
Long tail	Steers body in water

Notetaking and Graphic Organizers

Your Turn

Exercise Answer the following questions about the selection, the rough outline, and the analysis chart. Write your answers in complete sentences.

1. What sentence in the last paragraph expresses the main idea of the whole selection?

   _____

   _____

   _____

2. What is the main idea of paragraph 3 of the selection, and what details does the writer give to support it? (Hint: Remember that the topic sentence of a paragraph does not always come first.)

   _____

   _____

   _____

3. How does the writer conclude her essay? Explain.

   _____

   _____

4. What abbreviations and symbols are used in the rough outline?

   _____

   _____

5. Based on the chart on the previous page, what do you think is the purpose of an analysis chart?

   _____

   _____

   _____

   _____

78 AIM Higher! ISAT Language Arts Review

Notetaking and Graphic Organizers

Picture This!

Tools for Gathering, Organizing, and Presenting Ideas

Many human activities depend on effective communication. Certainly, there will be thousands of times in your own life when you will need to do one of the following:

1. gather information from something you read or hear
2. organize your ideas to create a speech or piece of writing
3. present ideas or information to others

Suppose that you become a city council member in your home town. You will have to take notes during council meetings and during meetings with local leaders and voters in your town. You will have to present your ideas to the council. You will have to prepare and present campaign speeches.

Suppose, instead, that you become a scientist. You will study at a university and take notes on class experiments and lectures. You will set up experiments of your own and record the results. You will analyze your results and read reports about similar scientific projects. You will need to write papers to present your findings at conferences or meetings.

Whatever career you choose, and certainly in your role as a student, you will need to gather, organize, and present ideas. You will achieve greater success in these activities if you know how to take notes using a rough outline form and how to arrange information using a graphic organizer. **Notes in rough outline form** and **graphic organizers** are excellent tools for gathering, organizing, and presenting information.

Meets ISAT Standards
1.B.3b
1.B.3c
1.B.3d
5.C.3c

Notetaking and Graphic Organizers

Notes in Rough Outline Form

Like computers, which can be used for doing mathematics, surfing the Web, sending an e-mail, writing a report, or playing a game, rough outlines can be used for many different purposes. For example, you can use a rough outline to take notes in class, to take notes on your reading, to present information, or to organize ideas before writing or speaking. A **rough outline** is simply a quick list of main ideas and supporting details. A **main idea** is any important point that you want to make. **Supporting details** are specific facts, opinions, examples, or other details that clarify the main ideas.

Look back at the example of a rough outline on pages 76–77. Notice that each main idea begins at the left margin. Supporting details for each main idea are written underneath that idea and are introduced by a dash (—).

Here are some hints to keep in mind when you are taking notes in the rough outline format:

Creating a Rough Outline

1. Do not try to write down everything. Write down only the main ideas and the supporting details.

2. Take notes in phrases, not in complete sentences. Begin each phrase with a capital letter.

3. Capitalize proper nouns, such as the names of people and places. You will find them easier to identify at a glance.

4. Use abbreviations and symbols, such as *Amer.* for *American,* = for *is,* → for *causes,* & for *and,* and *w/* for *with.* You may even want to abbreviate names using initials.

5. Begin main ideas at the left margin.

6. Write supporting details under the main ideas. Use a dash (—) at the beginning of each supporting detail.

7. Sometimes, you may find that supporting details relate to other supporting details. In such situations, you can indent them further and use dashes.

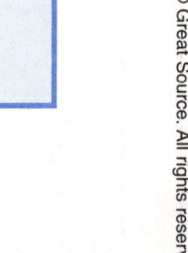

Your Turn

Exercise Read the following essay. As you read it, take notes on your own paper using the rough outline format.

Meets ISAT
Standards
1.B.3b
1.B.3c
1.B.3d
5.C.3c

Dark Passages: Stories of Sailors, Ice, and the Sea
by Norris MacLennan

"I knew that the gods could, should they have but the merest whim to do so, drown me anytime at their pleasure." So says writer and sailor Tristan Jones in his book-length memoir *Adrift*. It is a sentiment understood by all experienced sailors. Such men and women are well aware of the awesome power of the sea, of its changeableness, and of the potential for disaster. Throughout history, sailors have tempted the fates and tested their own physical and psychological limits by undertaking hazardous journeys. Among the most hazardous voyages have been those into the polar regions of the world. Examples of such journeys include ones taken by Willem Barents, Sir Ernest Shackleton, and John Patton.

For centuries, Scandinavian sailors have braved the treacherous, ice-riddled northern seas. One of the earliest recorded expeditions in this part of the world was made by Dutch explorer Willem Barents. After Christopher Columbus stumbled upon the Americas, many people assumed that there must be a "Northwest Passage" by water that cut through the northern part of the American continent from the Atlantic Ocean to the Pacific. Barents, on the other hand, set out to discover a "Northeast Passage" to the East Indies. He planned to sail north of Scandinavia and along the northern coast of Russia. He set sail in 1596. After rounding the coast of Spitsbergen, an island north of Norway, he found pack ice[1] blocking his way north. He decided to turn east and round the northern tip of Novaya Zemlya, an island north of western Russia. The captain of his accompanying ship refused to follow him. Barents, however, continued on. Soon, the ice closed in, choking his ship. Barents and his crew built a hut of driftwood on Novaya Zemlya and stocked the hut with food from their ice-locked ship. They killed Arctic foxes for meat and melted snow for fresh water. Spring brought sunshine during the day and slightly warmer weather, but the ice, like a gigantic nutcracker, had crushed their ship beyond repair. Barents and his crew left behind a letter telling their story to the world and set out

---

[1] **pack ice.** In the coldest parts of the world, the surface of the sea sometimes freezes, forming flat expanses of ice. The action of wind and waves often breaks up this ice into smaller pieces, which move about separately or refreeze and fuse together in unpredictable ways. Such surface ice is called pack ice. Pack ice can be extremely dangerous for boats attempting to move through it because it is unpredictable. After some time of moving freely through the ice, a captain and crew may find that suddenly the sea around them has frozen solid, leaving their boat stranded.

More ▶

Notetaking and Graphic Organizers 81

Your Turn

on the cold sea in two open boats. Almost immediately, they hit a storm, and Barents, already weakened by scurvy, died. His crew continued on. After traveling 1,600 miles across the icy sea, they eventually reached the Kola Peninsula in northwestern Russia. The body of water where Barents met his death is now called the Barents Sea.

General view, Archangel, Kola Peninsula, ca. 1890–1900. LC-DIG-ppmsc-03836. Library of Congress, Prints and Photographs Division.

A very well-known precarious journey into polar waters was made by Sir Ernest Shackleton. In 1914, Shackleton set out on a trans-Antarctic research expedition that was abandoned when his ship became trapped in ice. The crew camped out on an ice floe[2] for five months before Shackleton decided they must make a move to save themselves. He managed to transport the crew in three small, open boats to Elephant Island, southeast of Cape Horn, but the spot provided little refuge from the bitter, cold wind and miserable conditions. Shackleton realized that if he did not try to get help, he and his twenty-eight men would all die. Shackleton selected a small group of men and embarked on a desperate journey from Elephant Island to South Georgia Island, some eight hundred miles away. The odds were against Shackleton and his crew. Half of the route was entirely unknown, and the men were traveling in a boat that was only twenty-two feet long. Freezing waves soaked them every three to four minutes. Shackleton remained hopeful and in good spirits, although he suffered from leg and hip pain. Finally they spotted the island. They landed on the wrong shore, however, and had to hike to the whaling station on the other side of the island. This hike would carry them across glaciers and ice-covered mountains. Thirty-six hours after landing, they made it to the whaling station, frostbitten and half-conscious. No one recognized them. Shackleton's hair had even turned silver. As soon as they arrived, Shackleton organized a rescue team to return to Elephant Island to rescue the crew members he had left behind. Miraculously, every one of his men had survived the two-year ordeal.

---

[2]**ice floe.** A single piece, large or small, of floating sea ice

Another treacherous sea expedition involved the fisherman John Patton. In 1923, Patton and his crew were fishing near the North Cape, off the coast of Norway, when they saw a distress flare and went to investigate. The signal had come from the Scottish trawler *Ethel Nutton*, which was floating helplessly in icy waters. Patton's ship, *The Sargon*, had lost its lifeboats in raging waves; without a lifeboat, Patton had slim chances of helping the men. Nonetheless, he managed to save all eight men aboard the other vessel by maneuvering *The Sargon* until it was a few yards from the *Ethel Nutton*. Patton brought the men back to shore, and within twenty-four hours he was out on the seas again, looking for the next big catch; however, the fishing in the White Sea was poor, and Patton and his crew decided to turn back. Just then, they ran into an unexpected shoal of fish. After making the biggest catch of their lives, Patton and his crew headed for Tromso, where they would refuel and then head home. Unfortunately, winds and icy conditions held them back, and they ran out of fuel. Unable to escape, they endured violent snow squalls, and having run through their provisions, they survived on a diet of fish. Patton spent his time calculating the ship's position by studying the stars. One day, in anger and frustration, he threw away his sextant.[3] Without this vital navigating tool, Patton had no way of telling where they were. Their ship was locked in ice, and death seemed imminent. One day, with a sudden roar, the ice began to melt and *The Sargon* drifted out into the open sea. For four days, the ship drifted. On the fifth day, a German trawler rescued them. After four months, John Patton and his crew surprised everyone by appearing on the shores of Grimsby, England.

Shackleton, Barents, and Patton all faced extraordinary challenges at sea. Each set out with a specific goal, but in each case, that goal was set aside for the more important goal of simply surviving. Although they did not all succeed, they all showed unflagging determination and courage and so managed to make their mark in history.

General northward view, North Cape, Norway, ca. 1890–1900. LC-DIG-ppmsc-06197. Library of Congress, Prints and Photographs Division.

---

[3] **sextant.** An instrument for measuring the angle between the horizon and a heavenly body such as the sun or a star, used in conjunction with mathematical tables to calculate a ship's position

Notetaking and Graphic Organizers

Types of Graphic Organizer

A rough outline may not always be the best way to organize your ideas. Sometimes a graphic organizer is a more helpful tool. A **graphic organizer** is a type of chart or simple drawing with labels that is organized to show relationships among pieces of information. This chart lists some common graphic organizers. An example of each organizer is provided on the pages following the chart.

Types of Graphic Organizer

Word Web, or Cluster Chart	Column or Bar Chart
Cause-and-Effect Chart	Cycle Chart
Venn Diagram	Line Graph
Double-Entry Ledger, or T-chart	Pie Chart
Analysis Chart	Paragraph-Planning Chart
Character Analysis Chart	Tree Diagram
Pro-and-Con Chart	Reporter's Questions Chart
Comparison-and-Contrast Chart	Timeline
Sensory Detail Chart	Flow Chart

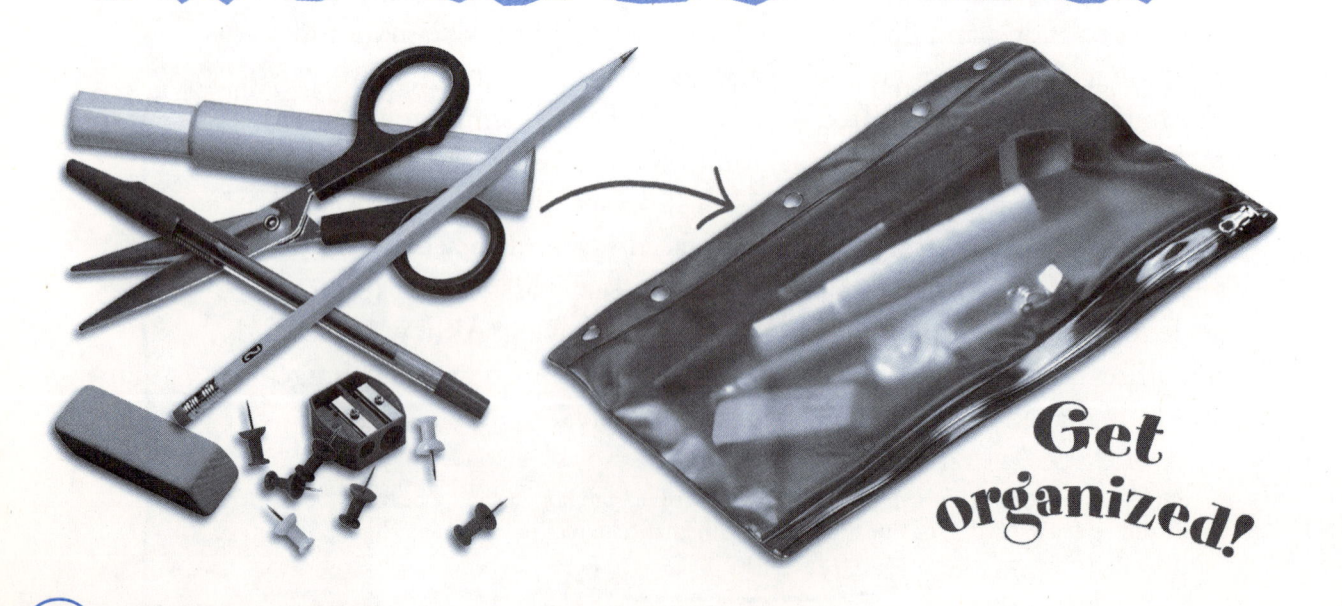

Get organized!

A | **Word Web, or Cluster Chart**

Meets ISAT Standards
1.B.3b
1.B.3c
1.B.3d
5.C.3c

Sailing

- **Sailboat Types**
  - Single-mast
    - Catboats
    - Sloops
    - Cutters
  - Double-mast, or split-rig
    - Yawls
    - Ketches
    - Schooners
- **Maneuvering**
  - Anchoring
  - Tacking
  - Mooring
  - Points of sail
  - Jibing
  - Balance
  - Stopping
  - Person overboard
  - Navigation
  - Right of way
- **Parts of Boat**
  - Shrouds
  - Transom
  - Hull
  - Rigging
  - Stays
  - Sheets
  - Keel
  - Rudder
  - Gunwales
  - Tiller
  - Cockpit
  - Mast(s)
- **Sails**
  - Reefing
  - Repairing
  - Sail Types
    - Mizzen
    - Jib
    - Mainsail
    - Genoa
    - Gaff
    - Spinnaker
    - Bermuda
- **Directions**
  - By wind
    - Windward
    - Leeward
  - By part of boat
    - Fore
    - Topsides
    - Port
    - Aft
    - Starboard
    - Below

B | **Cause-and-Effect Chart**

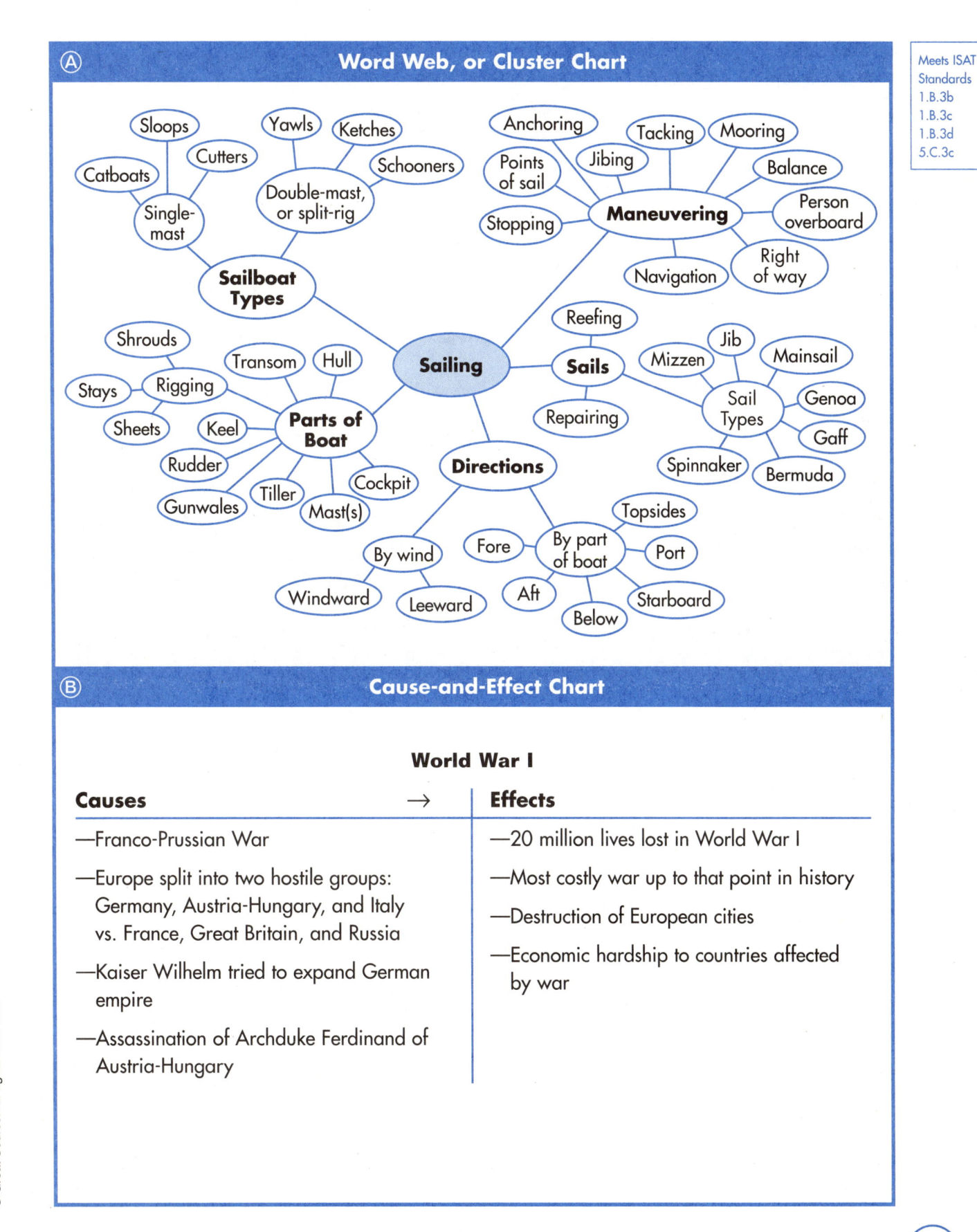

World War I

Causes →	**Effects**
—Franco-Prussian War	—20 million lives lost in World War I
—Europe split into two hostile groups: Germany, Austria-Hungary, and Italy vs. France, Great Britain, and Russia	—Most costly war up to that point in history
	—Destruction of European cities
—Kaiser Wilhelm tried to expand German empire	—Economic hardship to countries affected by war
—Assassination of Archduke Ferdinand of Austria-Hungary	

Notetaking and Graphic Organizers

Notetaking and Graphic Organizers

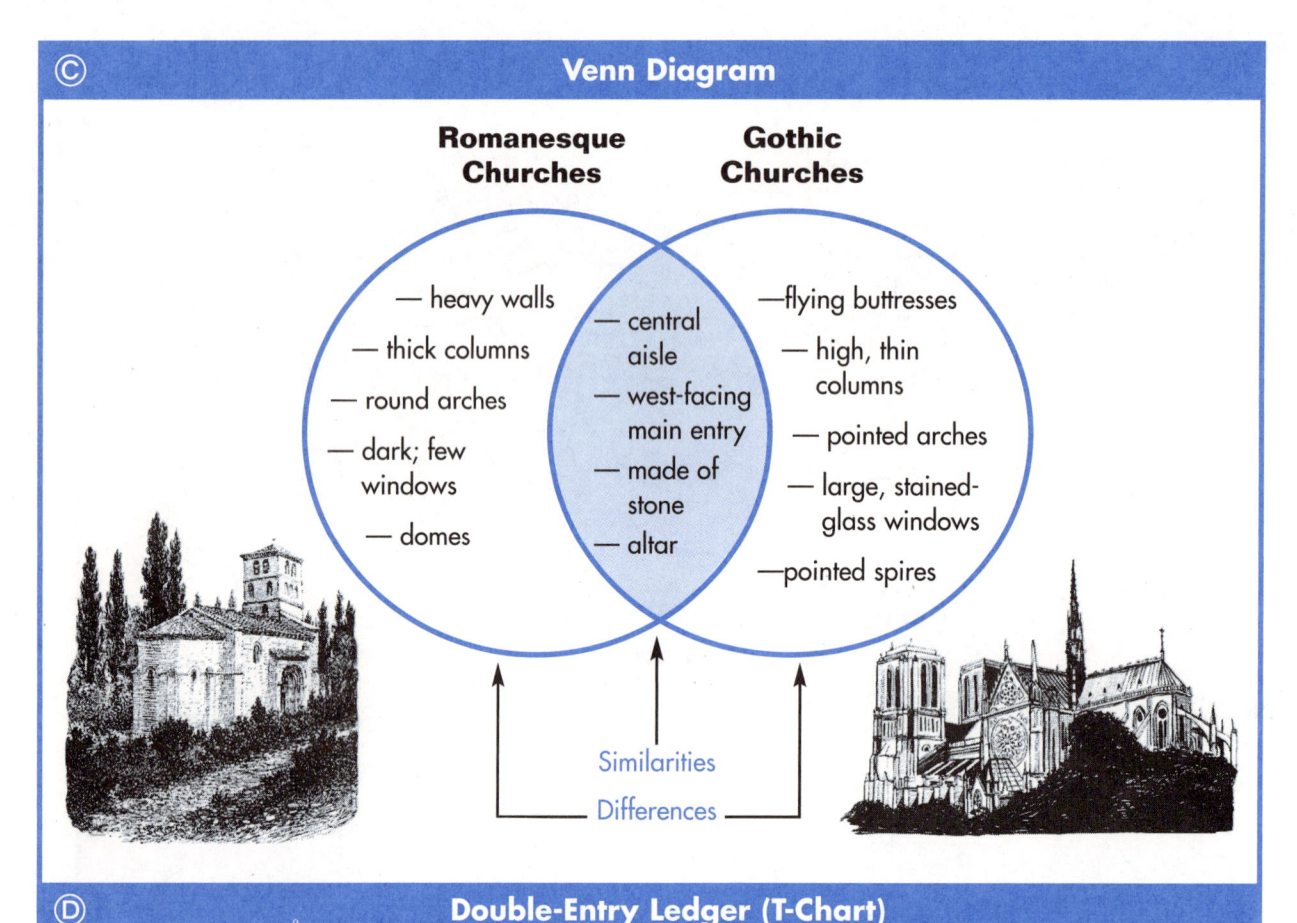

C ### Venn Diagram

Romanesque Churches
— heavy walls
— thick columns
— round arches
— dark; few windows
— domes

(Both)
— central aisle
— west-facing main entry
— made of stone
— altar

Gothic Churches
— flying buttresses
— high, thin columns
— pointed arches
— large, stained-glass windows
— pointed spires

Similarities
Differences

D ### Double-Entry Ledger (T-Chart)

from "Hop-Frog," by Edgar Allan Poe

"I never knew any one so keenly alive to a joke as the king was. He seemed to live only for joking. To tell a good story of the joke kind, and to tell it well, was the surest road to his favor. Thus it happened that his seven ministers were all noted for their accomplishments as jokers. They all took after the king, too, in being large, corpulent, oily men, as well as inimitable jokers."

Notes on "Hop-Frog" by Edgar Allan Poe

Text	Comment
—"keenly alive to a joke"	—Characterization of king
—"seemed to live only for joking"	—King's motivation
—telling a joke well = "surest road to his favor"	—Motivation of the king's ministers
—"large, corpulent, oily men"—all jokers, like the king	—Characterization of the ministers

86 AIM Higher! ISAT LANGUAGE ARTS Review

E) **Analysis Chart**

Parts of the Human Ear

Part	Function
Outer Ear	Catches and directs sounds
Tympanum	Vibrates when sound waves reach it
Malleus, Incus, Stapes	3 small bones in inner that pass on vibrations to cochlea
Cochlea	Generates a nerve impulse in the auditory nerve
Auditory Nerve	Sends electrical impulse to the brain

F) **Character Analysis Chart**

Ichabod Crane from "The Legend of Sleepy Hollow"

Characteristic/Trait	Description
Appearance	Tall, lanky, large feet/hands, huge ears, long nose, baggy clothes
Personality	Bookish, timid, nervous; liked scary stories; believed anything he heard; liked gossip
Background	Born in CT
Occupation	Teacher, singing master
Motivation	Looking for a girl to marry

Meets ISAT Standards
1.B.3b
1.B.3c
1.B.3d
5.C.3c

G) **Pro-and-Con Chart**

Pro and Con: Having an After-School Job

Pro	Con
—Can earn own money; don't have to ask for money from parents	—Can't participate in after-school activities
—Teaches good work ethic	—Might not have enough time for doing homework
—Good way to learn job skills not taught in school	—May not get enough sleep
—Looks good on college application; shows initiative and ambition	—Less time for social activities

Notetaking and Graphic Organizers 87

Notetaking and Graphic Organizers

Ⓗ **Comparison-and-Contrast Chart, by Characteristics**

Blue Whales vs. Sperm Whales

Characteristic	Blue Whale	Sperm Whale
Habitat	Ocean	Same
Animal order/class	Mammal/Cetacea	Same
Size	Up to 100 ft.	Up to 62 ft.
Physical features	Torpedo-shaped body	Same
Mouth	Plates of baleen	Teeth
Food	Krill	Squid
Range	Polar regions in summer; equatorial regions in winter	Temperate & tropical waters
Social behavior	Small groups	Same

Ⓘ **Comparison-and-Contrast Chart, by Similarities and Differences**

Blue Whales vs. Sperm Whales

Similarities	Differences
—Both cetaceans (ocean-living mammals) —Both valuable to whaling industry —Both live in small groups —Both have huge, torpedo-shaped bodies —Both are endangered (vulnerable to extinction)	—Blue whales are bigger—up to 100 feet long —Sperm whales grow up to 62 feet long —Sperm whales live in temperate & tropical waters; blue whales live in polar regions in summer, near equator in winter —Sperm whales have teeth; blue whales have baleen —Sperm whales eat squid; blue whales eat krill

Ⓙ Sensory Detail Chart

A Day at the Beach

Sight	Sound	Smell	Touch	Taste
— White waves crashing — Bright sun — Shells littering beach — Many big, colorful umbrellas & towels	— Hundreds of voices talking & laughing — Rhythmic splash of waves hitting shore — Bells of ice cream truck	— Salty air — Coconut smell of suntan lotion	— Cold shock of water — Rough feel of hot sand on hands & feet	— Mouth full of salty seawater — Sweet, smooth taste of chocolate ice cream

Meets ISAT Standards
1.B.3b
1.B.3c
1.B.3d
5.C.3c

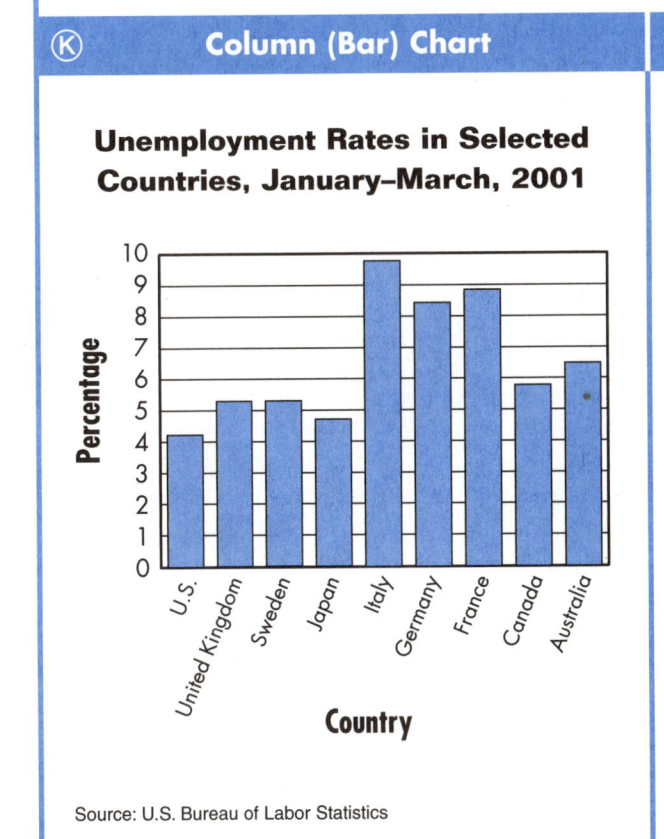

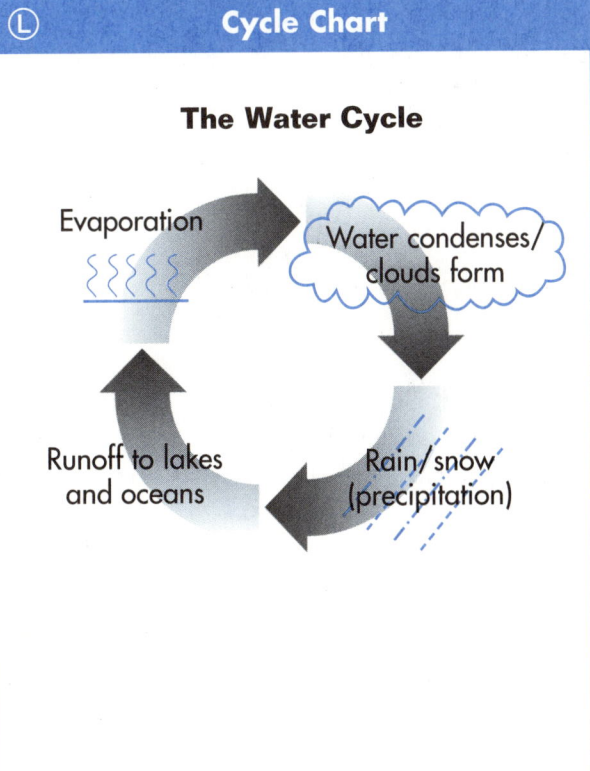

Ⓚ Column (Bar) Chart

Unemployment Rates in Selected Countries, January–March, 2001

Countries (x-axis): U.S., United Kingdom, Sweden, Japan, Italy, Germany, France, Canada, Australia

Percentage (y-axis): 0–10

Source: U.S. Bureau of Labor Statistics

Ⓛ Cycle Chart

The Water Cycle

Evaporation → Water condenses/clouds form → Rain/snow (precipitation) → Runoff to lakes and oceans → (back to Evaporation)

Notetaking and Graphic Organizers 89

Notetaking and Graphic Organizers

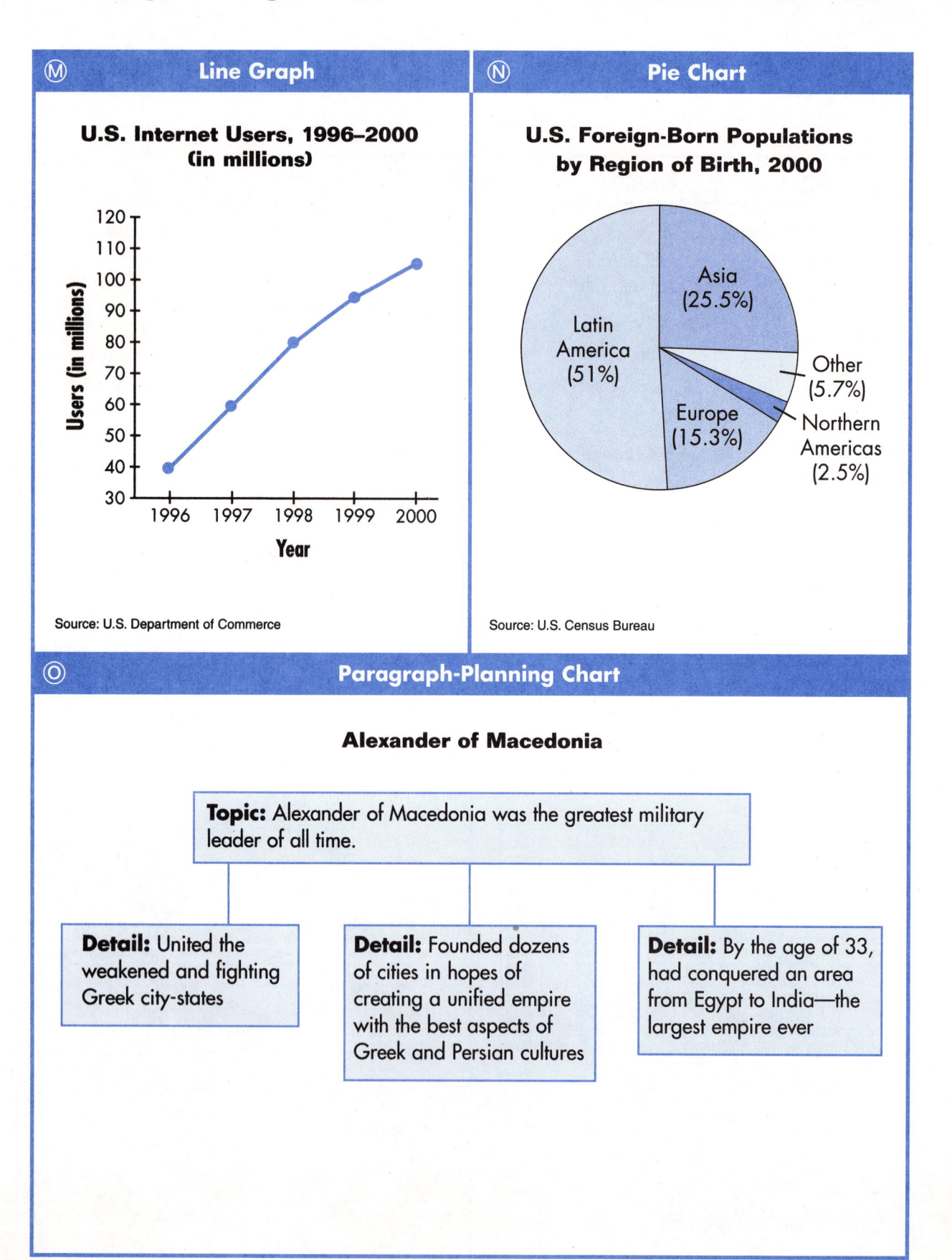

Ⓜ Line Graph

U.S. Internet Users, 1996–2000 (in millions)

[Line graph showing Users (in millions) on y-axis from 30 to 120, and Year on x-axis from 1996 to 2000. Data points: 1996 ≈ 40, 1997 ≈ 60, 1998 ≈ 80, 1999 ≈ 94, 2000 ≈ 105.]

Source: U.S. Department of Commerce

Ⓝ Pie Chart

U.S. Foreign-Born Populations by Region of Birth, 2000

- Latin America (51%)
- Asia (25.5%)
- Europe (15.3%)
- Other (5.7%)
- Northern Americas (2.5%)

Source: U.S. Census Bureau

Ⓞ Paragraph-Planning Chart

Alexander of Macedonia

Topic: Alexander of Macedonia was the greatest military leader of all time.

Detail: United the weakened and fighting Greek city-states

Detail: Founded dozens of cities in hopes of creating a unified empire with the best aspects of Greek and Persian cultures

Detail: By the age of 33, had conquered an area from Egypt to India—the largest empire ever

Tree Diagram

Some Major World Religions

- Christianity
  - Orthodox
  - Catholic
  - Protestant
- Buddhism
  - Theravada
  - Zen
  - Mahayana
- Judaism
  - Orthodox
  - Conservative
  - Reform
- Islam
  - Sunnite (Sunni)
  - Shiite

Meets ISAT Standards
1.B.3b
1.B.3c
1.B.3d
5.C.3c

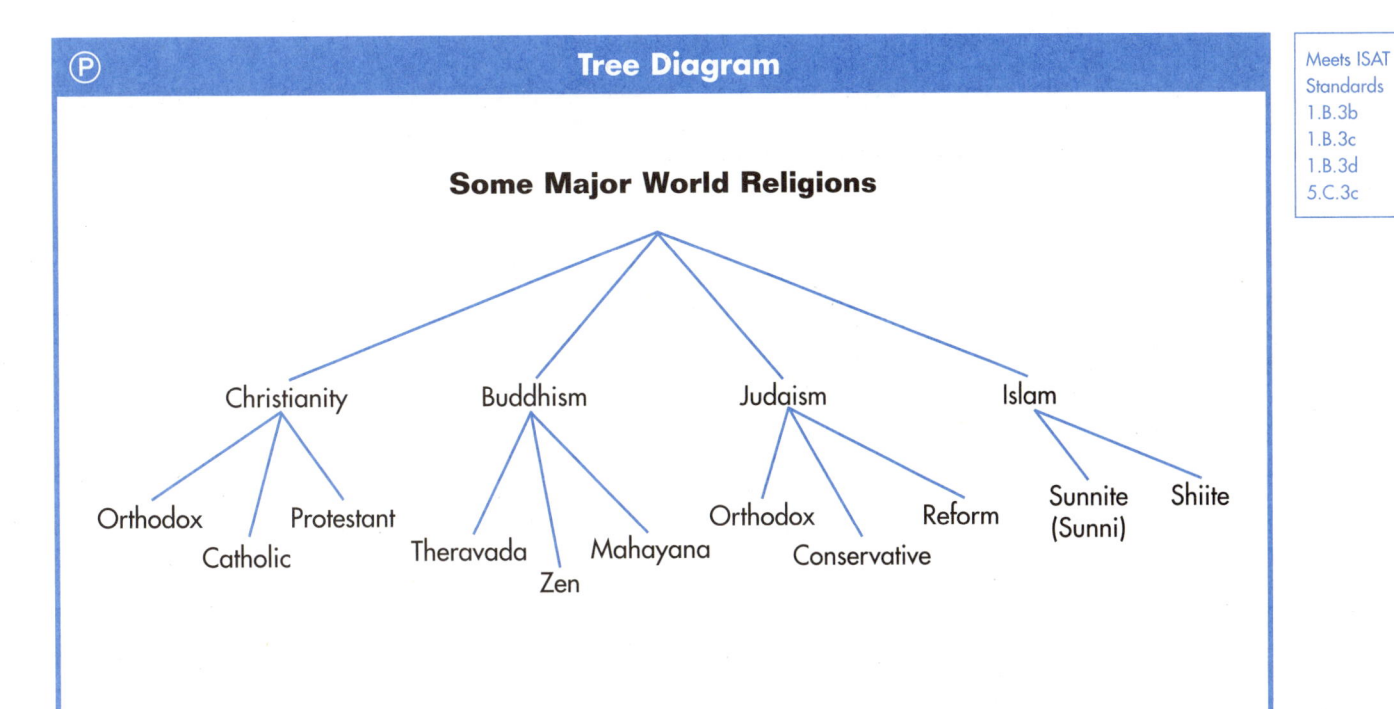

Reporter's Questions Chart

Queen Mother Passes Away: England Mourns Her Death

Who	What	Where	When	Why	How
Queen Mother of England	Mourning ceremony	Westminster Hall, London	Death—March 30, 2002; Mourning—April 5–April 9, 2002	Part of official mourning; people came to pay their respects before her funeral.	More than 50,000 people lined up to pass her coffin; they were in line all day and night.

Notetaking and Graphic Organizers

Notetaking and Graphic Organizers

Ⓡ Timeline

Chinese Dynastic and Later History, 960–1950

Yuan Dynasty (1279–1368)

Republic of China Established (1912)

950 1050 1150 1250 1350 1450 1550 1650 1750 1850 1950

Sung Dynasty (960–1279)

Ming Dynasty (1368–1644)

Qing Dynasty (1644–1911)

People's Republic of China Established (1949)

Ⓢ Flow Chart

Replacing Old Guitar Strings

Start → Examine highest-pitched string not yet examined → Is string corroded or dirty? —Yes→ Unwind string and remove → Attach new string of same weight → Tune string → Is this the last string? —Yes→ Stop

Is string corroded or dirty? —No→ (loop back to Examine)

Is this the last string? —No→ (loop back to Examine)

Legend:
- Start/stop
- Input or output
- Perform procedure
- Evaluate, test, or decide

© Great Source. All rights reserved.

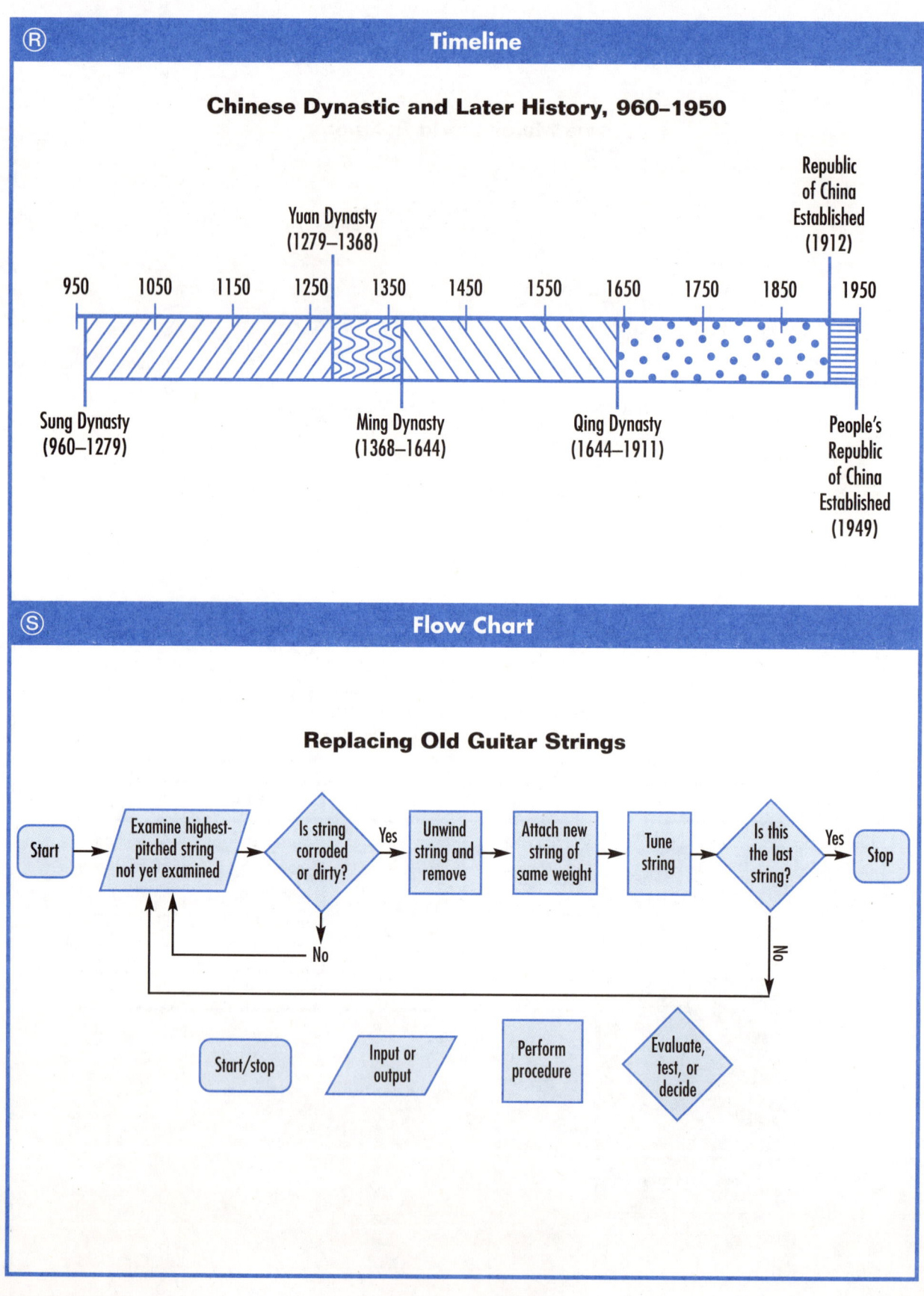

Your Turn

Exercise Review the types of graphic organizer listed on page 84. Then read each scenario below and explain which graphic organizer(s) would be appropriate to use.

Meets ISAT Standards
1.B.3b
1.B.3c
1.B.3d
5.C.3c

1. You are writing a report about your visit to a local dairy farm. What type of graphic organizer would you use to gather details? Explain why.

   _____

   _____

2. You are giving a report on the causes of crime. What graphic organizer might you use as you do your research? Explain.

   _____

   _____

3. You are creating a bulletin-board display comparing and contrasting the governments of the United States and Saudi Arabia. Choose two graphic organizers to collect the necessary information. What organizers would you choose and why?

   _____

   _____

4. You are giving a class presentation explaining how a bill becomes a law in the U.S. Congress. What type of graphic organizer might you use to support your presentation? Explain why.

   _____

   _____

5. You are on a panel selected to judge a debate on whether the space program is important to the United States. What graphic organizer would you choose to help you record the debaters' points? Why would you select this organizer?

   _____

   _____

Return to the exercises at the beginning of the chapter, revise your work as necessary, and submit the exercises to your teacher for grading.

Notetaking and Graphic Organizers

Chapter Project

Meets ISAT
Standards
1.B.3d
1.C.3a
1.C.3c
3.B.3a
3.C.3b
4.A.3d
4.B.3a
4.B.3c
5.A.3a
5.B.3a
5.B.3b
5.C.3b
5.C.3c

Choose one of the following topics or one of your own. Do research on your topic at the library or on the Internet, and create two graphic organizers to present your topic to the class.

✔ The history and achievements of the Aztec and Inca empires

✔ The story of Abraham Lincoln's childhood

✔ National monuments or national parks

✔ How the Renaissance influenced world exploration

✔ The growing popularity of women's soccer in the United States

✔ A favorite fictional character

✔ How to "burn" a compact disk (CD)

✔ Literacy rates in selected countries

✔ History of radio and television

✔ Life stages of a selected animal

Chapter 5
Talking Back to Books
Active Reading

First Encounter

Read this piece of informative writing about dolphins. Then try your hand at the exercises that follow the article. You will not be graded on the exercises at this time. At the end of the chapter, you will be directed to return to these exercises to revise and correct your work.

The Bottlenose Dolphin

by Deborah Hayes

One Student's Thoughts

1   Playful acrobats, dolphins have earned a place in the hearts of people around the globe. Each year, tens of thousands of tourists flock to see dolphins at parks like Sea World in Orlando, and tens of thousands more take excursions by boat to see dolphins and their larger relatives, whales, in the wild.

    Of the many kinds of dolphin around the world, the kind that people love most is doubtless the **bottlenose dolphin,** familiar as aquarium performers and as the television star Flipper. What makes the bottlenose so popular? One possible reason is that with its built-in "smile" and leaps above the waves, a bottlenose often looks as if it is having a very good time. Who can resist such a free-spirited creature? Dolphins are very entertaining to watch in the wild as well as in captivity. There are other reasons to be interested in dolphins, however, for they
2   are truly gifted, exceptional animals.

1. Predicting: This selection is going to be about dolphins, especially the bottlenose dolphin.

2. Questioning: What makes dolphins so exceptional?

Appearance, Range, and Habits

Most bottlenose dolphins are seven to eight feet long, with a streamlined body that is generally darker on top and lighter on the bottom. The upper body is generally dark bluish gray, becoming lighter on the sides and whitish or pinkish on the underside. This dolphin can be recognized by its distinctive short, stubby snout or beak, which gives the "bottlenose" its name. Like other dolphins, the bottlenose has small, cone-shaped teeth.

The bottlenose feeds on fishes, squid, and crustaceans.[1] Bottlenose dolphins are members of the order **Cetacea,**[2] which also includes whales, other dolphins, and porpoises.

Bottlenose dolphins are found throughout the world in temperate and tropical waters, but not in polar oceans. This dolphin lives in small groups (usually of less than ten or fifteen animals) when it is near shore. Naturally, dolphins living in inshore waters are fairly well known by humans, but the offshore-dwelling dolphins are less well understood. Some offshore dolphins have been seen in huge groups of hundreds of individuals.

3. Questioning: What is a crustacean? (**Predicting:** The first footnote will explain.)

4. Questioning: What is the order Cetacea?

5. Making Inferences: It seems to be some kind of group that includes whales and porpoises as well as dolphins. (**Predicting:** The second footnote will explain.)

6. Questioning: What does temperate mean?

7. Making Inferences: It seems to mean something other than tropical (very warm) and polar (very cold) waters. Maybe it means something in between—waters that are not too hot and not too cold.

8. Connecting: I have seen small groups of dolphins swimming (body surfing) just beyond the waves at Virginia Beach. I'm not sure if they were bottlenose dolphins, though.

9. Questioning: What does inshore mean?

10. Making Inferences: It seems to mean the opposite of offshore—in other words, near shore.

11. Questioning: I wonder why dolphins sometimes get together in such big groups offshore. Does anyone know?

---

[1]**crustaceans.** Hard-shelled animals (such as crabs and shrimps) with a segmented body and pairs of jointed limbs
[2]**order Cetacea.** A group of marine mammals that includes whales, porpoises, and dolphins. Cetaceans have nearly hairless bodies with flippers and a tail in place of fore- and hindlimbs.

First Encounter

Our fascination with dolphins is not just a modern phenomenon. Dolphins have captured our imaginations since ancient times. The ancient Greeks of the Homeric era, for example, incorporated dolphins into their myths. One myth describes how the god Dionysus, who had been captured by pirates, scared his captors, causing them to jump overboard and turn into dolphins. The ancient Romans pictured their god of the sea, Neptune, riding a chariot pulled by dolphins.

At birth, a bottlenose dolphin usually weighs from thirty-three to sixty-six pounds and can be almost four feet long. A dolphin baby is called a **calf** because it nurses on its mother's milk, just as other newborn mammals do. Within five weeks, the calf's teeth start to come in. After three or four months, it begins to eat fish. A dolphin calf may stay with its mother for five years or longer.

Dolphin Sizes and Weights

Birth Weight: 33–66 lb (15–30 kg)

Birth Length: 23–43 in. (70–130 cm)

Adult Weight: 330–1,430 lb (150–650 kg)

Adult Length: 62–128 in. (190–390 cm)

---

12. Visualizing: It would be really cool to see dolphins pulling a chariot.

13. Evaluating: Since these are myths, they are imaginary tales, not true stories.

14. Evaluating: That's a big baby!

15. Making Inferences: I didn't realize that a baby dolphin nurses on its mother's milk. That must be a bit tricky to do in the ocean, with waves.

16. Connecting/Extending: If dolphins are mammals, are there other similarities between them and other mammals that live on land, including humans?

17. Extending: I had no idea that an adult dolphin could get that big. I guess that it is more like a small toothed whale than I thought.

Dolphin Behavior

Dolphins are extremely social creatures that tend to live in **pods,** or groups. Males and females usually travel in separate pods, but pod membership is flexible. An individual dolphin may stay with a pod for a long or a short time, and some dolphins have been observed striking out on their own.

Most dolphins are not loners, however; in fact, they help each other in many ways. Dolphins often cooperate when they are hunting: Some of them herd fish into a tight circle while other dolphins take turns swimming into the midst of the fish to feed. When a dolphin calf is born, other dolphins will help the calf's mother boost the baby to the ocean's surface, so it can take its first breath of air quickly.

Dolphins also cooperate with each other for defense. Extremely athletic, dolphins can swim faster than twenty miles an hour in short spurts. If they are unable to escape a predator such as a shark or a killer whale, dolphins will work together to batter the enemy with their snouts or tails. If one member of a pod is injured, the other dolphins will hold the injured one at the water's surface so that it can breathe.

18. Questioning: I wonder why they form these groups and what makes the groups' membership change.

19. Summarizing: Dolphins depend on each other a lot.

20. Evaluating: That's amazing!

21. Paraphrasing: Dolphins depend on each other not only when they are hunting or starting a family but also for their survival.

22. Questioning: I wonder how the dolphins know when another dolphin needs help.

23. Making Inferences/Predicting: Dolphins must have some way of communicating with each other.

24. Making Inferences: Dolphins must be very smart to be able to figure out how to help each other that way.

Few people besides fishermen and scientists have seen what dolphins do offshore. Near shore, however, many people have seen them racing along the bow wave of a boat or riding in its wake. Dolphins also leap out of the water—a behavior known as **breaching**—and sail through the air. These forms of dolphin behavior, which are very athletic and seem like fun, are a key part of what has endeared dolphins to humans. People have seen dolphins bat around fish and pieces of seaweed as if they were playing ball. Observers have also seen dolphins make shimmering rings of bubbles linked together beneath the surface and then attempt to swim through them.

Although it may seem as if a bottlenose dolphin is smiling when we look at it, the "smile" of a bottlenose is not really a smile: The mouth of a bottlenose is always curved that way, even when the dolphin is in distress.

Intelligence, Communication, and Senses

Dolphins have very large brains for their size. Only humans have a larger brain-to-body ratio than dolphins do. Much of the scientific interest in dolphins is due to curiosity about what these creatures do with such large brains.

25. Visualizing: I can see them bounding through the water next to a boat. That must be great!

26. Evaluating: Wow—they really are athletic.

27. Questioning: I wonder if the dolphins really are doing these things for fun, or if they are doing them for some other reason.

28. Drawing Conclusions: This ability to leap out of the water and swim through bubble rings does not seem very different from the type of stunt that dolphins are trained to do in an aquarium show. They must be easy to train.

Certainly, dolphins are extremely intelligent. In careful scientific experiments, dolphins have been demonstrated to be self-aware, capable of recognizing themselves in mirrors.

29 Dolphins can recognize each other by their whistles. They communicate with one another using whistles and clicks that are sometimes higher in pitch than humans can hear. In addition to keen hearing, dolphins also have good eyesight. The one sense they appear to lack is a sense of smell. Like whales (and unlike humans), dolphins have another sense that is probably more useful

30 underwater: They use **echolocation**, bouncing sound waves off schools of fish and other prey to determine their size and distance. Once they have located their prey, dolphins can even use these bursts of sound as a weapon, stunning their prey for a moment to immobilize it.

As we have seen, dolphins justify our interest. They are truly amazing creatures who play, protect one another, share in child-rearing, cooperate in the hunt, communicate in ways that are still largely mysterious to us, are self-aware, and have very large brains. One wonders what dolphins think with those big

31 brains of theirs. Doubtless, much more can be learned about these astonishing, fellow big-brained inhabitants of planet Earth.

29. Summarizing: They <u>are</u> smart, and they can communicate with each other well underwater.

30. Connecting/Extending: I remember hearing about bats using echolocation in science class.

31. Predicting: I bet that scientists will learn more about how to communicate with dolphins as they study them more. Maybe we will even find out what they are thinking.

Active Reading

Your Turn

Exercise A Fill in the circle next to the correct answer to each multiple-choice question.

1. Which of the following would be MOST appropriate as another title for this selection?
   - Ⓐ "Play among Bottlenose Dolphins"
   - Ⓑ "Bottlenose Dolphins: An Introduction"
   - Ⓒ "Dolphins: Creatures of Mythology"
   - Ⓓ "Life in Various Kinds of Dolphin Pods"

2. How much does a dolphin calf weigh when it is born?
   - Ⓐ 33–66 pounds
   - Ⓑ 330–1,430 pounds
   - Ⓒ 75–100 pounds
   - Ⓓ 10–15 pounds

3. Which of the following senses is the dolphin missing?
   - Ⓐ the sense of hearing
   - Ⓑ the sense of smell
   - Ⓒ the sense of sight
   - Ⓓ the sense of touch

4. According to one ancient Greek myth, dolphins are
   - Ⓐ relatives of Proteus, the "The Old Man of the Sea."
   - Ⓑ demigods, or lesser gods.
   - Ⓒ pirates who jumped overboard to save themselves.
   - Ⓓ horses of the sea who pull the chariot of Jupiter.

5. Based on what you have learned about dolphin communication, which of the following statements do you think is MOST LIKELY to be true?
   - Ⓐ Shark language consists of whistles and chirps, too.
   - Ⓑ Scientists do not plan to learn more about dolphin language.
   - Ⓒ Scientists are trying to understand the whistles and chirps dolphins make.
   - Ⓓ People can hear the full range of dolphin signals.

102 AIM Higher! ISAT Language Arts Review

Exercise B Think about the social nature and playfulness of dolphins. They have often been compared to humans because of the complex social groups in which they live and the ways in which they play and interact. Write a paragraph in the space below describing specific ways in which dolphins are similar to human beings. Use additional paper if necessary.

Meets ISAT Standards
1.A.3a
1.A.3b
1.B.3a
1.B.3c
1.B.3d
1.C.3a
1.C.3c
1.C.3d
3.A.3
3.B.3a
3.C.3a

Active Reading 103

Active Reading

Talking Back to Books

A typical language arts test consists of reading selections, questions about the reading selections, and writing prompts (open-ended questions) related to the reading selections. One of the best ways to succeed on these tests is to read carefully. In the next several pages, you will learn some reading strategies that you can use to improve your reading skills.

Before Reading: Previewing a Selection

When you **preview** a selection, you look it over before you read it in depth. Previewing involves four steps: scanning, skimming, calling on your prior knowledge of the subject, and questioning.

1. Scanning

When you **scan** a selection, you look through it quickly to find specific parts or specific information. Begin scanning by looking for the title; author; direction line; headings; key words, which may be boldfaced, highlighted, or italicized; illustrations and captions; and special elements such as charts and boxed features. Once you locate a part, glance at it quickly to get the gist of it. Then go on to the next part.

Elements to Scan in Short Pieces of Nonfiction Writing

Direction Line	On reading tests, typically there will be a **direction line** telling you to read the selection. Often, the direction line will identify the type of selection you will be reading and explain what you should do when you finish reading. Here is an example: "Read this story by Isaac Asimov, and then answer the questions that follow."
Title	The **title** is the name of the selection. The title often provides a clue regarding what the piece of writing is about, or its main idea.
Author	The name of the **author** usually appears after the title. He or she is the person who wrote the selection.
Headings	**Headings** are the subtitles that appear within a selection. They mark the major parts of the selection and can indicate important ideas treated in the selection.

More ▶

104 AIM Higher! ISAT Language Arts Review

Key Words	**Key words** are especially important words that the author wants to emphasize. These words are central to the subject and often are defined in the text. They are usually highlighted in some way. They might be **boldfaced,** printed in *italics,* underlined, or printed in a different color.
Illustrations	**Illustrations** are pictures or graphics, including maps, charts, graphs, diagrams, drawings, and photographs.
Captions	A caption is usually included with an illustration. The **caption** is text that describes the illustration.
Charts or Boxed Features	**Charts** usually present information in rows and columns. **Boxed features** are set off from the text; they may appear against a shaded or colored background. These features contain text and/or graphics on some aspect of the subject.

Meets ISAT Standards
1.B.3a
1.B.3c
1.B.3d
1.C.3a
1.C.3d
1.C.3f

One Student's Response

As I scanned the selection on pages 96–101, I found the title ("The Bottlenose Dolphin"), the author (Deborah Hayes), the headings (Appearance, Range, and Habits; Dolphin Sizes and Weights; Dolphin Behavior; Intelligence, Communication, and Senses), and some key words (bottlenose dolphin, Cetacea, calf, pods, breaching, echolocation). I also glanced at the illustrations.

2. Skimming

When you **skim** a piece of writing, you read through it quickly to get the gist of it. You do not worry about getting every detail or idea. You are trying to get an idea of the overall concepts. Skim the first and last paragraphs of the selection (the introduction and conclusion) and the first and last sentences of the paragraphs. This will usually tell you the most important ideas in the selection.

Active Reading 105

Active Reading

One Student's Response

As I skimmed the introduction on dolphins on page 96, I located the writer's statement of her main idea (thesis): "There are other reasons to be interested in dolphins, however, for they are truly gifted, exceptional creatures." I can tell from this statement and from skimming the rest of the piece that Deborah Hayes is going to talk not only about the playfulness of the bottlenose dolphin but also about its intelligence. By skimming the first and last sentences of the paragraphs, I can see that some of the main ideas covered are the appearance of dolphins and how they live, how they communicate, the groups they establish and how they interact, their playfulness, and their large brains and well-developed senses. When I skimmed the conclusion, I saw that the author restated her ideas about what makes dolphins so special and worthy of interest.

3. Calling on Prior Knowledge

All new learning builds on the knowledge and experiences that you already have. A selection will be more meaningful to you and you will learn more from it if you relate it to yourself. As you preview a selection, think about what you already know and feel about the topic.

One Student's Response

I recall seeing movies and television shows about dolphins. I have even been to an amusement park where dolphins and other sea animals performed. I remember how athletic and smart the dolphins were. By thinking about these experiences, I can better relate to the information about the bottlenose dolphin.

4. Questioning

Scanning and skimming will give you an overview of the selection as a whole. The third step in previewing—calling on prior knowledge—will help you to connect the piece to your personal knowledge and experiences. Thinking briefly about what you already know about the topic can help you to read the selection in an active, engaged manner. Once you have connected the passage to your prior knowledge, you can ask yourself questions about the passage. The questions will help you to set a purpose for reading. You will be trying to answer your questions as you read.

As a final step in previewing a passage, ask yourself questions like these:

- What kind of selection is this? Is it persuasive? Informative? Narrative? A lyric poem? A newspaper article?
- What is this selection about? What is the author's topic?
- What can I expect this article to tell me about the topic?
- What is the main idea, or thesis, of the selection?
- What are the major supporting ideas or subtopics in the selection?
- What is the author's conclusion?

Meets ISAT Standards
1.B.3a
1.B.3c
1.B.3d
1.C.3a
1.C.3d
1.C.3f

One Student's Response

Looking over the selection, I see that it is about dolphins, specifically the bottlenose dolphin. I can tell from the headings and the facts and details about dolphins that the selection must be nonfiction, because dolphins are real animals. By skimming the introduction and conclusion, I can see that the main idea of the selection is that dolphins are very playful and intelligent animals. I can turn the headings into questions like these: Where do bottlenose dolphins live and what do they look like? How big do dolphins get? How do dolphins behave? How smart are dolphins? How do they communicate? What senses do they have and how do they use them? Then I can read the selection more carefully to find the answers to my questions.

Active Reading 107

Your Turn

Exercise A Scan the selection on pages 109–10 to answer the questions below. Do NOT read it closely. Then fill in the circle next to the correct answer to each multiple-choice question.

1. What is the title of this selection?
   - Ⓐ "All About Ancient Divers"
   - Ⓑ "Underwater Diving"
   - Ⓒ "The First Diving Equipment"
   - Ⓓ "All About Scuba Diving"

2. Which of the following is a heading in the selection?
   - Ⓐ "The First Scuba Mask"
   - Ⓑ "Divers in Ancient Times"
   - Ⓒ "The First Diving Equipment"
   - Ⓓ "The Water World"

Exercise B Skim the selection on pages 109–10. Do NOT read it closely. Then fill in the circle next to the correct answer to each multiple-choice question.

1. What is the MAIN topic of this selection?
   - Ⓐ famous underwater divers of today
   - Ⓑ the equipment of underwater diving
   - Ⓒ the history of diving
   - Ⓓ diving inventions of the past

2. Which of the following would be MOST appropriate as another title for this selection?
   - Ⓐ "Underwater Diving throughout the Years"
   - Ⓑ "Jacques Cousteau's Life under the Sea"
   - Ⓒ "The Development of the Aqua Lung"
   - Ⓓ "How to Choose the Right Diving Equipment"

Exercise C Write two statements about underwater diving on the lines below. These statements should be based on whatever you already know about the topic.

_____

_____

Exercise D On the lines below, write two questions that you think might be answered by this selection when you read it carefully.

_____

_____

AIM Higher! ISAT Language Arts Review

Exercise E Now that you have skimmed this selection, reread it carefully. Check to see whether your answers to Exercises A and B were correct. Also check to see whether the selection answered the questions that you wrote for Exercise D.

Meets ISAT Standards
1.B.3a
1.B.3c
1.B.3d
1.C.3a
1.C.3d
1.C.3f

Underwater Diving
by Jackson S. Tate

The exciting sport of underwater diving has been in existence for over five thousand years. Scuba diving is one form of underwater diving. The word *scuba* is an acronym. The letters of the word stand for the words in a phrase: S.C.U.B.A. stands for **s**elf-**c**ontained **u**nderwater **b**reathing **a**pparatus. Scuba divers are able to stay underwater for long periods of time because of the special breathing equipment they carry on their backs.

Divers in Ancient Times

Thousands of years ago, divers would hold their breath as they dived. They could only stay underwater for as long as they could hold their breath. The Greek historian Herodotus wrote of the first known diver, a Greek soldier named Scyllis, who used diving to help defeat the Persians at sea. Having been captured by the Persians, and overhearing their plan to attack the Greek navy, Scyllis jumped overboard and stayed underwater so long that the Persians assumed he had drowned. Then, using a hollow reed as a snorkel, he swam quietly among the enemy's ships. After he cut the anchor lines for the Persian ships, setting them adrift, Scyllis swam nine miles to rejoin the Greeks. Early divers such as Scyllis had to have strong lungs and good swimming skills. They did not have any diving equipment; it would be thousands of years before the S.C.U.B.A. was invented.

More ▶

Active Reading 109

Your Turn

Diving Equipment

The first piece of diving equipment was invented about five hundred years ago. It was called the diving bell. The diving bell was a large, bell-shaped bucket that was held in place several feet below the surface of the water, where it trapped air compressed by the water pressure. The diver could leave the bell to explore, and then return to it to breathe. The bell made it possible for divers to stay underwater for longer periods of time. The diving bell was improved over the next three hundred years. In the eighteenth century, a hand-operated air pump was invented. This was an exciting innovation. Air could be pumped through tubes to divers underwater. Then, in the 1940s, Jacques Cousteau, then a lieutenant in the French navy, along with an engineer named Emile Gagnon, developed the "Aqua-Lung." It was the first **portable**[1] S.C.U.B.A. unit. The Aqua-Lung allowed divers to carry air with them on their dives.

Scuba Diving Today

Modern scuba diving equipment looks very different from the diving bell. Today, divers wear special skin suits to keep them warm in the cold temperatures deep underwater. They also wear flippers that look like fish fins on their feet, making it easier to swim. Divers carry tanks filled with air on their backs.

People have been diving underwater for thousands of years. They have tried many different ways to stay underwater, and scuba diving has proved to be the most successful. It allows people to move freely underwater for long periods of time and enjoy the strange and beautiful animals that live deep below the surface of the ocean.

---

[1] **portable.** Capable of being carried or moved around easily

Active Reading

During Reading: Using Active Reading Strategies

For people who read well, reading is an extremely active process, one in which the reader is continually thinking about and interacting with the text. To get the most out of a selection as you are reading, use **active reading strategies.** For example, while reading a mystery selection, ask yourself "Who did it? Why did they do it? How did they get away so quickly?" and so on. As you continue reading, try to find the answers to your questions and then try to predict how the mystery will be solved. You can make inferences about the characters in the mystery to help to figure out who did it. Read on to see how your predictions and inferences compare with the outcome. If your prediction was different from the actual outcome of the story, think back and evaluate what you already read and the inferences you made from the clues provided. Then continue reading.

Meets ISAT Standards
1.B.3a
1.B.3c
1.B.3d
1.C.3a
1.C.3d
1.C.3f

What to Do While You Are Reading

Active Reading Strategy	Description
Questioning	Form **questions** about what you are reading by asking *Who? What? Why? Where? When?* and *How?* Then read to find answers to your questions.
Visualizing	A **visualization** is a picture in your mind. As you read, try to imagine the setting, characters, and objects that the author describes. Create a picture in your mind's eye of the actions and events.
Predicting	A **prediction** is an "educated guess" about something that might happen in the future. Based on clues in the selection and your own experience, you can make educated guesses about what will happen later in a selection that you are reading.
Making Inferences and Drawing Conclusions	An **inference** is an educated guess based upon what you already know. You make inferences while you read by using clues in the selection, in addition to your general knowledge, to draw conclusions not directly stated in the text.
Summarizing	A **summary** is a brief restatement of the main ideas in a selection. Often you will find the main ideas stated in the topic sentences of paragraphs or in the subheads in a selection.

More ▶

Active Reading 111

Active Reading

Paraphrasing	A **paraphrase** is a restatement of what you have read in your own words.
Evaluating	An **evaluation** is a judgment that you make about something in a selection.
Connecting and Extending	When you **connect,** you think about relationships between the ideas or events in the selection and experiences in your own life. When you **extend,** you think about relationships between ideas or events in the selections and other knowledge and information beyond the selection.

What *Not* to Do While You Are Reading

After Reading: Reflecting and Responding

After you read a piece, you should both **reflect** on it (think about it) and **respond** to it (make a connection or take some action based on it). Summarize the reading. Answer your prereading questions. Judge, or **evaluate,** the reading. Respond by talking about the reading with others, writing about it, or in some other way (such as making a poster or doing an oral report).

112 AIM Higher! ISAT Language Arts Review

Your Turn

Exercise Read the selection below. Use active reading strategies as you read. Write down at least five comments or questions in the right column. Try to use several of the active reading strategies listed on pages 111–12.

Meets ISAT Standards
1.B.3a
1.B.3c
1.B.3d
1.C.3a
1.C.3d
1.C.3f

Puffer Fish: Prickly Pets
by Aimee Evrist

One of the most interesting fish in the world is the puffer. A puffer fish can blow up its body to three times its normal size and shape. Imagine looking at a little fish one second and then, a moment later, at a giant, bug-eyed ball with spikes! Even though there are several different kinds of puffer fish, they all have big, bulging eyes and round bellies that can be inflated like a balloon.

The porcupine puffer is the most common puffer pet. It has an interesting personality and is fun to look at as well. It has prickly spines all over its body and an expressive face that appears almost human. Puffer pet owners claim that these unique fish even smile when they are happy. Porcupine puffers will swim to the side of the tank to greet their owners at the end of the day. They are also known to spit water at their owners if they do not get fed fast enough.

More ▶

Active Reading 113

Your Turn

Meets ISAT Standards
1.B.3a
1.B.3c
1.B.3d
1.C.3a
1.C.3d
1.C.3f

Perhaps the most interesting characteristic of the puffer fish is its habit of puffing up to protect itself from enemies. The puffer has a unique structure that enables it to expand: It has no rib cage or pelvic girdle, and its stomach contains a special sac that expands quickly as the fish gulps water and, if close enough to the surface, air. When the puffer senses danger, it automatically begins gulping, its body swells up, and its porcupine spines stick out. When its enemies see the puffer turn into a big, round, prickly ball, they usually lose their appetite!

There are many interesting aquarium fish, but puffer fish are among the most fascinating. They are particularly intriguing to watch as they puff up into big, prickly balls floating around a fish tank. Don't put your fingers into the tank—a puffer that is startled can quickly turn around and nip you! Puffers are also known for eating any smaller fish or animals in an aquarium. If you keep them in a tank by themselves, however, puffers are unusual fish that make entertaining pets.

Return to the exercises at the beginning of the chapter, revise your work as necessary, and submit the exercises to your teacher for grading.

Chapter 6
I Think I've Got It!
Reading Comprehension

First Encounter

Read the following story. Then try your hand at the exercises that follow the story. You will not be graded on the exercises at this time. At the end of the chapter, you will be directed to return to these exercises to revise and correct your work.

Rhythm and Blues

by Karen Leung

It has always seemed strange to me that people refer to seasons and nature when they talk about the rhythms of life—how the weather changes from cold to hot and then back to cold, how the trees lose their leaves each fall and grow new ones each spring. To me, the rhythms of life are the pulses and beats that I hear all around me. I'm always subconsciously tapping my fingers or feet to the various tempos I hear.

Last night, for instance, Dad was bringing me home from the final lacrosse game of the season. As he drove carefully through the drizzling rain, I felt hypnotized by the steady sound of the windshield wipers scraping back and forth against the windshield. Suddenly, I was awakened from my stupor by Dad clearing his throat.

"Karen! You're going to wear a hole in the dashboard with your drumming!" I hadn't even realized I'd been tapping my fingers.

After dinner that night, I joined Mom and Dad in the living room, where they sat quietly discussing their day. I didn't really hear their conversation because I was focused on the steady, constant drip of the faucet. Without realizing it, I was tapping my fingers to its rhythm.

"Tapping your fingers again? You just can't stop, can you?" observed Dad.

Then Mom asked me about what I wanted to do after school, now that the lacrosse season was over.

"I want to learn to play the drums," I announced without hesitation. I had been thinking about it a lot, ever since Miss Jaworski said I'd be good at it.

"You want to do what?" asked Dad.

Mom just sat there with her face all pinched up, as if she had smelled something foul.

"I want to play the drums," I repeated.

"But girls don't play drums. I mean, drums are so . . . *loud*. Why don't you take up the violin or the flute?" Dad suggested.

I couldn't believe him. The flute? He obviously didn't know me at all. Who says girls don't play drums? There are plenty of female drummers: Samantha Maloney, Phoebe Summersquash, Moe Tucker—and I was going to be one of them, one way or another.

One Saturday several weeks later, when I had saved up enough money, I visited the music store and bought a pair of drumsticks and a practice pad. On the way out of the store, I casually checked the notices posted on the bulletin board. One caught my eye: *"Drummer wanted."* Someone from my school had written the notice! It said that beginners were welcome, too! I ripped off one of the tabs with a phone number on it from the bottom of the notice and shoved it in my coat pocket.

I slowly reread the notice to make sure I had not missed anything. *"Good sense of rhythm required."* "No problem," I thought to myself, "I've got that." *"Must get along well with others."* Well, maybe Dad and I have had our differences lately . . . , but I generally get along well with people. *"M/F OK."* At least *they* didn't care if a girl wanted to play drums!

Suddenly, I discovered something I had missed the first time I read the notice: *"Must have own gear."* I let out an audible moan. I couldn't even try out for the band without a drum set. I was crushed.

Just then, a glint in the corner caught my eye, and I noticed the most beautiful set of drums—a shining altar of silver and black—beckoning me. I brandished my new sticks, straddled the "throne" (that's what drummers call their stools), and began to flail away. The crash and clang of the drums beneath my sticks was mesmerizing. I felt as if I were floating far above the ground, where no one could bother me or interrupt my rhythm.

More ▶

First Encounter

When my arms grew tired, I finally stopped. I looked up to find the store owner grinning at me. The other customers in the store stared. A couple of them even clapped!

The owner approached, still wearing his lopsided grin. "You handle those sticks pretty well," he said. "'Course, a good kit always helps. This here's one of the best starter sets. You looking to buy?"

"I wish," I mumbled. "But it costs a fortune, and I don't have much money."

"Hmmm," he said, twisting his mouth and rubbing the back of his neck, as if he were thinking hard.

"You interested in earning some?"

"How?" I said eagerly.

"I could use some help keeping track of inventory, cleaning up, that sort of thing . . . posting fliers for my band. I'm a drummer myself; maybe I could give you a few pointers when things are slow around here."

I was so excited I couldn't even speak; I nodded my head vigorously. We introduced ourselves—his name was Joe—and he took me around the stockroom and showed me what to do. As I was about to leave, I said, "So, how long do you think it'd take me to earn the kit?"

"'Bout six weeks."

"Oh," I sighed.

"Six weeks is not that long," he said. "You can play it here after hours."

"Yeah, but by that time they'll have already found a drummer," I said, motioning to the notice on the board. "Well, thanks a lot," I said as I shook his hand. "See you tomorrow around three."

All the way home, I thought about how I was going to break the news about my new job to Mom and Dad. If I brought it up at the wrong time, they might freak.

At dinner that night, I told a few funny stories from school and got Mom and Dad laughing. Then I eased into the topic of drums.

"There was a notice in the music store today," I said, slowly at first. The rest came out in a tumble: "A new band at school is looking for a drummer . . . it said beginners were welcome—girls, too." I glanced at Dad. "If they chose me, I'd have someplace to play. But," I sighed heavily, "I have to have a drum set even to try out." I paused. A strained silence settled over the table. "I saw the most awesome set at the store," I heard myself blurt out.

Mom and Dad gave each other a look across the table, and I panicked.

"I'm not asking you to buy it for me. I'm going to buy it myself. The manager at the store offered me an after-school job," I explained.

They freaked out, of course. "But what about your homework?" Mom said. "When will you get it done?"

I pointed out that my job wouldn't take up any more time than lacrosse and that I had always managed to get my work done during lacrosse season. They were quiet after that. Mom rubbed her hands together as Dad glowered at his plate. Finally he declared, "Well, you're not going to play the drums in this house."

"Fine," I replied coolly. "I'll practice at the store. It'll take me six weeks to earn enough money for the set anyway. By that time, the band will have already picked a drummer, but I'll find some other place to play." Then I stomped off to my bedroom and practiced drum rolls on my pillow until it began to spit out feathers.

The next morning, Dad said he was going to pick me up after school and drive me to the music store. I told him that he didn't have to. I could walk there from school, I assured him, but he insisted. He wanted to meet my boss and see the place where I was going to be spending so much time.

On the way over, he asked about the drum set. At first, I thought he was just looking for a way to get me to talk, but he kept asking questions as if he were really interested. He asked me to describe the set and tell him about the different drums and cymbals that came with it. By the time we got to the store, I was actually excited to show it to him. But when we walked through the door, the drum set—my drum set—was gone.

"What happened to my kit?" I cried. The store owner just grinned.

"Joe and I had a talk today," Dad said, slapping the store owner on the back. "He's agreed to give you an advance on your pay." Dad reached over and tore another one of the phone numbers off the notice on the board and handed it to me.

"Give them a call and see if you can try out today. We can head over after work with your new kit."

Your Turn

Exercise A Fill in the circle next to the correct answer to each multiple-choice question.

1. What is this story MOSTLY about?
   - Ⓐ how rhythms are an essential part of life
   - Ⓑ the importance of reading carefully
   - Ⓒ a determined girl's desire to play drums
   - Ⓓ a girl's love for the game of lacrosse

2. What do you think was the author's main reason for writing this story?
   - Ⓐ to show that people in families have disagreements
   - Ⓑ to explain that there have been some excellent female drummers
   - Ⓒ to explain how to play the drums
   - Ⓓ to show that determination is an important part of accomplishing goals

3. What part of the notice on the bulletin board FIRST catches Karen's eye?
   - Ⓐ "Drummer wanted."
   - Ⓑ "Good sense of rhythm required."
   - Ⓒ "Must get along well with others."
   - Ⓓ "M/F OK."

4. Why is Karen disappointed when she rereads the notice in the music store?
   - Ⓐ She has to get along with other people.
   - Ⓑ She does not have her own set of drums.
   - Ⓒ The notice is for a male drummer.
   - Ⓓ Her father wants her to study the violin.

5. Which event happens FIRST?
   - Ⓐ Karen practices drum rolls on her pillow.
   - Ⓑ Karen visits the music store.
   - Ⓒ Karen's lacrosse season ends.
   - Ⓓ Karen gets a job in the music store.

6. When does Karen visit the music store?
   - Ⓐ before lacrosse season ends
   - Ⓑ before she tells her parents she wants to learn to play the drums
   - Ⓒ two weeks after the faucet starts dripping
   - Ⓓ several weeks after she tells her parents she wants to learn to play the drums

7. Why does Karen practice drum rolls on her pillow?
   - Ⓐ She does not want to disturb her parents.
   - Ⓑ She is frustrated by the conversation with her parents.
   - Ⓒ She is practicing drum rhythms in time with the rain at her window.
   - Ⓓ She is trying to get the feathers out of her pillow.

8. What happens as a result of Karen's discussion with the music store owner?
   - Ⓐ She gives up wanting to study the drums.
   - Ⓑ She asks for a flute instead.
   - Ⓒ She gets a new job.
   - Ⓓ She reads the bulletin board.

9. What kind of person do you think Karen will be when she grows up?
   - Ⓐ determined and independent
   - Ⓑ silly and uncaring
   - Ⓒ rude and selfish
   - Ⓓ indecisive and distracted

10. Why do you think Karen's father convinces the store owner to let her take the drum set as an advance on her pay?
    - Ⓐ He is worried that the store owner will try to cheat her out of her pay.
    - Ⓑ He wants her to realize that she will not be any good as a drummer.
    - Ⓒ He wants to be supportive by making sure she can try out for the band.
    - Ⓓ He wants her to perform at a party he is giving that weekend.

Meets ISAT Standards
1.B.3c
1.B.3d
1.C.3a
1.C.3b
1.C.3d
2.B.3a
2.B.3c

Your Turn

Exercise B How successful do you think Karen will be in her attempt to learn how to play the drums? Use details from the selection and examples from your own experience to support your answer. Draft your response on a separate sheet of paper. Revise it using the Revision Checklist on pages 265–66. Then proofread it using the Proofreading Checklist on page 270. Finally, copy your final version onto the lines below.

Reading Comprehension

I Think I've Got It!

Reading comprehension occurs when a reader grasps, or fully takes in, the meaning of a selection. Reading tests like the ISAT for Reading contain lots of reading comprehension questions. In this chapter, you will learn strategies for answering many common types of questions from reading comprehension tests.

Meets ISAT Standards
1.B.3c
1.B.3d
1.C.3a
1.C.3b
1.C.3d
2.A.3a
2.A.3b
2.B.3a
2.B.3c
3.A.3
3.B.3a
3.B.3b
3.C.3a

Responding to Questions about the Main Idea

The **main idea** is the message or point that the selection as a whole is meant to get across. Questions about the main idea can be phrased in many ways:

- What is the main idea of this story?
- What is this selection mostly about?
- What is the author's purpose in writing this story?
- Which of the following titles is most appropriate for this selection?
- What is the theme of this selection?

Strategies for Answering Questions about the Main Idea

- Look at the question carefully for words that tell you it is asking about the selection as a whole. Some key words and phrases in the question may be *main idea, subject, theme, lesson, mostly about,* or *as a whole.*

- Look over the selection as a whole. Scan it, looking at the title, headings, first and last sentences, and so on. Ask yourself, "What is this mostly about?"

- Rule out any answers that are obviously incorrect. Then concentrate on the remaining choices.

- Make sure that the answer you choose refers to the *whole* selection, not just to part of it.

- Remember that an answer may be true, but it may not express the main idea.

Reading Comprehension

Take another look at this multiple-choice question about "Rhythm and Blues":

1. What is this story MOSTLY about?
   - Ⓐ how rhythms are an essential part of life
   - Ⓑ the importance of reading carefully
   - Ⓒ a determined girl's desire to play drums
   - Ⓓ a girl's love for the game of lacrosse

Here is how one student thought through the answer to Question 1:

One Student's Response

When I read the words <u>mostly about</u>, I knew that this question focused on the main idea. I read all the answer choices and then skimmed the story. I reread the beginning and ending paragraphs and glanced at the first and last sentences of each paragraph. I eliminated choices B and D because <u>reading</u> is not mentioned in the story at all, and <u>lacrosse</u> is definitely not the focus. Both of those choices were obviously incorrect, so I was able to narrow down the possible choices to A and C. Although A might have been correct in some ways, the rhythms of life did not seem to be the main focus of the story because they are talked about only in the opening paragraph. Choice C is correct because it summarizes the main idea of the story—a determined girl's desire to play drums. What made me especially confident that C is the answer is that when I skimmed, I noticed the word <u>drums</u> repeated many times, and I noticed that the story was presented from the girl's point of view.

Responding to Questions about Supporting Details

Supporting details are specific pieces of information about a person, character, event, place, topic, or idea that help get across the author's main idea. When you encounter a question about supporting details, follow these steps:

> **Strategies for Answering Questions about Supporting Details**
>
> - Choose a key word or phrase from the question or from one or more of the answers.
> - Scan the passage for the key word or phrase. When you find it, read carefully around the word or phrase to find the answer you need.
> - Use your finger, an index card, or a ruler to keep your place as you scan down a page.

Meets ISAT Standards
1.B.3c
1.B.3d
1.C.3a
1.C.3d

Here is a question about details from the story "Rhythm and Blues."

4. Why is Karen disappointed when she rereads the notice in the music store?
   - Ⓐ She has to get along with other people.
   - Ⓑ She does not have her own set of drums.
   - Ⓒ The notice is for a male drummer.
   - Ⓓ Her father wants her to study the violin.

Here is how one student thought through the answer to Question 4:

> **One Student's Response**
>
> I knew that this question referred to a supporting detail because it asked about one specific event—why Karen was disappointed when she reread the notice in the music store. I decided to scan for the word <u>disappointed</u>, but I couldn't find it. Then I decided to scan for the words <u>notice</u> and <u>music store</u>. I found the phrase <u>music store</u> and reread the entire passage about what took place at the music store. That passage did not mention anything about Karen's father wanting her to study the violin, so D was obviously incorrect. Then I examined the passage to see which part described something that had made Karen feel disappointed. Needing to get along with other people—choice A—did not seem to be a problem. Choice C could not be correct because the notice clearly said that males or females could apply. The only choice remaining was B. I checked the paragraph again to be sure and saw that Karen was <u>crushed</u> by the fact she did not own her own set of drums. Therefore, I was confident in selecting B as the answer.

Reading Comprehension

Reading Comprehension

Responding to Questions about Sequence

Reading comprehension questions often ask about the **sequence,** or order, of events, so it is important to be able to trace the events of a selection from beginning to end, even if some of the events are presented out of order. For example, a story might include a **flashback** to previous events or **foreshadowing** of events to come. It might be helpful to create a timeline or make a list of events as you read. Also note key words, like *first, finally,* or *in 1936,* that identify time.

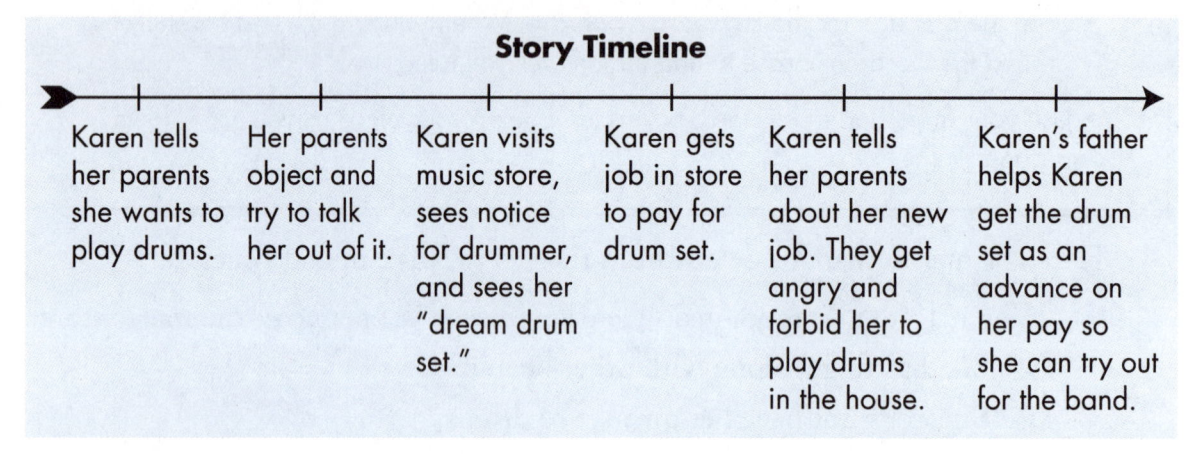

Story Timeline

| Karen tells her parents she wants to play drums. | Her parents object and try to talk her out of it. | Karen visits music store, sees notice for drummer, and sees her "dream drum set." | Karen gets job in store to pay for drum set. | Karen tells her parents about her new job. They get angry and forbid her to play drums in the house. | Karen's father helps Karen get the drum set as an advance on her pay so she can try out for the band. |

Strategies for Answering Questions about Sequence

- Remember that events are often, but not always, told in the order in which they happen. Be alert to variations in this order, such as flashbacks or foreshadowing.
- Look for key words like *first, next, last, then, before, after,* and *finally*. These words signal when things happen.
- Look for dates or times that tell when things occur in the selection.
- Create a timeline or list of events to keep track of the sequence of events in a story.

The fifth question about "Rhythm and Blues" asks you to identify the first event in a sequence:

5. Which event happens FIRST?
   - Ⓐ Karen practices drum rolls on her pillow.
   - Ⓑ Karen tells her parents that she wants to play the drums.
   - Ⓒ Karen's lacrosse season ends.
   - Ⓓ Karen gets a job in the music store.

Here is how one student thought through the answer to this question:

> **One Student's Response**
> The word <u>first</u> in this question indicates that it is about sequence. So, I scanned the story for each event that was mentioned as a possible answer and figured out the order in which those events occurred. The event described in choice C (the end of lacrosse season) happened early in the story. This led me to believe that C was the correct answer. To make sure, I thought about the timeline of the events in the story. I wanted to be certain that none of the events described in A, B, and D was an example of flashback or foreshadowing. I found that all the events in the story occurred in chronological order and that C was definitely the correct answer.

Meets ISAT Standards
1.B.3c
1.B.3d
1.C.3a
1.C.3d
2.A.3a

Responding to Questions about Cause and Effect

A **cause** is something that brings about or helps to bring about an event or a series of events. An **effect** is the event or events brought about by a cause. Cause and effect is one possible relationship between events in a story. For example, a fire alarm (*cause*) results in the postponement of a test (*effect*). A common type of reading comprehension question asks the reader to identify a cause-and-effect relationship between events in a selection.

A cause often comes just before its effect, but be careful! One event can come right after another event without the two events having a cause-and-effect relationship. For example, imagine that a story says: "Just as Marie picked up her books, the cat ran under her feet." Although the cat ran under her feet at the same time that Marie picked up her books, it did not run under her feet *because* she picked up the books. There is no cause-and-effect relationship between these events. On the other hand, if Marie tripped when the cat ran under her feet, then there would be a cause-and-effect relationship: The cat would have caused Marie to trip.

Be aware that a cause can have more than one effect, and an effect often has more than one cause. For example, imagine that a couple of friends take the bus to the park to ride their skateboards. They lose track of time trying out some new tricks and miss the last bus home. Because they spent

Reading Comprehension 127

Reading Comprehension

most of their money buying sodas and hot dogs from a vendor, they do not have enough money for a cab. They decide to walk home and end up getting lost. The facts that the friends skateboarded too long and missed the bus, that they spent all their money and did not have any left for a cab, and that they tried to walk home are all causes leading up to the effect: They got lost.

A particularly interesting example of a cause is motivation. A **motivation** is what moves a character to act or think in a certain way. Motivations can be **internal** (inside the character) or **external** (outside the character). For example, a girl might decide to try snowboarding because all her friends snowboard (*external cause*), or she might try snowboarding because she thinks it looks like more fun than skiing (*internal cause*). Sometimes characters are motivated by both internal and external causes, as when a girl tries snowboarding because all her friends are doing it and it looks like fun.

Questions about cause-and-effect relationships are often signaled by words or phrases such as *why, because, reason, therefore, as a result, cause, effect, consequently,* and *so*.

Read each question carefully to determine whether it asks about a cause ("Why did this happen?") or an effect ("What happened as a result of . . . ?"). Look for key words in the selection that indicate cause-and-effect relationships, such as *cause, effect, therefore, why, reason,* and so on.

When you encounter a cause-and-effect question, you can use one or more of the following strategies to help you to answer it correctly:

Strategies for Answering Questions about Cause and Effect

- Determine whether you are looking for a cause or an effect.

- Ask yourself, "Why did this happen?" (**cause**) and "What happened as a result?" (**effect**).

- Look for key words and phrases that signal cause-and-effect relationships, such as *cause, effect, because, why, reason, therefore, consequently, as a result,* and *so*.

- Remember that one event can follow another without being caused by it.

- Read carefully to determine the relationship between two events or facts. Ask yourself whether one causes the other or whether both events simply happen at about the same time.

- Look for multiple causes.

128 AIM Higher! ISAT Language Arts Review

The eighth question about "Rhythm and Blues" is a cause-and-effect question. It describes an event that occurred in the story and asks you to identify the result of that event:

8. What happens as a result of Karen's discussion with the music store owner?

   Ⓐ She gives up wanting to study the drums.
   Ⓑ She asks for a new flute instead.
   Ⓒ She gets a new job.
   Ⓓ She reads the bulletin board.

Here is how one student thought through the answer to Question 8:

Meets ISAT Standards
1.B.3c
1.B.3d
1.C.3a
1.C.3d
2.A.3a
2.B.3c
5.B.3a

One Student's Response

I knew that this was a cause-and-effect question because it included the key phrase <u>as a result</u>. This meant that it was asking for an <u>effect</u>. To answer this question, I looked at Karen's discussion with the music store owner and the events that followed the discussion. I was able to eliminate choices A, B, and D rather quickly. Choices A and B were clearly incorrect, based upon the facts of the story: Karen was determined to learn how to play drums throughout the story, and she definitely did not want a flute. She did read the bulletin board, but choice D was not an effect of the discussion that she had with the store owner. In fact, she did not speak with him until after she had read the bulletin board. I confidently chose C as the answer because after her discussion with the store owner, Karen walked home thinking about how she was going to tell her parents about her new job.

Responding to Questions That Require Inferences

Sometimes tests ask questions that are not answered directly in a selection. These questions are called **inference questions.** An **inference** is a reasonable conclusion or generalization based on evidence in the selection and your own experiences. It is an informed guess. In order to answer an inference question, you must read the selection carefully for evidence that supports your answer. You must figure out, based on the evidence and on your own general knowledge, which answer seems most reasonable.

A common type of inference question is one that requires you to draw a general conclusion from specific information. For example, suppose the text describes a person looking out a window at cars the size of ants and houses that look like pieces from a

Reading Comprehension 129

Reading Comprehension

board game. If you were asked where the person was, you would make an informed guess that the person was either in an airplane or a very tall building. If both of these were options among the answers, you would need to look for further evidence as to which answer was correct. The process of arriving at such a conclusion is called **making an inference.**

Another type of inference question is one based on general information provided in the selection; from that information, you are asked to draw a specific conclusion that is true. In such cases, this type of reasoning is known as **deduction.** For example, suppose that you know that the baseball coach in the story you are reading is a stickler about being on time and does not let team members play if they are late for a game. Suppose you also know that the main character is the best pitcher on the team and that they cannot win without him. If the player's car dies on

"Brilliant deduction!"

"Elementary, my dear test-takers."

his way to practice, you can reasonably deduce that his team will lose.

You may also be asked to make a prediction. A **prediction** is a reasonable guess about what you think will happen in the future. For example, if your class had scheduled an afternoon science outing to the park and a series of thunderstorms had been raging since the morning, it would be reasonable to guess that your trip would be postponed. This would be a prediction based on what you already know.

Use one or more of the following strategies to help you answer inference questions correctly:

Strategies for Answering Questions That Require Inferences

- First, try to rule out as many wrong answers as possible.

- Then, examine the choices that are left and look through the text for evidence that supports any of them. Think how you can put the facts from the story together with your own knowledge to come up with a reasonable inference.

- If more than one answer seems plausible, try to determine which one seems to be the *best* answer based on the evidence and your own knowledge.

- Check to make sure that your inferences and predictions are logical, based on your own knowledge and evidence from the text.

The following question about the main character in "Rhythm and Blues" asks you to make an inference, or prediction:

9. What kind of person do you think Karen will be when she grows up?
   - Ⓐ determined and independent
   - Ⓑ silly and uncaring
   - Ⓒ rude and selfish
   - Ⓓ indecisive and distracted

Meets ISAT Standards
1.B.3c
1.B.3d
1.C.3a
1.C.3d
2.A.3a
2.B.3c
5.B.3a

Here is how one student thought through the answer to Question 9:

One Student's Response

This question asked me to make a prediction about what Karen will be like when she grows up. First, I tried to rule out as many answers as I could. Choice D was clearly wrong because even though Karen seemed somewhat distracted in the beginning when she was drumming her fingers, she was never indecisive. I also eliminated choice B because I saw no evidence of silly behavior in Karen. Choice C seemed plausible because she could be considered somewhat selfish, in that she is fixated on learning how to play drums despite her father's wishes, and some people might consider the way she disagreed with her parents to be rude. Choice A seemed like a better answer, however, because Karen really was determined in her desire to learn how to play the drums despite her parents' disapproval. Moreover, she demonstrated her independence by getting a job in order to buy her own drum set. The evidence seemed to weigh more heavily in favor of Karen being determined and independent than rude and selfish, so I chose A as my final answer.

Reading Comprehension

Reading Comprehension

Now let's take another look at this question, which also asks you to make an inference:

10. Why do you think Karen's father convinces the store owner to let her take the drum set as an advance on her pay?

   Ⓐ He is worried that the store owner will try to cheat her out of her pay.

   Ⓑ He wants her to realize that she would not be any good as a drummer.

   Ⓒ He wants to be supportive by making sure she can try out for the band.

   Ⓓ He wants her to perform at a party he is giving that weekend.

Here is how one student thought through the answer to Question 10:

One Student's Response

I could tell that this question was asking me to make an <u>inference</u> based on the events of the story because it said, "Why do you think...." First, I tried to rule out as many answers as I could. Choice A seemed obviously wrong, since there was never any indication in the story that the store owner was dishonest or untrustworthy. Choice D also seemed wrong—there was no mention of a party in the story. Choice B was not supported by the text. In no place does the story say that Karen's father thinks she should realize that she won't be any good at playing the drums. In fact, at the end of the story, he seems quite supportive. Instead, choice C seems to be the correct answer. Considering what happens at the end of the story, when Karen's father suggests taking her to try out for the band after work, I can infer that he helped her get the drum set because he wanted her to have a chance to try out for the band.

Your Turn

Exercise Read each of the following selections. Then fill in the circle next to the correct answer to each multiple-choice question.

Meets ISAT Standards
1.B.3c
1.B.3d
1.C.3a
1.C.3d
2.A.3a
2.B.3c
5.B.3a

> When cameras were first invented, they were large, difficult to operate, and expensive. This meant that most people could not afford to own them. The introduction of smaller, less expensive, and easy-to-operate cameras in the early twentieth century opened up the field of photography to the general population. Today, we have affordable digital cameras that allow us to download images directly onto computers. When these digital cameras were first introduced, however, they too were very expensive. An overview of the history of cameras suggests that as a technology matures, it tends to become more affordable and thus more widely available.

1. What is the MAIN IDEA of this passage?
   - Ⓐ Most people cannot afford to own a camera.
   - Ⓑ The first cameras were large, expensive, and difficult to use.
   - Ⓒ Over time, a technology becomes cheaper and more widely accessible.
   - Ⓓ Digital cameras allow people to download images onto computers.

2. Which of the following events happened LAST?
   - Ⓐ Digital cameras became affordable.
   - Ⓑ Nearly anyone could afford to buy a camera.
   - Ⓒ Easy-to-operate cameras were introduced.
   - Ⓓ Smaller, less expensive nondigital cameras were invented.

More ▶

Reading Comprehension 133

Your Turn

Coach Peters called "Time out!" The team was behind by one point, with thirty seconds remaining in the game. Saleem thought back to the previous game, which he had lost by missing the final shot. "Don't put me in, Coach," he thought to himself. "I don't want another chance to blow the game." The coach's eyes settled on Saleem's lanky frame squirming near the end of the bench. "You're in!" barked Coach Peters. The clock ticked down, the basketball got loose, and there was a mad scramble on the court. Somehow, the ball ended up in Saleem's hands with three seconds left. It was too late to pass the ball—he had to shoot, and fast! Saleem lofted the ball up in the air, and it swished through the basket just as the clock ran out. His team had won.

3. How many seconds were left in the game when Coach Peters called "Time out"?
   - Ⓐ ten
   - Ⓑ twenty
   - Ⓒ thirty
   - Ⓓ forty

4. What happens BEFORE Saleem enters the game?
   - Ⓐ He makes the winning shot in the previous game.
   - Ⓑ He misses the final shot in the previous game.
   - Ⓒ There is a mad scramble for the ball.
   - Ⓓ He passes the ball to the opposing team.

> My neighbor, Jerry, is the best neighbor in the world. When I moved in next door to him five years ago, he took me around the block and introduced me to all my new neighbors. He also made a list of the best places to do my shopping and even included a map to each store. Back then, Jerry was in semi-retirement, but he was taking classes to learn how to be a kindergarten teacher. Just last year, however, his daughter had a baby, and he decided to quit school so he could spend more time with his granddaughter. Unfortunately, his daughter lives several miles away, and I do not get to talk to him as often as I used to. Despite all that, he still bakes pies for me and gives me flowers fresh from his garden. What a great neighbor!

Meets ISAT Standards
1.B.3c
1.B.3d
1.C.3a
1.C.3d
2.A.3a
2.B.3c
5.B.3a

5. Which detail shows you how Jerry makes the narrator feel welcome?

Ⓐ He takes classes at the local school.
Ⓑ He spends a lot of time with his granddaughter.
Ⓒ He introduces the narrator to everyone on the block.
Ⓓ He tells stories about semi-retirement.

6. Which of the following is NOT caused by the birth of Jerry's granddaughter?

Ⓐ He quits taking classes at the local school.
Ⓑ He gives baked pies and cut flowers.
Ⓒ He is not around as much as he used to be.
Ⓓ He does not talk to the narrator as much as he used to.

More ▶

Reading Comprehension 135

Your Turn

Meets ISAT
Standards
1.B.3c
1.B.3d
1.C.3a
1.C.3d
2.A.3a
2.B.3c
5.B.3a

> I think that it is important for people to consider adopting a dog from an animal shelter rather than purchasing one from a breeder. Because many dogs have not been spayed or neutered, there are more puppies than owners who are ready to raise them. As a result, many fine dogs sit in animal shelters and do not get adopted. Many dogs in animal shelters are not purebred, but some mutts are better behaved than purebreds. One final benefit of getting a dog from an animal shelter is that it is less expensive than purchasing a dog from a kennel. Adoption fees at a shelter tend to be quite low compared to the prices charged by for-profit kennels. Therefore, I implore anyone who is thinking about getting a dog to think about adopting one from a shelter instead of buying a purebred dog from a breeder.

7. What is the main idea of this passage?
   - Ⓐ The dog population is so large that many dogs do not get adopted.
   - Ⓑ Mutts are sometimes better behaved than purebred dogs.
   - Ⓒ Adoption fees in animal shelters are quite low.
   - Ⓓ People should consider adopting dogs from animal shelters.

8. Based on the information in the passage, what kind of person might the writer be?
   - Ⓐ a dog lover
   - Ⓑ a dog breeder
   - Ⓒ a kennel owner
   - Ⓓ a population expert

Return to the exercises at the beginning of the chapter, revise your work as necessary, and submit the exercises to your teacher for grading.

Chapter 7
A Tale to Tell
Understanding Fictional Narratives

First Encounter

Read this short story. Then try your hand at the exercises that follow the story. You will not be graded on the exercises at this time. At the end of the chapter, you will be directed to return to these exercises to revise and correct your work.

The Boom

by Tony Moore

My dad had been planning our sailing trip since I was eleven years old. He had spent two and a half years building a sailboat for our father-and-son adventure, and for two and a half years, he had been calling me out to the garage to help him. "C'mon skipper," he'd say. "Let's go work on *our* boat." But I never felt it was *our* boat. All I ever got to do was to hand him tools and get him glasses of iced tea. Once he actually let me help: I was supposed to sand some boards, and I worked really hard on them, but I guess I didn't do them right because as soon as I finished, he redid them. After that, I couldn't even breathe on the boat without being sent out of the garage on some errand.

It wasn't as if he did everything perfectly, either. The trip was supposed to have happened the previous summer, when I was twelve, but all kinds of things went wrong. First, he used the wrong sealant[1] and the whole front of the boat warped. Dad had to rebuild the entire hull.[2] Then he made the hole for the centerboard[3] too big. I tried to help. I even talked to the woodworking teacher at school, and we designed a wooden insert that would fit around the centerboard; Dad totally ignored our idea, of course, and did it his way. Just about the only thing he didn't make himself was the boom.[4] He ordered a custom-made boom that was constructed

---

[1] **sealant.** Substance used to prevent leaks
[2] **hull.** Outer body of the bottom part of a boat
[3] **centerboard.** Slab inserted at bottom center of a boat's hull that can be lowered into the water in order to stabilize a sailboat and lessen its sideways motion
[4] **boom.** Pole extending from a mast to hold or extend the bottom of a sail

out of some expensive aluminum alloy.[5] He insisted on researching the boom himself, but he made me come along on the two-hour drive to pick it up.

Finally, the boat came together, and the time for us to start our long-awaited trip arrived. Mom said that she was thrilled that Dad and I were going to "spend some quality time together." I think she was really thrilled to get rid of us, so that she and my sister Laurie could have the house to themselves. They were like best friends, the way they hung out together all the time—it was kind of creepy. I, on the other hand, was *not* eager to waste two weeks of my summer vacation in the middle of nowhere with Dad, following his orders. He wanted us to explore the islands in Lake Winnipeg and its interconnecting rivers. His plan sounded pretty ambitious to me, but I didn't say anything. He wouldn't have listened to me anyway. He gave me tourism packets about Canada and asked me to choose campsites, but then he ended up making the arrangements on his own. He was so obsessed with planning the trip and so excited about finally sailing his boat that it did not occur to him to ask whether I even wanted to go.

The night before we left, Dad stayed up half the night checking to make sure that he had packed everything that we needed. Again, I tried to help, but he said he had it all under control. I was really starting to dread going on this trip.

We hitched up the boat trailer and left at 5 A.M. When we crossed the border into Canada, the roads wound through trees and hills, and there were long stretches when we saw absolutely no sign of people anywhere. The forest looked different from the ones I was used to in southern Michigan. We were surrounded by towering evergreens as far as the eye could see. I felt as if we were driving down a long, dark tunnel. When I looked in the rearview mirror, it seemed as if the trees were closing in behind us, cutting us off from civilization.

I asked Dad if I could navigate and tried to find our campground on the map. There were many little dirt roads, though. It was hard to tell which numbers on the map went with the roads I was seeing, and I ended up getting us a little lost. Dad was furious. He wouldn't speak to me until we were on the right track again. I didn't mind the silence so much; it was better than some of the conversations we had.

During the three endless days of driving, our "conversations" were actually lectures from Dad. He kept telling me that I needed to develop a greater appreciation for nature: "'Simplify, Simplify, Simplify,' as Thoreau said. We are going to the woods to live 'close to the bone.'" Dad loved to speak in quotes. I felt like Bilbo Baggins listening to Gollum's riddles.[6] As he droned on and on, I thought about my friends hanging out at the arcade, wiping out all my high scores.

---

[5]**alloy.** Metal made stronger or better by addition of other metals; in this case, probably made lighter and more resistant to rust
[6]**Bilbo . . . Gollum.** Characters in J.R.R. Tolkien's *The Hobbit*

Understanding Fictional Narratives

First Encounter

When we finally reached Lake Winnipeg, we registered at the campground and then drove the boat trailer down to the water. The grayish blue lake was ruffled with white-capped waves. It was a beautiful blue-sky afternoon, with the wind flapping our clothes—a perfect day for sailing, Dad declared. He was in such a good mood that he even let me help raise the mast and secure the boom in place. We started talking in pirate voices and calling each other "Matey" as we lowered the boat into the water. We gazed toward the horizon with the eagerness of great explorers. It was a blast . . . for a while.

Once the boat was in the water and pointed into the wind, Dad said, "OK, Jared! Time to hoist the sails!"

I said, "Yes, sir, Cap'n," and we chuckled, even though it wasn't that funny. I grabbed the main halyard and then handed it to Dad. He deserved the satisfaction of raising the mainsail. I raised the jib and then climbed onto the foredeck to back it.[7] The white sails filled with air, as if puffing out their chests with pride. I imagine that's how Dad must have been feeling as we set sail in the boat he had built from scratch.

Once we got out in the middle of the lake, the wind was much stronger than it had been near the shore. We were flying along.

"Let out the main all the way and bring 'er down into a run,[8]" Dad said.

I guess I pushed the tiller[9] out too far, for suddenly Dad was yelling and the boom came swinging around, hard, from one side of the boat to the other. The boom hit him squarely across the shoulder, knocking him overboard.

Dad sputtered and splashed in the water as the boat sped past him. I think he was calling for help, but I couldn't seem to hear anything. He grew smaller and smaller as the boat and I were pushed away from him by the strong, steady wind. He began waving his arms frantically.

At last, the faint sound of his voice brought me out of my stupor. I had to turn the boat around and go get him. I panicked as I looked around at the parts of the boat: My mind went blank. I had never sailed alone before. When Dad did let me handle the tiller, he usually told me exactly what to do. He often took over and did everything by himself.

---

[7] **jib . . . back it.** The jib is the small sail at the front of a sailboat. A sailboat cannot sail when pointed directly into the wind. To move a sailboat that is stalled in this way, one can "back the jib," pushing the sail manually to one side or the other until it fills with air.
[8] **run.** Almost exactly opposite the direction from which the wind is blowing; sailing downwind; or *with* the wind
[9] **tiller.** Lever used to turn a rudder and thus steer the boat

I had watched him pretty closely. What could I do now but try?

I took a deep breath and grabbed the tiller and mainsheet.[10] I knew I had to push the tiller right to steer left and left to steer right. I was surprised at how nimbly the boat responded to my maneuvers as I swung it around and headed back toward Dad. I felt completely natural at the helm[11] as I headed back toward the head bobbing in the water. As Dad grew larger up ahead, it dawned on me that I had no idea how to stop the boat once I reached him. I grabbed one of the life jackets and tossed it to him as I sailed past.

"Turn her into[12] the wind," Dad yelled as he grabbed the jacket.

I whipped the boat around once again and sailed back toward Dad. I jammed the tiller to the right and turned directly into the wind. The boat halted like a horse whose reins had been pulled in. The thrill of satisfaction from my deft[13] command of the ship was squelched by terror as I watched Dad swimming toward me. He was going to kill me. No, worse than that, he was going to rant and rave about this for the rest of the vacation. He would be in a bad mood the whole time, and yet he would refuse to go home early.

I was resigned to a week and a half of torture as I extended a trembling hand and helped him climb into the boat. He took a towel from me in stern silence. I braced myself for a tirade, but nothing happened.

Dad just sat there quietly with his face buried in the towel. The sun was going down, and everything was cloaked in shadows. On shore, someone's laundry was flapping around on a clothesline between an RV and a pine tree.

"Dad, I'm really sorry," I said softly.

I was expecting him to fly into a rage, to start throwing things around the boat and yelling at me—that, or give me the silent treatment all the way back. I didn't know what to make of it when his shoulders started shaking. Was he crying? I looked away, embarrassed, toward the expanse of steely gray water that stretched before me. For a split second, I considered jumping ship. Suddenly, my father's head fell back from the force of a laugh so explosive that it is probably still echoing through the woods around Lake Winnipeg. Before I knew it, we were both doubled over with tears streaming down our cheeks. I didn't know why we were laughing; it didn't matter.

At last our howls died down. "Thanks for rescuing me, Mate," he said. We both chuckled, even though it wasn't that funny. Then Dad straightened up with a serious expression. He looked me in the eye and said, "Trust yourself when all men doubt you, but make allowance for their doubting too."[14] It was another riddle, but this time I knew what he was trying to say. He motioned toward the tiller. "Take us on home, Cap'n," he said.

---

[10] **mainsheet.** Rope controlling the mainsail
[11] **at the helm.** In charge of a boat (**helm** = tiller or steering wheel)
[12] **into.** Toward; facing the direction from which the wind is coming
[13] **deft.** Skillful
[14] **Trust . . . too.** Quotation from the British author Rudyard Kipling's poem "If"

Your Turn

Exercise A *Fill in the circle next to the correct answer to each multiple-choice question.*

1. What is Jared's attitude toward the trip to Canada?
   - Ⓐ He wishes he didn't have to go on the trip at all.
   - Ⓑ He is excited about helping his father plan the trip.
   - Ⓒ He wants his father to hurry up and finish the boat so they can leave.
   - Ⓓ He wishes he had more time to take sailing lessons before the trip.

2. Which of the following events happens AFTER all the others?
   - Ⓐ Dad stays up half the night checking his packing.
   - Ⓑ Dad is knocked out of the boat.
   - Ⓒ Dad rebuilds the boat's hull.
   - Ⓓ Dad plans a father-son trip to Canada.

3. When does Jared's father show that he has learned to respect his son?
   - Ⓐ when he asks Jared to sail the boat home
   - Ⓑ when he plans a long father-son adventure
   - Ⓒ when he asks Jared to sand some boards
   - Ⓓ when he lets Jared rebuild the hull of the boat

4. "I braced myself for a tirade, but nothing happened. Dad just sat there quietly with his face buried in the towel." What does the word *tirade* mean?
   - Ⓐ a loud, enthusiastic song
   - Ⓑ a long, angry lecture
   - Ⓒ a very generous gesture
   - Ⓓ an honest review or opinion

5. What do you think will happen on the drive home?
   - Ⓐ Dad will get mad at Jared for spoiling the trip.
   - Ⓑ Dad will tell Jared he is going to take Laurie next time.
   - Ⓒ They will get along well because they have resolved some problems.
   - Ⓓ They will get into an accident, and the boat will be damaged.

Exercise B Choose one of the following topics for an essay. In the space below, write a thesis statement. Then do a rough outline for your essay. Write the draft of the essay on your own paper. Revise it using the checklist on pages 265–66, and proofread it using the checklist on page 270. Then create the final draft.

Meets ISAT Standards
1.A.3b
1.B.3b
1.B.3c
1.B.3d
1.C.3a
1.C.3b
2.A.3b
3.A.3
3.B.3a
3.B.3b

1. How does Jared change as a result of his trip with his father? What do you think he has learned about himself by struggling to meet his father's expectations?

2. Summarize the plot of "The Boom." Describe how the conflict between Jared and Dad is introduced; what the crisis, or turning point, of the story is; and how the conflict is resolved.

THESIS STATEMENT: _____

_____

ROUGH OUTLINE:

Understanding Fictional Narratives 143

Understanding Fictional Narratives

A Tale to Tell

Elements of Narrative Fiction

A piece of writing that tells a story is called a **narrative.** A narrative may be **fiction,** an imaginary story, or **nonfiction,** a story about real people, places, and events. Novels are a type of fictional narrative, as are short stories like the one you just read.

All forms of fictional narrative have certain elements in common that can be thought of as their building blocks, or essential parts. When you come across a fictional narrative on a test, you may be asked to answer questions about the parts of a narrative. Learning about the elements of stories will help you to analyze, understand, and enjoy them.

Elements of a Narrative

1. **Setting.** The time and the place in which the events of a story occur. The setting in a narrative can sometimes be clear and well defined or, at other times, it can be left to a reader's imagination. The words "Outside the wind was blowing bitterly, and the snow was swirling all around the broken-down shack" describe a setting that helps to create in the reader a particular mood, or emotional response.

2. **Mood.** The overall feeling that a literary work or a part of a work creates in the reader. The mood of a story can change as the plot unfolds. The mood of a narrative is usually described by using adjectives such as *sad, suspenseful,* or *lighthearted.* The mood of the story that contains the setting described above might be described as bleak or gloomy.

3. **Tone.** The attitude of the writer or narrator toward ideas, events, or characters described in a story, or the attitude of a character toward ideas, events, or other characters. Tone is often described by such adjectives as *playful, ironic,* or *serious.* Writers create tone by carefully choosing specific words and details. In *The Adventures of Tom Sawyer,* Mark Twain says of Tom, "At this dark and hopeless moment an inspiration burst upon him. Nothing less than a great, magnificent inspiration." Twain's tone in this passage is *humorous* and *playful.* The phrases "dark and hopeless" and "great, magnificent" are exaggerations the author uses in order to poke gentle fun at the extremes of a young boy's emotions.

4. **Narrator.** The person or character who tells the story. An **internal narrator** is a character who tells a story. An **external narrator** is an observer who relates what happens to the characters. He or she is not a character or participant in the story's action.

More ▶

5. **Point of view.** The viewpoint from which the story is told

   - **First-person point of view.** The narrator tells the story using words such as *I* and *we* and often takes part in the narrative's action. "I listened closely and nodded as she tried to teach me all that she knew about riding" might be a line in a story told from the first-person point of view.

   - **Third-person point of view.** The narrator tells the story using words such as *he, she,* and *they* and does not participate in the narrative's action. "He stood frozen, watching the front door as it creaked open" could be a line in a story told from the third-person point of view.

6. **Characters.** The people, animals, or other creatures who take part in a story's action. The qualities or attributes of a character, such as personality, habits, appearance, and background, are called **characteristics.**

   - **Protagonist.** The main character in the selection. During the course of the story, that character experiences some conflict, or struggle, and usually goes through some important change.

   - **Antagonist.** The character (or force) with whom the protagonist has a conflict. Not all stories have an antagonist.

   - **Minor character.** A character who does not play a major role in the story

   - **Static character.** A character who does not change during the course of the action

   - **Dynamic character.** A character who changes in the course of the action

7. **Conflict.** A problem or struggle experienced by the protagonist

   - **External conflict.** A struggle between a character and an outside force. A sailor's struggle with a raging storm at sea is an example of an external conflict.

   - **Internal conflict.** A struggle experienced within a character. An example of an internal conflict might be a character's debate with himself about whether to report the risky behavior of a friend in order to keep the friend from getting hurt.

8. **Plot.** The series of events that occur in a story. Plots generally follow a particular pattern, which we will examine in more detail in the next section.

9. **Motivation.** A force that moves a character to act in a certain way. Like conflict, a motivation can be internal or external. A character might be motivated to go back to college by his desire to have a greater understanding of the world (**internal motivation**) or by pressure from his wife to get a better job that pays a higher salary (**external motivation**). The related term **motive** is often used

Meets ISAT Standards
1.B.3b
1.B.3c
1.B.3d
1.C.3a
1.C.3b
2.A.3b
2.B.3a
2.B.3c

More ▶

Understanding Fictional Narratives

Understanding Fictional Narratives

to describe a reason that a character has for acting in a certain way, as in "His motive was revenge."

10. **Theme.** A main idea or message conveyed by a literary work. Often, the theme is what the reader learns by observing the character's attempts to deal with the central conflict. The theme of a narrative should not be confused with the **subject,** or what the work is about. The subject of a story might be the friendship among a group of girls, whereas the theme might be that some friendships fade with time and distance, while others survive despite such obstacles.

Two Approaches to Analyzing a Story

When taking a test that involves reading comprehension, it is important to know how to analyze a story. Becoming familiar with the major elements of narratives is the first step in this process. The next step is to try to understand how these elements work together to create the overall effect of the story. Two common approaches are particularly helpful in coming to a greater understanding of a story: character analysis and plot analysis.

Character Analysis

You can learn a lot by thinking carefully about the characters in a story. As you read a fictional narrative, ask yourself questions like these about the characters:

Questions to Ask about Characters

Who is narrating the story? Is the narrator a character?

From what point of view is the story told?

What is the tone, or attitude, of the central character at the beginning of the story? How do you think he or she is feeling?

What is the challenge that the protagonist must overcome or the conflict that he or she faces?

Is this conflict internal, external, or both?

What are the protagonist's motivations? The antagonist's (if there is one)?

What are the major characteristics, or attributes, of the main character? Of the antagonist (if there is one)?

How does the protagonist meet his or her challenge, and what is the effect on him or her of the resolution of the conflict?

In the end, how has the protagonist changed, and what has he or she learned?

Who are the minor characters, and what roles do they play in the story?

When you do a **character analysis,** you take a closer look at a single character. Let's look at one student's character analysis of Jared, from the story "The Boom."

Meets ISAT Standards
1.B.3b
1.B.3c
1.B.3d
1.C.3a
1.C.3b
2.A.3b
2.B.3a
2.B.3c

Character Analysis: One Student's Process

The first sentence of the story, "My dad had been planning our sailing trip since I was eleven years old," uses the pronoun I, which suggests that the story is told from the first-person point of view. Jared is the one talking, so the reader knows immediately that Jared is the narrator of this story as well as the protagonist. Jared's tone, or attitude, toward the father-and-son sailing trip that his father has been planning is very negative. His dad thinks of the boat and the trip as their project, something that they are working on together, but Jared does not feel that way. He obviously resents the fact that his father won't let him help or do anything. The external conflict is that Jared's dad still thinks of Jared as a little kid and treats him that way. His father's lack of trust undermines Jared's confidence. Jared's greatest challenge in the story is sailing the boat by himself, which is made more difficult by his lack of confidence. He is strongly motivated by the desire to save his father, however, so he grabs the tiller. By successfully sailing the boat, Jared discovers that he is capable and proves this to his father as well. Therefore, the biggest change in Jared is that he gains confidence in himself. Jared also earns his father's trust. Jared's rescue of his father (who suddenly became the helpless one) ends the central conflict in the story. At the beginning of the story, Jared's characteristics include resentment and emotional distance from his father. Later in the story, Jared proves himself to have such characteristics as courage, resolve, and resourcefulness.

Understanding Fictional Narratives

Understanding Fictional Narratives

Meets ISAT Standards
1.B.3b
1.B.3c
1.B.3d
1.C.3a
1.C.3b
2.A.3b
2.B.3a
2.B.3c

Plot Analysis

As mentioned previously in the chapter, the **plot** is the series of events in a narrative. A plot usually involves the working out of a central conflict experienced by the main character, or protagonist. Although narratives do not always follow the same plot pattern, most will contain the main elements (see list below). When reading a narrative, look for the major plot elements. Be aware, however, that the selections on reading comprehension tests might be short passages or excerpts from longer narratives. In a short passage or excerpt, you might not find all the plot elements that would be present in a full-length narrative.

Elements of Plot

- **Exposition.** The part of the plot in which the characters and setting are introduced and background information is provided. The mood and tone are often established in this part of the plot.

- **Inciting incident.** The part of the plot in which the central conflict is introduced

- **Rising action.** The series of events by means of which the conflict intensifies, or builds

- **Climax.** The high point of interest or suspense in a story

- **Crisis.** The turning point in the story, when something decisive happens to determine how the conflict will be resolved or to bring about some kind of change in the main character. (In some stories, the climax and the crisis are the same event.)

- **Falling action.** The events that occur after the turning point. (Some narratives do not contain this element.)

- **Resolution.** The event that ends or that determines decisively the outcome of the central conflict

- **Dénouement.** The part of a story in which the loose ends of the plot are tied up. (Some narratives do not contain this element.)

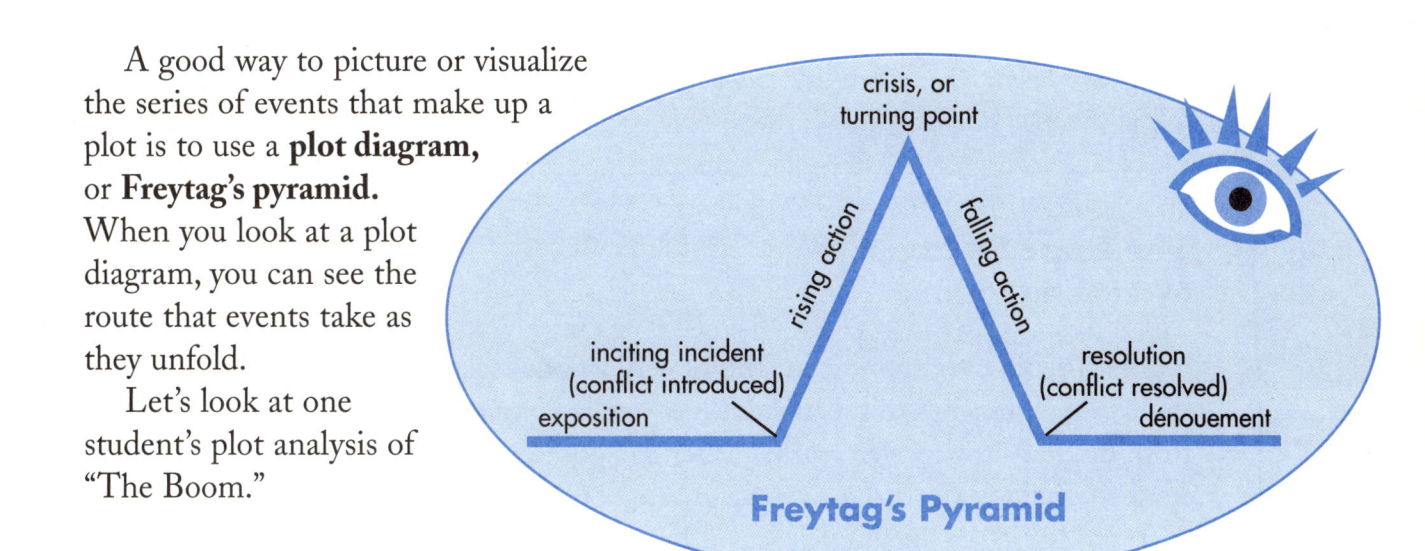

A good way to picture or visualize the series of events that make up a plot is to use a **plot diagram,** or **Freytag's pyramid.** When you look at a plot diagram, you can see the route that events take as they unfold.

Let's look at one student's plot analysis of "The Boom."

Freytag's Pyramid

- crisis, or turning point
- rising action
- falling action
- inciting incident (conflict introduced)
- exposition
- resolution (conflict resolved)
- dénouement

Plot Analysis: One Student's Process

In "The Boom," the <u>exposition</u> occurs in the first two paragraphs, in which Jared explains the history behind the sailing trip his father has been planning. This is the part of the story in which we learn why Jared is not thrilled about the trip, and we also get a sense of the issues that he has with his dad. The <u>inciting incident</u> is when they set off on the sailing trip. Clearly, the <u>central conflict</u>—the tension between Jared and his father—is going to come to a head on this trip. The <u>action rises</u> gradually as they travel to Canada, get lost along the way, finally arrive at the lake, get the boat all set, and begin sailing. As the wind picks up, so does the action, rising sharply toward a climax. The <u>climax</u> occurs when Jared's dad gets knocked out of the boat. This is definitely the most intense and exciting part of the action. The <u>turning point</u> is when Jared has to go back to rescue his father and manages to sail the boat on his own. There seems to be a change in Jared when he realizes that he has handled the boat pretty well by himself. The conflict is not fully resolved at this point, however, because Jared is still worried about what his father's reaction is going to be. The <u>resolution</u> of the conflict occurs when both Jared and his father laugh about the incident, releasing the tension that has built up. Then Jared's father, showing a new level of confidence in his son, asks him to sail the boat home. The <u>dénouement</u> is left to the reader's imagination, but it seems clear that the two characters are going to have a great time on the rest of their trip and will go home feeling much closer than they did before.

Understanding Fictional Narratives

Your Turn

Exercise A You have seen examples of a character analysis and a plot analysis. Read the story below. Then complete the character analysis and the plot analysis that follow the story.

The Rope Swing
by Victoria Fortune

Ben peered over the edge of the rickety wooden platform wedged high in the branches of the ancient oak tree. Thirty feet below, the frothing, red-brown river swirled around exposed roots that jutted out from the muddy riverbank like the gnarled bones of an old man's hand. A rotten log came hurtling along in the torrent and smashed against the jagged roots, shattering violently. The scattered remains were whisked away by the rushing current. Ben snapped his head back with a sharp gasp. His hands were slick with sweat—he'd never be able to hold on to the rope long enough to swing past the roots.

Ben glanced down at the jeering faces of Kenny and his friends, Eddie and Z Grissom.

"Hurry up!" Z demanded from the ground below. Kids at school joked that Z got his nickname because that was the only letter of the alphabet he could remember. Of course, they only said that behind his back. Z was a big, scary kid. He and his brother Eddie were the meanest, dumbest pair of bullies that Tallahatchie County had to offer. Yet, for some reason that Ben could not comprehend, his cousin Kenny had joined their ranks.

Ben had worshipped Kenny for as long as he could remember. Kenny was a couple of years older, but he had always let Ben hang out with him. They lived right down the road from each other. Ben's mom worked all the time, so Ben practically lived at his cousin's house. Kenny had taught Ben how to throw a ball, how to bait a hook, how to swim. Ben had learned just about everything he knew from Kenny.

Then Kenny started high school and things changed. He started hanging with the Grissom boys; the three of them were like a pack of hungry hyenas. They could smell fear and weakness from a mile away. Ben became the default victim of the pack when no other prey was available. Around his new friends, Kenny treated Ben like a mangy mutt.

If Ben tried to talk to him in public, he would make fun of Ben, embarrass him. Afterward, when the others were gone, Kenny would feel bad. He would say he was sorry, and Ben, eager for things to be the way they used to be, would forgive him. But Kenny never asked Ben to come along with him anymore. In fact, before long, Ben would find himself the victim of yet another scheme.

Once again, Ben had let himself be goaded by another dare. Well, this time he wasn't going to go through with it. He'd climb down. He gazed over the edge of the platform again at the row of boards that served as the ladder. They were nailed to the tree trunk all askew, and the distance between them looked much greater from this angle. Could he make it down that way, especially in his mud-caked sneakers? His tormenters stood at the bottom, glaring at him. Their mocking laughter drifted up on the hot summer breeze. If he climbed down, what would they do to him then? At least if he jumped, they would leave him alone, for a while.

A rush of fear and adrenaline surged through him, leaving his hands and feet tingling. He had heard the stories: One kid had jumped from the rope swing and been carried off by the current; no one ever saw him again. Another had slipped and fallen against the roots, cracking his skull open. That's why the river looks reddish, everyone said. The creaking of the boards beneath his sneakers, the roar of the river below, and the sing-song cadence of the boys' taunts swirled in Ben's brain. A strange sensation came over him, as if he were watching himself from a distance as his hands grasped the rope. He raised himself up on his tiptoes, leaned his weight back, and then flung himself forward off the platform.

He felt so free and light, soaring through the air, the wind in his hair, until a voice below him screamed, "Let go!" and he did. He was falling, flailing wildly, . . . and then, SMACK! His back hit the water so hard that it knocked the wind out of him. He gasped and choked, splashing and kicking frantically toward the shoreline that was slipping past like the view from a moving car. He couldn't breathe, even though his head was out of the water. He was sure he would drown.

His groping hands found a stray root, and he dragged himself onto the muddy riverbank. He grunted, coughed, and sputtered, gasping desperately for air. His back stung and his chest was heaving. He was battered and weak; he could barely feel his limbs, but as the sound of cackling laughter grew louder, he jumped up to protect himself from the approaching bullies.

"That was awesome!" Eddie snorted like a pig.

"Do it again," Z demanded.

More ▶

Your Turn

"Naw," Kenny mumbled. "He did it. Let him go."

"Well, I want to see him do it again," Eddie whined, his laughter fading.

"You heard him." Z stepped up in Ben's face. "Do it again, Benny. And this time . . . don't use the rope."

"C'mon guys," Kenny tried to sound nonchalant.

"Are you chicken, little Benny?" Eddie sneered.

"Leave him alone," Kenny said firmly.

Z narrowed his eyes and shifted his massive bulk into Kenny's path.

"You gonna make us?" he hissed, spewing saliva at Kenny through the huge gap in his front teeth. "How 'bout you jump with little Benny? You guys can hold hands." He and Eddie howled at the thought.

Watching Kenny being humiliated, something snapped in Ben. All the anger and rage of a hundred injustices boiled to the surface, blinding him to fear or consequences. "We'll jump," he declared, stepping between Kenny and Z and staring Z right in his beady black eyes. "In fact," Ben said, struck by the remarkable calmness of his own voice, "we'll even hold hands . . . , as long as you and Eddie jump first." He stepped back and waved his hand toward the platform, as if motioning politely for them to proceed.

Eddie and Z hesitated, glancing at one another blankly.

"Go on," Ben said, his courage mounting. "You're not scared, are you? If a scrawny kid like me could do it, you guys can. The platform is pretty shaky up there, but it'll probably hold your weight. I wouldn't look down, though, if I were you."

Z tried to look tough as he searched his vacant mind for a reply. Eddie was even paler than usual and clearly nervous.

"We gotta get home," he stammered. "C'mon, Z." He turned and plodded away without waiting for his brother. Z grumbled and slunk away after him.

"I'm sorry," Kenny said, "about everything."

"It's OK," Ben replied.

"Nice jump from the rope swing," Kenny added.

"Yeah, thanks."

"Hey, Ben . . . ." Kenny kicked at stones with the toe of his sneaker.

"Yeah?"

"Wanna grab some poles—see if the fish are biting?"

"Sure," Ben grinned. "You dig up the worms this time."

Part 1: Character Analysis

Who is the narrator of the story? From what point of view is the story told?
_____
_____

Who is the protagonist?
_____

What is the tone, or attitude, of the protagonist at the beginning of the story? How do you think he or she is feeling?
_____
_____
_____

What is the challenge or conflict that the protagonist must overcome? Is it an internal challenge, or an external one, or both?
_____
_____
_____

How does the protagonist overcome his or her conflict?
_____
_____
_____

In the end, how has the protagonist changed, or what has he or she learned?
_____
_____
_____

Meets ISAT Standards
1.B.3c
1.B.3d
1.C.3a
1.C.3b
1.C.3d
2.A.3a
2.A.3b
2.B.3a
2.B.3c

More ▶

Understanding Fictional Narratives

Your Turn

Part 2: Plot Analysis

Exposition: _____
_____
_____

Inciting incident: _____
_____

Rising action: _____
_____
_____

Climax: _____
_____

Crisis, or turning point: _____
_____
_____

Falling action: _____
_____
_____

Resolution: _____
_____
_____

Dénouement: _____
_____
_____

Exercise B Now that you have completed a character analysis and a plot analysis of the story, use that information to respond to the following extended-response questions. Make sure that you support your main ideas with evidence in the form of summaries, paraphrases, or quotations from the selection. Write your answers in complete sentences.

> Meets ISAT Standards
> 1.B.3c
> 1.B.3d
> 1.C.3a
> 1.C.3b
> 1.C.3d
> 2.A.3a
> 2.A.3b
> 2.B.3a
> 2.B.3c
> 3.A.3
> 3.B.3a

1. What do you think Ben has learned about human nature from his experience with Kenny and the Grissom boys? Do you think his relationship with Kenny will be different now? Why or why not?

   _____
   _____
   _____
   _____
   _____
   _____
   _____
   _____

2. In some stories, the climax and the turning point (crisis) are the same event; however, this is not always the case. What is the climax of "The Rope Swing," and what is the turning point? Explain your answer, using evidence from the text.

   _____
   _____
   _____
   _____
   _____
   _____
   _____
   _____

More ▶

Understanding Fictional Narratives

Your Turn

3. Taking a dare to perform a dangerous feat can have disastrous consequences. Every year, thousands of kids in the United States are injured as a result of taking dares. Given how dangerous it was to jump from the tree into the river, was Ben justified in daring Eddie and Z to take the leap? Why or why not?

Understanding Fictional Narratives

Presenting Evidence: Quotations, Paraphrases, and Summaries

When you are asked to write about literature, whether on a test or for a class, your response should contain both a main idea, which is expressed in a thesis statement, and evidence from one or more selections to back up your main idea. **Evidence** is information provided to prove or support a general statement. Three ways in which you can present evidence from a source are quotations, paraphrases, and summaries.

- A **quotation** includes words, groups of words, or whole sentences from the selection. When you quote from a selection, you pick up the material you want to include word for word, just as the author stated it, and you place that material in quotation marks in your essay.

- When you **paraphrase,** you restate the material from the selection in your own words, using roughly the same amount of detail as was used in the selection. Since you are describing the material in your own words, no quotation marks are needed.

- When you **summarize** material, you also restate material from the selection in your own words, but you condense it, using fewer words than were used in the selection. Whereas paraphrasing involves describing the material in detail, summarizing requires restating only the most important points, in as few words as possible.

It is important not to overuse paraphrases and summaries. Avoid simply retelling the selection. Retelling the selection is an easy mistake to make when writing about stories or nonfiction narratives. Rarely, however, will a writing prompt ask you simply to summarize the information in a selection. Rather, paraphrasing and summarizing should be used to provide specific evidence in support of points that you wish to make.

As you read a writing prompt, ask yourself, "What exactly am I being asked to do?" and "How can I best answer this question?" When you have determined what your answer will be, look back over the selection for specific evidence to support this answer. Then decide in which form this information would be most effectively presented in your answer—a quotation, paraphrase, or summary. You may want to use some combination of these.

Study the sample student response on the following page. It is a response to a writing prompt based on the story, "The Boom" at the beginning of this chapter. This response uses a combination of quotations, paraphrases, and summaries to present supporting evidence.

Meets ISAT Standards
1.B.3c
1.B.3d
1.C.3a
1.C.3b
1.C.3d
2.B.3a
3.A.3
3.B.3a
5.B.3a

Understanding Fictional Narratives 157

Understanding Fictional Narratives

WRITING PROMPT: *In Tony Moore's "The Boom," how does the main character change during the course of the story? What do you think he has learned about himself and his relationship with his father?*

Summary — In Tony Moore's story, "The Boom," Jared's experience on the sailboat helps him to develop a better understanding of his father as well as more confidence in himself. As the result of a scary crisis out on the lake, Jared finds out that he and his father can be closer than he would have imagined.

At the beginning of the story, the reader gets a glimpse of a father and son who do not work as a team or communicate well with each other. Jared's dad refers to the boat as "our boat," but building it is a one-sided project in which Jared's father builds while Jared feels useless and resentful. Jared

Quotation — says, "I couldn't even breathe on the boat without being sent out of the garage on some errand." When the boat is finally ready for the trip, Jared is "not eager to waste two weeks of my summer vacation in the middle of nowhere with Dad, following his orders." Though Jared's father is bossy and impatient, it also seems that Jared is partly to blame for the lack of communication: Not once does Jared tell his father what he thinks. Instead,

Summary — Jared keeps his resentment to himself. He listens to his father less than he would if he weren't so resentful.

At the moment the boom hits Jared's dad and knocks him into the lake, however, a real change begins. Jared has to act; left alone in the boat, he

Summary — has to take responsibility for the situation. Suddenly, his experience as a silent observer comes in handy, and Jared shows that he knows something about the boat after all. He turns it around, heads back to his father, and manages to rescue him.

Even as he is rescuing his Dad, Jared expects the worst. He says, "I was

Quotation — resigned to a week and a half of torture as I extended a trembling hand and helped him to climb into the boat." Jared does, however, speak to his dad at

Paraphrase — that moment. He says with sincerity that he is sorry for letting the boom knock his father into the water. Tension is released when Jared's dad lets out a huge, echoing laugh and Jared laughs with him. Father and son are relieved

Summary — by the rescue, and both can see the humor in what has just happened.

The ability to laugh together is just part of the change between Jared and his father. Suddenly, Jared has the sense that his father respects him.

Paraphrase — In fact, Dad tells Jared that he should trust himself even when others—including his own father—doubt him. Then he lets Jared steer the boat.

Summary — Jared learns many things on this trip: that he can drive the boat by himself, that his father appreciates what Jared can do, and that his father is more than just a critical pain in the neck.

Incorporating Quotations into Your Writing

1. Use quotation marks around direct quotations but not around paraphrases.

2. When quoting fewer than three lines from the selection, include the quotation in your paragraph and enclose it in quotation marks, as the writer did in the sample response on the previous page. When quoting three lines or more, set the quotation off in a paragraph of its own and indent the left and right margins five spaces (or one tab space) farther than the rest of the text. Indent the first line of the excerpt quoted only if it is indented in the original. Single-space the quotation and omit quotation marks, as in the following example from a story called "Leaving Taiwan":

   > Their ways and customs may seem strange at first, but think of all you will learn. You will make new friends with American boys and girls. You will learn to play their games.... You will even find that some of your games are the same. You can look forward to many exciting times.

3. When quoting more than one line from a poem, use a slash mark with spaces on either side to separate the lines. Capitalize and punctuate the quotation exactly as in the source.

   > The speaker of "A Birthday" has also experienced a rebirth but of a different kind. She says that she is overjoyed "Because the birthday of [her] life / Is come."

4. Make sure that quotations fit grammatically into your sentences. If you need to change a verb or pronoun to make it agree, as in the example above, place the changed material in brackets: [ ].

5. When the material quoted includes a direct quotation within a quotation, enclose the direct quotation in single quotation marks (' '), as in the following example:

   > It is clear from Jared's comments that he does not feel the boat is his at all: "'C'mon skipper,' [Dad would] say. 'Let's go work on *our* boat.' But I never felt it was *our* boat," Jared explains.

6. Conventionally, stories are written in the past tense, as in "Once upon a time, there was a young man who set out to seek his fortune." When writing about the events that occur in a literary work, however, you should use the *present* tense:

   > Jared sees the trip as a waste of two weeks. His father, on the other hand, seems excited.

   (The verbs *sees* and *seems* are in the present tense.)

More ▶

Meets ISAT Standards
1.B.3c
1.B.3d
1.C.3a
1.C.3b
1.C.3d
2.B.3a
5.B.3a

Understanding Fictional Narratives

Understanding Fictional Narratives

7. Sometimes you may wish to leave out some of the words within a quotation. Use an ellipsis (...) to indicate any words that are missing.

> Victoria Fortune writes, "The creaking of the boards beneath his sneakers... swirled in Ben's brain."

8. Use a period and an ellipsis (....) when omitting a sentence or more from a quotation, but be sure that complete sentences precede and follow the ellipsis.

> Ben had worshipped Kenny for as long as he could remember.... Ben's mom worked all the time, so Ben practically lived at his cousin's house.

9. Use a comma to set off a speaker's tag, such as *he says* or *he replies*.

> Ben says, "If a scrawny kid like me could do it, you guys can."

10. A colon may be used to introduce a quotation in a more formal way, especially after a phrase such as *the following*.

> Ben issues the following challenge to Eddie and Z: "Go on... You're not scared, are you?"

11. Periods and commas at the ends of quotations always go within the quotation marks. Other punctuation marks, such as colons, semicolons, question marks, and exclamation points go outside the quotation marks, except when they are part of the quotation. In the following sentence, the question mark is part of the quotation, so it goes *inside* the quotation marks.

> "Are you chicken, little Benny?" Eddie sneered.

Notice, however, that if the sentence in which the quotation appears is a question, but the quotation itself is not a question, then the question mark goes *outside* the quotation marks, as in the following sentence:

> Is Eddie telling the truth when he says, "We gotta get home"?

Your Turn

Exercise A Paraphrase, or restate in your own words, each of the sentences below.

1. Beauty is only skin deep.
   _____

2. A stitch in time saves nine.
   _____

3. Necessity is the mother of invention.
   _____

4. Neither a borrower nor a lender be;/For loan oft loses both itself and friend.
   _____

Meets ISAT Standards
1.B.3c
1.B.3d
1.C.3a
1.C.3b
1.C.3d
2.B.3a
3.A.3
3.B.3a
3.B.3b

Exercise B Choose one of the writing prompts below and write your response on your own paper.

1. What is the mood of the story "The Boom?" How does the author establish the mood? Does the mood change over the course of the story? Use evidence from the text to explain your answer.

2. In the story "The Rope Swing," how does Ben's attitude toward Eddie and Z change? At what point in the story does this change seem to occur? Use evidence from the text to explain your answer.

More ▶

Understanding Fictional Narratives

Your Turn

Exercise C The following paragraph contains some errors in the use of quotation marks. Read the paragraph carefully. Correct any errors that you find using the proofreading symbols on page 271.

Meets ISAT Standards 1.B.3c 3.A.3

PROMPT: In "The Rope Swing," how does the author show Eddie and Z to be bullies?

   In "The Rope Swing", author Victoria Fortune creates two hateful bullies, Eddie and Z. She does this by describing their actions and their words, which help us to understand their thinking (if it can be called that). Eddie and Z seem to think that other people exist only to be tormented and manipulated. At the very beginning of the third paragraph, Z is demanding that Ben take a dangerous jump into a swirling river from a rickety old rope swing platform. Hurry up," yells Z, eager for his own entertainment and indifferent to the fact that Ben could be hurt or killed. 'Z was a big, scary kid, the author writes. He and his brother Eddie were the meanest, dumbest pair of bullies that Tallahatchie County had to offer." After Ben jumps and somehow survives, the author describes Eddie's reaction in a way that hints at how she wants the reader to feel about Eddie: "That was awesome! Eddie snorted like a pig.' After Eddie and Z decide that Ben should jump again—this time without even using the rope—they begin to turn on Kenny for trying to protect Ben. Clearly, though, these two bullies have gone too far now: The author writes, All the anger and rage of a hundred injustices boiled to the surface, blinding [Ben] to fear or consequences. We'll jump, he declared," stepping between Kenny and Z, "...as long as you and Eddie jump first". The bullies, being cowards deep down, as many bullies are, back off and leave Kenny and Ben to themselves. This is what Ben wanted all along: an escape from two hateful bullies."

Return to the exercises at the beginning of the chapter, revise your work as necessary, and submit the exercises to your teacher for grading.

Chapter 8
Real People, Real Events
Understanding Nonfiction Narratives

First Encounter

Read this nonfiction narrative about an Olympic champion. Then try your hand at the exercises that follow the narrative. You will not be graded on the exercises at this time. At the end of the chapter, you will be directed to return to these exercises to revise and correct your work.

Wilma Rudolph: American Heroine

by Loretta Kane

Wilma Rudolph really did beat the odds. The seventeenth of nineteen children, she was born in 1940 in St. Bethlehem, Tennessee. A premature baby, she weighed only four pounds at birth. Soon after her birth, Wilma's family moved to Clarksville. When Wilma was still a small child, her parents learned that she had polio. The disease left Wilma with one weakened leg. At first, Wilma's family thought that she would never walk properly. Little did they know that Wilma would grow up to be one of the world's greatest runners.

Wilma Rudolph did not travel a smooth road. As a young child, she suffered from pneumonia and scarlet fever as well as polio. The polio left her leg so weak that she had to wear a leg brace in order to walk. Every day, members of her loving family would help her exercise and massage her bad leg.

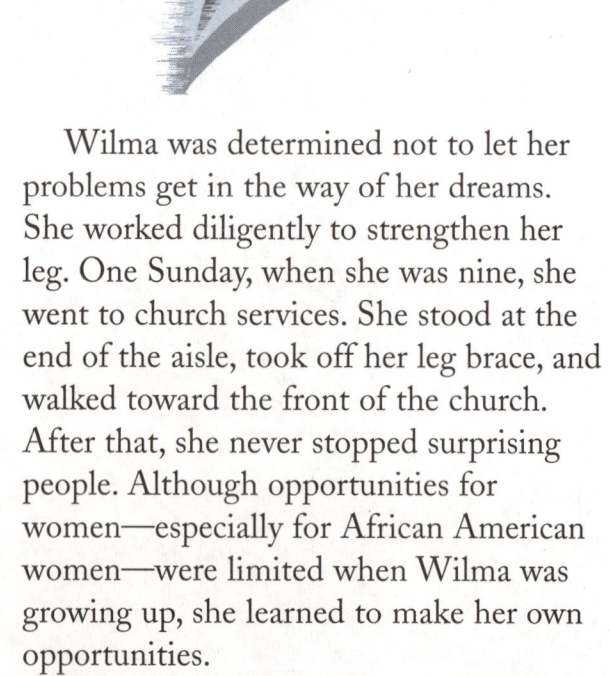

Wilma was determined not to let her problems get in the way of her dreams. She worked diligently to strengthen her leg. One Sunday, when she was nine, she went to church services. She stood at the end of the aisle, took off her leg brace, and walked toward the front of the church. After that, she never stopped surprising people. Although opportunities for women—especially for African American women—were limited when Wilma was growing up, she learned to make her own opportunities.

When she was in high school, Wilma became a star athlete. Her talents and fierce determination caught the eye of Ed Temple, the track coach at Tennessee State

University. Temple brought Wilma to his training camp for the track team. From that time on, Ed Temple coached Wilma Rudolph throughout her sports career.

In 1956, Wilma went to the Olympic Games in Melbourne, Australia. Though she did not win any individual races, her relay team took home the bronze medal. The 1960 Olympic Games in Rome, Italy, were different, however. During the Olympic trials, Wilma Rudolph set a record in the 200-meter dash. She received gold medals in both the 100-meter and 200-meter dashes, as well as in the 4 × 100-meter relay. She became the first American woman to win three gold medals in one Olympics. With her talent, determination, and smile, Wilma Rudolph had become a national heroine.

Until the 1960s, in many parts of the United States, blacks and whites were segregated in schools, restaurants, and hotels and on buses and other types of public transportation. In fact, most places in Rudolph's hometown had been segregated while she was growing up. As an African American woman who believed in equal rights for all, Rudolph refused to participate in any segregated events at her homecoming celebration after the Olympics. As a result, people of all ethnic backgrounds took part in Rudolph's homecoming parade and banquet. This was the first integrated celebration in the history of Clarksville, Tennessee. It was a landmark event in the struggle for civil rights.

After her success at the 1960 Olympics, Wilma Rudolph continued to fight for civil rights. She led protests over the next few years. Her work helped to strike down Clarksville's segregation laws. Later, she started the Wilma Rudolph Foundation, which helped underprivileged young people participate in sports. At the age of 54, Rudolph died of a brain tumor. She was arguably the greatest female runner in sports history. Her accomplishments and spirit continue to inspire young athletes today.

Your Turn

Meets ISAT Standards
1.B.3d
1.C.3a
1.C.3c
1.C.3d
2.A.3c
2.B.3a
2.B.3b
3.A.3
3.B.3a
3.B.3b

Exercise A Fill in the circle next to the correct answer to each multiple-choice question.

1. What is the main topic of this nonfiction narrative?
   - Ⓐ childhood polio
   - Ⓑ Olympic track events
   - Ⓒ segregation in Tennessee
   - Ⓓ Wilma Rudolph's life and accomplishments

2. What is most unusual about Wilma Rudolph becoming a world-class athlete?
   - Ⓐ She came from a small town.
   - Ⓑ She had a disability as a child.
   - Ⓒ She wore a leg brace throughout her life.
   - Ⓓ She was born in 1940.

3. The author explains that Wilma Rudolph "beat the odds," which means that she
   - Ⓐ had a difficult training routine.
   - Ⓑ succeeded despite obstacles.
   - Ⓒ could run quickly.
   - Ⓓ was politically active.

4. In which year did Wilma Rudolph win three gold medals at the Olympics?
   - Ⓐ 1952
   - Ⓑ 1956
   - Ⓒ 1960
   - Ⓓ 1964

5. What was unique about Wilma Rudolph's homecoming celebration?
   - Ⓐ It was held in Rudolph's hometown.
   - Ⓑ It involved many people.
   - Ⓒ It was an integrated event.
   - Ⓓ It was held in Tennessee.

AIM Higher! ISAT LANGUAGE ARTS REVIEW

Exercise B *Complete the activity below. Use additional paper if necessary.*

The title of the selection calls Wilma Rudolph an "American Heroine." Write a paragraph explaining the ways in which Rudolph demonstrated heroic qualities. Use evidence from the selection—in the form of quotations, paraphrases, or summaries—in your response. Revise your paragraph using the Revision Checklist on pages 265–66. Then proofread it using the Proofreading Checklist on page 270. Copy your final version onto the lines below. Use additional paper if necessary.

Understanding Nonfiction Narratives

Real People, Real Events

What Is Nonfiction?

The next three chapters of this text deal with nonfiction. **Nonfiction** is writing about real events, people, places, things, and ideas. When reading nonfiction, you should always pay attention to the following:

Aspects of Nonfiction

Subject	What the piece is about
Main Idea	The main point that the author makes about the subject
Audience	The reader or readers of the piece of writing
Tone	The overall attitude toward the subject or toward the reader communicated by the piece of writing
Purpose	What the writer wants to accomplish
Mood	The emotion created in the reader by the selection
Point of View	The vantage point from which the piece is told. A process essay or set of directions might be written from the **second-person point of view,** using the pronoun *you* to speak directly to the reader. Informative nonfiction, as in a news story, is often written from the **third-person point of view,** using pronouns such as *he, she, it,* and *they.* Personal anecdotes, diary entries, and autobiographies are usually written from the **first-person point of view,** using pronouns like *I, me, we,* and *us.*

More ▶

Mode The type of writing (classified by purpose). The main modes of nonfiction writing are as follows:

Expressive writing is personal and subjective. It expresses the thoughts and feelings of the writer. Examples include diaries, personal letters, dream analyses, journals, personal essays, and thank-you notes.

Narrative writing relates events or tells a story. Examples include biography, autobiography, and history.

Descriptive writing paints a picture in words. Examples include character sketches, travel guides, and field guides.

Expository, or **informative, writing** presents information. Examples include textbooks, how-to articles, consumer reports, cookbooks, encyclopedia articles, lab reports, and manuals.

Persuasive writing tries to convince the reader to adopt a particular point of view or to take a course of action. Examples include campaign speeches, letters to the editor, legal briefs, advice columns, and billboards.

Meets ISAT Standards
1.B.3c
1.B.3d
1.C.3b
1.C.3d
2.A.3a
2.A.3c

Understanding Nonfiction Narratives 169

Understanding Nonfiction Narratives

The following chart lists many of the most common types, or **genres,** of nonfiction:

Genres of Nonfiction

Acceptance speech
Advertising copy
Advice column
Almanac
Analysis essay
Annals
Annual report
Appeal
Application essay
Atlas
Autobiography
Bibliography
Billboard
Biography
Birth announcement
Book review
Brief
Brochure
Business card
Business letter
Business proposal
Bylaws
Campaign speech
Caption
Catalog copy

Cause-and-effect essay
Character sketch
Charter
Cheer
Classification
Classified ad
College entrance essay
Column, newspaper
Comeback speech
Comedic monologue
Commentary
Commercial
Community calendar
Comparison-and-contrast essay
Concordance
Constitution
Constructive speech, debate
Consumer report
Contract
Cookbook

Course description
Court decision
Credo
Critical analysis
Curriculum
Demonstration
Deposition
Diary
Diatribe
Dictionary entry
Directions
Dream analysis
Dream diary
Dunning letter
Editorial
E-mail
Employment review
Encyclopedia article
Epitaph
Essay
Eulogy
Explication
Exposé
Family history

Five-paragraph theme
Field guide
Filmstrip (documentary)
Flyer
Foreword
Fund-raising letter/ Solicitation
Graduation speech
Guidebook
Headline
History
How-to essay or book (guide)
Human interest story
Informative essay
Instructions
Interview questions
Introduction
Invitation
Journal
Keynote address
Lab report

More ▶

170 AIM Higher! ISAT Language Arts Review

Genres of Nonfiction (contd.)

Law (statute)
Learning log
Lesson
Letter of complaint
Letter of intent
Letter to the editor
Magazine article
Manifesto
Manual
Marketing plan
Memoir
Memorandum
Memorial plaque
Menu
Minutes
Monument inscription
Movie review
Music/Concert review
Nature guide
News story
Nomination speech
Obituary

Oral history
Oral report
Packaging copy
Paraphrase
Party platform
Pep talk
Personal essay
Persuasive essay
Petition
Police/Accident report
Political advertisement
Political cartoon
Prediction
Preface
Presentation
Press release
Process essay
Proclamation
Profile
Program notes
Prologue
Proposal

Protocol
Public service announcement
Radio spot
Rebuttal speech, debate
Recipe
Recommendation
Referendum question
Report
Research report
Resignation
Restaurant review
Resumé
Roast
Sales letter
Self-help book/ Column
Schedule
Science journalism
Scientific paper
Sermon
Sign
Slide show

Slogan
Specifications
Sports story
Storyboard
Summary
Syllabus
Technical writing
Test
Textbook
Thank-you note
Theater review
Toast
To-do list
Training manual, videotape, or slide show
Travel guide
Travelogue
Treaty
Vows
Want ad
Wedding announcement
Wish list

Meets ISAT Standards
2.A.3a
2.A.3c

Understanding Nonfiction Narratives

Understanding Nonfiction Narratives

Understanding Nonfiction Narratives

When you hear the word *story*, you probably think of fictional stories like *Harry Potter and the Sorcerer's Stone* or *The Lord of the Rings*. Not all stories, however, are fiction. Some are about real people, places, and events. Stories about real people, places, and events are known as **nonfiction narratives.**

Types of Narrative Nonfiction

Nonfiction narratives are one of the most common kinds of writing. You have probably read many nonfiction narratives without even knowing it! Two common types of nonfiction narrative are the autobiography and the biography. An **autobiography** is a story about a person's life, told by that person. A **biography** is a story about a real person's life, told by someone else. If you go to a bookstore, you will find that autobiographies and biographies are extremely popular. Bookstores are full of autobiographies and biographies about famous people, sports heroes, politicians, generals, movie stars, musicians, scientists, authors, and so on.

The following chart describes some of the most common types of narrative nonfiction:

Common Types of Narrative Nonfiction

Autobiography	Human interest story
Biography	Memoir
Captain's log	News story
Celebrity profile	Obituary
Diary or journal entry	Oral history
Family history	Police report
History	Sports story

172 AIM Higher! ISAT Language Arts Review

Purpose in Nonfiction Narratives

People love stories about other people. That is why, for example, *People* magazine is one of the most popular periodicals in the United States. We also love stories about recent events. That is one reason why people listen to or watch the news and read newspapers. Writers often create nonfiction narratives, therefore, to entertain and to inform. Nonfiction narratives can serve other purposes as well, such as to convey a message, to raise public awareness about an issue, or to illustrate a point through personal experience.

Elements of Nonfiction Narratives

Because nonfiction narratives are stories, they contain many of the same elements that are found in short stories, novels, and other fictional narratives. Be aware, however, that some nonfiction narratives do not contain all of these elements. For example, a nonfiction narrative may have more than one conflict or may lack a central conflict entirely. One major difference between fictional stories and nonfiction ones, of course, is that the actors in a fictional story are imaginary characters. The people in a nonfiction narrative are real people, identified by their real names. The chart on the next page describes some of the elements commonly found in nonfiction narratives.

> Meets ISAT Standards
> 1.A.3a
> 1.B.3c
> 1.B.3d
> 2.A.3a
> 2.A.3c

Understanding Nonfiction Narratives

Understanding Nonfiction Narratives

Meets ISAT
Standards
1.B.3a
1.B.3c
1.B.3d
1.C.3a
1.C.3c
1.C.3d
2.B.3a

The Parts of a Nonfiction Narrative

1. **Events.** The happenings or occurrences that make up the story
2. **People.** The participants in the events of the narrative
3. **Setting(s).** The place(s) and time(s) when the events occurred
4. **Chronological order.** Usually, the events in a nonfiction narrative are told in sequence, in the order in which they really happened
5. **Conflict.** Sometimes the events in a nonfiction narrative involve a struggle, or conflict
   - **External conflict.** A struggle between a person and an outside force
   - **Internal conflict.** A struggle that a person experiences within himself or herself
6. **Narrator.** The voice of the observer or the participant who tells the narrative. In short stories and novels, the writer often tells the story in the voice of an imaginary character. For example, a writer might tell a detective story using the voice of a character in the story, such as a detective or a victim of a crime. In a nonfiction story, the writer and the narrator are usually the same individual. Sometimes the narrator tells about events that he or she participated in personally. At other times the writer describes events that occurred to other people.
7. **Point of view.** The vantage point from which the narrative is told
   - **First-person point of view.** The narrator tells the story using words such as *I* and *we*
   - **Second-person point of view.** The narrator tells the story using the word *you*. This point of view is rarely used in nonfiction narratives.
   - **Third-person point of view.** The narrator tells the story using words such as *he, she,* and *they*
8. **Mood.** The overall emotional quality that the nonfiction narrative inspires in the reader (for example, suspense, joy, or anger)
9. **Tone.** The attitude that the writer has toward the subject or reader (for example, humorous, sarcastic, or authoritative)
10. **Theme.** The lesson or message that the narrative as a whole communicates

Actively Reading a Nonfiction Narrative

As you learned in the chapter on active reading, when you read, you need to do much more than just move your eyes across the page. To read well, you must continually think about what you are reading. The best readers use active reading strategies like the ones listed in the chart at right. As you read the following nonfiction narrative, notice what one student thought about while reading the selection.

Active Reading Strategies

- ✓ Question
- ✓ Visualize
- ✓ Predict
- ✓ Make inferences
- ✓ Draw conclusions
- ✓ Summarize
- ✓ Paraphrase
- ✓ Evaluate
- ✓ Connect and extend

Picasso and African Art
by Marti Bender

1. In the minds of most people, Pablo Picasso is synonymous with modern art. Certainly, Picasso was one of the most innovative and influential artists of the twentieth century.

2. Some people (especially those who like traditional art) find Picasso's art difficult to understand and appreciate. One key to understanding Picasso's work is understanding what he borrowed from African art. When

3. Picasso first saw African masks, in the first decade of the twentieth century, his reaction was immediate and strong. After seeing such masks, he painted out the faces in a work that he was creating.

4. Picasso replaced those faces with ones that have the same bold, or stylized, exaggerated features found in African tribal masks. That painting, *Les Demoiselles d'Avignon*, is now considered a modern

5. masterpiece. So, much of what is most modern in Picasso's painting—the exaggeration and distortion, for example—really comes from an ancient source in Africa!

One Student's Thoughts

1. Predicting This piece will tell how Picasso was influenced by African art.

2. Connecting/Extending I've seen some of Picasso's paintings. Some of them are pretty far out there.

3. Visualizing I can picture some African masks in my mind.

4. Questioning Why did Picasso replace the faces of the people in the painting?

5. Drawing Conclusions So, the exaggerated features that make Picasso's work look so modern were actually inspired by traditional African art.

Your Turn

Exercise A Read the selection. Then fill in the circle next to the correct answer to each multiple-choice question.

Making a Difference
by Janice Wong, Jefferson Middle School *Trumpet* Staff

Junior high school students in West Virginia helped to change the law. The eighth graders of Moorefield Middle School, in Moorefield, West Virginia, were shocked by the attacks on September 11, 2001. They decided to raise funds to help rebuild the Pentagon. Their goal was to collect one dollar from every eighth grader in the state.

There was one thing standing in their way: a law that prevented people from making donations to specific government programs. This law stated that people who donate money to the government have no control over how it is spent. The Moorefield students wanted their money to go toward rebuilding the Pentagon. They decided to call their congresswoman, Representative Shelley Moore Capito, to ask her for assistance. Representative Capito eventually drafted a new bill. Her bill proposed a new Show Your Pride in the Military Act. The new law would set up a government fund to help repair the Pentagon. It would also allow the Secretary of Defense to accept donations.

The bill passed easily in both houses of Congress and was signed into law. Now the Moorefield students have raised $5,000 to help rebuild the Pentagon. The actions of the Moorefield students show that in a democracy, the actions of ordinary citizens can make a real difference!

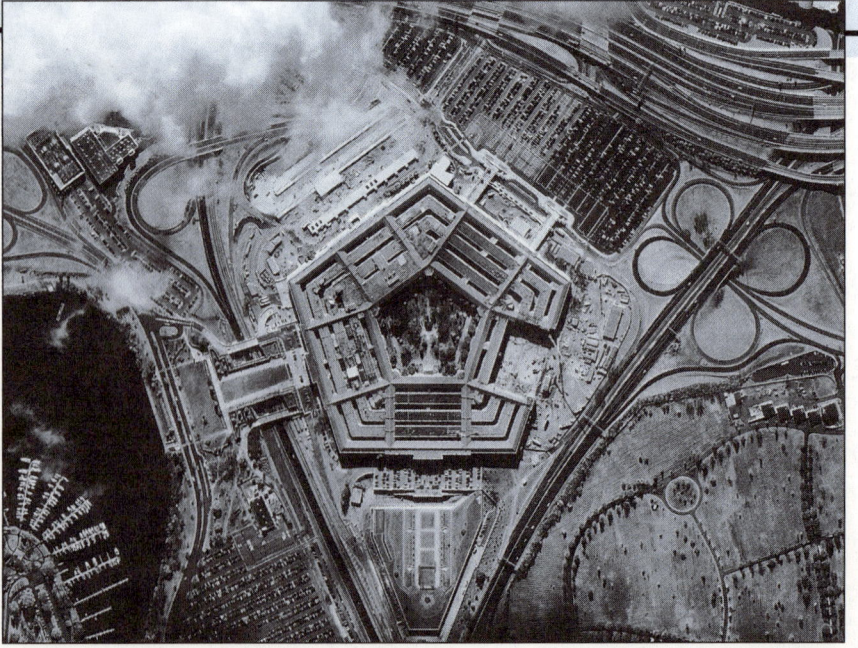

Pentagon photo: spaceimaging.com.

1. What is the MAIN focus of this selection?
   - Ⓐ the Moorefield students' fund-raising efforts
   - Ⓑ the Pentagon's architecture
   - Ⓒ Congresswoman Capito's election campaign
   - Ⓓ the West Virginia school system

2. What was the author's purpose in writing this selection?
   - Ⓐ to entertain
   - Ⓑ to describe, or create a portrait in words
   - Ⓒ to inform
   - Ⓓ to persuade readers to adopt a particular point of view

3. How did the Moorefield students help to rebuild the Pentagon?
   - Ⓐ by enlisting in the military
   - Ⓑ by collecting money from students in West Virginia
   - Ⓒ by going to Washington, D.C., and talking to politicians
   - Ⓓ by donating tools to reconstruct the damaged parts of the Pentagon

4. Who is the narrator of the piece?
   - Ⓐ a middle-school teacher
   - Ⓑ a middle-school student
   - Ⓒ a government official
   - Ⓓ a West Virginia congresswoman

Meets ISAT Standards
1.B.3c
1.B.3d
1.C.3a
1.C.3d

Understanding Nonfiction Narratives

Your Turn

Exercise B As you read the following selection, take notes in the space provided about what you are thinking. Use the active reading strategies: questioning, visualizing, predicting, making inferences, drawing conclusions, summarizing, paraphrasing, evaluating, connecting, and extending.

Making Changes
by Annie Sun Choi

César Estrada Chávez rose from obscurity to become one of the greatest labor leaders in the history of the United States. Before Chávez, many farm workers in this country lived miserable lives. They worked for very low wages, often in dangerous and squalid conditions. By creating a union and organizing farm workers, Chávez gave these people a voice with which to negotiate better conditions for themselves and their families.

Chávez was born in 1927 in Yuma, Arizona. When he was eight years old, some dishonest people cheated his father out of his land in a business deal. As a result, the Chávez family was forced to become migrant farm laborers to earn a living. They moved from farm to farm, harvesting crops. The work was very hard, yet the family barely earned enough to survive. They often had to live in crowded shacks without electricity or running water. Sometimes they lived in their car while they traveled from farm to farm. The experience of living in poverty due to a wrong that had been done to his father gave young César Chávez a keen sense of outrage at injustice.

Going to school was difficult for the Chávez children because the family moved so frequently, taking jobs as they became available. Young César and his

Your Notes and Comments

siblings consequently attended many, many different schools. In addition, the Chávez kids, like other children of migrant workers, experienced discrimination and humiliation at school. These negative experiences, combined with the need to earn money to help his family, led young César not to go to high school. Nonetheless, he continued to study hard all his life on his own and so became a well-educated man.

After a stint in the U.S. Navy at the end of World War II, Chávez married and moved with his family to East San Jose, California. There he became involved with the Community Service Organization, a self-help group for Chicanos. In 1962, Chávez founded the National Farm Workers Association (NFWA) and started organizing California farm workers into a union. Chávez found that though many workers wanted better pay and working conditions, some feared losing their jobs and did not want to protest. Nonetheless, the membership of the NFWA slowly grew, thanks to Chávez's organizing principles.

A gentle man, Chávez always insisted that people use nonviolent means to protest injustices around them. Between 1965 and 1970, under the leadership of Chávez, the union led a strike and a boycott against grape growers in California. Migrant workers went on strike, refusing to work until their employers agreed to improve their working conditions. Other people who were sympathetic to the migrant workers'

More ▶

Your Turn

cause participated in a boycott: They refused to buy grapes or grape products from California growers until the workers' conditions were improved. Millions of Americans joined the boycott, refusing to buy grapes until the growers agreed to negotiate with the union. During this time, the National Farm Workers Association merged with another union that was part of the AFL-CIO, and the United Farm Workers (UFW) was born.

César Chávez headed the United Farm Workers for many years. During that time, he took very low pay and worked tirelessly for workers' rights. On several occasions, he conducted long marches and held fasts to protest the mistreatment of workers. Fasting and long hours took a toll on his health. Still, Chávez persevered. "If you're outraged at conditions," he once said, "then you can't possibly be free or happy until you devote all your time to changing them and do nothing but that.... [You] can't change anything if you... avoid sacrifice."

In 1991, Chávez was awarded the Aztec Eagle, a high honor bestowed by the country of Mexico on people of Mexican heritage who have achieved greatness. In 1994, President Clinton awarded César Chávez the Presidential Medal of Freedom, the highest honor that a civilian can receive in the United States. Unfortunately, his family had to accept the Medal of Freedom for him, for Chávez had passed away quietly in his sleep the year before.

Exercise C *Answer the following questions on the lines provided.*

Meets ISAT
Standards
1.B.3a
1.B.3c
1.B.3d
1.C.3a
1.C.3b
1.C.3c
1.C.3d
2.B.3b
2.B.3c

1. Look at the chart of types of narrative nonfiction on page 172. What kind of piece is this selection about César Chávez?

   _____

   _____

2. What is the purpose of this selection?

   _____

3. From what point of view is this selection told?

   _____

4. What conflicts, or struggles, are described in the selection?

   _____

   _____

   _____

   _____

5. What lessons, or themes, are taught by this selection?

   _____

   _____

   _____

   _____

Understanding Nonfiction Narratives

Your Turn

Meets ISAT Standards
1.B.3d
1.C.3a
1.C.3d
2.B.3a
3.A.3
3.B.3a
3.B.3b

Exercise D What kind of person was César Chávez? Write a paragraph describing how his early experiences shaped him while he was growing up in California. Begin by stating your main idea in a topic sentence. Then support your topic sentence with specific details from the selection. Write your draft on a separate sheet of paper. Revise it using the Revision Checklist on pages 265–66. Then proofread it using the Proofreading Checklist on page 270. Copy your final draft onto the lines below. Use additional paper if necessary.

Return to the exercises at the beginning of the chapter. Revise your work as necessary, and submit the exercises to your teacher for grading.

Chapter 9
Just the Facts

Understanding Informative Nonfiction

First Encounter

Read these short pieces of informative nonfiction. Then try your hand at the exercises that follow the selections. At the end of the chapter, you will be directed to return to these exercises to revise and correct your work.

Creating a Möbius Strip

Can you imagine a figure that has only one edge or side? You can make one out of paper in just a few seconds. Here's how:

1. Cut a strip of paper that is about two inches wide and fourteen inches long.
2. Take the ends of the strip and bring them together. This will make an ordinary loop with two sides and two edges.
3. Before you glue the ends together, make a half turn in one end, so that the loop has a twist in it.
4. Glue the edges together. You now have a Möbius strip, a figure with one side!
5. Draw a line around the loop. Put your pencil on the strip, and keep pulling the strip along under the pencil until the mark meets the point where it began.
6. Now cut along your pencil mark. Instead of two loops, what did you end up with? You should have a single strip of paper.

Topology is a branch of math that investigates how geometric shapes are changed (and how they are not) by stretching, bending, or twisting. The Möbius strip is named after its discoverer, August Ferdinand Möbius (1790–1868). This loop has the interesting topological property of being a one-sided figure made from a two-sided one.

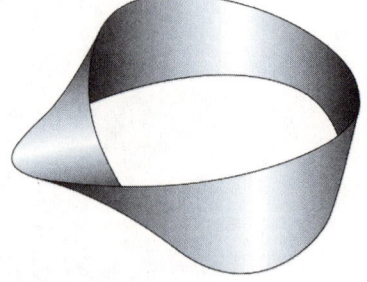

From a Math Activity Book

Special Numbers in Math

Counting Numbers. Also called the **natural numbers.** All whole numbers in the set {1, 2, 3, 4, . . .}. Zero is not a counting number.

Integers. The set of numbers that includes positive whole numbers, negative whole numbers, and zero {. . . −2, −1, 0, 1, 2, . . .}

Prime Number. A number that can be evenly divided only by itself and 1

Whole Numbers. All numbers in the set {0, 1, 2, 3, 4, . . .}; all numbers containing only digits to the left of a decimal point

Zero. The digit 0 that is used to show the absence of quantity

From a Math Textbook

A Short History of Zero
by Linda Cuervo-Sánchez

In the number 346, the digit 3 stands for three hundreds, the digit 4 stands for four tens, and the digit 6 stands for six ones. To write a number like 306, however, a zero is needed to show that there are no tens. Otherwise, there would be no way to tell the difference between 306 and 36. Zero plays a key role in our number system.

The Babylonians, who lived in what is now Iraq, developed a number system over 3,500 years ago. For more than a thousand years, however, their system had no symbol for zero. The Babylonians kept careful records of land, crops, and livestock. Not having a zero made the recordkeeping difficult. So eventually they began to use two slanting lines to mark an empty place, or position, in a number.

In Central America, the Mayans independently invented the concept of zero around A.D. 300. The Mayans created fine calendars, the most accurate in the world. In the Mayan time-keeping system, zero stood for the first year of a king's reign.

By A.D. 650, mathematicians in India had developed the numerals we use today, including zero. When counting, they placed round markers on a flat surface covered with sand. When a marker was taken away, a round impression was left in the sand. This open circle—called *shunya*, for "empty"—gave rise to our symbol for zero.

When Arabs conquered India after A.D. 1000, they quickly saw the value of *shunya*. Calling it *sifr*, they brought it and the other numbers home to the Middle East. By the 1200s, *sifr*, renamed *zepherium*, had reached Europe and began to revolutionize mathematics there. Our word *zero* probably comes from *zepherium*, as does *cipher*, a word that now means not only "zero" but also "any numeral" or "something secret."

From an Educational Magazine

First Encounter

Germain, Marie-Sophie. (1776–1831) French mathematician. Born in Paris, Germain decided to become a mathematician at thirteen years old. Her parents did everything possible to stop her. Like most people of the period, they believed that math was an inappropriate field of study for a woman. Her parents took away her mathematics books and even took away her candles so she could not read secretly at night. As a young woman, Germain used a man's name to correspond with leading mathematicians in Europe, such as Joseph-Louis Lagrange, Adrien-Marie Legendre, and Carl Friedrich Gauss. They were impressed by her intelligence and analytical skills and remained so even when they discovered her true identity. Still, Germain could not pursue a more formal education in mathematics. Largely self-taught, Germain tackled some of the most difficult math problems of her day. She is best known for her work on the theory of numbers and the vibrations of elastic substances.

From an Encyclopedia

Your Turn

Exercise A Fill in the circle next to the correct answer to each multiple-choice question.

1. Someone might consult the encyclopedia entry to
   - Ⓐ to find out when Marie-Sophie Germain was born.
   - Ⓑ learn the mathematics that describes vibrations of elastic substances.
   - Ⓒ find out about famous Greek mathematicians.
   - Ⓓ learn about the best way to study for math tests.

2. What is the difference between counting numbers and whole numbers?
   - Ⓐ Counting numbers include the number 0. Whole numbers do not.
   - Ⓑ Counting numbers do not include 0. Whole numbers do.
   - Ⓒ Counting numbers include negative numbers. Whole numbers do not.
   - Ⓓ Whole numbers include only prime numbers.

3. According to the educational magazine article, what did the Indians call the circle left in the sand after a counting marker was taken away?
   - Ⓐ zero
   - Ⓑ sifr
   - Ⓒ zepherium
   - Ⓓ shunya

4. What does a topologist study?
   - Ⓐ prime numbers
   - Ⓑ the history of zero and how its use has affected the development of mathematics
   - Ⓒ how geometric shapes are changed and how they are left unchanged by stretching, bending, or twisting
   - Ⓓ vibrations of elastic substances and number theory

Meets ISAT Standards
1.A.3a
1.A.3b
1.B.3c
1.B.3d
1.C.3a
1.C.3b
1.C.3c
1.C.3d
2.B.3a
3.A.3
3.B.3a
3.C.3a
5.A.3a
5.B.3b

Exercise B In a brief paragraph on your own paper, explain the purpose of the nonfiction piece about the history of zero. Do you think the author of the article was successful in accomplishing that purpose? Support your opinion with examples from the selection.

Understanding Informative Nonfiction 187

Understanding Informative Nonfiction

Just the Facts

Informative Writing in Everyday Life

Almost everything around you tells you information. A can of fruit juice tells you how many calories it contains. A newspaper tells you the important events that happened yesterday. A letter or e-mail tells you about your friend's day. Because you are continuously surrounded by information, one of the most important skills you must develop in school is the ability to read informative nonfiction well.

A piece of **nonfiction** writing tells about real events and real people. A piece of **informative nonfiction,** or **expository writing,** focuses on facts and information about a subject. Your science and social studies textbooks are examples of informative nonfiction. So are any reference books you use in the library. There are many, many types of informative nonfiction. You have already learned about biographies and autobiographies, two common forms of informative nonfiction. Biographies and autobiographies are nonfiction narratives. They communicate information about people and about events in their lives.

Here are some other types of informative nonfiction:

Types of Informative Nonfiction

- Almanac, atlas, encyclopedia, field guide, dictionary, travel guide, or other reference work
- Constitution of a country or charter of a corporation or club
- Factual essay or research report created for a class
- Police report or accident report
- Newspaper article reporting about a current event
- Recipe, set of directions, technical manual, how-to book, or any other work that presents directions or instructions for a process
- Scientific paper or lab report
- Textbook
- Wedding or birth announcement

Accuracy in Informative Writing

Informative nonfiction focuses on communicating facts, so it is important that these facts be accurate. Suppose that you read an article about dogs that claimed that all dogs bark. That statement is not accurate. The basenji is a breed of dog that does not bark. (It does make noises that sound like a yodel.) Now imagine reading a newspaper article that names the wrong candidate as the winner of an important election. In 1948, *The Chicago Daily Tribune* did precisely that. The paper ran on its front page the headline "Dewey Defeats Truman," though Harry S. Truman had already won the presidential election by a small margin.

Because incorrect information can have serious consequences, it is important to make sure that the source that you are reading is reliable. Make sure that it is possible to **verify,** or double-check, the facts presented in the work.

Pieces of informative nonfiction should be **objective.** This means that they should present only facts and not opinions. A newspaper story should not contain opinions presented as though they were facts. Opinions should be saved for the newspaper's editorial page. Opinions are also expressed in columns and in letters to the editor.

When reading informative writing, ask yourself questions like these:

> Meets ISAT Standards
> 1.A.3a
> 1.A.3b
> 1.B.3c
> 1.B.3d
> 1.C.3f
> 5.A.3a
> 5.B.3a

Thinking about the Accuracy of Informative Writing

1. Do you know anything about the author? Is he or she reliable? Is he or she objective? Is the author an expert in the field about which he or she is writing? What were the writer's sources of information? How good are these sources?

2. Can the facts presented be verified, or checked? Are they true by definition? Can they be proved by observation or by consulting an expert or a reference work?

3. Is the information in the piece of writing up-to-date? (Sometimes, this can be very important. A twenty-year-old science book, for example, might tell you that no mammal has ever been cloned. That "fact" would be wrong.)

4. Does what you are reading contradict something you know or have experienced?

5. Has the author left out important facts that relate to the topic? If so, why? Is this the whole truth, or only part of it?

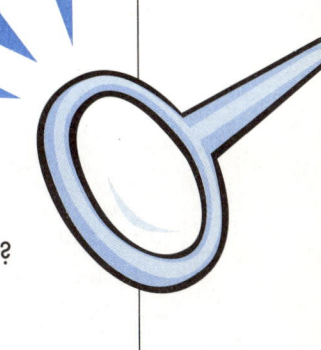

Understanding Informative Nonfiction

Understanding Informative Nonfiction

Evaluating Web Sites and Other Sources of Information

When you read pieces of informative nonfiction, you should ask yourself questions about the text and person who wrote it. Think about where the author got his or her facts. Did the author use **authoritative,** or knowledgeable, sources? Authoritative sources include encyclopedias, almanacs, atlases, and articles written by experts. The Internet provides a lot of information. It is a useful tool for verifying sources or researching information. Many Web sites, however, contain incorrect or out-of-date information. Use authoritative Web sites, such as those developed and maintained by universities, government agencies, news providers, or knowledgeable experts, such as university professors. In general, use caution when using the Internet to research a topic. Always verify facts by using more than one good source.

Main Ideas, Supporting Details, and Conclusions in Informative Writing

When you read informative nonfiction, keep your eye out for main ideas and the specific details used to support them. The **main idea** is the author's primary point. **Supporting details** are specific facts that support or prove the main idea in the text.

Here is a main idea:

> Camels, which were brought to Australia in the late nineteenth century, have had an enormous impact on the Outback.

Here are specific details that support the main idea:

- Camels were brought to Australia in the late 1800s to help pioneers develop the dry interior region of the country. When trucks and offroad vehicles made camels obsolete, more than ten thousand camels were released into the wild.
- Because camels have no natural predators in Australia, the camel population of the country has increased significantly. The number of camels has soared to about half a million.
- Although they are peaceful animals, camels cause damage to plants and soil. This threatens crops grown by Australian farmers and prevents native plants from growing.

Here is how the main idea and specific details that support it can be combined to form a paragraph:

> Camels, which were introduced to Australia in the late 1800s, have had an enormous impact on the Outback. They were first brought to Australia to help pioneers develop the dry interior region of the country. When trucks and offroad vehicles made camels obsolete, more than ten thousand camels were released into the wild. Because camels have no natural predators in Australia, their numbers have increased significantly, soaring to about half a million. Although they are peaceful animals, camels cause damage to plants and soil, threatening cropland and preventing native plants from growing.

Always ask yourself the following questions when you read informative nonfiction: Are the author's main ideas and the conclusions that he or she draws supported by the specific details (the facts) presented in the piece? Are these details facts or opinions?

Your Turn

Exercise Jack is interested in the wild camel herds in Australia and wants to do a report on them. He needs to do some research and wants to use a computer to look up the information on the Internet. He types "camels in Australia" in a search engine and comes up with a list of possible sources. When he tries to check the number of wild camels in Australia, he finds out that some of the sources contradict each other.

Meets ISAT Standards
1.B.3c
1.B.3d
1.C.3d
1.C.3f
3.A.3
3.B.3a
3.C.3a
3.C.3b
5.A.3a
5.B.3a
5.C.3a

- The first Web site is mainly about camel racing. It says that 10,000 to 12,000 camels were originally brought to Australia, and that about 20,000 camels were released into the wild in the 1920s when they were not needed anymore. It does not say how many wild camels there are now, but it says that the number of camels doubles every decade (every 10 years). This would mean that the number has doubled eight times since about 20,000 camels were released in 1920. (Jack has to figure out the math himself.)

- The second Web site says that there are 500,000 (half a million) wild camels in Australia now. The article on this Web page is about exporting camels to other countries where people like to eat camel meat. This Web site is maintained by a news organization. The reporter who wrote the article interviewed ranchers and a meat-exporting association in Australia.

- The third Web site is maintained by an environmental group in Australia. It estimates that there are about 200,000 wild camels in Australia but points out that no one has actually counted the number of camels.

- The fourth Web site is maintained by an organization of ranchers in Australia who are promoting the export of camels for meat. They believe that the grazing land in Australia should be reserved for their livestock, not camels. They say that there are now over half a million camels competing with livestock and native wild animals for food.

- The fifth Web site is about travel to Australia. It says that there are thousands of wild camels in the dry interior, and that the Outback could not have been explored and settled without them.

On your own paper, write a letter to Jack recommending how he could check the information from these Web sites. Are all of these Web sites equally reliable? Explain which sources might provide more accurate information than others, and tell Jack why he needs to be careful about using information from some sources.

Understanding Informative Nonfiction

Understanding Informative Nonfiction

Strategies for Informative Writing

A writer can communicate facts about a subject in many different ways. This section presents the most common strategies authors use to inform their readers. Following an example of each approach, you will find a short list of questions you can ask yourself to evaluate that type of informative writing.

Nonfiction Narratives

You have probably read a biography or autobiography of a famous person. Perhaps you have read about the amazing life of Leonardo da Vinci in your history class or about the career of a famous musician in a magazine. When an author wants to write about real events or people, he or she might write a **nonfiction narrative.** The writer usually focuses on one event or a series of events, organizing them in chronological order. A story about how John Wheeler and a group of dedicated Vietnam War veterans came up with the idea of building a Vietnam War memorial is an example of a nonfiction narrative. The selection below describes the experience of an elevator operator of a clock tower:

> Nancy Sias looks at her watch. It is two minutes before nine in the morning. Ten seconds before the clock strikes nine, she stuffs a finger in each ear. The bells ring at exactly nine o'clock. Though the sound is muffled, it is still extremely loud. Nancy counts the gongs of the clock, wincing with each bell. Though she has worked as the elevator operator of Sather Tower for two years, she is still not accustomed to the deafening rings.
>
> Sather Tower is the tall clock tower that overlooks the campus of the University of California at Berkeley. As an elevator operator, Nancy takes visitors up to the observation deck. She answers their questions and gives a little of the history behind Sather Tower to eager tourists. The clock tower was built in 1914 and has a carillon of sixty-one bells. A carillon is a set of tuned bells that a musician strikes in order to play a song. The smaller bells of the tower weigh about nineteen pounds, while the larger ones weigh over ten thousand pounds. Nancy always explains to visitors that the most unusual feature of the tower is the floors between the lobby and the observation deck. On those private floors, the university's paleontology department stores fossils and bones of prehistoric animals. The tower is the perfect storage cabinet for the department.

When you read a narrative essay, ask yourself the following questions:

Questions to Ask about Nonfiction Narratives

1. Who are the major characters involved?
2. What is the **setting,** or time and place, of the story?
3. What is the **sequence,** or order of events, of the story?
4. What issues or struggles (if any) are involved? How are they resolved?
5. What is the importance of the events in the essay?

Writing about Processes

Some authors want to inform readers about a process. A **process** is any activity that involves steps. For example, a writer might describe how doctors transplant a heart or how bees make honey. A how-to essay is one common way to describe a process. A **how-to essay** teaches the reader how to do an activity, such as throwing a curve ball or building a kaleidoscope. The following selection describes how to build a raft:

> Building a timber raft can be an exciting, fun project. Here's how to go about creating one: You will need log poles about nine feet long that have similar diameters. Six inches is a good width. Lash together enough logs to create a nine-by-nine foot square (probably about eighteen logs). Use clove-hitch and half-hitch knots, as shown in the diagram below.
>
> Clove hitch   Half hitch   Clove hitch
>
> Next, choose two logs of slightly smaller diameter, and lash these perpendicularly above the cut ends of the larger logs. Fill in the second layer of logs.
>
> Finally, add a third layer of logs perpendicular to the second. You may wish to lash logs to the top of the raft to serve as siderails or a bench. You can even add a sail to your raft. If you decide to test your raft on the water, bring other people along and make sure that everyone knows how to swim. Test the raft only in a calm, shallow area that is not near any rapids. Be sure to wear a life jacket.

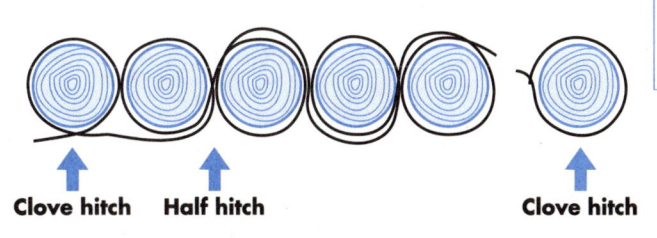

Meets ISAT Standards
1.B.3c
1.B.3d
1.C.3a
1.C.3c
1.C.3d

Questions to Ask about Writing That Describes Processes

1. What process is the writer describing?
2. What are the **stages,** or steps, in the process?
3. In what **sequence,** or order, do the steps occur?
4. Has the writer left out any important steps?

Understanding Informative Nonfiction 193

Understanding Informative Nonfiction

Writing about Classes (Classifying)

One strategy that a writer can use to communicate information is to organize the information into **classes,** or groups. This method helps the writer to present information about many subjects in a clear, well-ordered manner. For example, an article about collecting rocks or shells can tell readers about the different types and where they can be found. By dividing information into classes, the writer can explore the different kinds of shells in an orderly fashion. The same approach can be applied to other topics, as shown in the selection below:

> For hundreds of years, people and horses have worked together on farms, plowing fields or clearing land. Horses have also carried soldiers to battle and transported people and materials. Using selective breeding, people have helped develop different breeds of horse for different purposes.
>
> Horses used for work, especially for pulling heavy loads, are called draft horses. Such horses include the Clydesdales and the Belgians, both known for their great strength. Other horses have been bred primarily for speed: Thoroughbreds, for example, gallop at speeds over thirty miles an hour in races such as the Kentucky Derby, while Quarter Horses are the fastest sprinters over shorter distances such as a quarter-mile. The Quarter Horse's speed and ability to turn quickly also makes that breed useful for herding cattle.
>
> Now that most horses no longer work for a living, however, the light (non-draft) breeds are mostly used for sports and recreation. Because of their athletic ability, Thoroughbreds and Quarter Horses compete in many sports, including jumping. Arabians, originally bred to carry people swiftly across the desert, now are more likely to be found on a trail ride or in the show ring. In their efforts to find the perfect partner for whatever type of riding they like best, some people have crossed one breed of horse with another, hoping to get the best characteristics of both.

Questions to Ask about Writing That Classifies

1. Into what **classes,** or groups, does the writer divide the subjects?
2. What is the basis of the writer's system of classification?
3. Why did the writer put an item into one group instead of another?

Comparing and Contrasting

Often a writer wants to describe the similarities and differences between two or more subjects. An excellent way to achieve this goal is to compare and contrast the subjects. When you **compare,** you describe similarities. When you **contrast,** you describe differences. For example, a restaurant reviewer for a newspaper might compare and contrast two restaurants. She might discuss how both restaurants serve the same type of food, are moderately priced, and are in the same neighborhood. Then the writer might explain how one restaurant has faster service and larger portions, while the other has better food.

The selection below discusses the similarities and differences between Greenland and Iceland:

> Greenland and Iceland are both Arctic countries located near the North Pole. Both of their economies rely heavily on fishing because both countries have long coastlines on the North Atlantic. Both countries also have significant mineral deposits. Greenland and Iceland also have close cultural, political, and economic ties to northern Europe and Scandinavia, especially to Denmark.
>
> While Greenland and Iceland are similar in some ways, they are strikingly different in others. Greenland, despite its name, is a country of glaciers and ice. Its icecap is approximately three-quarters of a mile thick in some places. The landscape can be harsh and stark, especially in winter. Greenland is colder than Iceland: Many Greenlandic people consider fourteen degrees Fahrenheit a comfortable temperature. Because of the ice and permanent frost (permafrost), very little of the country's land can be used to grow crops or raise sheep. Greenland is still part of Denmark and relies heavily on support from the Danish government. Iceland became independent from Denmark in 1944.
>
> Iceland, on the other hand, is much greener than Greenland. In general, summer temperatures are much milder in Iceland, reaching about fifty degrees Fahrenheit. Iceland is a volcanic island with a stunning landscape that includes mountains, glaciers, volcanoes, and waterfalls. Much of the country is powered by geothermal heat, found deep below the surface.
>
> Both countries are sparsely populated, with most of the people living near the coast. Iceland is home to roughly 279,000 people, while only about 56,000 live in Greenland.

Meets ISAT Standards
1.B.3c
1.B.3d
1.C.3a
1.C.3c
1.C.3d
1.C.3e

Questions to Ask about Writing That Compares and Contrasts

1. What subjects are being compared and/or contrasted?
2. What are their similarities?
3. What are their differences?

Understanding Informative Nonfiction

Understanding Informative Nonfiction

Writing about Causes and Effects

Another excellent strategy a writer can use to communicate facts to the reader is to explain how one event or series of events (the **cause** or **causes**) brings about another event or series of events (the **effect** or **effects**). For example, a weather forecaster might explain the effects of a shift in the jet stream or ocean currents on our weather patterns. By exploring cause-and-effect relationships, a writer can help the reader to understand the event fully.

When you read writing that explores causes and effects, it is important to recognize necessary and sufficient causes. A **necessary cause** is one that must occur in order for a particular effect to happen. For instance, unprotected exposure to ultraviolet, or UV, light is a necessary cause of a sunburn. A person must be exposed to UV light in order to get a sunburn. A **sufficient cause** is a single cause that, by itself, is enough to bring about an effect. For example, a power blackout is sufficient cause to prevent a refrigerator from running.

The selection below discusses the causes and effects of a weather phenomenon known as "El Niño":

In 1997 and 1998, the weather phenomenon known as "El Niño," a warming of waters in the Pacific Ocean, produced wild weather all over the globe. As the waters of the eastern Pacific Ocean near the equator became warmer, heat and moisture from the ocean rose into the atmosphere, altering weather patterns in far-flung places. El Niño brought drought and forest fires to Hawaii, Australia, Southeast Asia, and Central America. It created typhoons in Indonesia and caused flooding and landslides in California and the Pacific Northwest. It produced heat waves in western Canada and ice storms in New England and eastern Canada. El Niño blew frigid Arctic air into Texas and Georgia and fueled tornadoes in Florida, Alabama, and Tennessee. Although El Niño did bring pleasant weather to places like North Dakota, many of its effects were extreme and destructive.

Questions to Ask about Writing That Describes Causes and Effects

1. What cause or causes does the writer identify? What are the effects?
2. Has the writer correctly identified all the causes and effects?
3. Has the writer provided enough evidence to establish a causal relationship?

Analyzing

One method a writer can use to inform the reader is to **analyze** a subject by breaking it down into its parts and explaining how the parts are related to the whole and to each other. Analysis is a common writing strategy used in essays, articles, and books. A chapter from a science book, for example, might analyze the water cycle by describing its parts: evaporation, condensation, and precipitation. Then the chapter might show how the three processes move water back and forth from Earth's surface to the atmosphere.

The selection below analyzes the food web:

> The food web is a system that involves four main players: the sun, producers, consumers, and decomposers. The sun provides most of the energy used by living things on our planet. Producers get from the sun the energy that they use to produce food. These producers include all plants on land and in the sea, from the giant sequoias to tiny, ocean-dwelling phytoplankton. Consumers are organisms that eat other organisms. Consumers, such as humans, insects, mammals, amphibians, reptiles, and fish, eat both producers and other consumers. Decomposers, which are mostly bacteria and fungi, are organisms that convert dead matter into minerals and gases, including carbon and nitrogen. These nutrients are released back into the air, soil, and water. Decomposers are necessary parts of the food web because they recycle nutrients back into the system, making them available again to the producers. All the players of the food web are incredibly important parts of our planet and live together in a delicate balance.

Meets ISAT Standards
1.B.3c
1.B.3d
1.C.3a
1.C.3c
1.C.3d

Questions to Ask about Writing That Analyzes

1. What is the whole subject being discussed?
2. What are the parts of the subject?
3. How are the parts related to one another?
4. What function does each part serve?
5. How are the parts related to the whole?

Defining

Another common strategy used by writers of informative nonfiction is definition. For example, a medical pamphlet might define asthma, or a science article might define acid rain. Writers can define a word or concept in several different ways. The author might collect and present several definitions from different sources, such as a dictionary, encyclopedia, or almanac. A writer might give synonyms for a given term or provide quotations that tell how other people have defined the term. Often, writers include many

Understanding Informative Nonfiction

Understanding Informative Nonfiction

examples that illustrate the topic in a concrete way.

The selection below defines a heart disorder:

> An arrhythmia is a heart disorder characterized by fast, inconsistent heart rhythms caused when the upper chambers of the heart quiver instead of beating normally. When someone is experiencing arrhythmia, the upper chambers of the heart beat between 350 and 600 times per minute. Normal hearts beat between 60 and 80 beats per minute.
>
> In a person with arrhythmia, the pumping function of the upper chambers does not work properly. As a result, blood is not completely emptied from the heart's chambers, causing it to pool and sometimes to clot, or thicken. People who suffer from arrhythmia are at a greater risk for stroke and heart attack than people whose hearts function normally. Some symptoms of arrhythmia include an irregular heartbeat, shortness of breath, chest discomfort, and dizziness.
>
> Though arrhythmia can be serious, many cases are mild. In fact, some people with the disorder are entirely unaware that they have it. With a proper diet and exercise and regular visits to doctors and cardiologists, people with the disorder can live normal, healthy lives.

Questions to Ask about Writing That Defines

1. What term or terms are being defined?
2. What methods of definition are being used?
3. Are the definitions concrete and precise?
4. Are alternative definitions discussed?
5. Do the definitions presented seem to be accurate? Why or why not?

Mixing It Up

When writing informative nonfiction, most authors use a combination of strategies. One writer might create an essay that incorporates elements of definition, analysis, and classification. Another might write a nonfiction narrative that compares and contrasts two subjects. When you read informative nonfiction, identify the strategies the author uses to inform the reader. Then ask yourself active reading questions, such as the ones given in the charts in this chapter.

The following selection about the U.S. Postal Service incorporates elements of process, analysis, and classification:

Whether you are mailing a letter down the street or around the world, the journey a piece of mail takes is complicated. First, a postal carrier picks up the letter from your mailbox along his or her route through several neighborhoods. The carrier then returns the letter to your town's post office, where a postal worker stamps it with the name of your town or city. Finally, a postal truck collects letters and packages from the town post office and transports them. Some letters and packages are sent to an airport and flown over long distances, while others are loaded on large trucks to be transported across state lines. The Postal Service uses planes, trains, and automobiles to transport letters and packages, as well as mules to transport letters down to the bottom of the Grand Canyon!

There are roughly 38,000 post offices in America, and the U.S. Postal Service delivers mail to over 134 million addresses. About 1 million more addresses are added each year. A single postal carrier might deliver as many as 2,300 pieces of mail a day to over 500 addresses. In order to operate effectively, the Postal Service employs a team of nearly 800,000 people.

Depending on how fast you want your letter to get to its destination, you can choose among several options, including first class, priority, express, and parcel post. The most popular services people use are first class and priority mail. Though the two are similar, there are several differences. First class mail is used for personal and business correspondence. Any item can be sent first class, but the item must weigh 13 ounces or less. Priority mail is used for documents, gifts, and merchandise. Any item may be sent as priority mail. The maximum weight for priority mail is 70 pounds. Both services will usually get a piece of mail to its destination between one and three days. Priority mail, however, is guaranteed to arrive within this time.

The U.S. Postal Service is an important service that millions of Americans depend on for business and for personal correspondence. Hospitals, companies, and schools rely on the service to help them function effectively. Perhaps the most important function of the Postal Service is that it brings people together. For just a few coins in your pocket, you can send a letter to a friend down the street or to an uncle across the country.

Meets ISAT Standards
1.B.3c
1.B.3d
1.C.3a
1.C.3c
1.C.3d

Understanding Informative Nonfiction 199

Your Turn

Exercise A *Read this essay. Then answer the questions that follow it.*

Introduction to the European Middle Ages
by Sherman Cole

The **Middle Ages,** or Medieval Era, in European history is the period from the fall of Rome, in A.D. 476, to the beginning of the Renaissance, in the early 1400s. During this long period—almost a thousand years—social and political life was much more structured and rigid than it is today.

Social Classes

In the Middle Ages, almost all people belonged to one of three social classes.[1] The **nobility,** or **noble class,** included all who held titles such as *king, earl, duke,* or *knight.* Members of this class possessed wealth and power. Their wealth came from control over land. Their noble status was hereditary, meaning that it passed automatically to their sons and daughters. The **clergy,** or **clerical class,** included the pope, bishops, priests, and members of religious communities such as nuns, monks, and friars. These were people who served the Church. People who were not nobles or clergy were members of the class of **common people,** or **commoners.** This class included **freemen,** or **yeomen,** and **serfs,** or **villeins.** Freeman, to some extent, could control their own lives. Serfs could not. Like cattle and land, serfs were owned by the nobility. A serf could not move or marry or do much of anything important without the consent of his or her master.

Within each social class, there were strict ranks. A king was higher in rank than an earl. A bishop was higher in rank than a priest. A freeman was higher in rank than a serf. Rarely did anyone move from one rank to another. There were some exceptions, however. A freeman might be made a knight by a powerful noble. A serf might be freed by his or her noble master and become a freeman. A freeman or a younger son or a daughter from a noble family might enter the Church to follow the religious life.

Social and Political Institutions

Rigid order marked the social classes in the Middle Ages, and the same was true of social and political institutions. The three great institutions of the period were the Church, the feudal manor, and the guilds.

Almost all people in Europe during the Middle Ages belonged to the **Roman Catholic Church,** which was headed by the pope. Medieval people were very devout. They attended mass, took sacraments such as confession, and prayed to saints and the Virgin Mary for favors and forgiveness of their sins. Extremely wealthy and powerful, the Church built great cathedrals throughout Europe.

---

[1]**almost all people . . . classes.** There were some exceptions. Medieval legends of "wolfmen," for example, probably come from isolated cases of people who lived like animals, outside of society, in the woods. Such wild men of the woods are featured in some medieval tapestries and folktales.

Every village had its priest, who took his orders from a bishop, who in turn reported to the pope. The great wealth of the Church came from various sources. Everyone was expected to pay a tithe, or a portion of his or her income, to the Church. In addition, the Church owned large amounts of land.

Very few nobles or commoners could read or write. Many members of the clergy, however, could read and write Latin, the official language of the Church and of the Vulgate Bible (a Latin translation of the Bible prepared by St. Jerome in the fourth century A.D.). Not surprisingly, then, almost all scholarship in the Middle Ages was religious in nature. Monks and priests compiled books of saints' lives, prayers, and commentaries on the Bible. Occasionally, they prepared more secular works, such as histories or books on gardening, medicine, and other arts and crafts.

Outside the Church, the most important institution was the **feudal manor**—a large tract of land ruled over by a lord or baron. The political system of the Middle Ages is known as **feudalism.** Under this system, all land belonged to the king. The king granted use of large tracts of land to the lords, or barons, who in turn owed loyalty and service to the king. For example, the lord would be required by law to provide soldiers and arms to the king for a certain amount of time each year. A person who received land and was obligated to return this gift through service was called a **vassal.** The great landholders (lords or barons) were vassals of the king.

These lords, in turn, granted land to lesser nobles, and these lesser nobles became their vassals. The wealth of the lords was based on the land and the serfs that they owned. Serfs and freemen would work the land and pay rent to the lord, often in the form of crops or livestock. All the wild game of the manor, however, belonged to the lord. In order to wage war or put down a rebellion, the king would call on his lords, who in turn would raise an army of lesser nobles, or knights. Warfare in those days was a savage business, fought on foot and on horseback, hand to hand, with lances, swords, daggers, and maces. The knight clad in chain mail and armor is a readily recognizable figure from the Middle Ages.

As the Middle Ages progressed, some villages became large cities, and within the cities and villages, yeomen craftspeople, such as goldsmiths, tinkers, weavers, carpenters, and masons, organized themselves into associations called **guilds.** The guilds had several purposes. They controlled the prices of goods and services. They limited competition. They organized entertainment for their members and supported members who became ill or fell into poverty. The guilds also oversaw the training of young craftspeople. A full guild member was known as a **master.** Young people who were learning a craft were called **apprentices.** An apprentice had to work for many years as an unpaid servant to the master in exchange for learning the craft and attaining guild membership.

More ▶

Understanding Informative Nonfiction

Your Turn

Meets ISAT Standards
1.A.3a
1.A.3b
1.B.3b
1.B.3c
1.B.3d
1.C.3a
1.C.3c
1.C.3d
3.A.3
3.B.3a
5.B.3a

Fill in the circle next to the correct answer to each multiple-choice question.

1. Which statement below presents the essay's thesis or main idea?
   - Ⓐ Medieval life was hard and dreary because of the feudal system.
   - Ⓑ The king owned all the land.
   - Ⓒ Bishops and barons were powerful noblemen who owed loyalty to the king.
   - Ⓓ Social and political life in the Middle Ages was highly structured and rigid.

2. Which event happened FIRST?
   - Ⓐ The guilds developed.
   - Ⓑ The Middle Ages ended.
   - Ⓒ Rome fell.
   - Ⓓ The church built great cathedrals throughout Europe.

3. A feudal king gave land grants to the barons and bishops because
   - Ⓐ these noblemen were highly literate.
   - Ⓑ he expected loyalty and support from these people in return.
   - Ⓒ he wanted to raise taxes from the noblemen.
   - Ⓓ the noblemen worked for the Church, and the king wanted the Church on his side.

4. A person who served a master and learned from him a trade such as carpentry or weaving was called
   - Ⓐ a serf.
   - Ⓑ an apprentice.
   - Ⓒ a villain.
   - Ⓓ a noble.

Exercise B When you analyze something, you break it down into its parts and tell how all the parts function. On your own paper, create a rough outline of the selection "Introduction to the European Middle Ages." Then, write a paragraph in which you define the term *analyze* and explain how the author analyzed the topic of life in the Middle Ages.

Return to the exercises at the beginning of the chapter, revise your work as necessary, and submit the exercises to your teacher for grading.

Chapter 10
A Matter of Opinion

Understanding Persuasive Nonfiction

First Encounter

Read this persuasive essay about the possibility of life on other planets. Then try your hand at the exercises that follow the essay. You will not be graded on the exercises at this time. At the end of the chapter, you will be directed to return to the exercises to revise and correct your work.

Is Something Out There?

by Baer Levin

Aliens. The entertainment industry loves them. Practically every television season features some new program involving creatures from outer space. In recent years, television studios have given us, to name just a few, the smash-hit series *The X-Files*, the amusing comedy series *Third Rock from the Sun*, and the latest installments in the *Star Trek* series. Movie studios, if anything, are even more alien obsessed. The 1950s gave us such classics as *The Day the Earth Stood Still* and *It Came from Outer Space*. The last decades of the twentieth century gave us the *Alien* films, *E.T., Close Encounters of the Third Kind, Independence Day, Mars Attacks!, Men in Black*, and *Star Wars*. In short, aliens visit American movie screens as commonly as they visit the Mos Eisley Cantina on Tatooine (for you *Star Wars* fans) or Douglas Adams's *Restaurant at the End of the Universe* (for those of you who prefer your aliens in novels).

Aliens fill our fantasies, but is there any reason to believe that aliens are anything more than fantasy? Could life actually exist out there, in the darkness of space? The answer, most definitely, is yes. That life exists on other planets seems a reasonable conclusion, given the chemical composition of the universe, the sheer number of places where other life could exist, the general ability of life to prosper in spite of the most extreme conditions, and the evidence for ancient life on Mars.

First, the chemical composition of the universe makes it possible for life to exist elsewhere. By shining light from a distant star through a prism, scientists can break that light into its **spectrum**—a rainbow of colors ranging from low-frequency red light to high-frequency purple light. The chemicals that make up the burning material (gases) from a star or other light source create lines in the spectrum that are like a signature or fingerprint: They allow scientists to identify the chemicals that are being emitted by the star or light source. By studying these characteristic lines, scientists have learned that the materials found in our part of the universe are found throughout the rest of the universe as well. Living creatures on Earth are made up primarily of carbon and the hydrogen-and-oxygen mixture known as water (H_2O). Carbon is widespread throughout the universe, and hydrogen is the most abundant element of all. Oxygen is a bit more scarce, but it has been found in water both on our moon and on Mars. If water can be found as far away as Mars, it seems likely that it exists in many other places in the universe as well. So, the chemicals necessary for life are present, and perhaps even abundant, in other parts of the universe.

Second, the sheer number of planets in the universe suggests that there are other planets that could be inhabited by some form of life. In his book *Probability 1: Why There Must Be Intelligent Life in the Universe,*[1] Amir Aczel estimates that our galaxy, the Milky Way, contains as many as 300 billion stars and that the universe as a whole contains as many as 100 billion galaxies, each with its own stars. Therefore, the number of stars in the universe is in the neighborhood of 30 trillion! Aczel further points out that, according to Michel Mayor, an astronomer at the University of Geneva who specializes in looking for other planets besides those that revolve around our sun, it is likely that "every star has at least one planet." As recently as 1991, the existence of planets outside the solar system was speculative. By April of 2002, however, astronomers had confirmed the existence of approximately 77 planets outside our solar system. If Mayor's idea that there is at least one planet for every star is correct, there could be more than 30 trillion planets in the universe. If that is the case, it seems reasonable to assume that at least some of these planets would be of the right size and distance from their own stars to support life.

Third, we know from observations on Earth that life is able to exist in extremely hostile environments. Thomas Brock of the University of Wisconsin at Madison found bacteria living in acidic hot springs in Yellowstone National Park at temperatures that reached 85°C (185°F). Karl Stetter of the University of Regensburg, in Germany, has found bacteria living near thermal vents on the ocean floor at temperatures up to 113°C (235.4°F). James T. Staley of the University of Washington has found bacteria in ice from the Antarctic sea that thrive at temperatures of −15.5°C (4°F).

Diana Northrup of the University of New Mexico is a microbiologist who is studying SLIME (Subsurface Life in Mineral Environments). Deep inside caves like Lechuguilla (in New Mexico) and Cueva de Villa Luz ("Cave of the Lighted House," in Mexico), Northrup and other cave scientists have discovered goopy strands of bacteria that thrive in acidic conditions "and live in an environment that's just like the inside of your car battery."

SPECTRUM:
Long Wavelength
Low Frequency
Low Energy

Radio waves

Microwaves
Radar

Infrared light

Visible

Ultraviolet light

X-rays

Gamma-rays
Short Wavelength
High Frequency
High Energy

---

[1] New York: Harcourt, 1998.

First Encounter

Discovery of these extremophiles, or creatures that thrive in extreme conditions, has led some scientists to believe that the planetary conditions necessary to support life may not have to be as Earthlike as people once thought. NASA is studying the possibility of sending a space probe to Europa, one of the moons of Jupiter, to look for extremophile life. The surface of Europa is covered with ice, but there may well be a liquid sea beneath the surface. The probe would drill through the ice. If there is a buried "ocean" on Europa, the probe would release a robotic submarine to explore it. Some scientists have suggested that extremophiles might live in other unlikely places, such as the atmospheres of giant planets like Jupiter, or underground aquifers[2] on planets like Mars.

Fourth, the recent discovery of evidence of ancient life on Mars lends additional support to the idea that life exists elsewhere. On August 7, 1996, NASA announced that evidence of fossil bacteria had been found on a meteorite from Mars. The meteorite, which fell to Earth in Antarctica, is about 4.5 billion years old. Within the meteorite were traces of chemicals and fossil outlines consistent with bacteria. The fossil bacteria have been dated to about 3.6 billion years ago. While some controversy remains over interpretation of the findings about the Martian meteorite, it may well be that life existed on Mars billions of years ago, when the surface of Mars contained running water and when Mars had a thicker atmosphere. If ancient life did exist on our nearest planetary neighbor in space, then it seems very likely that life exists on some of the 30 trillion other planets in the universe.

Does all this mean that someday soon we shall be traveling off to Tatooine for a root beer float at the Mos Eisley Cantina? Probably not. It does mean, however, that the idea of alien life has finally gained some scientific respectability.

[2] **aquifer.** An underground layer of porous rock or sand containing water

Photos courtesy of NASA/JPL/Caltech

Your Turn

Exercise A *Fill in the circle next to the correct answer to each multiple-choice question.*

Meets ISAT Standards
1.A.3a
1.A.3b
1.B.3c
1.B.3d
1.C.3a
1.C.3d
1.C.3e
2.B.3a

1. What is the thesis, or main idea, of this persuasive essay?
   - Ⓐ that there is intelligent life on other planets in the universe
   - Ⓑ that there may be life on other planets in the universe
   - Ⓒ that there is a cantina, or restaurant, on a planet called Tatooine
   - Ⓓ that there is life on Mars

2. Which idea is NOT presented by the author as evidence for the existence of life elsewhere in the universe?
   - Ⓐ the similarity in chemical composition of various parts of the universe
   - Ⓑ the large number of planets in the universe
   - Ⓒ the idea that living organisms may have traveled to Earth, in the past, aboard meteorites or asteroids
   - Ⓓ the discovery of evidence of bacterial life in a meteorite from Mars

3. According to the essay, some bacteria are able to live at temperatures
   - Ⓐ as low as 4°F and as high as 235.4°F.
   - Ⓑ as low as 14°F and as high as 135°F.
   - Ⓒ as low as 114°F and as high as 23°F.
   - Ⓓ as low as −15.5°F and as high as 113°F.

4. Which of the following would be the BEST alternative title for this essay?
   - Ⓐ "Alien Flicks"
   - Ⓑ "The Martian Meteorite"
   - Ⓒ "Life on Other Planets?"
   - Ⓓ "Planets beyond Our Solar System"

More ▶

Understanding Persuasive Nonfiction

Your Turn

5. Amir Aczel estimates in his book that the number of stars in the universe is more than
   - Ⓐ 30 thousand.
   - Ⓑ 30 million.
   - Ⓒ 30 billion.
   - Ⓓ 30 trillion.

6. By April of 2002, scientists had discovered how many planets outside our solar system?
   - Ⓐ more than 100
   - Ⓑ about 100
   - Ⓒ none
   - Ⓓ 77

7. *Extremophiles* are organisms that can live
   - Ⓐ on other planets.
   - Ⓑ in extreme conditions.
   - Ⓒ at the far reaches of the Earth.
   - Ⓓ on Tatooine.

8. Which event would have happened FIRST?
   - Ⓐ The Martian rock fell to Earth as a meteorite.
   - Ⓑ Organisms similar to bacteria lived on Mars.
   - Ⓒ Fossils of bacteria were formed in a Martian rock.
   - Ⓓ Scientists discovered fossil bacteria in a Martian rock.

9. According to the essay, life is made up mostly of
   - Ⓐ carbon and nitrogen.
   - Ⓑ silicon and oxygen.
   - Ⓒ carbon and water.
   - Ⓓ silicon and water.

10. A surface made of ice is a feature of
    - Ⓐ Mars.
    - Ⓑ Earth.
    - Ⓒ Europa.
    - Ⓓ Triton.

Exercise B What is the thesis statement of the essay you have just read? Is this thesis statement a fact or an opinion? Explain.

Meets ISAT
Standards
1.B.3c
1.B.3d
1.C.3a
1.C.3d
2.A.3a
2.A.3c
2.A.3d
2.B.3a
3.A.3
3.B.3a
3.C.3a

Understanding Persuasive Nonfiction

Understanding Persuasive Nonfiction

A Matter of Opinion

According to the Federal Communications Commission, by the time a person in the United States reaches the age of eighteen, he or she will have watched between 15,000 and 20,000 hours of television. According to the Association of National Advertisers, approximately 16 minutes of every hour of television time is made up of commercials. So, by the age of eighteen, an American has watched between 4,000 and 5,300 hours of television commercials.

Each one of those commercials is an example of **persuasion,** writing and speech created to encourage people to think or act in a particular way.

Persuasion plays an important role in modern life, not only in the areas of marketing and advertising but also in politics and social life. Children attempt to persuade their parents to let them adopt pets. Teenagers attempt to get their friends to go to particular movies, concerts, or sporting events. Politicians continually attempt to persuade voters to vote for them or to support their positions on issues. Workers attempt to persuade their employers to give them promotions, better working conditions, or better pay and benefits. Employers attempt to persuade their workers to take pride in their work and to work more productively. Defense lawyers attempt to persuade judges and juries that their clients have done no wrong. Occasionally, drivers attempt to persuade police officers not to give them tickets! Persuasion is everywhere in the contemporary world. Therefore, learning to interpret and evaluate persuasive writing and speech is extremely valuable.

Every act of persuasion involves attempting to get someone to accept a particular opinion. So, the first step in understanding persuasion is to understand what opinions are all about.

Understanding Facts and Opinions

A statement that can be proved to be true is a **fact**. A statement that cannot be proved, absolutely, to be true or false is an **opinion**. Though not absolutely provable, opinions are nonetheless really important. Your opinions tell what you like and dislike, what you believe, what you care about, and what you want. To a large extent, they define who you are.

Distinguishing Facts and Opinions

Consider the following sentences:

1. Internet 2 is a high-bandwidth network created for use by university research centers.
2. Internet 2 allows people to send life-size moving images instantaneously over long distances.
3. Internet 2 is really cool.

The first two sentences state facts. These facts could be proved to be true by direct observation. A person could go to a university research center where Internet 2 is installed and observe it in action. An easier way to prove these facts would be to consult a reliable source, such as an expert, a reference work, or someone else who has made a direct observation. In the case of Internet 2, you could read about it in one of the back issues of the magazine *Scientific American*.

The third sentence states an opinion. Making observations and checking reference works will not tell you whether the statement is true, because it is not a statement about something that is or is not the case in the world. It is a statement about how the speaker feels about Internet 2. Some people might have different feelings about the new technology and thus different opinions.

Meets ISAT Standards
1.A.3a
1.A.3b
1.B.3c
1.B.3d
1.C.3a
1.C.3c
1.C.3e
2.A.3c

REMEMBER:

A fact can be proved by direct observation or by consulting a reliable source.

Understanding Persuasive Nonfiction 211

Understanding Persuasive Nonfiction

Common Reference Works (for Checking Facts)

1. **Almanacs.** Collections of information and statistics, often in chart or table form, on a wide variety of topics, such as populations of countries, flags, sports records, and awards. Almanacs are updated periodically, generally every year.

2. **Atlases.** Collections of maps and related information.

3. **Dictionaries.** Collections of words and phrases, along with definitions; etymologies, or word histories; pronunciation guides; and usage notes. An **unabridged dictionary** is a large, comprehensive collection of the words of a language. An **abridged dictionary** is a shorter work containing fewer and generally shorter entries. A **thesaurus** is a dictionary of synonyms and antonyms.

4. **Encyclopedias.** Collections of articles, usually by experts, on a variety of topics. There are general-purpose and subject-specific encyclopedias. Encyclopedias are available in both print and electronic formats.

5. **Literary reference works.** This general category includes many types of reference work, such as the *Readers' Guide to Periodical Literature,* which lists magazine and journal articles by author, subject, and title; dictionaries of quotations; biographical dictionaries; digests, which give summaries of works; handbooks of literary terms; literary encyclopedias; concordances, or directories of words and phrases used in particular works or by particular authors; and much, much more.

6. **Online reference works.** Most of the types of reference work listed above are available online. Many of the best reference sites, unfortunately, charge usage or subscription fees. Nonetheless, the Web can be a really valuable source of information. See "Evaluating Information Found on a Web Site" on the following page.

Types of Fact

As you have just learned, a fact is a statement that can be proved to be true. Some facts are true by definition.

> **Fact that is true by definition:**
> A *trompe l'oeil* painting is one that is so realistic that it fools the eye.

You can tell that this fact is true because the phrase *trompe l'oeil* (pronounced *tromp loy*) means "a painting so realistic that it fools the eye." Looking up the word in a dictionary will confirm this fact. All the facts that make up mathematics are of this kind. They are true by definition:

> **Facts that are true by definition:**
> A right triangle is a triangle with one 90° angle.
> $5 \times 3 = 15$.

212 AIM Higher! ISAT Language Arts Review

Now consider this fact:

> **Fact that can be proved by observation:** The Great Pyramid of Khufu, in Egypt, is carefully placed so that its sides face due east, west, north, and south.

You can prove this fact by going to Giza, in Egypt, and looking at the Great Pyramid with a compass in hand. (If you actually did this, you would have to compensate for the fact that true north and the magnetic north measured by a compass are not exactly the same, but you get the idea.) Of course, that is not the most practical approach. Instead, you would probably look up the Great Pyramid in a reference work, such as an encyclopedia or atlas or in an online Web site devoted to Egypt or to ancient history and architecture. Of course, you can also prove a fact by talking to an expert who has made observations or who has learned about observations made by others. For example, you might telephone an Egyptologist at a university to ask him or her about the Great Pyramid.

Meets ISAT Standards
1.B.3c
1.B.3d
1.C.3a
1.C.3c
1.C.3e
2.A.3c
5.A.3a
5.B.3a
5.B.3b

Evaluating Information Found on a Web Site

Some Web sites are more reliable than others. Unfortunately, you cannot always depend on what you read on the Web. Some sites contain misinformation and mistakes. When you use a Web site for information, do the following:

1. When using a search engine to look for information on a topic, do not simply pick the first site that pops up. Look through the sites that appear in response to your search query to find ones that seem most likely to have reliable information.

2. Check to see what individual or organization is responsible for producing the Web site. Ask yourself whether that person or organization is expert in the field that you are researching. Often, the author of a page will not be identified, but sometimes that information is provided.

3. Look to see if the Web site lists sources for the information that it presents, and check to see if those sources are reliable.

4. Make sure to use current Web sites when you do research. Look to see if the site is dated. The authors of some Web pages will put dates on their pages to indicate when they were posted, revised, updated, or modified. Some browsers have "Page Info" commands that let you view when a page was last modified. Unfortunately, not all pages are dated, so you will not always be able to find this information.

5. Check particular facts by consulting more than one source. In this way, you will often be able to identify mistakes on Web sites. If the information from one site seems to contradict that from another, always go with the facts as presented by your most reliable sources.

Understanding Persuasive Nonfiction

Understanding Persuasive Nonfiction

These days, there are many Web sites that allow students to ask questions that will be answered, directly, by experts. Keep in mind, however, that behind every expert and every reference work there are direct observations. Also keep in mind that some Web sites are more reliable than others. Always make sure that your source is reliable.

Types of Opinion

Opinions come in many varieties. The following chart describes the most common types:

Some Kinds of Opinion

Judgment, or Statement of Value	An opinion that tells what a person cares about	EXAMPLE: The short stories of Ray Bradbury are fascinating!
Statement of Belief	An opinion that tells something that a person thinks is true but that he or she cannot prove beyond a shadow of a doubt	EXAMPLE: Ray Bradbury is right to believe that at one time, there might have been life on Mars.
Statement of Obligation	An opinion that tells what one or more people should do	EXAMPLE: You ought to read Ray Bradbury's story "The Veldt."
Statement of Policy	An opinion that tells what organized groups of people, such as governments, societies, companies, or the students in a school, should do	EXAMPLE: Middle schools should include Ray Bradbury on their required reading lists.
Prediction	An opinion about what will happen in the future	EXAMPLE: Ray Bradbury will be awarded the Nobel Prize in Literature.

Your Turn

Exercise A Tell whether each of the following sentences is a statement of fact or a statement of opinion.

1. The Aswan High Dam in Egypt holds back a reservoir containing 5.97 trillion cubic feet of water.

   _____

2. The Aswan High Dam in Egypt is one of the most amazing structures in the world.

   _____

3. The Egyptian government should not have built the Aswan High Dam.

   _____

4. Ninety-five percent of Egypt's population lives within twelve miles of the Nile River.

   _____

5. The Aswan High Dam provides flood control and generates electricity.

   _____

Meets ISAT Standards
1.B.3c
1.B.3d
1.C.3a
1.C.3c
1.C.3e
2.A.3c
5.A.3a
5.B.3a
5.B.3b

Exercise B Tell whether each of the following statements of fact is true by definition or can be proved to be true by observation.

1. A dam is a barrier constructed across a waterway to control the flow or raise the level of the water.

   _____

2. The Aswan High Dam generates ten billion kilowatt-hours of electricity every year.

   _____

3. A turbine is a machine that converts energy from a moving fluid into mechanical or electrical power.

   _____

More ▶

Understanding Persuasive Nonfiction

Your Turn

4. An embankment dam is a dam that consists of a mound of dirt and rock.

   _____

5. The Aswan High Dam is one of the largest embankment dams in the world.

   _____

Exercise C *On the lines provided, write five opinions—a statement of value, a statement of belief, a statement of policy, a statement of obligation, and a prediction.*

EXAMPLE: Commercial television should be banned from schools. (statement of policy)

1. a statement of value: _____

   _____

2. a statement of belief: _____

   _____

3. a statement of obligation: _____

   _____

4. a statement of policy: _____

   _____

5. a prediction: _____

   _____

Exercise D Explain which secondary source you might use to prove or disprove each of the following statements. (See list of reference works on page 212.)

1. The Spanish word *bambalear* means "to sway."
   _____

2. Australia is slightly smaller than the contiguous[1] United States.
   _____

3. In 1927, Babe Ruth hit sixty home runs.
   _____

4. It was Oscar Wilde who wrote that "It is absurd to divide people into good or bad. People are either charming or tedious."
   _____

5. Benjamin Franklin invented bifocals, the lightning rod, and a stove for heating homes.
   _____

Exercise E Make a list of opinions with which you agree and opinions with which you disagree. Look over your list. What do these opinions tell you about yourself—about what you value and believe?

Opinions with Which I Agree	Opinions with Which I Disagree

What these tell about me: _____
_____
_____
_____

---
[1]**contiguous.** Touching, sharing a common border

Understanding Persuasive Nonfiction

Understanding Persuasive Nonfiction

Supporting Opinions

It is important to respect other people's opinions. It is also important that people be allowed to express their opinions freely and openly, in debates and discussions. You should realize, however, that all opinions are not created equal. Some opinions make sense. Others do not. A **reasonable opinion** is one that is supported by facts and that is consistent with acceptable values. Think about this opinion:

> **Reasonable Opinion:** You should stay in school and study hard.

That opinion is reasonable because it is supported by facts like these:

- In 1998, the median annual income of high-school graduates working full-time and year round was $31,477 for males and $22,780 for females.
- The average 1998 median annual income for full-time year-round workers with a bachelor's degree was $51,405 for men and $36,559 for women.
- Between 1990 and 1995, the income of men who were year-round, full-time workers with four or more years of college increased by 1 percent (after adjustment for inflation), compared with a 9 percent drop for men with one to three years of high school.
- The annual income for men who had completed high school dropped by 5 percent between 1990 and 1995.

Source: National Center for Education Statistics

The opposite opinion is unreasonable because it is contradicted by the facts:

> **Unreasonable opinion:** Staying in school and studying hard is not worth it.

The first opinion is also reasonable because it is consistent with important values like taking personal responsibility and not being a quitter.

If an opinion is not supported by facts, or **evidence,** then it probably is not worth holding. If an opinion contradicts your core **values,** or what you care about or believe deeply, you should also view it with suspicion.

REMEMBER:

All opinions are not created equal. An opinion is as good as the facts and the values that support it.

Your Turn

Exercise A *Read each of the following examples of persuasive writing. In each case, tell what opinion is being stated and name two facts being used to support the opinion.*

Meets ISAT Standards
1.B.3c
1.B.3d
1.C.3a
1.C.3c
1.C.3d

1. Last month, administrators at Bentley Junior High School decided to place twenty-four hour padlocks on the two rear doors of the school building. The reason for the padlocking was to increase security at the school. I believe, however, that the padlocks should be removed for the following reasons: First, if a fire were to occur, it would take a student in a classroom near the locked doors at least three minutes to walk from the classroom to one of the remaining open doors. Second, the two locked doors are the closest ones to the bus drop-off and pickup area and are therefore the most convenient exits for students to use.

OPINION BEING EXPRESSED: _____

ONE FACT THAT SUPPORTS THIS OPINION: _____

_____

ANOTHER FACT THAT SUPPORTS THIS OPINION: _____

_____

2. It's time for Americans to become serious about wasting less paper. According to a report from the Worldwatch Institute, Americans recycle only about 45 percent of the paper that they use, so more than half of it is wasted. Furthermore, the average American uses nineteen times as much paper as the average person in the developing world.

OPINION BEING EXPRESSED: _____

_____

ONE FACT THAT SUPPORTS THIS OPINION: _____

_____

ANOTHER FACT THAT SUPPORTS THIS OPINION: _____

_____

Understanding Persuasive Nonfiction

Your Turn

Exercise B Write two opinions. Beneath each opinion, write two facts that support it.

1. OPINION: _____
   _____

   SUPPORTING FACT: _____
   _____

   SUPPORTING FACT: _____
   _____

2. OPINION: _____
   _____

   SUPPORTING FACT: _____
   _____

   SUPPORTING FACT: _____
   _____

Understanding Persuasive Nonfiction

Understanding Persuasion

If you have ever tried to convince someone else to think or act in a certain way, then you have attempted the art of persuasion. In the modern world, persuasive writing and speech can be found everywhere. The following chart lists some examples of persuasion in everyday life:

Examples of Persuasive Writing and Speech

- Advertisement
- Book review
- Campaign speech
- Commercial
- Debate
- Editorial
- Letter to the editor
- Movie review
- Opinion column
- Press release
- Restaurant review
- Talk show on radio or television
- Television review

Analyzing Persuasive Writing and Speech

When you **analyze** something, you study its parts to see how they are related to one another and to the whole. The most important part of a piece of persuasion is the thesis statement, which is always an opinion. Recall that an opinion is a statement that cannot be proved absolutely to be true but that can be supported by facts.

In a piece of persuasive writing, the main opinion presented in the thesis statement is often supported both by facts and by other opinions. The following are some questions to ask yourself whenever you read or listen to a persuasive piece:

Meets ISAT Standards
1.B.3c
1.B.3d
1.C.3a
1.C.3c
1.C.3d
2.A.3d
2.B.3a

Thinking about Persuasive Writing and Speech

1. What is the main opinion, or thesis, that is being supported?
2. What facts are presented in support of that opinion?
3. Is the opinion consistent with your own beliefs and values?
4. Are the facts presented by the writer or speaker reliable? Are they up to date? Are they based on direct observation or authoritative sources?
5. If the writer or speaker presents other people's ideas or opinions, are these people recognized experts or authorities?
6. Does the writer or speaker appeal mostly to reason or just to people's emotions?
7. Does the author make a fair, unbiased presentation, or has he or she presented a one-sided, narrow, skewed argument, ignoring important facts and values just to make his or her case?
8. Does the author's argument make sense? Is it reasonable and logical? Is it well supported?

Understanding Persuasive Nonfiction 221

Your Turn

Exercise Review the persuasive essay at the beginning of this chapter (pages 204–06). Then answer these questions about it.

1. What main idea, or opinion, is the writer supporting?

   _____

   _____

2. What facts does the writer use to support that opinion?

   _____

   _____

   _____

   _____

   _____

3. What expert sources does the writer refer to in support of his opinion?

   _____

   _____

4. Does the writer appeal mostly to reason or just to emotions? Explain.

   _____

   _____

   _____

Understanding Persuasive Nonfiction

Constructive and Rebuttal Arguments

Sometimes, when attempting to persuade others, writers or speakers use both constructive and rebuttal arguments. A **constructive argument** presents the writer or speaker's reasons for accepting his or her point of view. A **rebuttal argument** presents reasons for not accepting the opposing point of view. Suppose that a writer is creating a persuasive essay that argues this main idea:

> The government should place high taxes on sport utility vehicles (SUVs).

A constructive argument in favor of this opinion might point out that sport utility vehicles get lower gasoline mileage than ordinary cars do and that they therefore cause more air pollution and make the United States more dependent on foreign oil. Opponents of this opinion might argue that big families, farmers, coaches, and others need SUVs and other large vehicles, and that people already pay too much in taxes. They also might argue that Americans should be able to drive the vehicles they want to drive without government interference. To present a complete argument, someone who favors higher taxes on SUVs would want to present rebuttal arguments—ones that counter the arguments of the opposition. For example, he or she might argue that the government could create an exemption from the higher taxes for people who demonstrate a real need for a large vehicle.

Meets ISAT Standards
1.B.3c
1.B.3d
1.C.3a
1.C.3c
1.C.3d
2.A.3d
2.B.3a
3.B.3a

Understanding Persuasive Nonfiction

Literary Techniques in Persuasive Writing

For persuasive writing or speech to be effective, it needs to appeal not only to reason but also to emotion. Two ways in which people appeal to emotions are through figurative language and rhetorical devices. **Figurative language** is writing or speech that is not meant to be taken literally. **Rhetorical devices** are words and phrases used in special ways to create an emotional impact on a reader or audience.

Other important elements in persuasive writing are the author's tone and voice. **Tone** is the author's attitude toward the subject. **Voice** is all the qualities that make an author's writing sound unique and human.

Techniques Used in Persuasive Writing

Figurative Language

Metaphor. Description of one thing as if it were another
EXAMPLE: "Overuse of freshwater resources is a time bomb that eventually will blow up in the face of American agriculture."

Simile. A comparison between two unlike things using *like, as,* or *than*
EXAMPLE: "Letting a kitchen or bathroom faucet run while brushing your teeth is incredibly wasteful. It's like taking one bite of a plate full of food and dumping the rest in the trash."

Rhetorical Devices

Antithesis. A strong contrast between two ideas
EXAMPLE: "Clean water is the source of all life. Polluted water is a major source of disease and death."

Loaded words. Words that have strong emotional content
EXAMPLE: "Already, our harbors are full of *foul, disgustingly polluted* run-off and *muck* from our city *sewers.*"

Parallelism. Use of similar grammatical forms to give items equal weight
EXAMPLE: "Clean, fresh water is essential *for good health and for long life.*"

Repetition. The use, again, of any element, such as a sound, word, phrase, clause, or sentence
EXAMPLE: "We need *to clean up our act and clean up our harbors.*"

Rhetorical question. A question that is not meant to be answered because the answer is presumed to be clear or self-evident
EXAMPLE: "Are we going to allow a few polluters to destroy, irretrievably, our harbor ecosystems?"

Persuasive Reasoning

As you have already learned, effective persuasion appeals both to people's emotions and to reason. Two kinds of reasoning that are used in persuasive writing and speech are induction and deduction. **Inductive reasoning** is the process of drawing a general conclusion from specific observations.

Consider this example:

> **Specific observation:** On April 11, two cars collided at the intersection of Greene and Hewlett Streets, where there is no traffic light.
> **Specific observation:** Similar accidents have occurred in the same intersection several times during the past two years.
> **General conclusion:** A traffic light should be installed to reduce the number of collisions at the intersection of Greene and Hewlett Streets.

Deductive reasoning is the process of drawing a conclusion that has to be true if the facts on which the conclusion is based are true.

Consider this example:

> **Fact:** According to the ordinances, or local laws, of the city of Leeville, owners must keep their dogs on a leash when walking them in city parks; people who violate this ordinance are subject to a $100 fine.
> **Fact:** Mr. Calvados walked his dog in Lindsey Park, in Leeville, without a leash.
> **Conclusion:** Mr. Calvados is subject to a $100 fine.

Notice that if the two facts on which this conclusion is based are both true, then the conclusion has to be true. Because this is so, the argument is an example of valid deductive reasoning.

Meets ISAT Standards
1.B.3c
1.B.3d
1.C.3a
1.C.3c
1.C.3d
1.C.3e
1.C.3f
2.A.3a
2.A.3d
2.B.3a
3.B.3a

Understanding Persuasive Nonfiction

Understanding Persuasive Nonfiction

Fallacies in Reasoning

Some arguments are not reasonable. They contain errors in reasoning, or **fallacies.** The following chart describes some of the most common fallacies found in persuasive writing and speech:

Common Fallacies

False analogy. In a **false analogy,** the writer compares two things that are similar in one way and then assumes, without justification, that they are alike in other ways

EXAMPLE: Writing is like singing. You either have the talent for it or you don't.

EXPLANATION: These sentences make a false analogy between writing and singing. The ability to write is not something with which a person is born. It is something that can be learned. There are many people who are tone deaf or otherwise incapable of learning how to sing, but almost all people can learn to write reasonably well if they read and practice their writing often.

Post hoc ergo propter hoc. This expression is Latin for "after this, therefore because of this." It is often false to claim that because one event follows another, the first event causes the second. Whenever you come across a cause-and-effect argument, ask yourself whether the cause(s) and effect(s) are really related.

EXAMPLE: Jaime visited Layla, who has a cat, and a week later he broke out in a rash. Jaime must be allergic to cats.

EXPLANATION: It is not necessarily the case that exposure to the cat caused the rash. In fact, because the rash occurred long after the exposure to the cat, it probably had some other cause.

Non sequitur. This expression is Latin for "It does not follow." A *non sequitur* is a conclusion that simply does not follow from the facts presented.

EXAMPLE: I don't like plays, so we should go skating.

EXPLANATION: The conclusion (*we should go skating*) is not a necessary consequence of the premise (*I don't like plays*).

Ad hominem. This expression is Latin for "to the person." Someone making an *ad hominem* argument attempts to cast doubt on an opposing opinion by attacking the person holding the opinion rather than by addressing the opinion itself.

EXAMPLE: Senator Luker supports the mandatory seat belt law, but everyone knows that he's one of those wealthy people who's out of touch with ordinary citizens.

More ▶

EXPLANATION: Even if Senator Luker is wealthy and out of touch, these observations have nothing to do with whether it makes sense to require people to wear seat belts. This statement attacks the senator instead of giving a good argument against the law.

False dichotomy, or "either/or" argument. This type of argument falsely assumes that only two alternatives are possible

EXAMPLE: Make up your mind! You're either for the idea of requiring all students to wear uniforms or against it.

EXPLANATION: This statement does not allow for a range of possible opinions. Some people might favor uniforms only under certain conditions (for example, that they be made available at low cost or that they be attractive and comfortable).

Overgeneralization. Overgeneralization is the act of making an **inference,** or informed guess, based on too little evidence

EXAMPLE: My cat has a tail, and so does every other cat that I've seen. Therefore, all cats must have tails.

EXPLANATION: The speaker has based a conclusion about all cats on a few observations. However, there are breeds of cat, like the Manx, that do not have tails, so the speaker is wrong.

Stereotyping. Stereotyping is the act of unfairly attributing a particular quality or characteristic to a whole group of people. When people make generalizations about whole groups of people (all girls or all boys, for example), they are almost always wrong in particular cases. Stereotyping leads to discrimination and prejudice. It is one of the most dangerous of all logical fallacies.

EXAMPLE: Amrit is from India, and he is a really good chess player. Those Indians must be really good at strategy and logical thinking.

EXPLANATION: The speaker has based a conclusion about all people from India on an observation of a single individual. Obviously, the speaker is guilty of stereotyping.

Meets ISAT Standards
1.B.3c
1.B.3d
1.C.3a
1.C.3c
1.C.3d
1.C.3e
1.C.3f
2.A.3d

As you may have guessed from the examples given in the chart, fallacies can have extremely negative consequences. Racial prejudice and consumer fraud are two examples of what can happen when people accept fallacies as true. Learning to recognize fallacies can help you to avoid being duped by shoddy thinking and dishonest double talk.

Understanding Persuasive Nonfiction

Your Turn

Exercise A *Choose one of the following persuasive topics or one of your own. Write a statement of opinion based on the topic. Next, list two arguments supporting your opinion and two arguments opposing your opinion. Then, think of arguments that you could use in rebuttal against the opposing arguments.*

Possible Topics:

- Should all students be required to study a foreign language every year during middle school and high school?
- Should people be required to put muzzles on their dogs when they take them out in public?
- Should the speed limit on the nation's highways be 55 miles per hour?

1. YOUR OPINION: _____
   _____

   ARGUMENTS SUPPORTING YOUR OPINION:

2. _____
   _____

3. _____
   _____

   ARGUMENTS OPPOSING YOUR OPINION:

4. _____
   _____

5. _____
   _____

   REBUTTALS OF THE OPPOSING ARGUMENTS:

4a. _____
   _____

5a. _____
   _____

Exercise B Read the following arguments. After each argument, identify the type of fallacy or fallacies used in each argument and explain why they make the conclusions false.

Meets ISAT Standards
1.B.3d
1.C.3c
1.C.3d
2.B.3a
5.B.3a

1. The year that star basketball center Mike Tower started wearing ALLWORLD basketball shoes, his team went on to win the district championship. How can you argue with that kind of success! Don't be a loser. Buy ALLWORLD!

_____
_____
_____
_____

2. The Great Pyramid in Egypt is made of stones weighing thousands of pounds. The people who created the pyramid had really primitive technology, so they must have had help from aliens who visited the Earth during ancient times.

_____
_____
_____
_____

3. Michelle wants to hold the prom at the Stardust Ballroom, but she's just a freshman, and a teacher's pet at that, so what does she know?

_____
_____
_____
_____

Return to the exercises at the beginning of the chapter, revise your work as necessary, and submit the exercises to your teacher for grading.

Understanding Persuasive Nonfiction

Chapter Project

Meets ISAT
Standards
1.B.3a
1.B.3d
1.C.3c
1.C.3d
1.C.3e
2.A.3a
2.A.3c
2.A.3d
2.B.3a
3.C.3b
4.B.3a
4.B.3b
4.B.3c

To gain a better understanding of how persuasive writing works, try this project with a group of your classmates:

✔ Gather editorials, letters to the editor, and advertisements from local or national newspapers.

✔ Study these to find examples of the following literary techniques and logical fallacies:

Literary techniques
  Figurative language:
    Metaphors
    Similes
  Rhetorical devices:
    Antithesis
    Loaded words
    Parallelism
    Repetition
    Rhetorical questions

Logical fallacies
  False analogies
  Post hoc ergo propter hoc arguments
  Non sequiturs
  Ad hominem arguments
  False dichotomies, or either/or arguments
  Overgeneralizations
  Stereotyping

✔ Present your findings to your class in an oral report or on a bulletin board.

230 AIM Higher! ISAT Language Arts Review

Chapter 11
Step by Step
The Writing Process for Examinations

First Encounter

Below and on the next four pages you will find the following: a writing prompt from a test, a student's rough outline based on the prompt, and a piece of writing based on the outline. Read these materials. Then try your hand at the exercises that follow. You will not be graded on the exercises at this time. At the end of the chapter, you will be directed to return to these exercises to revise and proofread your work.

> A wealthy graduate of your school has recently left $400,000 to fund an after-school program. The graduate has promised that if the program is successful, there will be additional money to keep it going in future years.
>
> Your principal has asked students, their parents, and teachers for suggestions about activities for the after-school program. In essay form, describe the activities you would like to see in the program. Explain why, backing up your opinions with reasons.

Writing Prompt from a Test

232 AIM Higher! ISAT Language Arts Review

Here is one student's rough outline in response to the prompt:

One Student's Rough Outline

"Our After-School Program"

Introduction
Main Idea: Stress diverse needs of students
Thesis: We must realize that students have a variety of skills and
   interests, and we should try to make sure that our program
   addresses as many needs as possible.

Sports/Athletics
—Need exercise
—Work on physical skills alone or together
—Organized sports/competitions
—Non-organized sports
—Indoor activities for bad weather

Creative arts
—Make up for cuts in art & music programs
—Chance to play instruments/sing/draw/paint

Computers & woodworking/auto shop
—Make & fix things (maybe for school)
—Make useful items
—Computer time, esp. for kids who don't have one at home

Extra help/Study hall
—Help other students
—Help kids with homework
—Teachers don't have time

Conclusion: How to run program
—Have students sign up for activities
—Allow different choices on different days
—Let students change their minds after that
—Could have more choices if volunteers help out

First Encounter

After making an outline, Julio wrote a rough draft of an essay about the topic specified in the prompt. Then he revised his draft for content and proofread it for errors in grammar, spelling, capitalization, and punctuation.

One Student's Rough Draft

Julio Ortega

English 8

"Our After-School Program"

Recently, our school re(ci)eved a wonderful gift: $400,000 to set up an after-school program. Now we have a chance to make important *help* decisions about how ~~we~~ *our school* will use the money. If our program is successful, we can get *more* money to continue it in future years. The most important thing to realize is that we ~~can't~~ *cannot* satisfy everybody~~s~~ *student's* needs. We must realize that students have a variety of skills and interests, and we should try to make sure that our program addresses as many needs as possible. *While* ~~S~~some students may wish to parti(ci)pate in something they already know how to do, ~~Some~~ *others want to* will try something new. ~~Some~~ *Still others* can use the time to get extra help with their school work.

~~I think that~~ *I*t is important to include ~~sports~~ *athletics*. Everybody says that kids need more exercise. Some students could use *the time* to practice their skills on their own. ~~Some~~ *Others* will enjoy playing on teams. our school could orgize competitions with other middle schools for the first time. Others ^an students^

will want to play sports just for fun. ~~I have heard people say that~~ an

athletics program would be fine in good weather, but what would the kids

who play sports do in bad weather? ~~I say that~~ we should figure ~~that~~ out

some indoor options ~~and not let it keep~~ athletics ~~out~~. ^rather than leave out^

    Another area of importance ~~are~~ is the creative arts. We no longer have

art classes ^or music^ in school. ~~I know that my cousin, who goes to another~~

~~school, also does not have art.~~ I for one like to draw and paint ~~and~~. ^know a lot of students who would^ They would

like to have someone show ~~me~~ them how to use different techniques and

materials. ~~We also no longer have a music program.~~ Students who like

to play a musical instrument or sing should also have a chance to do

that after school.

    Some students are really good at working with tools. ~~They~~ These students would like to

fix cars and make ~~stuff~~ ^things out of wood^. They could make things, ~~such as signs~~

for the school or scenery for the school play. They could also make

birdhouses or other things to take home. Some students ~~who like~~

~~computers are called something I won't say. These~~ ^would rather spend time on a computer^ students who really

like computers or who don't have a computer at home could work in the

media center after school. Anyone who needs more time or information

to finish a paper or project could work on it there.

More ▶

First Encounter

Finally, Some students do not have anyone at home who can help them with

their
~~there~~ school work. Those students who have trouble reading or doing

math could get help from other students or from tutors. Other

students just need a lot of help with their homework. Teachers often do

not have the time to go over homework in class. It is one thing to come up with all these ideas but another thing to make them work.
Here's how I would run the program: I would have students sign up for

~~a certain number of weeks. I would have~~ different choices on different

be somewhere else on certain days,
days. That way, if a student had to ~~baby-sit or go to piano lessons~~, he

or she would not have to miss a big chunk of the program. Students

would sign up for an activity for a certain number of weeks. After that

either   ¶
time, they could continue or choose something else. One thing that

help would be to have   who could   e
would ~~be great is if~~ people ~~might~~ volunteer their time. Than we would not

have to use all the money from the gift to pay instructors or coaches.

We could use more of the money on equipment and supplies—and on

providing interesting choices for students. Even then, we might not

do
be able to offer everything everyone wants, but we could ~~get~~ a lot

more than we do now!
~~closer!~~

Your Turn

Exercise On your own paper, answer the following questions. Use complete sentences.

1. What purpose is the piece of writing supposed to accomplish?

2. According to the writing prompt, what must the piece of writing include?

3. What does this student mention at the beginning of his essay to get his readers' attention?

4. What is the thesis statement of this piece of writing? Where does it appear?

5. Julio divided the rough outline for the body of his piece of writing into four parts. What is the subject of each of these four paragraphs?

6. Why did Julio remove the phrase *I say that* from the last sentence of the second paragraph?

7. What are three examples of spelling errors corrected by the writer?

8. Why did he place a / and a # sign between *a* and *lot* in the fifth paragraph?

9. What are two examples of transitions that Julio added to make the connections between his ideas clearer and smoother?

10. What are two examples of words that he replaced with new words that are more concrete and precise?

11. What is an example of an irrelevant detail that Julio cut from the essay?

12. List an example of a punctuation error Julio corrected when he revised his piece of writing.

13. What is an example of a run-on sentence that Julio corrected? How did he correct it?

14. Why did Julio change the last paragraph to two separate paragraphs? (Hint: What is the main idea of each paragraph?)

Meets ISAT Standards
1.B.3b
1.C.3e
2.A.3d
3.A.3
3.B.3a
3.B.3b
3.C.3a

The Writing Process 237

The Writing Process

Step by Step

Have you ever received a present or bought something that you had to put together? If so, you probably recall having to go through a process to assemble the item. The first step might have involved reading through some directions. Then you were probably instructed to make sure that all the pieces were there and to gather any tools you would need for the assembly process. Next, you might have followed each step in the proper order until the item was completely assembled. If you are like a lot of people, however, you might have just jumped in and started trying to assemble the item without reading the directions first or gathering all the necessary pieces and tools. In this case, you probably encountered many glitches along the way. You most likely had to look back and reread the directions repeatedly to figure out why some pieces did not fit together properly. You probably had to stop periodically to go find tools. Perhaps you even had to take apart items that were put together in the wrong order. The assembly process is usually much more difficult and generally takes longer when approached in this way. The writing process is very similar.

Stages in the Process of Writing

Writing is another process that is best approached with some forethought and planning. Good writers rarely just sit down and begin writing, write until they have filled the page, and then stop. Much of the work of writing, in fact, is done in the planning stage, before the first word is written. Even after a piece has been written, there is still a lot of work to be done revising and proofreading it. Finally, after all of these stages of the process, the piece is ready to be shared with others.

The following chart shows the stages in **the process of writing.**

Prewriting

Choose subject, genre, purpose, audience

⬇

Narrow/focus topic
  Use graphic organizer

⬇

Write thesis statement

⬇

Gather ideas
  Brainstorm   Observe
  Discuss   Recall
  Freewrite   Research
  Interview   Use graphic organizer

⬇

Organize ideas/plan the piece
  Use rough outline
       or
  Use graphic organizer

⬇

Graphic Organizers*

Analysis chart
Cause-and-effect chart
Comparison-and-contrast chart
Cycle chart
Double-entry ledger (T-chart)
Flow chart
Paragraph-planning chart
Pro-and-con chart
Reporter's questions chart
Sensory detail chart
Timeline
Tree diagram
Venn diagram
Word web/cluster chart

*For examples of these graphic organizers, see Chapter 4, "Picture This! Notetaking and Graphic Organizers."

Meets ISAT Standards
1.B.3b
1.C.3e
2.A.3d
3.A.3
3.B.3a
3.B.3b
3.C.3a

Drafting

Get it all down roughly
       or
Get main ideas down and fill in supporting details and examples later
       or
Create a careful, complete draft, revising as you go

⬇

"Don't think of a draft as a finished sculpture. Think of it as raw clay—the material you will shape into the finished piece."

More ▶

The Writing Process **239**

The Writing Process

Revision

Evaluate and revise . . .
   for audience.
   for purpose.
   for focus and elaboration.
   for structure and organization.
   for style and voice.
     for word choice.
     for sentence variety.
     for sound and for figurative language.

"Good writing is rewriting."

Note: Extensive revision is called *rewriting*.

Proofreading

Proof
   for manuscript form.
   for grammar and usage.
   for mechanics.
     for capitalization.
     for punctuation.
   for spelling.

Note: Another name for proofreading is *copyediting*. Together, revision and proofreading are called *editing*.

Publishing

- Give a copy to a relative or friend.
- Read it aloud.
- Bind it into a book.
- Put it on a bulletin board.
- Send it to the school or local paper.
- Put it in your portfolio.
- Enter a writing contest.
- Post it online.
- Record or perform it.

Variations on the Writing Process

Keep in mind that this standard writing process can vary from person to person and from one type of writing to another. For example, most people usually do not revise their informal e-mails to friends or the entries that they write in their diaries. A quick note, like "Don't forget to buy milk," is generally written with no prewriting, evaluation, or revision. Some writers do revision and proofreading at the same time, in a single read-through. This is not recommended, however, as it is easy to miss errors this way. Some writers follow the process straight through from beginning to end, while others pause in the middle of writing to gather more ideas (prewriting) or to edit (revise) some of what they have already written. It is not uncommon for a writer to discover while revising that he or she does not like part of a piece. Consequently, he or she might return to the drafting or even the prewriting stage. So, the writing process really looks something like this:

The Writing Process

- Prewriting
- Evaluation and Revision
- Drafting
- Proofreading
- Publishing/Sharing

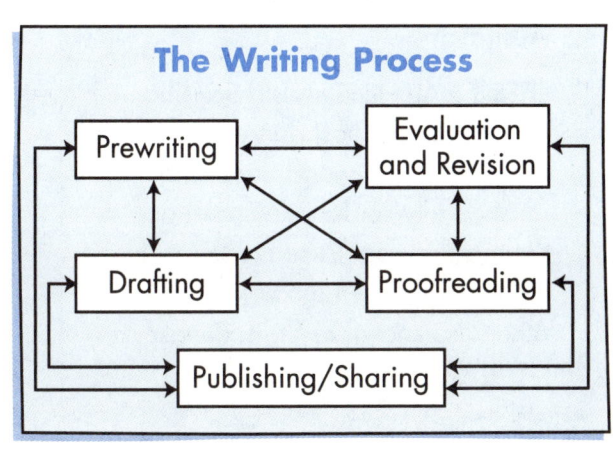

Prewriting

Prewriting, as the chart indicates, is the first step in creating a piece of writing. The prewriting process has its own series of steps.

Meets ISAT Standards
1.B.3b
1.C.3e
2.A.3d
3.A.3
3.B.3a
3.B.3b
3.C.3a

Prewriting: Choosing Your Subject, Genre, Purpose, and Audience

The first step in the prewriting process is to choose your subject, genre, purpose, and audience. The **subject** is the general topic that you will write about. The **genre** is the type of writing you will do. For example, will you be writing a short story (fiction) or an essay about events that really happened (nonfiction narrative)? The **purpose** is the reason for your writing. Is it intended to inform? Persuade? Entertain? Describe? Convey a moral? You should also think about your **audience**—the person or people who will read your work. Will you be writing for children, other students your age, adults, or some combination of these? How much will your readers know about your subject already? Thinking about the audience can help you to determine the style for the piece, such as how formal it should be, how sophisticated your vocabulary and sentence structure should be, and how much background information you will have to include.

The Writing Process

The Writing Process

Prewriting: Narrowing, or Focusing, Your Topic

Once you have established these four basic elements, you may need to **narrow**, or **focus**, your topic. For example, suppose you are given an assignment to write about music. The entire subject of music is so vast that you would not be able to cover it all, even if you wrote a bookshelf worth of books. Therefore, you must narrow the topic.

Here is an example of one way the general subject of music could be narrowed to come up with a topic suitable for a short essay:

> GENERAL SUBJECT: Music
>
> FOCUSED: Women in music
>
> MORE FOCUSED: Women who have had a huge impact on music history
>
> EVEN MORE FOCUSED: Aretha Franklin, the "Queen of Soul," essentially created the genre of soul music

A graphic organizer, such as a word web or a T-chart, can help you to narrow your topic. For example, look at the word web on page 85. Notice how the word web narrows the general subject of sailing to a number of specific topics, such as parts of boats and the different types. These topics are narrowed even further to such specific topics as single-mast and double-mast, or split-rig, boats. There are many graphic organizers that are also helpful in narrowing topics, including Venn diagrams (see page 86) and analysis charts (see page 87). The type of graphic organizer that is most useful will depend on the topic and the purpose of your writing.

Prewriting: Creating a Thesis Statement

The next step, after focusing your topic, is to write the thesis statement. The **thesis statement** expresses the main idea of your piece in one or two sentences. A thesis statement helps you to keep your writing focused on your central idea.

The following chart shows an example of a general subject, a focused topic, and a thesis statement about the topic:

> SUBJECT: Deadly creatures
>
> FOCUSED TOPIC: Deadly creatures of Australia
>
> THESIS STATEMENT: Australia is home to some of the most dangerous creatures in the world, including the most deadly spider and snake and the most poisonous sea creature known to man—the box jellyfish, otherwise known as the sea wasp.

Your Turn

Exercise A Study the following writing prompt. Identify the subject, the purpose, the genre, and the audience. Write those on the lines provided. NOTE: Do NOT create a piece of writing in response to the writing prompt. You are simply being asked to identify parts of the prompt!

Meets ISAT
Standards
1.B.3b
1.C.3e
2.A.3d
3.A.3
3.B.3a
3.B.3b
3.C.3a

> **WRITING PROMPT:** Read the excerpt about the Navajo ritual of the Blessing Way. This ceremony is performed to ensure good luck, good health, and a good life for a young person who is coming of age. Think of another ritual that people follow to bring good luck. In an essay, compare the Blessing Way ceremony with another ceremony that is used to bring good luck.

1. SUBJECT: _____

2. PURPOSE: _____

3. GENRE, OR TYPE, OF WRITING: _____

4. AUDIENCE: _____

Exercise B The writing prompts on tests are often very general. Usually, you will need to narrow the broader topic to a more specific topic that you will write about. For each of the writing prompts given below, create a narrow topic suitable for a short essay. Write your narrowed topic on the line provided. NOTE: Do NOT write essays in response to the writing prompts. You are simply being asked to create narrowed topics!

1. > **WRITING PROMPT:** The African-American educator Booker T. Washington once said: "Success is to be measured not so much by the position that one has reached in life as by the obstacles which he has overcome." Think about the obstacles you have overcome. In a speech, identify an experience in which you overcame some obstacle in order to reach a particular goal successfully.

   NARROWED TOPIC: _____
   _____

More ▶

The Writing Process **243**

Your Turn

Meets ISAT Standards
3.B.3a
3.C.3a

2. **WRITING PROMPT:** Most people have in mind a place they would most like to visit, if they could. For some people, this might be a place where they could take on a great challenge, such as climbing Mount Everest. For others, it might be a place where they could relax and enjoy the beauty of nature, such as the Hawaiian Islands. Still others might choose to visit a ranch in the West and ride the range, to walk along the Great Wall of China, or to visit one of the great cities of the world. Think of a place that you would love to visit. It can be a place that you have learned about in school or in books or through friends or relatives, or it could a place you have visited before. Describe the place you would like to visit, and explain at least three reasons why you would like to go there.

NARROWED TOPIC: _____

_____

3. **WRITING PROMPT:** What is your favorite type of music? Define your favorite genre of music and explain how it differs from some other types of music. Also, describe what it is that you like about this type of music. If you do not have a single favorite genre of music, then describe one of the genres that you like.

NARROWED TOPIC: _____

_____

Exercise C Now that you have come up with a focused topic for each of the writing prompts in Exercise B, write a thesis statement for an essay on each of these topics:

An obstacle you have overcome

A place you would like to visit

Your favorite genre of music

Write your thesis statements on your own paper.

The Writing Process

Prewriting: Gathering Ideas

When you have developed a strong thesis statement, it is time to gather ideas and information to support your main idea. There are many ways to gather ideas and information.

The following chart describes a few helpful techniques:

Techniques for Gathering Ideas

Brainstorm   When you **brainstorm,** you bring up as many possible ideas as you can, quickly, without worrying about whether they work. You can brainstorm alone, but this technique works best with partners. For example, suppose your task is to write about the role of communication in the modern world. Here are some of the results you might get from brainstorming with a partner or a small group:

—Communication vital in modern world
—Satellites
—Instant access everywhere, not just in cities
—Cell phones
—Internet
—TV/Radio
—People around world can share ideas, info

Freewrite   When you **freewrite,** you write whatever comes to mind about your topic for a given time—perhaps five minutes. Try to cover many angles of the topic without stopping to evaluate your thoughts. Your goal is to get as much material down on paper as possible. When you are done, you can select your best ideas and examples and choose the best way to reorganize them. Here is an example of one student's freewriting about the values he or she thinks are important in the world today:

Everybody wants peace, justice, etc. We all want wars to end. Different ideas about how to stop them. People now have more leisure than before. But people seem to work hard, too. Maybe it's that people expect to work hard but they also expect to be rewarded for it. They're working for something. Respect for individual. The idea of human rights can never be lost now. Lots of dangers in today's world because of high tech, but lots of new excitement, opportunity, too. Everybody can get in on it. Education for everyone is the thing that has to be kept up.

More ▶

The Writing Process

Interview Create a list of questions you could ask people who know a lot about your topic.

Discuss Arrange a group discussion about the topic. This technique works best if the people in the group are knowledgeable about the topic and if they receive ahead of time a list of items for discussion.

Research Use reference works, such as encyclopedias, atlases, almanacs, and dictionaries; refer to books and to articles from magazines, newspapers, and journals; look at reputable, authoritative Web sites.

Use Graphic Organizers Possibilities include word webs (cluster charts), Venn diagrams, timelines, flow charts, tree diagrams, double-entry ledgers, comparison-and-contrast charts, pro-and-con charts, and analysis charts. These are excellent ways to gather and organize information. Here is an example of a word web that a student made for an essay on the subject of Africa:

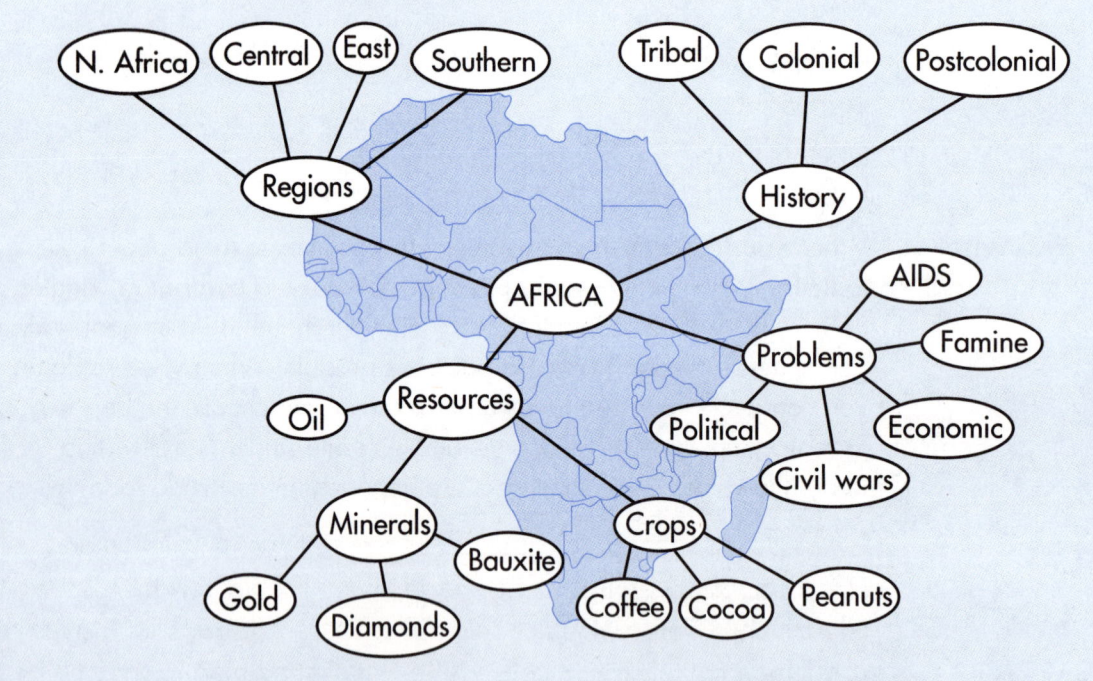

For more information on other ways to organize ideas, see Chapter 4, "Picture This! Notetaking and Graphic Organizers."

More ▶

List Make a list, in one or more columns, of information about your topic. Here is an example of a list that a student made of what she knew and wanted to find out about fuel:

Meets ISAT Standards
1.B.3b
3.B.3a
3.C.3a
5.A.3a
5.B.3a
5.B.3b
5.C.3c

1. Oil is a fossil fuel—comes from the ground, from decayed prehistoric plants & animals.
2. Coal & natural gas are also fossil fuels.
3. Major oil reserves in Middle East, Russia, U.S., Canada, North Sea, Nigeria, Venezuela.
4. Crude oil is shipped in tankers.
5. Crude oil is refined—how?
6. Pollution, global warming—What happens when we burn coal, oil, or natural gas?
7. How much fossil fuel is left underground?
8. How can we make it last longer?
9. What did people use before coal & oil?
10. What can people use now instead of fossil fuels?

Observe Use your five senses to study your subject carefully. This is an excellent method for topics that require description, such as "a tropical rain forest" or "my favorite day."

Recall Think back on your previous experience and try to remember as much detail as you can. Write down everything that you can remember. Often, it is helpful to try to remember things in the order in which they occurred. Sometimes it is helpful to concentrate on memories of particular places or people. For example, if you are asked to research and write about how canyons are created and you have actually visited one, your firsthand experience could provide useful insight and information.

The Writing Process 247

Your Turn

Exercise A *Suppose that you have been asked to write a paper about a topic related to one of the following subjects. Circle the subject you have chosen. Then, in the space provided, make a word web, or cluster chart, based on the subject. Then, choose a specific topic from your word web and write it on the line provided.*

1. Possible subjects (circle one):

   fascinating historical or fictional characters   hobbies

   sea life   mythology

   current events   the future

2. Create a word web to explore ideas about your subject.

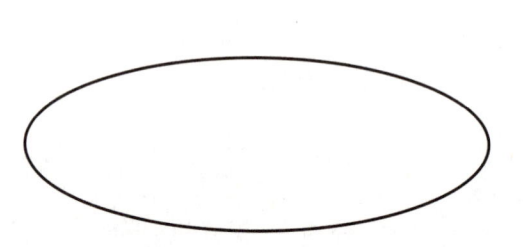

3. Choose one of these ideas as your specific topic: _____

   _____

248   AIM Higher! ISAT Language Arts Review

Exercise B On the lines provided, do some freewriting based on the specific topic that you chose in Exercise A on the previous page. Simply write whatever comes into your mind about the topic. For now, do not worry about your grammar, usage, mechanics, or spelling.

Meets ISAT
Standards
3.B.3a
5.C.3a
5.C.3c

_____

_____

_____

_____

_____

_____

_____

_____

_____

_____

_____

_____

_____

_____

Exercise C Based on your freewriting, create a thesis statement for an essay about the topic you have chosen.

THESIS STATEMENT: _____

_____

_____

The Writing Process

The Writing Process

In a test-taking situation, you will approach the prewriting process differently than you would when writing on your own or for a class assignment. Here are some of the major differences:

Prewriting in a Test-Taking Situation

1. **Manage your time.** Some writing tests are timed. Even if the test is not timed, you will usually have a limited amount of time in which to complete the test. Wear a watch or make sure you can see a clock, and check it often. Be sure to allow yourself enough time to do your prewriting, create a draft, and then revise and proofread your answer. Some students make the mistake of not taking enough time for prewriting when writing for a test. Do not be one of those students! In some writing situations, you can take an unlimited amount of time for revision. When you take a writing test, that will not be the case. Therefore, it is especially important to have a clear plan for what you want to write before you begin drafting.

2. **Analyze the writing prompt carefully to determine your subject, genre, purpose, and audience.** The **writing prompt** is the set of directions that tell you what you are supposed to write. Usually, the writing prompt will determine your subject, purpose, and audience. It probably will also specify the genre (type of writing) and the form your response should take, such as a letter, a single paragraph, or an essay consisting of more than one paragraph. Consider the following writing prompt:

   The legislature in your state is considering passing a law requiring all public school students to wear uniforms. [**Subject**] Identify three reasons why this law should or should not be adopted. Write a letter [**Form**] to your local representative [**Audience**] persuading [**Purpose**] him or her to vote for or against a law requiring public school students to wear uniforms. Be sure that the reasons you state in your letter show why uniforms would have a positive or negative effect on all or most public school students, not just yourself. Choose reasons that would be convincing to a state representative.

   More ▶

This prompt tells you that the **subject** of the piece of writing should be school uniforms. More specifically, you must identify three arguments for or against school uniforms. The **form** and **genre** of the response will be a letter. Your **purpose,** of course, will be to persuade. The hypothetical (imaginary) **audience** for your writing will be your state representative, though your real audience will be the people who will be evaluating and scoring your answer. Remember to study the writing prompt carefully to make sure that you understand what your subject, genre, purpose, and audience will be, as well as the form your response should take.

Meets ISAT Standards
1.B.3a
1.C.3a
1.C.3c
2.A.3c
3.B.3a
3.C.3a

3. **Pay particular attention to action words in the writing prompt.** There are certain **verbs,** or **action words,** that play a particularly important role in the prompt. These are key words that set the purpose for your writing: They tell you exactly what you are supposed to do. Here are some examples of action words to look for in writing prompts:

Key Action Words in Prompts

Compare. When you are asked to **compare** people, places, or things, you must show how they are alike.

Contrast. When you are asked to **contrast** two people, places, or things, you must point out how they differ. (You might be asked to compare and contrast them, which means you must describe similarities and differences.)

Define. When you are asked to **define** a term, you must tell what it means. A good way to do this is to identify the group or category to which it belongs and explain how it differs from other things in that group or category. Then you can elaborate on your basic definition, perhaps by giving one or more specific, detailed examples.

Describe. When you are asked to **describe** something or someone, you must paint a portrait of your subject in words, showing how it looks, feels, sounds, smells, or tastes and perhaps explaining what it does.

Discuss. When you are asked to **discuss** a topic, you must look at the topic from various angles and come to some conclusion about it. When discussing a topic in writing or in speech, it is sometimes easy to get off track if there are a lot of angles or aspects to explore. Be sure to stick to the central idea or focus created by your thesis statement.

More ▶

The Writing Process 251

The Writing Process

Evaluate. When you are asked to **evaluate** something, you must make a judgment about it based on specific criteria.

Explain. When you are asked to **explain,** you must give reasons, examples, or step-by-step details to tell what something means, why something happens, or how something works.

Identify. When you are asked to **identify** someone or something, you are simply being asked to select and describe some person, place, or thing. Try to do this as precisely and accurately as possible, by answering *who, what, when, where,* and *why* questions.

List. When you are asked to **list,** you are being asked for a collection of items, given one after another.

Persuade. When you are asked to **persuade,** you must convince the reader to adopt a point of view or to take a particular course of action. To do that, you will have to present reasons and evidence.

Relate. When you are asked to **relate,** you are usually being asked to tell a story or to show how two or more items are connected.

Review. When you are asked to **review,** you must look something over carefully, discuss its most important points, and, usually, provide an evaluation of it.

Summarize. When you are asked to **summarize,** you must restate something using fewer words. The keys to summarizing are to include only the most important details or events and to generalize, or make broad statements that cover a number of specific details.

4. Respond to the entire prompt. Sometimes students make the mistake of responding to only part of a writing prompt. For example, consider this prompt:

> Think of a time when you learned an important lesson the hard way. Perhaps you made a mistake for which you paid dearly. For example, you forgot to do something important, or you did something you knew you shouldn't have done and regretted it. Describe what happened, and explain what you learned from the experience.

This prompt requires that the students do three things: First, the student must think about an event or time in his or her life when he or she learned an important but difficult lesson. Second, the student must describe exactly what happened. Third, the student must explain the lesson that he or she learned from this experience. An essay that simply described the event without explaining what lesson the student learned from it would receive a low score.

More ▶

Meets ISAT
Standards
1.B.3a
1.C.3a
1.C.3c
2.A.3c
3.B.3a
3.C.3a

5. **Gather information from the prompt, from your own knowledge and experience, and (if applicable) from the selection or selections provided.** In an ordinary writing situation, there are many ways to gather information. You can go to the library, use the Internet, interview experts or eyewitnesses, and so on. In a testing situation, your options for gathering the details to use in your piece of writing will be extremely limited. Sometimes, information will be provided in the writing prompt itself. That is another reason to look at the prompt carefully. On some tests, you are likely to encounter writing prompts that are based on one or more reading selections. In such situations, you must pick relevant details from the selections to use in the piece that you are writing. Information from the selections can be summarized, paraphrased, or quoted directly. At other times, you will have to gather information entirely from your own knowledge and experience. A word web, timeline, or other graphic organizer can help you to do this. Be sure to gather details that are specific and related to your main idea.

6. **Make sure that you write a thesis statement that is a general, one- or two-sentence answer to the writing prompt.** An extremely important part of good writing is **focus**—keeping to the point and avoiding irrelevant details. The best way to keep your focus is to write a thesis statement that states the central idea of your piece—the main point that you wish to make. The thesis statement should be a general, one- or two-sentence response to the writing prompt. Consider the writing prompt on the previous page. A good thesis statement for a response to this prompt would be the following:

   I had to learn it the hard way, but my experience taught me a valuable life lesson that I will not soon forget.

7. **Create a rough outline or a graphic organizer to plan the piece.** In a testing situation, you generally will not be able to rewrite your piece extensively, as you might in an ordinary writing situation. Therefore, you need to plan very carefully before you begin drafting your answer. Do this by creating a rough draft or a graphic organizer to provide a map of the information you will include and the general order in which you will discuss it. Make sure that your outline or organizer includes material that responds completely to the writing prompt. In a high-pressure writing situation, such as writing for a test, people are sometimes tempted to skip this important step. Do not be one of those people!

Your Turn

Exercise Read the writing prompt below. Do NOT produce a piece of writing in response. Instead, simply fill in the circle next to the correct answer to each multiple-choice question.

> **WRITING PROMPT:** The school board is considering eliminating the school yearbook in order to cut costs. As an editor of the school yearbook, write a letter to the school board that states your viewpoint on eliminating the school yearbook. In your letter, cite quotations from other students who work on the yearbook committee to support your viewpoint.

1. The topic of this writing prompt is
   - Ⓐ whether the school yearbook should be eliminated.
   - Ⓑ the benefits of having a school yearbook.
   - Ⓒ how eliminating the school yearbook would help cut costs.
   - Ⓓ what it's like to be an editor of the yearbook.

2. The purpose of your response will be to
   - Ⓐ explain whether a school yearbook is important.
   - Ⓑ present your opinion about eliminating the yearbook.
   - Ⓒ list other students who work on the yearbook committee.
   - Ⓓ explain why you like working as a yearbook editor.

3. The key question this prompt asks is,
   - Ⓐ will cutting the school yearbook cut school costs?
   - Ⓑ why does the school board want to eliminate the yearbook?
   - Ⓒ should the school yearbook be eliminated?
   - Ⓓ how else could the school board save money for the school?

4. The form of the response should be
   - Ⓐ an essay.
   - Ⓑ a list.
   - Ⓒ a letter.
   - Ⓓ a story.

5. The audience for your response is
   - Ⓐ the school board.
   - Ⓑ your classmates.
   - Ⓒ the yearbook committee.
   - Ⓓ other editors of the yearbook.

The Writing Process

Organizing Your Ideas

Once you have gathered ideas and information for your piece, you will need to arrange them in a logical order. While many students are tempted to skip this step and begin drafting immediately, organizing your ideas before you write is one of the most crucial steps in creating a successful piece of writing. It is much more difficult to revise a disorganized piece of writing than it is to organize the information in the first place. Since organization is one of the main standards on which your writing will be evaluated, it is worth taking the time to complete this step in the process. In order to score well on a writing test, your writing must have logical and coherent organization. **Logical organization** means that the ideas are arranged in an order that makes sense. **Coherent organization** means that each idea follows reasonably from the one before it and leads reasonably to the one after it.

Methods of Organization

This section shows eight major methods of organizing information in your writing. If you study these approaches and learn how to use them, you will be able to write your own essays with confidence.

1. Chronological Order When you use **chronological (time) order,** you write about events in the order in which they took place. This method works well in essays about a series of events. Chronological order is the method of organization used in most narrative writing, such as stories, biographies, and histories. Note the use of chronological order in the following paragraph about the great African leader Sundiata:

> Sundiata was the son of the king of the Malinke people and a woman who had a hunchback. A soothsayer had predicted that if the king had a son with a hunchbacked woman, he would grow up to be the greatest of his people's heroes. However, when Sundiata was a small child, he disappointed many people. According to legend, he could not walk until he was seven years old. Then, his mother made braces for his legs. He learned to walk, and he also became a fine horseman. In later years, this skill would prove crucial.

Chronological order is appropriate for this paragraph because the writer focuses on a series of developments in a hero's life.

Meets ISAT Standards
1.B.3a
1.C.3a
1.C.3c
2.A.3c
3.B.3a
3.C.3a

The Writing Process

There are also ways of making detours from strict chronological order. One variation in time order is **flashback,** in which you temporarily stop the clock of the narrative in order to tell about something that happened in the past. Another variation is **foreshadowing,** in which you hint about something that will happen in the future. Writers often use foreshadowing to build suspense—that "What will happen next?" feeling. In the paragraph about Sundiata, the phrase, "A soothsayer had predicted" signals a flashback. The last sentence of that paragraph ("In later years,…") is an example of foreshadowing.

2. Spatial Order When you use **spatial order,** you present visual details in the order of their appearance. The order should follow a consistent principle, such as top to bottom, bottom to top, far to near, or outside to inside. This method works well for describing places, people, and objects. Note the use of spatial order in the following paragraph about the great wall of Zimbabwe:

> The stone ruins stand in a forest valley. The first thing that greets your eye is a wall of large stones, put together without nails or mortar. The ruins form a broken circle that once measured more than 800 feet around. The wall is 17 feet thick in some places, and it rises to more than 30 feet in height. Walking through a break in the wall, you come to the Conical Tower. Though damaged, its top rises above the top of the wall.

This description is organized from outside to inside. This helps the reader feel as if he or she is approaching the wall, entering the ruin, and exploring.

Just as flashbacks and foreshadowing are variations of chronological order, zoom ins, zoom outs, and order of impression are variations of spatial order. In a **zoom in,** you describe the subject from far away at first, then from closer and closer positions, focusing on smaller details the closer you get. The sample paragraph about the ruins uses a zoom in. A **zoom out** is the opposite. It begins close up and gradually moves away from the subject.

When you use **order of impression,** you start with what an observer would notice first about the thing being described. Then, you go on to write about less obvious details. For example, if you wanted to describe a happy person, you might start with his or her sunny grin and then proceed to how the person enters a room, how he or she is dressed, and so on.

3. Comparison-and-Contrast Order When you need to describe the ways in which two things are similar and/or different, **comparison-and-contrast order** is the best way to organize the information. There are several ways to arrange the information:

- You can organize the material by **subject,** discussing one subject completely and then comparing or contrasting the second subject with the first.

- You can organize the material by **similarities and differences,** first discussing all the ways the two subjects are alike and then describing all the ways in which they differ.
- You can organize the material by **features,** comparing and contrasting both subjects characteristic by characteristic. First, you mention one characteristic and explain how the two subjects are similar or different with respect to that characteristic. Then, you mention another characteristic and do the same, and so on, until you have described all the characteristics that you want to discuss.

The following paragraph compares and contrasts two different peoples of southern Africa. Notice the way the writer has organized the material by subject:

> The Khoisan, a hunting and gathering people, occupied much of southern Africa until the Late Iron Age, which lasted from about A.D. 1000 to about 1600. The Khoisan lived in small groups without formal leaders. They were nomads, moving continually in search of food. Men hunted with bows and arrows. Women collected plant foods such as nuts, roots, and berries. During the Late Iron Age, Bantu farmers and herders from farther north settled in southern Africa. Their iron tools and weapons were superior to those of the Khoisan. The Bantu lived in large family groups called clans, and had strong leaders.

This paragraph focuses on two contrasting ways of life. First, the writer describes the Khoisan ways of making a living and of forming groups. Then the writer discusses the same two aspects of the Bantu lifestyle.

4. Organization by Classification and Division When you use this method of organization, you **classify** various topics that you want to discuss into groups, using standards such as features or membership in a specific class. This method is useful when you are discussing several related topics. For example, an article about ice skating might be divided into sections on figure skating, speed skating, and hockey.

Notice the way the writer classifies topics in the following paragraph about the regions of Africa:

> The clearest regional boundary in Africa is the Sahara desert. This vast ocean of sand separates North Africa from sub-Saharan Africa. North Africa contains several Muslim nations, including Egypt, Libya, Algeria, and Morocco. Sub-Saharan Africa can be divided into at least four regions of its own. The eastern grasslands of Tanzania and its neighbors are quite different from the rain forests of central Africa or the coastal forests of western Africa. Southern Africa, including nations such as Zimbabwe, Zaire, and South Africa, is notably rich in minerals.

The writer classifies the subject geographically. Each detail supports the main idea—that the continent is made

Meets ISAT Standards
1.B.3a
1.C.3a
1.C.3c
1.C.3e
2.A.3c
3.B.3a
3.C.3a

The Writing Process

The Writing Process

up of distinct regions, each with its own unique traits.

5. Organization by Degree This method of organization is especially useful when you want to describe to what extent (how much or how often) a particular trait or feature occurs in several persons, places, or things.

The following paragraph about African rock art is organized by degree:

> Paintings and rock carvings of varying artistic complexity can be found across Africa. Perhaps the finest examples have been found in the mountains of Algeria. There, a rock carving known as "The Crying Cows" shows a group of cattle with long, curving horns. These beasts seem to jump out of the rock, ready to gore the viewer. In Libya, a herd of giraffes more than six feet tall and more than 7,000 years old decorates the side of a cliff. Although this carving is more primitive than the crying cows, it is nonetheless, an impressive and fairly accurate rendering. In Chad, flat drawings of human figures nine feet tall were carved on rock, their bodies patterned with lines. In the Air Mountains of Niger, artists scratched at dark rock to reveal the light rock beneath, creating simple pictures that look like the stick figures drawn by children.

In this case, the writer has ranked the examples of rock art according to his or her opinion of their quality.

Another writer might not agree with the order used here. You can see, however, that the listing represents an order of degree in the writer's mind.

You can vary order of degree in a couple of interesting ways. In **organization by familiarity,** you begin with a detail that will probably be familiar to your readers. You then continue with information that may be less well known. In **organization by order of importance,** you begin with the most important fact or idea about a subject. Then you go on to information that is less and less important. Newspaper articles often use order of importance. A news article usually includes the most important fact about the story in the first sentence or paragraph. That "lead" answers some of the five *W*'s: *Who? What? Where? When? Why?* Organization by order of importance can be shown graphically as an inverted (upside-down) pyramid.

Who? What? Where?
When? Why? How?
Most important detail
↓
Next most important
↓
Less important
↓
Least important

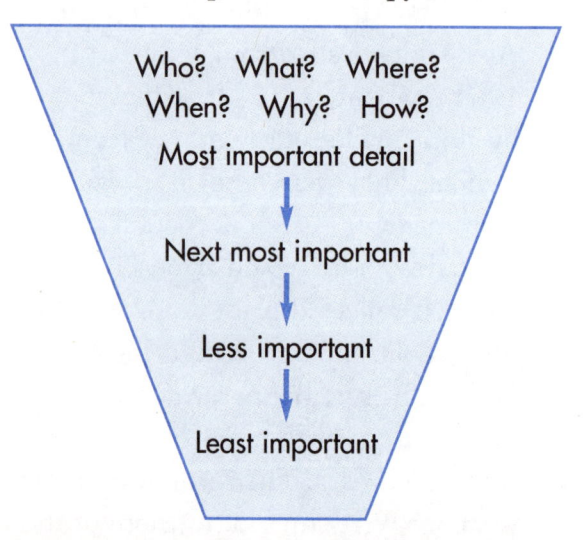

Inverted Pyramid Organization

6. Cause-and-Effect Order A **cause** is something that makes something else happen. An **effect** is what happens as a result of the cause. In a cause-and-effect essay, you might begin by stating a cause of an event. Then, you might discuss the effects. In contrast, you might start by stating an effect and then discuss its causes. Any one cause may have many effects, and any one effect may have more than one cause.

Read the following cause-and-effect paragraph about the role of the diamond trade in African countries:

> Diamonds mean wealth. The nation of Botswana has three large diamond mines. Together, they produce more than a billion dollars' worth of diamonds per year. As a result, Botswana has one of the highest standards of living in Africa. For those who can afford to buy them, diamonds mean rings and baubles. For the people who dig uncut diamonds in mines, they mean hard work for a tiny share of the profits. Unfortunately, in many impoverished African countries, the struggle to obtain valuable diamonds has led to civil war and horrific human rights violations. In Botswana, however, the government has managed to maintain fairly tight control over the diamond mines and has used the profits to create one of the most stable countries on the continent.

This paragraph discusses several different effects for one cause—diamonds. It spans a number of effects, from jewels for the rich, to work for the poor, to a stable government in Botswana.

7. Dialectic Organization When you use this method of organization, you present two sides of an issue and seek a middle ground. First, you state one view (the **thesis**), then an opposing view (the **antithesis**). Then you describe a compromise between the two views (the **synthesis**).

Notice the dialectic organization of the following paragraph about old and new civilizations:

> For sheer splendor, ancient civilizations are hard to beat. The ruins of ancient Egypt are more awesome than most of the intact buildings of our time. What have we built that can rival the hanging gardens of Babylon, the Great Wall of China, or the fabled temple of Solomon? Yet modern times have seen splendid ideas come forth. The idea of individual freedom is perhaps the greatest of these. How did average people live in ancient Babylon or Egypt? Were they free to earn a living in whatever way they chose? Could a despot have them killed at whim? Perhaps it is best to say that every

Meets ISAT Standards
1.B.3a
1.C.3a
1.C.3c
1.C.3e
2.A.3c
3.B.3a
3.C.3a

The Writing Process **259**

The Writing Process

civilization has something to contribute to the greatness of the human race. Some civilizations do so with stone and wood. Others do so with art and ideas. Others do so with might and money.

The passage begins with praise for ancient civilizations. Then it presents an opposing view claiming that modern times are better. The writer ends up taking a middle ground. This dialectic approach is particularly useful in persuasive writing. Presenting two sides of an issue and then arguing a middle-of-the-road position often proves to be very convincing, because the reader feels as if he or she has heard both sides of the story and is able to make an informed decision.

8. Deductive and Inductive Organization
When you use **deductive organization,** you start with a general statement. Then you give specific facts and details to support the generalization. When you use **inductive organization,** you do the opposite. You start with specific facts or examples and then present a general conclusion based on those details.

The following paragraph is organized deductively:

> East Africa was one of the major trading centers of the ancient world. Its coastal towns and islands linked Asia, Africa, and the Middle East. Ships from China and India came to port there to do business with Arab traders. By A.D. 1200–1500, the people along the coast of East Africa had created a Muslim culture that blended the ways of all three regions. There, the Swahili language developed. (*Swahili* comes from the Arabic word for "coast.") It became the shared tongue of people all over East Africa.

The following paragraph presents the same material inductively:

> The islands and coast of East Africa were the homeland of Swahili, the shared language of people of this region. (The word *Swahili* comes from the Arabic word for "coast.") Ships from China and India came to port there. Arab traders had been arriving there for centuries. By A.D. 1200–1500, a Muslim-Swahili culture emerged. Its language was used throughout the region for business among different peoples. Its culture combined the ways of Africa, Arabia, and Asia. East Africa, in short, was a major trading center of the ancient world.

Which method is preferable—deductive or inductive? It depends on the subject and what you are trying to say. Consider which method you think might be more interesting to your audience.

One way to organize your ideas before you write is to make a rough outline (see pages 76–77). Another option is to create a chart or other graphic organizer (see pages 84–92). Alternatively, you might choose to put all your ideas on note cards and to arrange the cards in a logical order.

Your Turn

Exercise A Read the two paragraphs below. Then fill in the circle next to the correct answer to the multiple-choice questions that follow each paragraph.

Meets ISAT
Standards
1.B.3a
1.C.3a
1.C.3c
1.C.3e
2.A.3c
3.B.3a
3.C.3a

> Shaka Zulu, the mighty leader of his people, had an unhappy childhood. His mother was an orphan named Nandi, whose father had been the chieftain of the Langeni clan. She married the son of a chieftain of the Zulu clan and bore him a son, Shaka Zulu. For one reason or another, however (versions of the story vary), Shaka and his mother were rejected by Shaka's father when Shaka was a still a young boy. They were forced to leave the Zulu clan and sought refuge among the Langeni, who took them in but weren't exactly welcoming. The other children laughed at Shaka and teased him for being small. Those were lonely years for Shaka and his mother. Shaka spent the time building himself into a strong, powerful warrior. It seems likely that the cruelty and rejection he suffered as a youth contributed to Shaka's ruthlessness as a leader.

1. This paragraph is organized using
    - Ⓐ spatial order.
    - Ⓑ dialectic order.
    - Ⓒ cause-and-effect order.
    - Ⓓ comparison-and-contrast order.

> The rock art of Africa is under siege by all kinds of destructive forces. In addition to the natural forces of wind and sand that eat away at these precious works of art, thieves chip away at them in order to sell the pieces in the marketplace. Soldiers use these works of art as practice targets. Vandals deface the rocks by carving their initials on them or making lewd additions to the ancient images. Tourists splash water and corrosive, carbonated beverages on the rock carvings to make them show up more clearly in photos. People seeking magic power also chip away at the rocks. Officials say that almost half of the engravings in the Sahara have been damaged. These facts lead to just one conclusion: Governments and citizens must work together to save the rock art of Africa.

2. The writer of this paragraph used
    - Ⓐ organization by classification and division.
    - Ⓑ order of degree.
    - Ⓒ inductive order.
    - Ⓓ deductive order.

The Writing Process

Your Turn

Exercise B *The paragraph below is supposed to be organized according to spatial order. It should describe the river from its beginning to its end, where it meets the ocean. One of the sentences in the paragraph is out of order, however. Place the sentence in the proper order by circling it and drawing an arrow to the place where it should appear in the paragraph.*

The Zambezi River runs west to east, spanning 1,700 miles through the eastern part of southern Africa. It begins in the mountains where Zambia borders Angola. After the falls, it is dammed to form Lake Kariba, one of the largest manmade lakes in the world. Curving south, it nourishes Zambia's Western Province. When it reaches the southern border of Zambia, it turns east again and forms the border between Zambia and Zimbabwe. Along this eastward path, it soon reaches Victoria Falls, where it falls 350 feet straight down. Then the river enters Mozambique, where it flows southeast until it reaches the Indian Ocean.

Exercise C *The steps below are supposed to be organized in the order in which they should be completed, but at least one of the steps is out of order. Place the steps in the correct order by circling any item that is out of order and drawing a line to where it should appear in the rough outline.*

How to Varnish Furniture

—Apply tape to protect any area of furniture that you don't want varnished

—Use coarse sandpaper to sand the area where varnish will be applied

—Wait for varnish to dry

—Apply varnish

—Sand the varnished area lightly with fine sandpaper

—Gather the necessary supplies

Exercise D Read the writing prompt below and one student's freewriting based on that prompt. The student has underlined the information in the freewriting that she wants to use in her essay, but she needs to organize it before she can begin writing. Take the underlined items from the freewriting and arrange them in a more logical order in the pro-and-con chart below the freewriting.

Meets ISAT
Standards
1.B.3d
1.C.3d
1.C.3e
2.A.3a
3.B.3a
3.C.3a

> WRITING PROMPT: The school board will be considering a proposal that would make 35 hours of community service per year for each year of high school a requirement for graduation.
>
> Decide whether or not you support this proposal. Then write a letter to the school board in which you state your opinion, give reasons supporting it, and try to persuade the school board to agree with your opinion.

One Student's Freewriting:

Students have <u>no time</u> to do community service. Can hardly get our homework done as it is—(<u>too much homework</u>!) Kids need to study. Plus, almost <u>everyone has after-school activities</u> and practice—games on weekends. On other hand, kids <u>might learn new skills</u> they wouldn't learn in school—<u>could lead to career for some kids</u>. But, <u>some kids already work</u>—have after school jobs—not fair to make them work for free. Some kids need to <u>learn to be less selfish</u>, though. They think they're entitled to everything—need to develop some <u>sense of responsibility</u>. <u>Community does need free help</u> and we <u>should all pitch in</u>. Benefits each one of us if community is in better shape. Maybe <u>service could be optional</u>. Could <u>encourage it</u> and <u>offer choices</u>—<u>reward students who do volunteer</u>—but not require it.

After you fill out this chart, write a short proposal for a compromise between these views on the lines provided below.

Reasons against Requiring Community Service	Reasons for Requiring Community Service

COMPROMISE: _____

_____

The Writing Process

Drafting

When you draft, you put your ideas down on paper. One approach to drafting (and this one works best for most people in ordinary writing situations) is to get your ideas down on paper quickly, without worrying too much about grammar, usage, mechanics, or spelling. Then, when you are done, you can go back to rewrite and refine your work. Another approach to drafting (which works best in a test-taking situation, when there is little time for rewriting) is to begin with a well-organized outline and to work carefully, thinking through each piece of information as you write. Some people who work in this way also like to revise and proofread as they go.

Drafting in a Test-Taking Situation

When writing for a test, follow these guidelines for drafting:

1. **Draft carefully.** Some writing tests allow time and space for rewriting. More commonly, however, you will be given a certain amount of time and a certain amount of space in a test booklet for your response. Usually, you will have no opportunity for a full-scale rewrite. Therefore, you will need to make sure that most of what you put down the first time is what you want to say, in the order in which you want to say it.

2. **Follow your rough outline or graphic organizer.** Instead of writing a quick, sloppy draft, organize your ideas first. Choose a thesis statement that is a one-sentence answer to the prompt. Next, make a rough outline or graphic organizer. Then, as you draft, follow the outline or organizer. Begin by grabbing your reader's attention and stating your overall idea in a thesis statement. Then develop this idea. Before you begin each paragraph, think clearly about what you want to put into it. Think about the main idea you want to express in your topic sentence. Then choose the supporting details you will include to support the main idea. Make sure that you present your ideas in a clear, logical order. As you write, use words or phrases to connect your ideas (see the list of transitions on pages 312–13).

3. **Write as neatly as you can.** On a written test, neatness counts! The scorers who will read your work need to be able to make out what you are saying, so be careful about your handwriting. Do not write too small or squeeze letters or words together. Be sure to indent paragraphs as you go. If you need to cross something out, draw a single line through the middle of it. Do not scratch it out messily.

   INCORRECT: Mrs. Reed ~~tried to~~ calmly le̶a̶d the panicked children to the closest fire exit.

   CORRECT: Mrs. Reed ~~tried to~~ calmly le̶a̶d the panicked children to the closest fire exit.

264 **AIM Higher! ISAT Language Arts Review**

Evaluation and Revision

Good writing is rewriting. Few people produce great or even very good writing the first time around. Even professional writers go back over their work once, twice, even three times or more until they get the results they want. Once you have written a draft, there are several additional steps you need to take to produce a finished piece of writing. The first two of these steps are evaluation and revision.

Evaluation is the process of looking over a piece of writing to determine what changes if any, need to be made in it. **Revision** is the process of making changes in the organization and content of your work.

Evaluating Your Work

Ideally, when you do a piece of writing for class, you can take advantage of your teacher's evaluation, perhaps a peer's evaluation, and a self-evaluation before creating the final draft. When you are writing in a test-taking situation, however, self-evaluation is your only option.

Here are some useful questions to ask when you evaluate any piece of writing:

Meets ISAT Standards
1.B.3d
3.A.3
3.B.3a
3.C.3a

Evaluation and Revision Checklist

Questions to Ask about Any Piece of Writing

✔ **Audience:**
- ❑ Is the piece appropriate for the intended audience?
- ❑ Will the language be clear to the audience?
- ❑ Is the writing appropriately formal or informal?
- ❑ Has the necessary background information been included?
- ❑ Has unnecessary background information been left out?

✔ **Purpose:**
- ❑ Does the piece fulfill the purpose for which it was written?
- ❑ On a test, does the piece answer the test prompt completely?

More ▶

The Writing Process 265

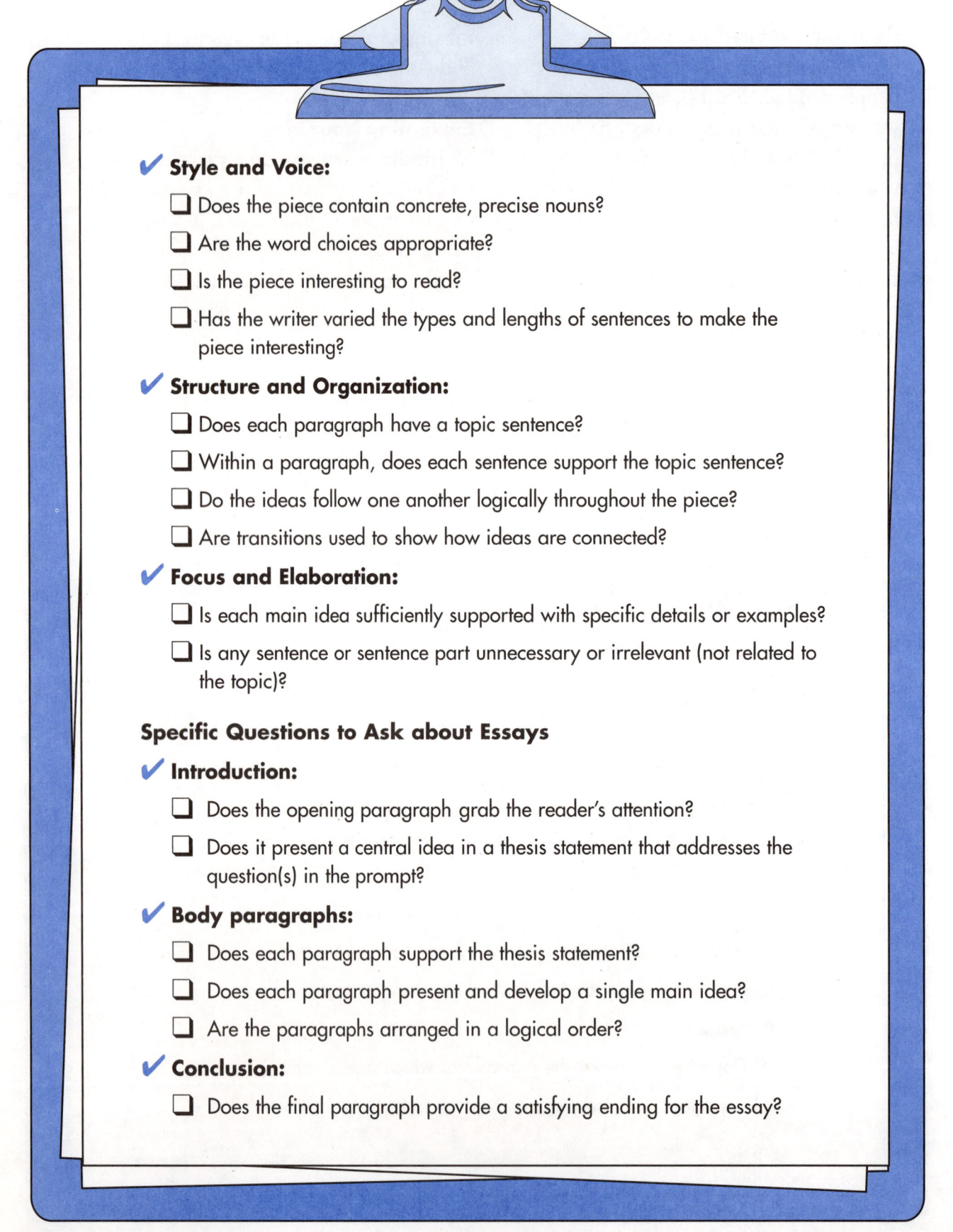

The Writing Process

✔ **Style and Voice:**
- ☐ Does the piece contain concrete, precise nouns?
- ☐ Are the word choices appropriate?
- ☐ Is the piece interesting to read?
- ☐ Has the writer varied the types and lengths of sentences to make the piece interesting?

✔ **Structure and Organization:**
- ☐ Does each paragraph have a topic sentence?
- ☐ Within a paragraph, does each sentence support the topic sentence?
- ☐ Do the ideas follow one another logically throughout the piece?
- ☐ Are transitions used to show how ideas are connected?

✔ **Focus and Elaboration:**
- ☐ Is each main idea sufficiently supported with specific details or examples?
- ☐ Is any sentence or sentence part unnecessary or irrelevant (not related to the topic)?

Specific Questions to Ask about Essays

✔ **Introduction:**
- ☐ Does the opening paragraph grab the reader's attention?
- ☐ Does it present a central idea in a thesis statement that addresses the question(s) in the prompt?

✔ **Body paragraphs:**
- ☐ Does each paragraph support the thesis statement?
- ☐ Does each paragraph present and develop a single main idea?
- ☐ Are the paragraphs arranged in a logical order?

✔ **Conclusion:**
- ☐ Does the final paragraph provide a satisfying ending for the essay?

Revising Your Work

After evaluating a piece of writing, you should revise it to correct any problems you have identified. When you revise, you can mark changes on your draft, as shown in the following chart:

> ### Types of Revision
>
> When revising, you can . . .
>
> - ADD material Mr. Mugrat lived in the ^*great, green* Okefenokee Swamp
>
> - DELETE (CUT) material He was known for his lassitude. ~~You should know that~~ *lassitude* is just a fancy word for a combination of weariness and laziness.
>
> - MOVE material Given the dangerousness of the Okefenokee, you might be wondering how he managed to survive. ~~The swamp is~~ (snake-and-alligator-infested).
>
> - CHANGE (REPLACE) material Well, his secret was just plain old garden variety ^*orneriness* ~~meanness~~.

Be sure to mark your revisions neatly. When you add material, use a caret (∧) below the line, and then write in the added material neatly above the caret. When you cut material, draw a single line through the text to be removed. When you move material, circle it and draw an arrow to the place to which the material should be moved. When you replace material, draw a single line through the text to be replaced, and then write the new material above the old text.

Meets ISAT Standards
1.B.3d
3.A.3
3.B.3a
3.B.3b
3.C.3a

The Writing Process **267**

The Writing Process

Read the following example of a rough draft and study the revisions that the writer made. Pay especially close attention to the analysis below, which explains why the revisions were made.

Sample Paragraph with Revisions

First Draft with Revisions

Writers use satire to mock vices or flaws. ~~The satire can attack~~ the behavior of individuals or ~~the flaws~~ in society as a whole. Mark Twain's novel <u>The Adventures of Tom Sawyer</u> includes a number of examples of light-hearted satire. One target of Twain's mocking humor ⁀for instance⁀ is superstitious beliefs. ~~Superstitions are held~~ ⁀not only on the part of⁀ by the boys ~~and by~~ but also on the part of many of the adult characters. ⁀In addition,⁀ In his portrayal of the ⁀harsh, narrow-minded⁀ schoolmaster, Twain ~~also~~ attack*s* some of the educational trends of his day.

Clean Revised Draft

Writers use satire to mock vices or flaws in the behavior of individuals or in society as a whole. Mark Twain's novel <u>The Adventures of Tom Sawyer</u> includes a number of examples of light-hearted satire. One target of Twain's mocking humor, for instance, is superstitious beliefs, not only part of the boys but also on the part of many of the adult characters. In addition, in his portrayal of the harsh, narrow-minded schoolmaster, Twain attacks some of the educational trends of the day.

Analysis of the Revision

This paragraph about satire in *The Adventures of Tom Sawyer* has a clear topic sentence, as well as suitable support; however, the original paragraph lacks transitions and contains a number of short, choppy sentences that are lacking in variety. In the revised draft, the writer has added these transitions to connect ideas logically: *for instance, not only . . . but also,* and *in addition.* In the final sentence, the addition of the phrase *harsh, narrow-minded* makes the portrayal of the schoolmaster more vivid. The writer has also used the techniques of combining and expanding sentences to make the paragraph more varied and interesting to read.

268 AIM Higher! ISAT LANGUAGE ARTS REVIEW

Proofreading Your Work

In school, you are not likely to receive a good grade on a paper that is full of grammatical mistakes and spelling errors. English teachers are picky about such things because they matter in real life. Imagine that you are an employer looking through a stack of resumés for potential employees. Would you be likely to hire the person whose resumé is full of mistakes in grammar, spelling, or punctuation? If a college admissions board can accept only 2,000 of the 20,000 students who apply, are they likely to accept a student whose application is full of errors?

Everyone makes mistakes, but if your writing is full of careless errors, there is a strong likelihood that those who read it will make negative judgments about you. Therefore, it is important to find and correct as many errors as possible. Generally, by the time you proofread, you have already evaluated and revised the content and organization of the piece of writing. **Proofreading** involves reading through the piece of writing again in order to check for errors in grammar, usage, mechanics, spelling, and manuscript form.

As you proofread, you should correct the errors you find using the proofreading marks shown in the chart on page 271.

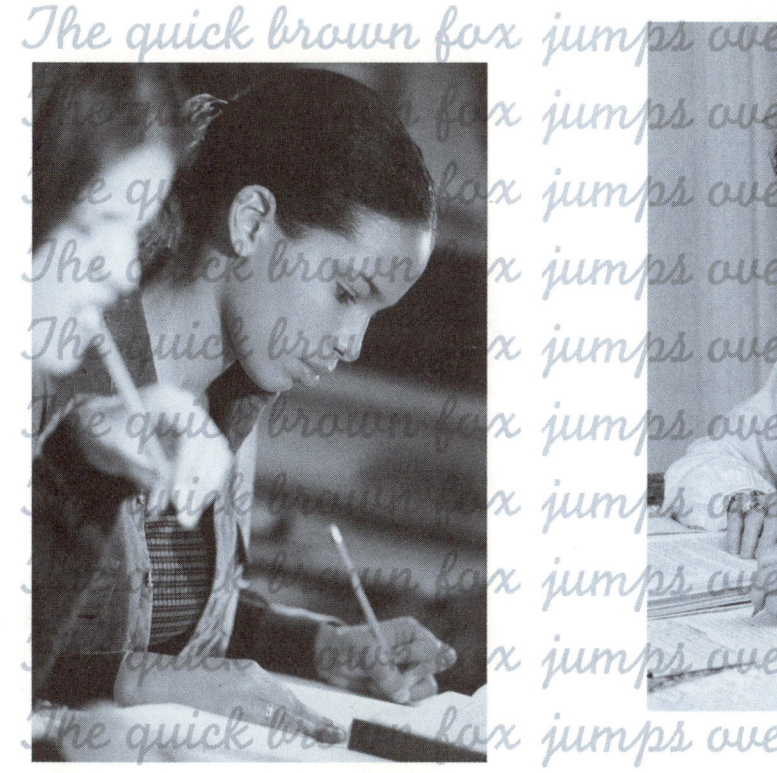

Meets ISAT Standards
1.B.3d
3.A.3
3.B.3a
3.B.3b

The Writing Process

The Writing Process

Below is a checklist for the proofreading process. Read the list carefully.

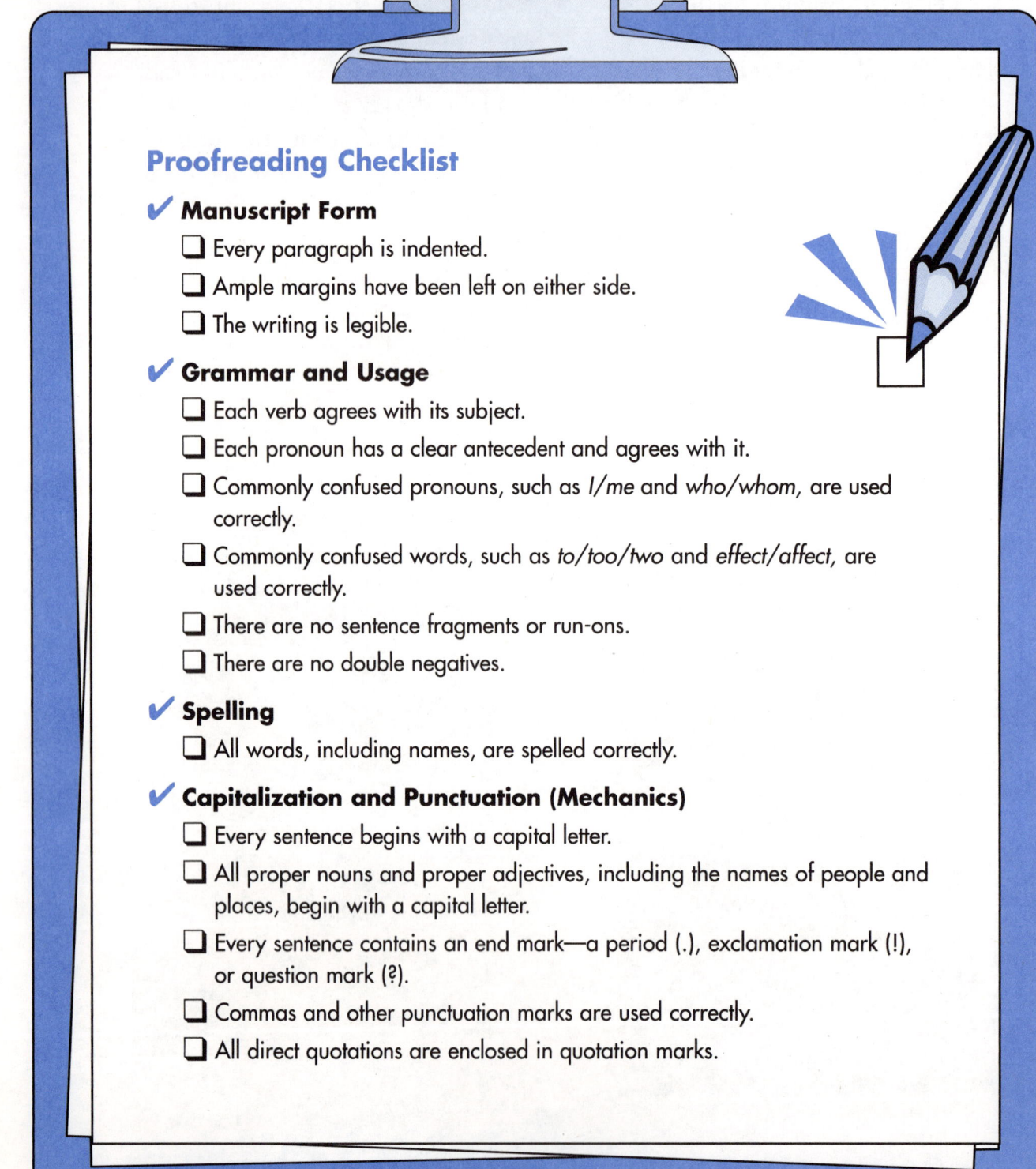

Proofreading Checklist

✓ **Manuscript Form**
- ❑ Every paragraph is indented.
- ❑ Ample margins have been left on either side.
- ❑ The writing is legible.

✓ **Grammar and Usage**
- ❑ Each verb agrees with its subject.
- ❑ Each pronoun has a clear antecedent and agrees with it.
- ❑ Commonly confused pronouns, such as *I/me* and *who/whom*, are used correctly.
- ❑ Commonly confused words, such as *to/too/two* and *effect/affect*, are used correctly.
- ❑ There are no sentence fragments or run-ons.
- ❑ There are no double negatives.

✓ **Spelling**
- ❑ All words, including names, are spelled correctly.

✓ **Capitalization and Punctuation (Mechanics)**
- ❑ Every sentence begins with a capital letter.
- ❑ All proper nouns and proper adjectives, including the names of people and places, begin with a capital letter.
- ❑ Every sentence contains an end mark—a period (.), exclamation mark (!), or question mark (?).
- ❑ Commas and other punctuation marks are used correctly.
- ❑ All direct quotations are enclosed in quotation marks.

You should use the standard proofreading symbols to mark corrections in your writing. Because they are standard, these marks make clear to any reader the changes that you want to make in the text. On a test, your answers will be graded according to the corrected version, as long as the corrections can be clearly understood by the person evaluating your writing.

Study the chart below to learn the standard proofreading symbols used for making corrections. The meanings of most of the symbols are obvious. Once you become familiar with them, you will find them very easy and convenient to use. As you proofread, keep in mind that attention to these details will make your writing more effective. You will convey your ideas more clearly, and as a result, your writing will be more powerful.

Meets ISAT Standards
1.B.3d
3.A.3
3.B.3a
3.B.3b

Revision and Proofreading Symbols

Symbol and Example	Meaning of the Symbol
∧ bicycle built *for* two	Insert (add) something that is missing.
ℓ Paris in the ~~the~~ spring	Delete (cut) these letters or words.
/ e/xtreme skiing	Replace this letter.
— Say it ~~ain't~~ *isn't* so.	Replace this word.
∽ the glass delicate slippers	Transpose (switch) the order.
⤴ give to the needy gifts	Move this word (or group of words)
⌒ chair person	Close up this space.
⌿ truely	Delete (omit) this letter and close up the space.
≡ five portuguese sailors	Capitalize this letter.
lc / a lantern and a Sleeping bag	Lowercase this letter.
¶ waves. "Help me," she cried.	Begin a new paragraph here.
⊙ All's well that ends well⊙	Put a period here.
∧, parrots macaws, and toucans	Put a comma here.
ˇ childrens toys	Put an apostrophe here.
: There are three good reasons:	Put a colon here.
# the grand#opening	Put a space here.

The Writing Process 271

The Writing Process

Read the example below of a sample student response that has been corrected using proofreading marks:

Some of the most unusual birds in the world are ratites. Ratites are flightless birds. ~~These are birds that~~ Unlike other birds, they cannot fly. The breastbone of these birds is smooth, ~~It is~~ like a raft. In fact, the word "ratite" comes from a Latin word meaning "raft." At present, there are five major types of ratite. ~~Ratites~~ including ostriches, ~~Ostriches~~ which are found in Africa and ~~are~~ the largest living ~~bird~~ species. Emus are also ratites. ~~Emus live in Australia.~~ which are native to Australia. They are the second-largest species of bird. ~~More~~ of bird is the ostrich. Some other ratites are cassowaries in Australia, rheas in South America, and kiwis in New Zealand. ~~I am also interested in cardinals.~~

Evaluating, Revising, and Proofreading in a Test-Taking Situation

When writing for a test, follow these guidelines for drafting:

Meets ISAT
Standards
1.B.3d
3.A.3
3.B.3a
3.B.3b

1. **Do your evaluation, revision, and proofreading in separate passes.** Remember that on a writing test, you will rarely have the opportunity to rewrite your piece completely. Therefore, after doing a careful draft, you will have to make any revision and proofreading corrections on your draft copy. Save time to read through your response carefully. As you read it the first time, look for changes that you can make to improve its content, style, and organization. Ask yourself questions like those in the Evaluation and Revision Checklist on pages 265–66. Then, mark your revisions. Finally, read the piece through again to look for errors in grammar, usage, mechanics, spelling, and manuscript form, and mark those corrections as well.

2. **Mark all revision and proofreading corrections neatly. Use standard proofreading symbols.** Use the standard revision and proofreading symbols shown in the chart on page 271 to make your corrections. Do not scratch out material that you wish to cut or replace. Draw a neat line through it. Write replacement material neatly above the line where it is supposed to go. If you need to move material to improve the organization, circle the material to be moved, and draw a neat arrow to show where the material should be moved.

3. **Do a quick check for paragraph indents.** If you have forgotten to indent a paragraph, mark the place where a paragraph indent should appear using a caret (∧) and a paragraph symbol (¶).

4. **Do a quick check for initial capital letters and end punctuation.** Make sure that every sentence begins with a capital letter and ends with a period, exclamation mark, or question mark.

The Writing Process

Your Turn

Exercise A Rewrite the following paragraph on your own paper. Incorporate all the corrections that are indicated by the revision and proofreading symbols.

The name kiwi comes from the maori language and refers to the loud call of the ~~mail~~ ^male bird^. There are three species of kiwi in new Zealand: the common kiwi, the little spotted kiwi, and the great spotted kiwi. Kiwis are about the size of a chiken and are ~~colored~~ grayish brown ^in color^. These birds have only traces of ~~the~~ wings which are hidden beneath ~~they're~~ ^their^ plumage. (lc) Oddly, the Nostrils of a kiwi are at the tip of it's bill rather then the base.

Exercise B Use the revision and proofreading symbols on page 271 to correct all the errors in the following sentences.

1. Kiwis live in the forests of new Zealand where they thrive on a diet of worms in sects and berries.

2. by day they sleep in burrows, at night, search for food.

3. Kiwis have large, well-developed claws on all four toes of each foot which the birdsuse to defend theirselves.

4. The eggs of kiwis are the largest of any bird species relative to the size of the bird, a kiwi egg can way up to one pound (450 grams.)

5. The female lays one or to large eggs in the burrow. Than the male tends the eggs for a period of up to about 80 days.

6. when the chicks hatch from the eggs, they are full featherd. And their eyes are open. However they do not eat for a week after hatching.

Return to the exercises at the beginning of the chapter, revise your work as necessary, and submit the exercises to your teacher for grading.

Chapter 12
Sentence Sense
Constructing and Editing Sentences

First Encounter

The essay about baseball below contains a number of problems in sentence construction. Read the essay and note the problems as you read. Then try your hand at the exercises that follow the essay. You will not be graded on the exercises at this time. At the end of the chapter, you will be directed to return to these exercises to revise and correct your work.

The Beginnings of Baseball

by Alan Sewall

¹What is the origin of the game that is our "national pastime," and where did it come from? ²Some people say that baseball was invented by Abner Doubleday in 1839 in Cooperstown, New York. ³Today, however, most historians do not believe that Doubleday invented the game. ⁴Instead, think that baseball developed from an old English game called "rounders." ⁵In rounders, fielders put out base runners by throwing the baseball at them, if the baseball hit the runner, the runner was out. ⁶This method of putting out runners was called "soaking."

⁷The first true baseball club was founded in 1845 in New York City by Alexander Cartwright. ⁸The club was called the Knickerbocker Base Ball Club of New York. ⁹Cartwright wrote the original set of official baseball rules. ¹⁰The baseball diamond used today was set up by Cartwright's rules. ¹¹Also, under Cartwright's rules, fielders put base runners out by tagging them with the baseball instead of to soak them.

¹²The Knickerbockers played their first game against the New York Nine on June 19, 1846. ¹³The game took place just across the Hudson River from New York, so many people sailed over. ¹⁴The Knickerbockers lost the game 23 to 1.

¹⁵Soon other baseball clubs were formed in other cities. ¹⁶Soldiers from all over the country learned about the game during the Civil War a few years later. ¹⁷In 1869, the Cincinnati Red Stockings became the first professional baseball team. ¹⁸Other professional teams were soon formed, and in 1876, eight of these teams formed the first major league, the National League.

¹⁹During the late 1800s, baseball officials introduced several new rules. Making the game into the one we play today. ²⁰In 1857, the length of the game was set at nine innings. ²¹Later, the distance from home plate to the pitcher's mound was increased and lengthened, and pitchers, who originally threw underhanded, were allowed to throw overhanded. ²²Under a rule adopted in 1864, fair balls caught on the first bounce were no longer counted as outs.

²³In 1901, a second major league, the American League, was formed, like the National League, it had eight teams. ²⁴For the next fifty years, there were sixteen major-league teams in cities stretching from Boston to St. Louis, and the rules of the game were almost exactly like those used today. ²⁵Baseball's so-called "modern era" had begun.

Top: Champions of America (the Atlantics of Brooklyn baseball club), Brooklyn, c. 1865. LC-USZ62-94553. Bottom: Union prisoners playing baseball at Salisbury, N.C., c. 1863. LC-USZ62-38. Library of Congress, Prints and Photographs Division.

Constructing and Editing Sentences

Your Turn

Exercise Fill in the circle next to the correct answer to each multiple-choice question.

1. Which change, if any, should be made in sentence 1?
   - Ⓐ Eliminate repetition by removing *and where did it come from.*
   - Ⓑ Change *origin* to *beginnings.*
   - Ⓒ Capitalize the *n* in *national.*
   - Ⓓ Make no change.

2. You can correct an error in sentence 4 by
   - Ⓐ removing the word *Instead.*
   - Ⓑ changing the *E* in *English* to a small letter.
   - Ⓒ adding the word *they* before *think.*
   - Ⓓ changing *think* to *thought.*

3. How would you improve sentence 5?
   - Ⓐ Capitalize the *f* in *fielders.*
   - Ⓑ Place a period after *them,* and start a new sentence with *If.*
   - Ⓒ Change *them* to *they.*
   - Ⓓ Add the phrase *to put them out* after *them.*

4. The best way to improve sentence 10 is to
   - Ⓐ capitalize the *r* in *rules.*
   - Ⓑ add the words *and tomorrow* after *today.*
   - Ⓒ change *was set up by Cartwright's rules* to *Cartwright's rules set up,* and move that new phrase to the beginning of the sentence.
   - Ⓓ add a comma after the word *today.*

5. How would you improve sentence 11?
   - Ⓐ Put an exclamation point at the end of the sentence.
   - Ⓑ Add a comma after *out.*
   - Ⓒ Change the words *to soak* to *soaking.*
   - Ⓓ Make no change.

6. What is the best way to improve sentence 13?
   - Ⓐ Add the words *to watch* at the end of the sentence.
   - Ⓑ Add a comma after *River*.
   - Ⓒ Add the words *and was played* after *place*.
   - Ⓓ Make no change.

7. What is the best way to revise sentence 16 to emphasize when the event happened?
   - Ⓐ Revise the sentence to read, "A few years later, soldiers from all over the country learned about the game during the Civil War."
   - Ⓑ Revise the sentence to read, "Soldiers from all over the country learned about the game a few years later during the Civil War."
   - Ⓒ Revise the sentence to read, "During the Civil War a few years later, soldiers from all over the country learned about the game."
   - Ⓓ Make no change.

8. What change should be made in sentence 19?
   - Ⓐ Add *toward the latter part of the century* after *During the late 1800s*.
   - Ⓑ Add a period after *1800s*.
   - Ⓒ Change the period after *rules* to a comma, and make the *M* in *Making* lowercase.
   - Ⓓ Change *baseball officials introduced several new rules* to *several new rules were introduced by baseball officials*.

9. What change should be made in sentence 21?
   - Ⓐ Change *threw* to *throws*.
   - Ⓑ Remove the words *and lengthened*.
   - Ⓒ Add a comma after *mound*.
   - Ⓓ Make no change.

10. What change should be made in sentence 23?
    - Ⓐ Add a period after *formed*, and start a new sentence with *Like*.
    - Ⓑ Change *was formed* to *is formed*.
    - Ⓒ Add the words *the same number as in the National League* at the end of the sentence.
    - Ⓓ Make no change.

Meets ISAT Standards
1.B.3c
1.B.3d
2.A.3d
2.B.3a
3.A.3
3.B.3b

Constructing and Editing Sentences

Sentence Sense

If you wanted to build a bookcase, you would not use balsa wood, the light but flimsy material used for model airplanes. You would choose an attractive and strong material like pine or maple or oak. What is true of building bookcases is also true of building paragraphs and essays: Good materials make good products. Good paragraphs and essays are made of strong, clear, varied, and interesting sentences. In this chapter, you will learn how to create effective sentences—the building blocks of well-crafted writing.

Sentence Types

Sentences can be classified in different ways. One way to classify sentences is by their **function,** or what they do. Another way to classify them is by their **structure,** or how they are put together.

Sentence Function

Sentences can be classified as declarative, imperative, interrogative, or exclamatory. Notice how these types of sentence differ in their function, or what they do.

A **declarative sentence** makes a statement. It is followed by a period.

> EXAMPLES: Rugby shares characteristics with football and soccer. Rugby players love their rough-and-tumble game.

An **imperative sentence** gives a command or makes a request. Such a sentence usually ends with a period; however, a strong or urgent command may end with an exclamation point.

> EXAMPLES: Kick the ball down the field. Catch that pass!

An **interrogative sentence** asks a question. It ends with a question mark.

> EXAMPLES: Who invented rugby? Where was the game first played?

An **exclamatory sentence** expresses strong feeling. It is followed by an exclamation point.

> EXAMPLES: How they enjoy playing rugby! What a close match that was!

280 AIM Higher! ISAT Language Arts Review

Read the following paragraph:

Rugby is a fast-moving game. It is not that different from football. Players can can carry, kick, and throw the ball. Players score points by getting the ball over the other team's goal line. They can also score points by kicking the ball over the crossbar and through the goal posts. The sport is named for the Rugby School in England, where it was first played in 1823.

This paragraph contains only declarative sentences. Now read a revised version of this paragraph. Notice how including sentences of different types makes the same material more interesting.

Rugby is a fast-moving game. Imagine football with a British accent. In rugby, players can carry, kick, and throw the ball. How does a player score points? Every rugby player knows the answer to that: Get the ball over the other team's goal line, or kick it over the crossbar and through the goal posts. How did the sport get its name? It was named for the Rugby School in England, where it was first played in 1823.

Meets ISAT Standards
1.B.3c
1.B.3d
2.A.3d
2.B.3a
3.A.3
3.B.3b

Sentence Structure

A **simple sentence** contains at least one subject and verb and expresses a complete thought. The following chart shows some patterns for forming simple sentences:

Types of Simple Sentence

Subject + verb: **S V** The player runs.

Subject + linking verb + predicate noun: **S LV PN** The captain is Josh.

Subject + linking verb + predicate adjective: **S LV PA** The match is close.

Subject + verb + direct object: **S V DO** The player threw a pass.

Subject + verb + direct object + indirect object: **S V DO IO** Justin handed the glove to me.

Subject + verb + indirect object + direct object: **S V IO DO** Justin handed me the glove.

Subject + verb + direct object + objective complement:
S V DO OC Joanna called the match exciting.

Constructing and Editing Sentences 281

Constructing and Editing Sentences

Each type of simple sentence can be combined or expanded by adding new parts:

COMBINING: Justin handed me the glove, **and** I put it on my left hand.
ADDING PARTS: The **new** player threw an **outstanding** pass.

A **clause** is a group of words that has a subject and a verb. An **independent clause** expresses a complete thought and can stand alone as a sentence. A **dependent clause**, or **subordinate clause**, does not express a complete thought and cannot stand alone as a sentence.

INDEPENDENT CLAUSE: Rugby is a demanding sport.
DEPENDENT CLAUSE: because you need strength and stamina

A **compound sentence** contains at least two independent clauses but no dependent clauses. The clauses in a compound sentence are usually joined by a comma and a **coordinating conjunction,** such as *and, or, nor, for, but, so,* or *yet.*

INDEPENDENT CLAUSE + COORDINATING CONJUNCTION + INDEPENDENT CLAUSE

             — IC —   CC
William Webb Ellis picked up a soccer ball in 1823, **and**
   — IC —
the sport of rugby was born.

             — IC —   CC
The version called Rugby League has thirteen players on a side, **but**
             — IC —
the more traditional version, Rugby Union, has fifteen.

A **complex sentence** contains one independent clause and one or more dependent clauses.

DEPENDENT CLAUSE + INDEPENDENT CLAUSE:

             — DC —
When rugby teams huddle together in a "scrum,"
             — IC —
the players look like a huge spider with many legs.

INDEPENDENT CLAUSE + DEPENDENT CLAUSE:

             — IC —
Many rugby players wear special soccer shoes with high sides
   — DC —
that support the ankles.

INDEPENDENT CLAUSE WITH EMBEDDED DEPENDENT CLAUSE:

⎡——IC——⎤ ⎡————————DC————————⎤
A rugby ball, which is made of leather panels stitched together,
⎡——————IC——————⎤
looks quite similar to a football.

A **compound-complex sentence** has two or more independent clauses and at least one dependent clause.

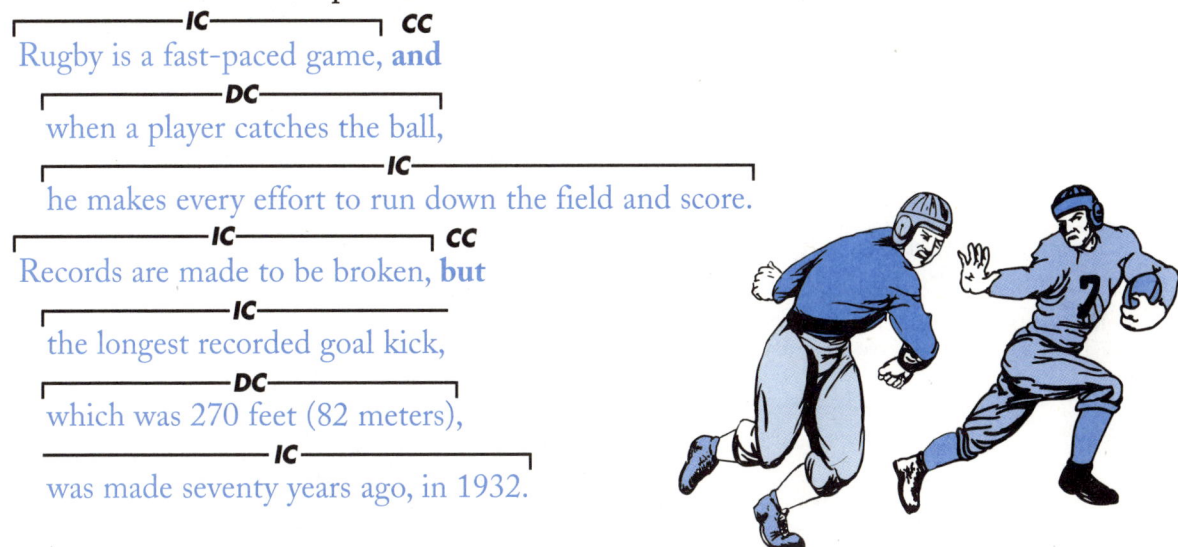

⎡————IC————⎤ CC
Rugby is a fast-paced game, **and**
⎡————DC————⎤
when a player catches the ball,
⎡————————IC————————⎤
he makes every effort to run down the field and score.

⎡————IC————⎤ CC
Records are made to be broken, **but**
⎡————IC————⎤
the longest recorded goal kick,
⎡————DC————⎤
which was 270 feet (82 meters),
⎡——————IC——————⎤
was made seventy years ago, in 1932.

Read the following paragraph:

The name *hockey* probably comes from a French word. That word is *hoquet*. It means "hooked stick." There are many versions of hockey. The various types include ice hockey, field hockey, and hurling. Hurling is played in Britain. My favorite is field hockey. Each team in field hockey has eleven men or women. No physical contact is permitted. Lacrosse resembles field hockey. Lacrosse players use sticks with nets to carry, throw, and catch the ball.

The paragraph contains only simple sentences. Notice how the paragraph becomes less monotonous and more interesting to read when it is rewritten to include sentences with a variety of structures.

The name *hockey* probably comes from the French word *hoquet*, which means "hooked stick." The many versions of hockey include ice hockey, field hockey, and hurling, which is played in Britain. My favorite is field hockey. Each team in field hockey has eleven men or women, and no physical contact is allowed. Lacrosse resembles field hockey, but players use sticks with nets to carry, throw, and catch the ball.

Meets ISAT Standards
1.B.3c
1.B.3d
2.A.3d
2.B.3a
3.A.3
3.B.3b

Constructing and Editing Sentences

Your Turn

Exercise A *In the space provided, write the letter of the item in Column B that correctly matches each type of sentence listed in Column A.*

Column A	Column B
_____ 1. declarative sentence	a. gives a command or request
_____ 2. interrogative sentence	b. expresses strong feeling
_____ 3. imperative sentence	c. makes a statement
_____ 4. exclamatory sentence	d. asks a question

Exercise B *In the space provided, write two original sentences in each of the forms described. Label the parts for your first three pairs of sentences as shown in the example.*

EXAMPLE: S   LV   PA
Rattlesnakes are venomous.

1. Simple sentence: Subject + linking verb + predicate adjective

    A. _____

    B. _____

2. Simple sentence: Subject + verb + direct object

    A. _____

    B. _____

3. Simple sentence: Subject + verb + indirect object + direct object

    A. _____

    B. _____

4. Compound sentence: Independent clause + conjunction + independent clause

    A. _____

    B. _____

AIM Higher! ISAT Language Arts Review

5. Complex sentence: Independent clause + dependent clause (in either order)

A. _____

_____

B. _____

_____

6. Compound-complex sentence: At least 2 independent clauses + 1 dependent clause

A. _____

_____

B. _____

_____

Meets ISAT
Standards
1.B.3c
1.B.3d
2.A.3d
2.B.3a
3.A.3
3.B.3b

Constructing and Editing Sentences

Constructing and Editing Sentences

Expanding and Combining Sentences

Sophisticated writers use a wide variety of sentence structures. You can make your sentences more varied and, therefore, more interesting by using two simple techniques: expanding and combining. When you **expand** a sentence, you add details. When you **combine** sentences, you join two or more sentences together to create a single sentence.

Expanding Sentences

You can add words, phrases, and clauses to a sentence to make it clearer and more descriptive.

Techniques for Expanding Sentences

- Add **modifiers,** or words that make the meanings of other words more definite.

    ORIGINAL: Players use sticks to strike a disk called the puck.

    EXPANDED: Ice hockey players use long sticks to strike a rubber disk called the puck.

- Add **prepositional phrases,** or groups of words beginning with a preposition and ending with a noun or pronoun.

    ORIGINAL: Play begins.

    EXPANDED: Play begins with a face-off in the middle of the ice.

- Add **appositive phrases,** or groups of words made up of an appositive and its modifiers. An **appositive** is a noun or pronoun placed next to another noun or pronoun to identify or explain it.

    ORIGINAL: Our team won the state championship.

    EXPANDED: Our team, the Centerville Ravens, won the state championship.

- Add **predicates,** or verb phrases.

    ORIGINAL: Hockey sticks are sturdy.

    EXPANDED: Hockey sticks are sturdy and measure 53 inches from the handle to the heel.

- Add **dependent clauses,** or groups or words containing a subject and a verb that add further information to the sentence.

    ORIGINAL: Hockey pucks are often kept frozen before a match.

    EXPANDED: So that they will keep their original form, hockey pucks are often kept frozen before a match.

Read the following paragraph:

> Tennis is a sport played on a court divided by a low net. The goal is to hit the ball over the net so that the opponent cannot return it. Tennis probably began during the Middle Ages. It became very popular in Europe; however, it was some time before the game of lawn tennis developed. The older versions of tennis used a ball made of sheepskin. This ball would not bounce on grass. For lawn tennis, a new type of ball had to be invented.

Notice how the paragraph becomes more concrete, precise, and interesting when it is rewritten with expansion:

> Popular with both men and women, tennis is a sport played on a court divided by a low net. The goal is to hit the ball over the net so that it bounces into the opponent's court and cannot be returned. The sport, which was first known as "real" (or royal) tennis, probably began in France during the Middle Ages, and it quickly became very popular in Europe among the nobility; however, it was not until the nineteenth century that lawn tennis, the modern game, was developed. The older versions of the game used a ball made of sheepskin, which would not bounce on grass. For lawn tennis, a new ball made of vulcanized rubber and covered with flannel had to be invented.

Combining Sentences

In the film *Groundhog Day,* Bill Murray wakes up every morning and must relive the same day, again and again and again. Without some variety, a day can become very boring. The same is true of your writing.

An effective way to achieve variety is to combine short sentences to make longer ones. Including a mix of short and long sentences to your writing will make the writing more interesting to read.

Meets ISAT Standards
1.B.3c
1.B.3d
2.A.3d
2.B.3a
3.A.3
3.B.3b

Constructing and Editing Sentences 287

Constructing and Editing Sentences

Here are some ways to combine sentences:

Techniques for Combining Sentences

✔ **Move individual words.**

SEPARATE: The game of cricket is played in England. The game is popular.

COMBINED: The popular game of cricket is played in England.

✔ **Turn sentences or sentence parts into a phrase; then move the phrase.**

- **Use a participial phrase.**

SEPARATE: The bowler in cricket throws the ball. He uses an overarm motion like that of a baseball pitcher.

COMBINED: Using an overarm motion like that of a baseball pitcher, the bowler in cricket throws the ball.

- **Use an appositive phrase.**

SEPARATE: Lord's Cricket Ground is located in London. It is the "home of cricket."

COMBINED: The "home of cricket," Lord's Cricket Ground, is located in London.

- **Use a prepositional phrase.**

SEPARATE: This cricket ground was established by Thomas Lord. He established it in 1787.

COMBINED: This cricket ground was established by Thomas Lord in 1787.

✔ **Adapt and/or move clauses.**

- **Use two main (independent) clauses to form a compound sentence.**

SEPARATE: Cricket players use special bats. Two teams take turns to bat and field.

COMBINED: Cricket players use special bats, and two teams take turns to bat and field.

- **Use two or more clauses to form a complex sentence.**

SEPARATE: Two batsmen must defend the "wicket" with their bats. They score by running up and down the "pitch," a narrow strip of grass.

COMBINED: Two batsmen, who must defend the "wicket" with their bats, score by running up and down the "pitch," a narrow strip of grass.

Read the following paragraph.

    The wickets in cricket are made of wood. They are at each end of the cricket pitch. The wood is usually ash. The wickets are twenty-eight inches high. Each wicket has three stumps. On top of these posts are placed two "bails." The bails are small and rounded. They connect the stumps horizontally. The bowler tries to knock one or both of the bails off the stumps with the ball. If he succeeds, the batsman is "bowled out."

Notice how combining sentences adds to the variety and interest of the paragraph.

    The wooden wickets at each end of the cricket pitch are usually made of ash and are twenty-eight inches high. Each wicket consists of three stumps that are connected horizontally at the top by two small, rounded "bails." If the bowler succeeds in knocking one or both of the bails off the stumps with the ball, the batsman is "bowled out."

Meets ISAT Standards
1.B.3c
1.B.3d
2.A.3d
2.B.3a
3.A.3
3.B.3b

Constructing and Editing Sentences

Your Turn

Exercise A Follow the directions in italics to combine the sentences below.

1. *Combine this pair of simple sentences into a compound sentence.*

    Lacrosse sticks used to be made of hickory wood.

    Many are now made of aluminum and plastic.

    _____

    _____

    _____

2. *Combine this pair of simple sentences into a complex sentence.*
   [Hint: Use the word *which*.]

    The ball does not become stuck in the net.

    The net is tightly strung to prevent that from happening.

    _____

    _____

    _____

3. *Combine these simple sentences into a compound-complex sentence.*
   [Hint: Use *which* or change *measure* to *measuring*.]

    Field hockey is played both indoors and outdoors.

    The goals are quite small.

    The goals measure just twelve feet wide and seven feet high.

    _____

    _____

    _____

Exercise B Read the following paragraph. Then, on your own paper, rewrite the paragraph. Follow the instructions for expanding some of the numbered sentences.

¹Football is played by two teams of eleven players each. ²The object is to score points by crossing the opposing team's goal line. ³Players run with the ball for a touchdown. ⁴Football involves a great deal of physical contact.

Meets ISAT Standards
1.B.3c
1.B.3d
2.A.3d
2.B.3a
3.A.3
3.B.3a
3.B.3b

1. Use the appositive phrase *a popular sport in America* (with commas before and after it) to expand sentence 1.

2. Use the phrases *at the other end of the field* to expand sentence 2.

3. Use the verb phrase *and pass it to other players* to expand sentence 3.

Exercise C Read the following paragraph. Then, on your own paper, rewrite the paragraph. Follow the instructions for combining the numbered sentences.

¹The first versions of American football were played in the mid-1800s. They were played at American colleges. ²At that time, football was a very rough sport. It had no official rules except to get the ball past the opposing team. ³Princeton was the first college to establish rules of the game in 1867. Princeton was where football originated. ⁴Rutgers College also established rules that same year. Rutgers is located close to Princeton. In 1869, Rutgers and Princeton played the first intercollegiate football game. ⁵By the end of the century, the game had become so dangerous that many colleges were banning it. President Theodore Roosevelt called on Harvard, Princeton, and Yale to save the game by instituting stricter rules.

1. Combine the pair of sentences labeled (1) in the paragraph by moving a prepositional phrase from one sentence to the other.

2. Using the word *which*, form a complex sentence to combine the pair of sentences labeled (2).

3. Use an appositive phrase to combine the pair of sentences labeled (3).

4. Use the words *which* and *and* to form a compound-complex sentence from the three sentences labeled (4).

5. Using the word *so*, form a compound sentence to combine the pair of sentences labeled (5).

Constructing and Editing Sentences

Constructing and Editing Sentences

Editing and Proofreading Sentences

Whenever you write, you should take the time to revise and proofread. When you **revise,** you make changes in organization and content. When you **proofread,** you correct errors in grammar, usage, mechanics, and spelling. After you finish a piece of written work, especially if it is writing done for a test, look over your sentences to see if you can improve their style. Also check to see if your sentences contain any errors that need to be corrected. The following chart describes some changes that you can make in individual sentences to improve their style and to correct common errors.

> **Creating Sentences with Style**
>
> ✓ **Vary sentence openings.**
>
> - BEGIN WITH A MODIFIER: *Officially,* baseball is our national sport.
> - BEGIN WITH A PHRASE: *With a leap,* the center fielder caught the ball.
> - BEGIN WITH A SUBORDINATE CLAUSE: *Unless we score in the ninth inning,* they will win the game.
>
> ✓ **Vary sentence length.**
>
> - You can add interest to your writing by using a combination of short and long sentences.
>
>   VARIED SENTENCES: Baseball players must wear plastic helmets. Given that the speed of a baseball pitch may exceed one hundred miles per hour, this is a sensible regulation.
>
> ✓ **Vary sentence structure.**
>
> - You can add interest to your writing by using a variety of sentence structures—simple, compound, and complex.
>
>   ORIGINAL: My older brother is not a sports fan. He will occasionally watch a game. (**simple sentences**)
>
>   REVISED: Although my older brother is not a sports fan, he will occasionally watch a game. (**complex sentence**)
>
>   or
>
>   My older brother is not a sports fan, but he will occasionally watch a game. (**compound sentence**)
>
>   More ▶

✓ **Change passive-voice sentences to the active voice.**

- You can make your writing more lively by changing the **passive-voice** sentences (declarative sentences in which the doer of the action follows the verb or does not appear) into **active-voice** sentences (declarative sentences in which the doer of the action comes before the verb).

    ORIGINAL IN PASSIVE VOICE: If the ball is hit out of the park (**passive**), the batter scores a home run.

    REVISED: If a batter hits the ball out of the park (**active**), he scores a home run.

✓ **Correct faulty parallelism.**

- You can make your writing less awkward by making similar ideas **parallel,** or similar, in structure.

    ORIGINAL: If you are used to playing baseball, you will notice some differences when you play softball: The ball is larger, and there is a small field.

    REVISED: If you are used to playing baseball, you will notice some differences when playing softball: The ball is larger, and the field is smaller.

✓ **Use effective repetition.**

- Repetition should usually be avoided. Sometimes, however, it can be used effectively to emphasize an idea.

    The announcer said, "Hank Aaron has just set a new world record!" Wow! A new world record—you don't see that every day.

✓ **Use inverted word order for emphasis.**

- You can emphasize an idea by moving it to the beginning (or end) of a sentence.

    ORIGINAL: If only Pedro can strike out this last batter, the series will belong to the Red Sox.

    INVERTED TO EMPHASIZE "THE RED SOX": The Red Sox will clinch the series, if only Pedro can strike out this last batter.

Meets ISAT Standards
1.B.3c
1.B.3d
2.A.3d
2.B.3a
3.A.3
3.B.3a
3.B.3b

Constructing and Editing Sentences 293

Constructing and Editing Sentences

Editing Sentences to Correct Common Errors

✔ **Correct wordiness.**

- In writing, less is usually more.

    ORIGINAL: I firmly believe that the history of the game of basketball is really quite interesting.

    REVISED: The history of basketball is quite interesting.

✔ **Avoid sentence fragments.**

- A **fragment** is a group of words that does not express a complete idea.

    ORIGINAL: 1891, the year in which modern basketball was invented

    REVISED: Dr. James Naismith invented modern basketball in 1891.

✔ **Correct run-on sentences.**

- A **run-on** is two sentences written, incorrectly, as one.

    ORIGINAL: Naismith attached a peach basket to the balcony at each end of a gym in Springfield, Massachusetts, this game, called "basket ball," rapidly grew into a popular sport.

    REVISED: Naismith attached a peach basket to the balcony at each end of a gym in Springfield, Massachusetts. This game, called "basket ball," rapidly grew into a popular sport.

More ▶

✔ **Revise stringy sentences.**

- A **stringy sentence** contains a lot of elements loosely connected by *ands*.

    ORIGINAL: Volleyball is a sport that combines some elements of basketball and some elements of badminton, and volleyball is played with teams of six players, rather than the five players on a team in basketball, and the players hit a ball over a net, and they use their hands, arms, or any other parts of their upper bodies.

    REVISED: Volleyball is a sport that combines some elements of basketball and badminton. Unlike basketball, which has five players on a team, volleyball has teams of six. Using their hands, arms, or any other parts of their upper bodies, volleyball players hit a ball over a net.

✔ **Correct dangling modifiers.**

- A **dangling modifier** is one that modifies the wrong element in the sentence.

    ORIGINAL: Reaching the stadium in the early afternoon, our seats were perfect. (The phrase *Reaching...afternoon* incorrectly modifies *seats*.)

    REVISED: Reaching the stadium in the early afternoon, we found that our seats were perfect. (The phrase now correctly modifies *we*.)

✔ **Correct misplaced modifiers.**

- A **misplaced modifier** is one that is not placed close enough to the word that it is supposed to modify.

    ORIGINAL: Our team organized a fund drive needing new equipment. (The phrase *needing new equipment* is too far from *team*, the word that it modifies.)

    REVISED: Needing new equipment, our team organized a fund drive.

Meets ISAT Standards
1.B.3c
1.B.3d
2.A.3d
2.B.3a
3.A.3
3.B.3a
3.B.3b

Constructing and Editing Sentences 295

Your Turn

Exercise Read the following sentences. Then fill in the circle next to the item that BEST corrects each sentence.

1. A fastball was thrown by the pitcher, and the ball was swung on by the batter and was missed.
    - Ⓐ The pitcher threw a fastball, and the ball was swung on by the batter and missed.
    - Ⓑ The pitcher threw a fastball, and the batter swung and missed.
    - Ⓒ The pitcher's fastball was swung on and missed by the batter.
    - Ⓓ A fastball was thrown by the pitcher, which the batter swung on and was missed.

2. When the backhand shot sliced down the line.
    - Ⓐ When the backhand shot down the line.
    - Ⓑ Down the line when the ball was hit backhand.
    - Ⓒ When the backhand shot sliced down the line, I silently cheered.
    - Ⓓ I hit the ball backhand it sliced down the line.

3. In the sport of netball, teams have seven players each the nets are supported by poles rather than backboards.
    - Ⓐ In the sport of netball, teams have seven players each, and the nets are supported by poles rather than backboards.
    - Ⓑ In the sport of netball, seven players each, and the net is supported by poles. Not backboards.
    - Ⓒ In the sport of netball, teams have seven players each, the nets are supported by poles rather than backboards.
    - Ⓓ In the sport of netball, teams have seven players each. The nets supported by poles, rather than backboards.

AIM Higher! ISAT Language Arts Review

4. In golf, the object of the game is to hit the ball into each hole and using as few strokes as possible.
   - Ⓐ In golf, the object of the game are to hit the ball into each hole and to use as few strokes as possible.
   - Ⓑ In golf, the object of the game is hitting the ball into each hole and to use as few strokes as possible.
   - Ⓒ In golf, the object of the game is to hit the ball into each hole and to use as few strokes as possible.
   - Ⓓ In golf, the objects of the game is to hit the ball into each hole and using as few strokes as possible.

Meets ISAT Standards
1.B.3d
3.A.3
3.B.3b

5. While washing my uniform, some of the buttons came off.
   - Ⓐ Some of the buttons came off while washing my uniform.
   - Ⓑ When my uniform was washing, some of the buttons came off.
   - Ⓒ Some of the buttons, while washing my uniform, came off.
   - Ⓓ Some of the buttons of my uniform came off in the wash.

6. Tricia is lucky because she can always talk about her problems with her coach.
   - Ⓐ Tricia with her coach is lucky because she can always talk about her problems.
   - Ⓑ Tricia is lucky with her coach because she can always talk about her problems.
   - Ⓒ Tricia is lucky because she can always talk with her coach about her problems.
   - Ⓓ With her coach about her problems, Tricia is lucky because she can always talk.

7. Like golf, croquet was a fashionable and stylish amusement and pastime during the nineteenth century over a hundred years ago.
   - Ⓐ Over a hundred years ago, croquet was a fashionable and stylish amusement and pastime.
   - Ⓑ Like golf, croquet was a fashionable amusement during the nineteenth century.
   - Ⓒ Fashionable and stylish, croquet was like golf in the nineteenth century over a hundred years ago.
   - Ⓓ During the nineteenth century, which was over a hundred years ago, croquet and golf were stylish amusements and pastimes.

More ▶

Constructing and Editing Sentences

Your Turn

Meets ISAT Standards
1.B.3d
3.A.3
3.B.3b

8. We could see the golfers teeing off from our car window.
   - A From our car window, we could see the golfers teeing off.
   - B We could see the golfers teeing off. From our car window.
   - C We looked out of our car window we could see the golfers teeing off.
   - D From our car window, golfers teeing off.

9. Good foul-line shooting must be mastered by all basketball players.
   - A All basketball players must master good foul-line shooting.
   - B Good foul-line shooting must be mastered by any and all basketball players.
   - C By all basketball players, good foul-line shooting must be mastered.
   - D Good foul-line shooting. Must be mastered by all basketball players.

10. Invented by a British army officer in India. The game of snooker is similar to pool.
    - A The game of snooker is similar to pool, it was invented by a British army officer in India.
    - B The game of snooker. Invented by a British army officer in India. Is similar to pool.
    - C Invented by a British army officer in India, the game of snooker is similar to pool.
    - D The game of snooker, similar to pool, invented a British army officer in India.

Return to the exercises at the beginning of the chapter, revise your work as necessary, and submit the exercises to your teacher for grading.

Chapter 13
Perfect Paragraphs
Main Ideas and Supporting Details

First Encounter

Read this informative essay about language games. Then try your hand at the exercises that follow the essay. You will not be graded on the exercises at this time. At the end of the chapter, you will be directed to return to these exercises to revise and correct your work.

Words at Play

by Robin Shulka

Many animals communicate, but only human beings use language, which is a breathtakingly complex combination of sound and meaning and grammar. Humans also love to play. When the automobile was invented, it was a sure bet that auto racing would not be far behind. It's also not surprising that humans have combined their instinct for language with their penchant for play to create many, many kinds of language games.

One of the most widely practiced of all word games is the **pun.** Technically, the art of punning is called *paronomasia.* It consists of using the similarity between different words or more than one sense of a single word in a humorous or imaginative way. Examples of the first kind of pun are found in this story: A maharajah, or king, in India decrees that henceforth no one but he is to hunt animals. The people get upset by this and kick him out of office, creating the first instance of the *reign* being called on account of the *game.* An example of the second kind of pun is the fatally wounded Mercutio, in *Romeo and Juliet,* telling Romeo, "Ask for me tomorrow and you shall find me a *grave man.*" Some people consider puns a low form of humor, but many pundits[1] consider them to be quite punny.

Another quite common word game is the creation of palindromes. A **palindrome** is one or more words that read the same from right to left as from left to right. The word *palindrome* comes from two ancient Greek words—*palin,* meaning "backward," and *dromos,* meaning "running." So, a palindrome runs both forward and

---

[1] **pundit.** An expert on some subject. As used here, the word is a pun on the word *pun.*

Alien Spacecraft

backward. Examples of one-word palindromes include *pep, pop, noon, peep, Bob, level,* and *radar.* Language lovers have collected many longer palindromes, including this sentence about Teddy Roosevelt, the president who helped create the Panama Canal: "A man, a plan, a canal: Panama." Another example is an imaginary quotation from the emperor Napoleon, who was exiled to the island of Elba: "Able was I ere[2] I saw Elba."

Yet another common word game is creating anagrams. An **anagram** is a word or group of words formed by rearranging the letters that make up another word or group of words. For example, the letters of the name *Daniel* can be rearranged to form the words *denial, nailed,* and *DNA lie.* The name *Clint Eastwood* can be rearranged to create the words *Old West Action.* The word *education* can become *a coed unit.* The word *democracy* can become *YMCA credo.*

A variation on anagrams is **laddergrams,** in which one word is transformed into another by changing a letter at a time to create a new word at each step. For example, the word *cat* can become *dog* in this way:

CAT → COT → COG → DOG

And you can transform *lead* into *gold* in this way:

LEAD → HEAD → HELD → HOLD → GOLD

See if you can create a laddergram to transform the word *heat* into the word *cold* and the word *wild* into *tame.*

Of course, puns, palindromes, and anagrams are just a few of the many thousands of word games that people have invented, from Botticelli, charades, crossword puzzles, cryptograms, hangman, jumble, knock-knock, pig Latin, and riddles, to twenty questions, wacky wordies, and word searches. People who design games for fun and profit are constantly experimenting with new variations on these traditional word games. Sometimes, it can be fun simply to come up with interesting arrangements of words. At right is one example of a word square. Can you create one of your own?

T	R	O	T
H	O	P	E
A	P	E	S
T	E	N	T

---

[2]**ere.** Previous to; before

Main Ideas and Supporting Details

First Encounter

How to Play Botticelli

One of the most interesting of word games, and an excellent game for parties, is Botticelli, which is named after the Italian painter Sandro Botticelli. Here's how to play this wonderful game:

For the purposes of the game, one person is the Knower, and everyone else is a Seeker. A Name is the name of a person or animal, alive or dead, real or imaginary, whom most people would know. For people with first and last names, the Name is usually the last name, or surname, except when the person or animal is generally known by his or her first name or by a single name. So, for example,

Mohandas Gandhi = Gandhi
Gordon Sumner = Sting
Madonna Louise Veronica Ciccone = Madonna
Kermit the Frog = Kermit

The Knower thinks of a Name and gives the Seekers its first letter. So, for example, the Knower might think of Ludwig van Beethoven and say the letter "B."

The Seekers then take turns trying to stump the Knower. The first Seeker thinks of a Name beginning with a B and gives a clue. For example, the Seeker might think of George Bush, Jr., and say, "Are you a politician?" The Knower then has to come up with a Name beginning with B that fits the clue. So, for example, the Knower might say, "No, I am not Senator Barbara Boxer." If the Knower cannot come up with a name that fits the clue, then the Seeker can ask a yes/no question about the Name, such as "Are you male?" or "Are you alive?"

Play continues in this manner until the Seekers learn enough clues that one of them is able to figure out the Name that was chosen to begin with by the Knower.

Sandro Botticelli (A.D. 1445–1510) is best known for his work "The Birth of Venus."

Your Turn

Exercise A The opening essay about word games contains six paragraphs—an introduction, four body paragraphs, and a conclusion. Study the third paragraph of the essay. Then, on your own paper, answer these questions about it.

1. What is the topic sentence of the paragraph?
2. What are three supporting ideas presented in the paragraph?
3. What are two transitions used in the paragraph to connect ideas?

Exercise B Paragraphs can serve a number of different functions in pieces of writing. On your own paper, answer the following questions about the paragraphs in the essay on word games.

1. What function does the first paragraph perform? What topic does the paragraph introduce?
2. What is the topic of the second paragraph? What sentence introduces this topic?
3. What is the topic of the third paragraph? What sentence introduces this topic?
4. What is the topic of the fourth paragraph? What sentence introduces this topic?
5. What function does the final paragraph perform?

Meets ISAT Standards
1.B.3c
1.B.3d
1.C.3d
1.C.3e
2.B.3a
3.B.3a

Main Ideas and Supporting Details

Perfect Paragraphs

What Is a Paragraph?

A paragraph is a lot like a room in a house. Just as a house can include rooms of many types, a piece of writing may include paragraphs of many types. Some are large and well furnished, like a living room or library or den. One may lead or connect directly to the next. Others are tiny but functional, like closets or utility rooms. Longer pieces of writing, like newspaper stories, magazine articles, essays, and novels, contain a variety of paragraph types. These paragraphs work together to make up the whole in the same way that the various rooms make up a house.

A good working definition of a paragraph is this: A **paragraph** is a unit of writing, usually containing more than one sentence, that communicates a main idea. Let's look at some of the many kinds of paragraphs that you will find in the world of real writing.

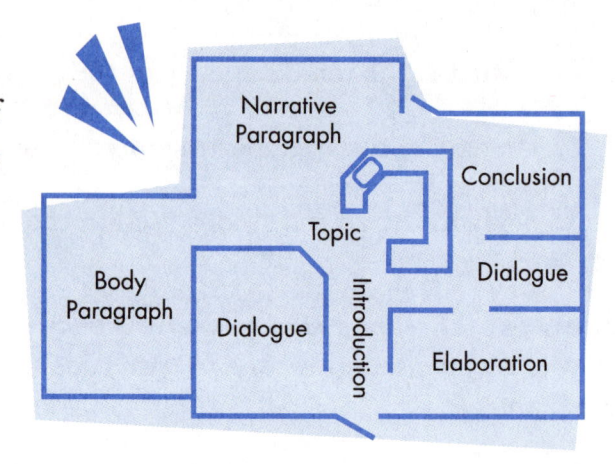

In newspaper articles, paragraphs often contain only one or two sentences. In most forms of writing, however, paragraphs contain several sentences that are related to a single main idea. In short stories and other narrative writing, a paragraph can simply present a series of events, one after the other.

Drought Predicted
by Curtis Donner
Herald Staff

In a radio address Tuesday evening, Governor Tindale warned that the state may be facing a severe drought this coming summer.

"Unless we see some relief soon," said the Governor, "we shall probably need to start rationing water by June."

Excerpt from newspaper article containing one-sentence paragraphs

One minute the fire was miles off—an acrid scent in the air, a distant mass of dark clouds of smoke. Then the wind picked up and shifted to the southwest. Like a cat, the fire leapt across the road to the edge of town. First to catch fire was the gas station at one end of Fairview Avenue. The convenience store building crackled and erupted into flame. Then, before anyone could shut off the gas pumps, the gasoline fumes exploded.

A narrative paragraph that presents a series of events

Often stories relate dialogue between characters. A new paragraph begins when a new person starts speaking.

> Sitting at his desk in the Town Hall at the other end of town, Mayor Lumino called out to his assistant. "What on earth was that?"
>
> "Beats me," said Martha, who had served as the Mayor's assistant through six terms of office. "Sounded like the whole town just exploded."
>
> At that moment, someone came running down the hallway, yelling, "The gas station just blew up!"

Excerpt from a narrative with paragraphs of dialogue

As the examples above show, some paragraphs have only one or two sentences. In most of the informative and persuasive writing that you do for school, however, paragraphs should follow standard paragraph form.

A **paragraph in standard form,** or a **standard paragraph,**

1. contains a **main idea,** which is expressed in the topic sentence, and

2. contains at least two or three **supporting sentences** related to the main idea.

The paragraph might also contain a **clincher sentence,** or **concluding sentence**, that sums up the ideas presented in the paragraph.

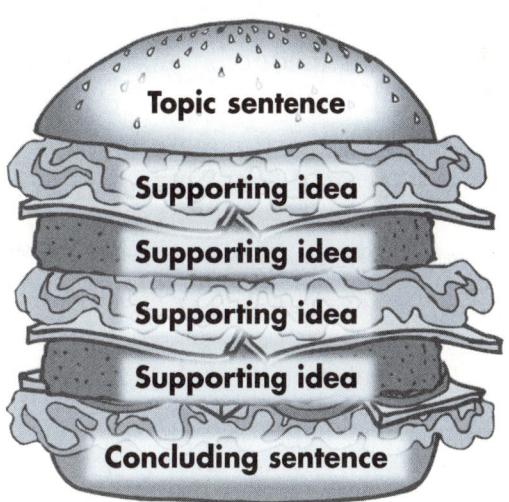

Meets ISAT Standards
1.B.3c
1.B.3d
1.C.3d
1.C.3e
2.B.3a
3.A.3
3.B.3a

Topic sentence
Supporting idea
Supporting idea
Supporting idea
Supporting idea
Concluding sentence

Main Ideas and Supporting Details 305

Main Ideas and Supporting Details

Topic Sentences

The most important part of a standard paragraph is the **topic sentence.** It not only states the main idea of the paragraph but also reflects the writing's purpose. Often, the topic sentence comes first, as in the paragraph below:

> Those who wish to paint can choose from among many different media, including oils, tempera, acrylics, gouache, and watercolors. Oil paints contain pigment in an oil base. On the positive side, oils are easily mixed and can create subtle effects. On the negative side, oils can be smelly and require paint thinner or turpentine for cleanup. The other types of paint all have a water base. Tempera paints contain egg yolk and have a dull finish. They are appropriate for posters and other painting involving large, flat areas of color. Acrylics are much like oils, except that the colors tend to be more highly saturated, or intense. Watercolors are typically much thinner in texture than acrylics. Gouaches are somewhere between acrylics and watercolors. For all the water-based media, cleanup is relatively easy, involving only water and soap.

Paragraph in standard form with an introductory topic sentence

Sometimes the topic sentence comes later in the paragraph:

> You may never have given much thought to the subject of time. Time, like air, seems to be simply there—a given—and so not particularly noticeable, complicated, or interesting. Those who have thought seriously about time, however, have realized that it is far from simple and obvious. The physicist Albert Einstein showed over a hundred years ago that time slows down for objects in motion. The effect is not noticeable, however, for speeds significantly less than the speed of light. Some physicists today—notably Julian Barbour, author of *The End of Time,* believe that all time exists at all time and that our experience of time as unfolding or going forward is an illusion. Such ideas seem very strange but are really quite good contemporary science.

Paragraph in standard form with a topic sentence embedded in the middle

In still other paragraphs, the topic sentence comes at the end:

> At the Watersports Shop, one can rent kayaks, small sailboats, catamarans, and snorkeling gear. One can also sign up there for SCUBA trips and diving instruction. At the Inner Self Center, one can take classes in yoga and meditation. At the Activities Desk, one can arrange for sailing trips, gourmet meals, hikes around the island, and ferry rides to other islands nearby. **Certainly, a visitor can keep himself well occupied while at the Caneel Bay resort on St. John.**

Paragraph with topic sentence at end

Occasionally, a paragraph may have an **implied topic sentence,** which means that the writer does not state the main idea directly. You must determine (infer) the main idea based on information in the paragraph. Look at the next example, which comes from a guidebook for tourists:

> It is always a good idea to keep your money and identification somewhere safe and secure, such as in your front pocket or in a small pouch hung around your neck. Back pockets are easy to pick. Also, keep your eyes up and look around you. Criminals are much more likely to prey upon people who aren't paying attention to their surroundings. Finally, make sure you know the area you are exploring or have a map on hand. Getting lost in an unfamiliar place can be dangerous and frightening.

Paragraph with implied topic sentence

The topic sentence of this paragraph could be "Whenever you travel to an unfamiliar place, there are a few common-sense rules that you should follow."

The Art of Building Paragraphs

You have learned that a standard paragraph contains a topic sentence and at least two or three sentences that relate to the topic sentence. The sentences that make up the rest of a paragraph support the main idea presented in the topic sentence. These sentences, called **supporting sentences,** provide details and examples that help explain the main idea, which may be reinforced in a **clincher sentence** at the end of the paragraph. The art of supporting a topic sentence is called **elaboration.**

Meets ISAT Standards
1.B.3c
1.B.3d
1.C.3d
1.C.3e
2.B.3a
3.A.3
3.B.3a

Main Ideas and Supporting Details

The chart below lists various types of elaboration that can be used to illustrate or expand the main point a writer is making in a paragraph.

Types of Elaboration

Analogy	A comparison of the subject to some other thing that shares some of the same characteristics
Causes	Statements that tell why something has happened, why it exists now, or why it will happen
Effects	Statements that tell what happened, is happening, or will happen as a result of something else
Events	Statements that describe what has happened, is happening, or will happen
Facts	Statements that can be proved to be true
Figures of Speech	Descriptive statements that are not literal, including metaphors, similes, and personifications
Illustrations and Examples	Statements about items that are particular instances of the topic of the paragraph. (For example, a paragraph about world religions might have separate sentences about Christianity, Islam, Hinduism, Buddhism, and Judaism.)
Negations	Statements that contradict other statements
Opinions	Statements of obligation, belief, judgment, or value
Paraphrases	Ideas from one or more sources, restated in different words
Qualifications	Statements that limit the range or scope of a statement or observation. (Qualifications often contain a negation like *but* or *however*.)
Quotations	The words of another person, repeated exactly and placed in quotation marks
Reasons	Statements explaining why something happens or should happen
Sensory Details/Description	Sentences or details that tell how things look, taste, smell, sound, or feel
Statistics	Statements presenting information in numerical form
Summaries	Brief retellings of material from a source

Your Turn

Exercise A Write a topic sentence for a paragraph about each of the following topics. As you develop each topic sentence, remember the purpose of the paragraph: to persuade, inform, describe, or define. Save your topic sentences for use in another exercise later in this chapter.

Meets ISAT
Standards
1.B.3d
1.C.3d
3.A.3
3.B.3a

1. Write a topic sentence for a persuasive paragraph about placing restrictions on the hours that school-aged people are allowed to work. (Take a position for or against this idea.)

   _____

   _____

2. Write a topic sentence for an informative paragraph that explains the duties of someone playing a particular position on a sports team (for example, a tight end in football, a catcher in baseball, or a goalie in soccer).

   _____

   _____

3. Write a topic sentence for a descriptive paragraph about an unusual building, such as a geodesic dome or an ice palace, or an unusual vehicle, such as the space shuttle or an electric car.

   _____

   _____

4. Write a topic sentence for a paragraph that gives an extended definition of an abstract term, such as *progress*, *hope*, *honesty*, or *love*. A paragraph of definition might begin with a question about the meaning of the term. It could also start with a sentence that defines the term in a general way. You might want to consult a dictionary to help you explain what your term means.

   _____

   _____

Main Ideas and Supporting Details

Your Turn

Exercise B Choose one of the following subjects and circle it. Narrow the general subject to a more specific topic that you know a lot about. Write your topic on the line provided for that purpose. Then, come up with five sentences about your topic using the instructions below. Write these sentences on your own paper. (What you are doing in this exercise is practicing how to create different types of elaboration.)

GENERAL SUBJECTS: film and television
celebrities
popular music
books

YOUR NARROWED TOPIC: _____

1. Write a sentence about your topic that expresses an opinion.

2. Write a sentence about your topic that states a fact.

3. Write a sentence about your topic that describes a cause and/or an effect.

4. Write a sentence about your topic that contains a figure of speech.

5. Write a sentence that describes some part or feature of your topic.

Exercise C Write a paragraph in standard form about the topic you chose for the previous exercise. Create a topic sentence and several sentences that support your topic sentence. You may use some or all of the sentences that you created for the previous exercise, but make sure that they support your topic sentence. Review the chart on page 308 for other types of elaboration you may include. Write a rough draft of your paragraph on your own paper. Next, revise your draft using the Revision Checklist on pages 265–66. Finally, proofread your paragraph using the Proofreading Checklist on page 270, and make a clean final copy.

Main Ideas and Supporting Details

Ordering and Organizing Ideas in a Paragraph

Normally, you will write paragraphs by coming up with an idea for a topic sentence and then generating a list of details to use in the body of the paragraph. The details in the body can be any of the kinds listed in the chart on elaboration on page 308. After coming up with the details that will support the main idea of the paragraph, you will need to organize those details in a logical way.

As you saw in Chapter 11, "Step by Step: The Writing Process for Examinations," there are many ways to organize details. You can organize them in **chronological (time) order,** or order of occurrence.

You can organize details in **spatial order,** left to right, right to left, top to bottom, bottom to top, front to back, back to front, near to far, far to near, or in the order in which they are encountered or noticed.

You can organize details in **degree order,** from most to least (or least to most) important, common, valuable, exciting, and so on.

In addition to chronological, spatial, and degree order, you can use part-by-part order to organize your ideas. In **part-by-part order,** you do not follow an overall organizational pattern. Instead, you connect each idea in some way to the idea that preceded it and to the one that follows it.

There are many other ways to organize a piece of writing. In **problem-solution order,** you first present a problem. Then you present a solution to it. In **cause-and-effect order,** you first present a cause (or an effect) and then present its effect (or cause). For more information on organization, see pages 255–60.

Using Transitions to Clarify Organization

Transitions are words and phrases used to show how ideas are connected to one another. They help readers to understand how ideas are related. For example, when you write a paragraph in chronological order, you might start sentences with the words *first, second, then,* or *next.* When you write a paragraph that classifies information, you might start sentences with *the first type, one kind, another type,* or *another group.*

Meets ISAT Standards
1.B.3c
1.B.3d
2.A.3a
2.A.3d
3.A.3
3.B.3a
3.B.3b
3.C.3b

Main Ideas and Supporting Details

The following chart describes some transitions that you can use to connect ideas in your writing.

Transitional Words and Phrases

Transitions to Show Time/Narration

after	eventually	next
at last	finally	then
at once	first	thereafter
before	meanwhile	when

Transitions to Show Place/Description

above	beyond	into
across	down	next to
around	here	over
before	in	there
behind	inside	under

Transitions to Show Importance/Evaluation

first	mainly	then
last	more important	to begin with

Transitions to Show Cause and Effect

as a result	for	so that
because	since	therefore
consequently	so	

Transitions to Compare Ideas

also	as well	moreover
and	like	similarly
another	likewise	too

Transitions to Contrast Ideas

although	in spite of	on the other hand
but	instead	still
however	nevertheless	yet

More ▶

© Great Source. All rights reserved.

Transitions for Classification

| the first type | one kind | other sorts |
| another group | other kinds | other types |

Transitions to Introduce Examples

| for example | one example | one sort of |
| for instance | one kind | another example |

Transitions to Introduce a Contradiction

| however | instead | on the contrary |
| in spite of this | nonetheless | otherwise |

Transitions to Introduce a Conclusion, Summary, or Generalization

| as a result | in general | therefore |
| in conclusion | in summary | thus |

Pronouns (such as the word *these*) that refer to people, places, things, or ideas introduced in preceding sentences are also transitions. **Repeated words** can also serve as transitions.

Meets ISAT Standards
1.B.3d
2.A.3d
3.A.3
3.B.3a

Read the paragraph below and notice how the author uses transitions, which have been set in **boldface,** to connect the ideas:

While many people think of birds as flying creatures, there are actually about forty known species of flightless bird. **These flightless birds** have unique characteristics. **For instance,** flightless birds have relatively small wing bones and flat breastbones. **These qualities** are unique because most birds have relatively large wing bones and large breastbones that support the muscles used for flying. **Since** it cannot fly, a flightless bird must escape predators in **other ways. For example,** the kiwi, a flightless bird native to New Zealand, has the ability to run quickly. Penguins move awkwardly on land but can swim swiftly under water. **Although** an ostrich cannot fly away from predators, it is taller than most predators and can defend itself with its long, sharp claws.

Main Ideas and Supporting Details 313

Main Ideas and Supporting Details

Concluding a Paragraph

Many paragraphs end with a **clincher sentence,** or **concluding sentence,** that gives the reader a satisfying sense of an ending. This sentence might restate the main idea in different words or summarize the evidence presented in the rest of the paragraph. The concluding sentence might also extend or elaborate on the main idea. It might connect the main idea of the paragraph to the reader's life. It might draw a conclusion, make a suggestion, or call on the reader to take some action. Some concluding sentences pose a question or leave the reader with something to ponder.

When you write a paragraph-length response, use your own judgment to decide whether you need a clincher sentence at the end of the paragraph. The last sentence in a paragraph might simply be the last in a series of ideas.

Look at the following version of the paragraph about flightless birds. Notice how the concluding sentence summarizes the ideas and sheds new light on the topic:

> While many people think of birds as flying creatures, there are actually about forty known species of flightless bird. These flightless birds have several unique characteristics. For instance, flightless birds have relatively small wing bones and flat breastbones. These qualities are unique because most birds have relatively large wing bones and large breastbones that support the muscles used for flying. Since it cannot fly, a flightless bird must escape predators in other ways. For example, the kiwi, a flightless bird native to New Zealand, has the ability to run quickly. Penguins move awkwardly on land but can swim swiftly under water. Although an ostrich cannot fly away from predators, it is taller than most predators and can defend itself with its long, sharp claws. Each species of flightless bird has adapted to its own environment, showing yet again the remarkable inventiveness and flexibility of nature.

Your Turn

Exercise A Read each paragraph below. Underline the topic sentence, circle the transitional words and phrases, and double-underline the concluding sentence.

> Meets ISAT Standards
> 1.B.3d
> 2.A.3d
> 3.A.3
> 3.B.3a

1. The science of language, which is called linguistics, has a long history. One of the first true linguists was the ancient Hindu expert on grammar, Panini. This scholar lived sometime during the period from the sixth century to the third century B.C. Panini studied the grammar of Sanskrit, the language of ancient India, and wrote a grammar book consisting of about four thousand rules. A few centuries later, in ancient Rome, the scholar Marcus Terentius Varro (116–c. 29 B.C.) wrote a book entitled *On the Latin Language*. During the Middle Ages, many linguists thought that all the languages of the world had their origins in Hebrew, the language of the Bible. By the late 1700s, however, linguists were working on a solid, scientific base to study how languages have developed over time. These experts compared the world's languages with each other, noting similarities and differences. As a result of such comparisons, experts could group languages into families such as Indo-European. Throughout the ages, remarkable individuals with a deep love for language have shaped linguistics and contributed to our knowledge of people, culture, and history.

2. Like people and animals, language comes in a wide variety of forms. For instance, some linguists believe that there are about six thousand languages spoken in the world today. However, only about two hundred of these languages are spoken by as many as a million speakers. Only twenty-three languages, moreover, have fifty million or more speakers each. Of these languages, English, Hindi, Mandarin Chinese, and Spanish are the most widely spoken. Within many of the languages spoken, there are countless dialects, or relatively close variations. This enormous variety of languages and dialects reflects the diversity of cultures around the world.

Main Ideas and Supporting Details

Your Turn

Meets ISAT Standards
2.A.3d
3.A.3
3.B.3a
3.B.3b
3.C.3a
5.A.3a
5.B.3a

Exercise B Look back at Exercise A on page 309. Create a paragraph-length response using one of the topic sentences you wrote for the exercise. You might have to do some research in the library or on the Internet. Remember to use specific details to support your topic sentence, and connect your ideas with transitional words and phrases. Use a concluding sentence to end your paragraph. Write your rough draft on a separate sheet of paper. Revise it using the Revision Checklist on pages 265–66. Then proofread it using the Proofreading Checklist on page 270. Copy your final version onto the lines below.

Return to the exercises at the beginning of the chapter, revise your work as necessary, and submit the exercises to your teacher for grading.

AIM Higher! ISAT Language Arts Review

Chapter 14
Excellent Essays
Introduction, Body, and Conclusion

First Encounter

Read the writing prompt. Then read the essay a student wrote in response to it. Also try your hand at the exercises that follow the essay. You will not be graded on the exercises at this time. At the end of the chapter, you will be directed to return to these exercises to revise and correct your work.

SAMPLE WRITING PROMPT: Write a five-paragraph essay on a topic related to some animal or group of animals. Discuss the appearance and behavior of your favorite animal or group of animals. These may be animals that you have observed in the wild or at a zoo. They may be pets such as cats, dogs, or tropical fish. Your essay should contain information about the behavior of the animal or group of animals you choose.

The Magic of Birds
by Sylvia Bernstein

What is the most popular hobby in the United States? The answer may surprise you. It is birdwatching! More than 30 million Americans have chosen as their hobby exploring the magic of birds. Birdwatching is popular for several reasons. It is simple. It is relatively inexpensive. It involves getting exercise in the outdoors. Birds are fascinating both to amateur birdwatchers and to scientists. By observing birds in the wild, you can learn about their behavior and habits, including migration, courtship displays, and songs.

Bird migration is one of the wonders of the animal kingdom. In the spring and fall, many North American birds set off on long trips. These migrations give birdwatchers chances to observe the birds along their flyways, or migration routes. Scientists believe that birds migrate to find better temperature conditions, to seek food, and to return to their breeding grounds. Some birds migrate many thousands of miles, from one continent to another. One example is the Arctic tern, which migrates more than 20,000 miles a year between the northern part of North America and Antarctica. Migrating birds often travel at night, sometimes over open water. How do the birds know what route to take each year? Scientists are not yet sure exactly how they do it.

Courtship displays are another interesting feature of bird life. In many bird species, the males display colorful feathers to attract a mate. One of the most amazing displays is that of the peacock. The tail feathers of the male peacock are especially beautiful. The bowerbirds of Australia and New Guinea use another type of courtship display. Male bowerbirds build elaborate structures called "bowers" to attract their mates.

Finally, scientists have devoted much attention to birdsong. About half of the roughly 9,600 known species of birds are songbirds. These birds regularly produce calls or songs. However, the songs of birds differ greatly in their length and variety. Simple calls, such as a chip alarm call, consist of a single note. Songs are more complex. Robins, mockingbirds, and nightingales, for example, produce more elaborate songs. Each one of these songs has many notes. Scientists are still not certain about the functions of birdsong. Many experts believe that male birds "sing" to advertise their presence and to attract mates. The songs warn competitors not to intrude on the singer's turf.

Migration, breeding habits, and songs of birds are lively topics for experts and amateur birdwatchers alike. The next time you find yourself in a park, a forest, or just looking out your window, take a close look. Maybe you, too, will be caught up in the magic of birdwatching!

Your Turn

Exercise Use the lines provided below to answer the following questions about the essay on the preceding pages. Answer in complete sentences.

1. Where does the writer's thesis statement appear? What is the central idea?

2. In the first body paragraph, what is the topic sentence? Identify three details that help to support the topic sentence in this paragraph.

3. In the second body paragraph, what is the topic sentence? Identify two details that help to support the topic sentence in this paragraph.

4. What is the topic sentence of the third body paragraph? What are three details that support the topic sentence?

320 AIM Higher! ISAT Language Arts Review

5. What are the three main ideas that support the writer's thesis? (Hint: Look for the topic sentences in the body paragraphs.)

   A. _____

   _____

   B. _____

   _____

   C. _____

   _____

6. In the third body paragraph, what transitions does the writer use to make the ideas in the paragraph easy to follow?

   _____

   _____

7. Which sentence in the concluding paragraph summarizes the thesis and the most important supporting ideas of the essay? What else does the writer do in her conclusion?

   _____

   _____

   _____

   _____

Meets ISAT Standards
1.A.3a
1.A.3b
1.B.3c
1.B.3d
1.C.3a
1.C.3d
2.A.3a
2.B.3a
3.A.3
3.B.3a

Introduction, Body, and Conclusion

Excellent Essays

You are wandering past your local newsstand. You spot a magazine. It might be a sports magazine. It might be a fashion magazine. An article title on the cover grabs your attention. You pick up the magazine. You thumb through the pages until you find the article. Then for several minutes, you are completely caught up in what you are reading. What happened? You most likely just read and felt the magic of one form of the essay.

What Is an Essay?

An **essay** is a short piece of writing that deals with part of a larger subject. An essay needs to be focused. It is *not* an extended or complete treatment of a subject. For example, Ingrid Wickelgren's 144-page book *Ramblin' Rabbits: Building a Breed of Mechanical Beasts* is *not* an essay. Instead, an essay is a work that treats a small part of a subject in a focused way. For example, the subject of virtual reality games in the future might be covered in an essay, but not completely. That is usually the case with essays. An essay does not attempt to cover every aspect of a subject. An essay should grab and keep your attention, and you should be able to read it in a relatively short amount of time.

Here are two examples of focused ideas appropriate for essays: You might write an informative essay about recent changes in the profession of nursing. You could also write a humorous essay on the language that young people use for instant messaging.

The idea of focus is central to what an essay is. A good essay does not wander off onto unrelated topics. It presents a sharply focused main idea and then expands on or supports that idea.

Essays can be written on a wide range of topics. Magazines, for example, are full of essays on every possible topic. There are also many ways to develop essays. In this chapter, you will learn one simple model for putting together an essay. The chapter will teach you to create what is sometimes called the **standard classroom theme**. As you grow as a writer, you will learn to write essays that are more complicated. However, even in the more complex essays that you write in the future, you will still want to focus on a single overall idea—your **thesis**.

The ability to write essays is an important test-taking skill. Most state examinations require essay writing. For language arts tests, you will sometimes be required to write essays on reading passages. At other times, you will have to write essays that present your own ideas or your own prior knowledge and experience. Here are some of the types of essay you may be asked to write:

Meets ISAT Standards
1.A.3a
1.A.3b
1.B.3c
1.B.3d
1.C.3a
1.C.3d
2.A.3a
2.B.3a
3.A.3
3.B.3a

Types of Essay

- **Narrative essays** based on real-life events
- **Personal essays** about experiences you have had
- **Persuasive essays** that attempt to convince others to take a certain action or to adopt a certain point of view
- **Informative** or **expository essays** that define, analyze, compare and contrast, classify, or describe

Introduction, Body, and Conclusion

Introduction, Body, and Conclusion

Whatever type of essay you are asked to write on a test, you will generally do well if you can construct an essay in the format of the standard classroom theme. This type of essay has the following features:

Essay Model: The Standard Classroom Theme

Characteristics

1. It is four or five paragraphs long.
2. It gives details to support a central idea, or **thesis.**
3. It contains a clear beginning (introduction), middle (body), and end (conclusion).

Structure

—**Paragraph 1: Introduction**

The introduction has two purposes or goals:
- to grab the reader's attention
- to state the essay's main idea, or **thesis**

—**Paragraphs 2, 3, and 4 (if present): Body Paragraphs**

Each body paragraph presents a major idea in support of the thesis statement. The main idea of each body paragraph is presented in a **topic sentence.** The topic sentence is supported by sentences that present additional information and details.

The topic sentence can appear at the beginning, at the end, or somewhere in the middle of a body paragraph. Sometimes the topic sentence can be implied. (See Chapter 13, "Perfect Paragraphs: Main Ideas and Supporting Details.")

—**Paragraph 4 or 5: Conclusion**

The conclusion should "wrap things up." It should give the reader a feeling of closure. There are many ways to write a conclusion. These will be discussed later in this chapter.

Prewriting: Planning an Essay

The prewriting process includes the thinking and planning you do before you write. Study the graphic organizer for essays shown below. This graphic organizer shows clearly the parts of a standard classroom theme. It is a helpful tool for planning an essay for a writing test.

Meets ISAT Standards
1.B.3d
1.C.3f
3.A.3
3.B.3a
3.B.3b

Introduction

Topic: _____

Thesis Statement: _____

Body Paragraphs

Body Paragraph 1
Topic Sentence:
_____
_____
_____

Supporting Details:
_____
_____
_____
_____
_____

Body Paragraph 2
Topic Sentence:
_____
_____
_____

Supporting Details:
_____
_____
_____
_____
_____

Body Paragraph 3
Topic Sentence:
_____
_____
_____

Supporting Details:
_____
_____
_____
_____
_____

Conclusion

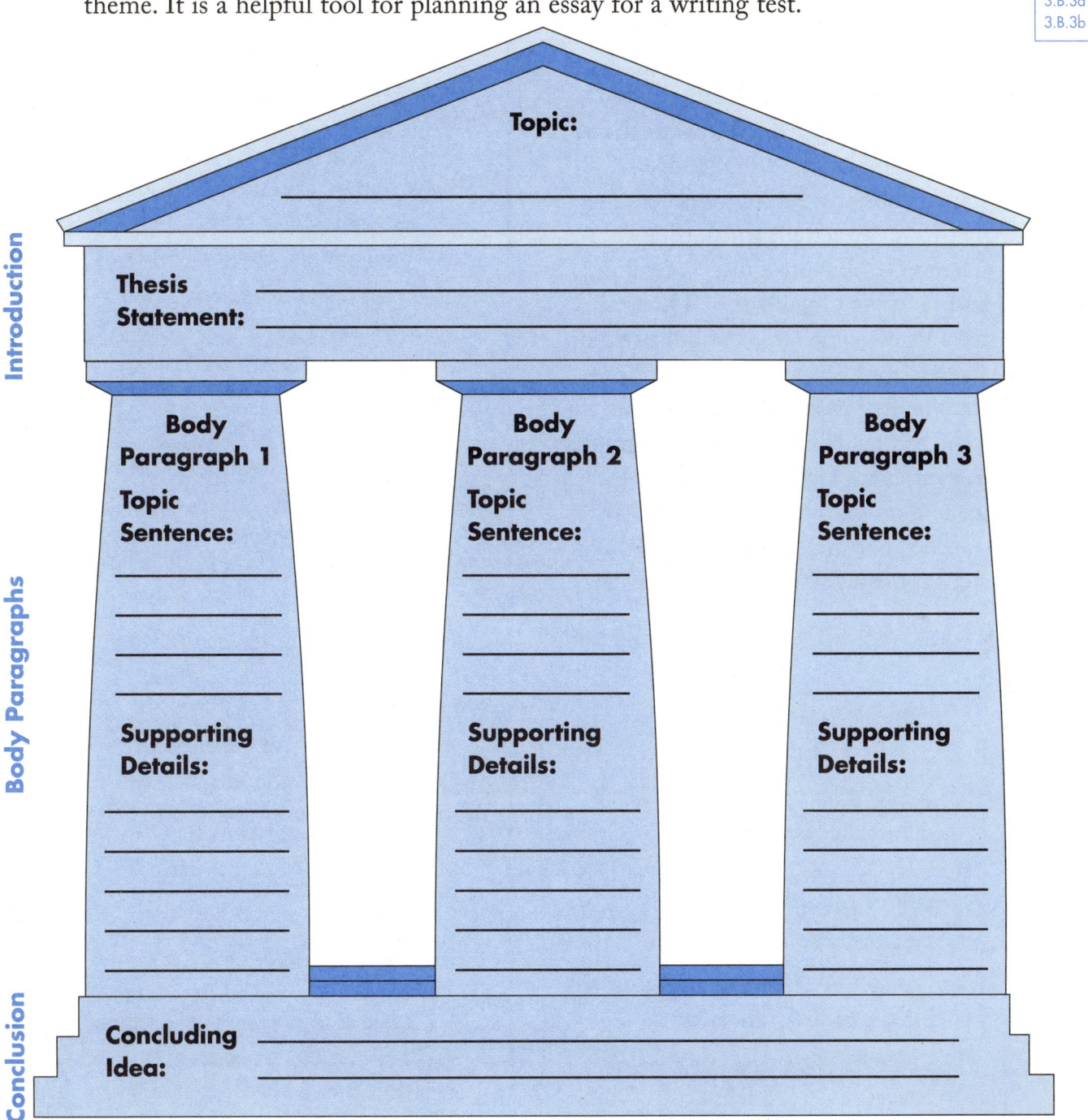

Concluding Idea: _____

The first step in the prewriting process is to analyze the assignment or writing prompt (on your exam). Make sure you understand what you are supposed to write about and what your writing should contain. (See Chapter 11, "Step by Step: The Writing Process for Examinations.")

Introduction, Body, and Conclusion

The next step is to develop a thesis statement for your essay. The **thesis statement** presents the central idea that your essay will discuss. It should be a one- or two-sentence general response to the writing prompt.

The third step is to gather ideas and information related to your thesis statement. Use one or more of the standard brainstorming or notetaking methods you have learned. (See Chapter 4, "Picture This! Notetaking and Graphic Organizers.") Once you have listed some ideas, look for two or three main ideas related to the thesis statement. These ideas will become the topic sentences of the body paragraphs in your essay. Now you are ready to make a rough outline for your essay.

The chart below summarizes the steps for essay writing covered so far.

Prewriting Steps for Writing Essays in Response to Test Prompts

1. Analyze the writing prompt to find out what it is asking.
2. Write a one- or two-sentence answer to the prompt. This will serve as the thesis statement for your essay.
3. Gather ideas for the essay (perhaps using a graphic organizer).
4. Organize your ideas into a rough outline.

Here is a rough outline by the student who wrote the opening selection about birds.

One Student's Rough Outline

The Magic of Birds
Intro
 —No. of birdwatchers
 —Reasons why birdwatching is popular
 —Thesis statement—birds are fascinating to scientists & amateurs
Bird Migration (1st Body ¶)
What:
 —Long-distance flights
When:
 —Spring & fall
 —Many fly at night
Why:
 —Reasons for migration (food supply, favorable climate for raising young)
Where and how:
 —Navigation over land & water—scientists not sure how
Courtship Displays (2nd Body ¶)
 —Peacock
 —Bowerbirds (Australia & New Guinea)
Birdsong (3rd Body ¶)
 —Variations in length & complexity (calls = short, simple; songs = longer, more elaborate)
 —Poss. functions of songs
Conclusion
 —Summary—recap main ideas
 —Suggest readers become involved

Your Turn

Exercise A Choose one of the following general subjects and circle it (or choose a subject of your own).

Animals	Exercise/Sports	School/Education	Careers
Teenagers	Movies	Music	Art
Politics	Computers	Parks	Vacation

OTHER SUBJECT: _____

Meets ISAT
Standards
1.B.3b
1.B.3d
1.C.3f
3.A.3
3.B.3a
3.B.3b

Exercise B In the space provided, make a word web of specific ideas based on the general subject that you chose in Exercise A. If necessary, look back at the word web on page 85 as a model.

Introduction, Body, and Conclusion

Your Turn

Exercise C Using the word web you created in Exercise B, choose a narrowed, focused topic appropriate for a five-paragraph essay (a standard classroom theme). Write your topic on the line provided.

NARROWED, FOCUSED TOPIC: _____

Exercise D Based on your narrowed, focused topic, write a single sentence that states the central idea, or thesis, of your essay. Save this thesis statement for use in another exercise later in this chapter.

_____

_____

_____

Exercise E On the line provided below, tell what the purpose of your essay will be (to narrate, or tell a story; to persuade; to describe; to inform; to entertain; etc.).

_____

Introduction, Body, and Conclusion

Drafting: Writing the Introduction

Writing is a process. It involves continual shifts and changes. New thoughts pop into a writer's mind all the time, and different writers carry out specific tasks in different ways and in different sequences. Therefore, the writing process varies from individual to individual. Writers differ considerably, for example, in their approach to drafting.

Some writers begin drafting an essay by writing an introduction. Other writers prefer to write the introduction last. You can choose either method. However, when you write an essay in response to a prompt on a test, you may find it easier to begin with the introduction. You can then continue through to the end, following your rough outline.

The introduction should grab the reader's attention. It should also present the thesis statement, the central idea or main point of your essay. There are many ways you can grab the reader's attention. Study the methods listed below, together with the example given for each method.

Meets ISAT Standards
1.B.3d
1.C.3e
3.A.3
3.B.3a
3.C.3a

"Hooking" the Reader

- **Begin with a startling or interesting fact.**

    This is the strategy followed by the writer of the essay on birdwatching (pages 318–19). The writer begins by challenging the reader to identify the most popular hobby in America and then surprises the reader with the information that the most popular hobby is birdwatching.

- **Begin with a quotation or proverb.**

    My grandfather used to say, "I rarely see anything more beautiful than a bird." I grew up on a farm. That made it easy for me to see what he meant. I started to take a serious interest in birds when I was only five. Later, I discovered that birdwatching is the most popular hobby in the United States. There are three kinds of bird behavior that I find especially interesting. These include migration, courtship, and songs.

- **Begin with an anecdote, or very brief story.**

    Last week, I saw the first cardinal of the season—a flashy red male. He was in my friend Frieda's backyard. We were both delighted to watch the brilliantly colored bird. He hopped around looking for seeds. After a few minutes, we saw him shoot up to the top of the garage. There he sat and

More ▶

Introduction, Body, and Conclusion

preened his feathers. I suddenly realized how much pleasure I get out of watching and reading about birds. Three aspects of bird behavior I find especially interesting are migration, courtship displays, and birdsong.

- **Begin with an analogy to something else.** (An **analogy** is a comparison presented to make a point.)

   It is hard to convince a stamp collector or a model ship builder to try another hobby. However, it is *impossible* to convince a birdwatcher to put down the binoculars! I know this is true. How do I know? I am passionate about birdwatching. So are a lot of other people. In fact, there are about 30 million birdwatchers in America alone. For most birdwatchers, there are three especially interesting aspects of bird behavior. These include migration, courtship displays, and birdsong.

- **Begin by posing a question.**

   The writer of the essay on pages 318–19 used the question strategy. The writer combined this strategy with the strategy of presenting an interesting fact.

Your Turn

Exercise On the lines below, write the introduction for an essay using the thesis statement you wrote for Exercise D on page 328. Revise your introduction. Then copy the revised version on your own paper.

Meets ISAT
Standards
1.B.3d
1.C.3e
3.A.3
3.B.3a
3.B.3b
3.C.3a

Introduction, Body, and Conclusion

Introduction, Body, and Conclusion

Drafting: Writing the Body Paragraphs

Look back at the graphic organizer on page 325. You can see that developing an essay is like constructing a building. The thesis statement is like the roof of the building. The thesis is held up or supported by the body paragraphs. The body paragraphs must provide strong support, or the thesis will not be convincing or persuasive and your argument may come crashing down!

Each body paragraph in a non-narrative essay should consist of the following parts:

- a main idea in the form of a topic sentence
- at least two or three sentences that support the main idea
- transitions to show how your ideas are connected

Look at the main headings in your rough outline. They state the ideas that will become topic sentences in the body paragraphs of the essay. In each body paragraph, the topic sentence should directly support the thesis statement, or the overall focus. The topic sentence of a body paragraph may appear at the beginning of the paragraph, in the middle, or at the end. In some paragraphs, the topic sentence may be implied rather than explicitly stated. It is best to avoid using implied topic sentences, however, until you become a more experienced writer.

One good way to plan a body paragraph is to construct a word web. Below is an example of a word web for the first body paragraph of the essay about birds on pages 318–19. The topic sentence for this paragraph appears in **boldface type** in the middle of the web. Related or supporting ideas are placed around the topic sentence.

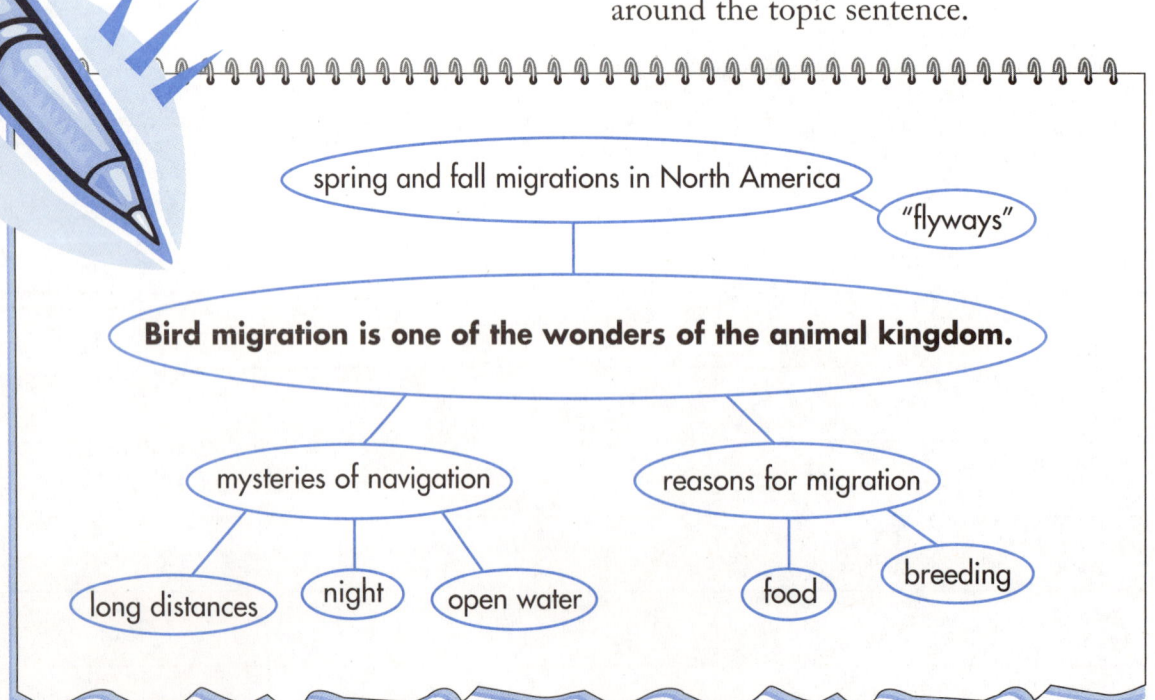

- spring and fall migrations in North America
  - "flyways"
- **Bird migration is one of the wonders of the animal kingdom.**
  - mysteries of navigation
    - long distances
    - night
    - open water
  - reasons for migration
    - food
    - breeding

332 AIM Higher! ISAT Language Arts Review

Organizing Body Paragraphs and Using Transitions

The ideas in a body paragraph of an essay should be presented in a logical order. In addition, the paragraphs themselves should be presented in an order that makes sense. (For information on methods of organization, see pages 255–60 of Chapter 11, "Step by Step: The Writing Process for Examinations.") As you write, you should use transitional words and phrases whenever you can in order to connect ideas and to show their logical relationship to each other. (See the list of transitions on pages 312–13 of Chapter 13.)

Using Supporting Ideas and Details in Body Paragraphs

You have learned that you can use many types of **elaboration,** or details, within a paragraph. The same is true within the body paragraphs of an essay. The chart below shows some of these options.

Meets ISAT Standards
1.B.3d
1.C.3f
3.A.3
3.B.3a
3.C.3a

Types of Detail That Can Be Used for Elaboration within Essays

- Analogies
- Anecdotes
- Causes
- Comparisons/contrasts
- Descriptions/sensory details
- Effects
- Events
- Facts
- Figures of speech
- Illustrations/examples
- Negations
- Opinions
- Paraphrases
- Qualifications
- Quotations
- Reasons
- Statistics
- Summaries

Introduction, Body, and Conclusion

Introduction, Body, and Conclusion

For a test like the ISAT for Writing, you may have to write essays based on material in selections that you have read or to which you have listened. In such cases, the body paragraphs of your writing must contain evidence from the selections. This evidence can take the form of **direct quotations**. Direct quotations should be placed in quotation marks (see "Incorporating Quotations in Your Writing," below and on pages 159–60). Your evidence can also be in the form of paraphrases or summaries. When you **paraphrase,** you restate an idea or a passage in your own words. When you **summarize,** you restate an idea in fewer words.

For example, a body paragraph in the essay about birds might have included evidence in the form of a quotation. It might also have used paraphrase and summary:

> Professor Ricardo Ortega is a scientist at our local university. I asked him how birds navigate. He told me that there is still some mystery about bird migration. Flying over the water at night, for example, seems to require some special navigation ability. "One theory is that the birds are able to navigate by orienting themselves to the Earth's magnetic field," Professor Ortega said.

To incorporate direct quotations into your writing, follow these guidelines:

Incorporating Quotations into Your Writing

1. Use quotation marks around direct quotations but not around paraphrases.
2. Sometimes you may wish to leave out some of the words within a quotation. Use an ellipsis (. . .) to indicate any words that are missing.
3. Use a period followed by an ellipsis (. . . .) when omitting material after a complete sentence.
4. Always use a comma to set off a speaker's tags in dialogue. **Speaker's tags** include all expressions like *he says* or *she replies.*
5. Periods and commas at the end of quotations always go within the quotation marks. Other punctuation marks go outside. These include colons, semicolons, question marks, and exclamation points. If the punctuation mark is part of a quotation, it should appear within the quotation marks.
6. To quote more than one line from a poem, use a slash mark (/). Put spaces on either side of the slash to separate the lines. Capitalize the quotation exactly as in the source.

334 AIM Higher! ISAT Language Arts Review

Your Turn

Exercise A In the space below, create a graphic organizer to gather ideas and information for your essay. You may use one of the graphic-organizer formats shown in Chapter 4, "Picture This! Notetaking and Graphic Organizers."

Meets ISAT
Standards
1.B.3d
1.C.3f
3.A.3
3.B.3a
5.B.3b

Introduction, Body, and Conclusion

Your Turn

Exercise B Based on the information from your graphic organizer, make a rough outline of the body paragraphs of your essay by filling in the outline below.

Body ¶1 Topic: _____

_____

—Supporting detail: _____

_____

—Supporting detail: _____

_____

—Supporting detail: _____

_____

Body ¶2 Topic: _____

_____

—Supporting detail: _____

_____

—Supporting detail: _____

_____

—Supporting detail: _____

_____

Body ¶3 Topic: _____

—Supporting detail: _____

_____

—Supporting detail: _____

_____

—Supporting detail: _____

_____

Meets ISAT
Standards
3.A.3
3.B.3a
3.B.3b
3.C.3a
5.C.3c

Exercise C Review the rough outline you created for the previous exercise. Make sure that your ideas are presented in the most logical order. Then, on your own paper, draft the body paragraphs of your essay. Next, revise and proofread those paragraphs using the checklists on pages 265–66 and 270.

Introduction, Body, and Conclusion 337

Introduction, Body, and Conclusion

Writing the Conclusion

There are many ways of concluding an essay. In a conclusion, aim to give the reader a satisfying sense of an ending. The chart below shows some possible strategies for concluding an essay.

Strategies for Concluding an Essay

1. Restate the thesis in different words. Summarize the main ideas presented to support the thesis.

2. Restate the thesis. Call attention to its importance or interest.

3. Relate the thesis to the reader's life or to some broader context.

4. Call on the reader to adopt some belief or to take some action related to the thesis.

5. Tie together any loose ends.

6. Briefly touch on the consequences of what was discussed in the essay.

Sometimes writers end an essay with their last point. Sometimes they end with the final event they want to describe. This kind of ending without a formal conclusion is especially common in nonfiction narrative writing. This kind of ending is also commonly found in newspaper stories. When you write for an examination, do not end your essays in this way. The scorer will be looking for a formal conclusion.

A conclusion begins with a transition. The transition signals that the essay is about to end. Examples of such transitions include *In conclusion, In summary, As the preceding paragraphs show, Finally, Thus,* or *As we have seen.*

Here is an example of a concluding paragraph from an informative essay. The essay discusses stamp collecting. The rest of the essay deals with how to start and maintain a stamp collection. In the concluding paragraph, the author shifts the focus to the reader and calls upon the reader to take an action:

> In summary, stamp collecting can give you hours of fun. It can teach you about geography, history, and foreign cultures. Trading stamps and exchanging information can also help you to make new friends. Next time you see a colorful stamp, why not make it Exhibit No. 1 in your new stamp album?

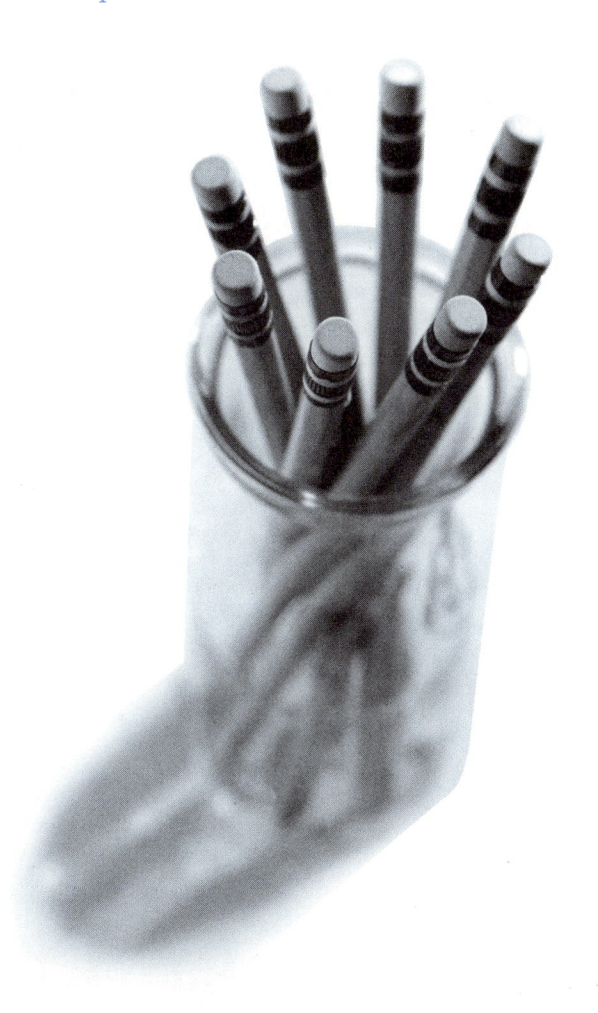

This concluding paragraph comes from a persuasive essay. The essay argues against censorship by school administrators of articles in student newspapers. Notice how the writer concludes her essay by restating the thesis (in the first sentence) and then summarizes the main ideas from the body of the essay.

> In summary, censorship by administrators of school newspapers should be avoided for several reasons. First, such censorship in the form of prior restraint is inconsistent with democratic principles. Second, such censorship shifts responsibility for content from students to administrators and thus interferes with the learning of responsibility. Third, such censorship decreases the diversity of speech within the school, silencing some voices that perhaps should be heard.

Meets ISAT
Standards
1.B.3d
1.C.3f
3.A.3
3.B.3a
3.C.3a

Introduction, Body, and Conclusion

Your Turn

Meets ISAT Standards
3.A.3
3.B.3a
3.B.3b
3.C.3a

Exercise On the lines below, draft the concluding paragraph of your essay. Next, revise and proofread your conclusion. Finally, put all the pieces of your essay together to create a final draft using the checklists on pages 265–66 and 270.

Return to the exercises at the beginning of the chapter, revise your work as necessary, and submit the exercises to your teacher for grading.

Chapter 15
Stylin'
Voice and Style in Writing

Photo courtesy of NASA/JPL/Caltech.
This is a composite image and is not to scale.

First Encounter

Read these two articles about Europa, a moon of Jupiter. Then try your hand at the exercises that follow. You will not be graded on the exercises at this time. At the end of the chapter, you will be directed to return to these exercises to revise and correct your work.

Moonstruck Scientists Eye Europa

by Robin Lamb

Everyone—even the most unimaginative, dull-witted person among us—has at some time looked up at the night sky and wondered, "Are we alone in the universe?" or "Is there intelligent life out there?" (When I read the papers in the morning, I sometimes wonder if there's intelligent life down here, but that's another story.) Europa, one of the moons of Jupiter, might help us to answer the first of those questions. We may well share our solar system with little, squiggly ocean-dwelling aliens.

When we look into the night sky, we see one moon. If you could stand on Jupiter (which you can't, because it's made of gas), and could look up at the night sky (which you couldn't, because the atmosphere is too thick), you would see sixteen moons. How's that for unfair? We get one. Jupiter gets sixteen. Go figure.

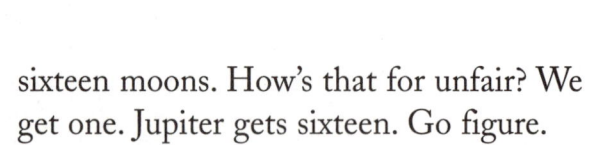

At any rate, the four largest of Jupiter's moons are called the Galilean satellites. That's because about four hundred years ago (in 1610, to be exact), Galileo Galilei turned what was then a new-fangled invention—the telescope—on Jupiter. In those days, people thought that the planets were stuck (sort of like raisins in a plum pudding) into crystal spheres that revolved around the Earth. What Galileo saw blew that view to smithereens. He saw four moons circling Jupiter like flies around a rotting peach. Galileo called his moons the "Medicean stars" because (being no fool) he hoped to win the favor (not to mention the money!) of the Medici, a fabulously wealthy and powerful family of Renaissance fat cats.

The third largest of the four Galilean moons of Jupiter, Europa is almost the same size as our own beloved near-Earth companion, lovely Luna. Although our moon and Europa could be mistaken for twin sisters, anyone could see at a glance that Europa is the cold one. In fact, the whole surface of Europa is covered with ice. What makes scientists excited enough to conga around their laboratories shaking their TI 30 scientific calculators is what may lie beneath all that ice. Many believe that the Europa's icy blanket covers a vast submerged ocean.

A few years ago, scientists discovered on Earth, way down in the deepest part of the ocean, a whole culture of living things—strange giant tubeworms and weird crustaceans—that get their energy entirely from heat released through cracks in the sea floor. Some scientists believe that on Europa, in the ocean under the ice, there may exist living creatures that get their energy in the same way. For that reason, NASA is planning expeditions to Europa to drill beneath the surface and take a peek.

Now, here's the interesting thing: Where you find water, you find life. It is well known, for example, that around 70 percent of our bodies is made up of water (and, in my case, diet soda). Ponds, creeks, rivers, streams, oceans, and even rain puddles—all are teeming with microorganisms (or "low life," as I like to call them). Advertisers love to remind Americans that even the water in the toilet bowl has living things in it!

I know what you're thinking: Those NASA scientists are just a bunch of loons like the people who think that little green men are drawing gangland symbols in the wheat fields of Kansas and Yorkshire.[1] But consider this: On Earth, buried in frozen glaciers in Antarctica, we have found—well, I haven't exactly looked myself, but you know what I mean—we human beings who go traipsing around Antarctic glaciers and those of us who read

---

[1] **Yorkshire.** Section of northern England

Voice and Style in Writing

First Encounter

about people who do that kind of thing—we have found microorganisms. That's right—we've found creatures living inside glaciers, and those little guys actually like it when the temperature hovers around, say, minus four degrees Fahrenheit.

Interestingly, one of the biggest lakes on Earth—Lake Vostok, in Antarctica—is also completely sealed under ice, and scientists are now debating whether to drill into pristine Lake Vostok to release a small robot submarine. This remote-controlled device would swim around, looking for microorganisms, as practice for a mission to Jupiter's frozen moon.

When Galileo dared to suggest that the planets did not revolve around the Earth, he was placed under house arrest. People didn't like the idea of humans not being the center of celestial attention. Wouldn't it be ironic if the next blow to our oversized egos turned out to be that one of the Galilean moons of Jupiter, Europa, harbored life? Me, I'm ready to believe it does, but then, like most human beings, I'm ready to believe any improbable thing, as long as it brings me pleasure to think it. In fact, if scientists do discover microbugs on Europa, I want to be among the first to meet them. I imagine putting them in a cooler, down in the water under the ice and the diet soda, and carrying them off to the park with me. "What do you have in the cooler?" people would ask. "Nothing much," I'd say. "Just some diet soda and some aliens."

Europa: Sixth Moon of the Jovian System[2]

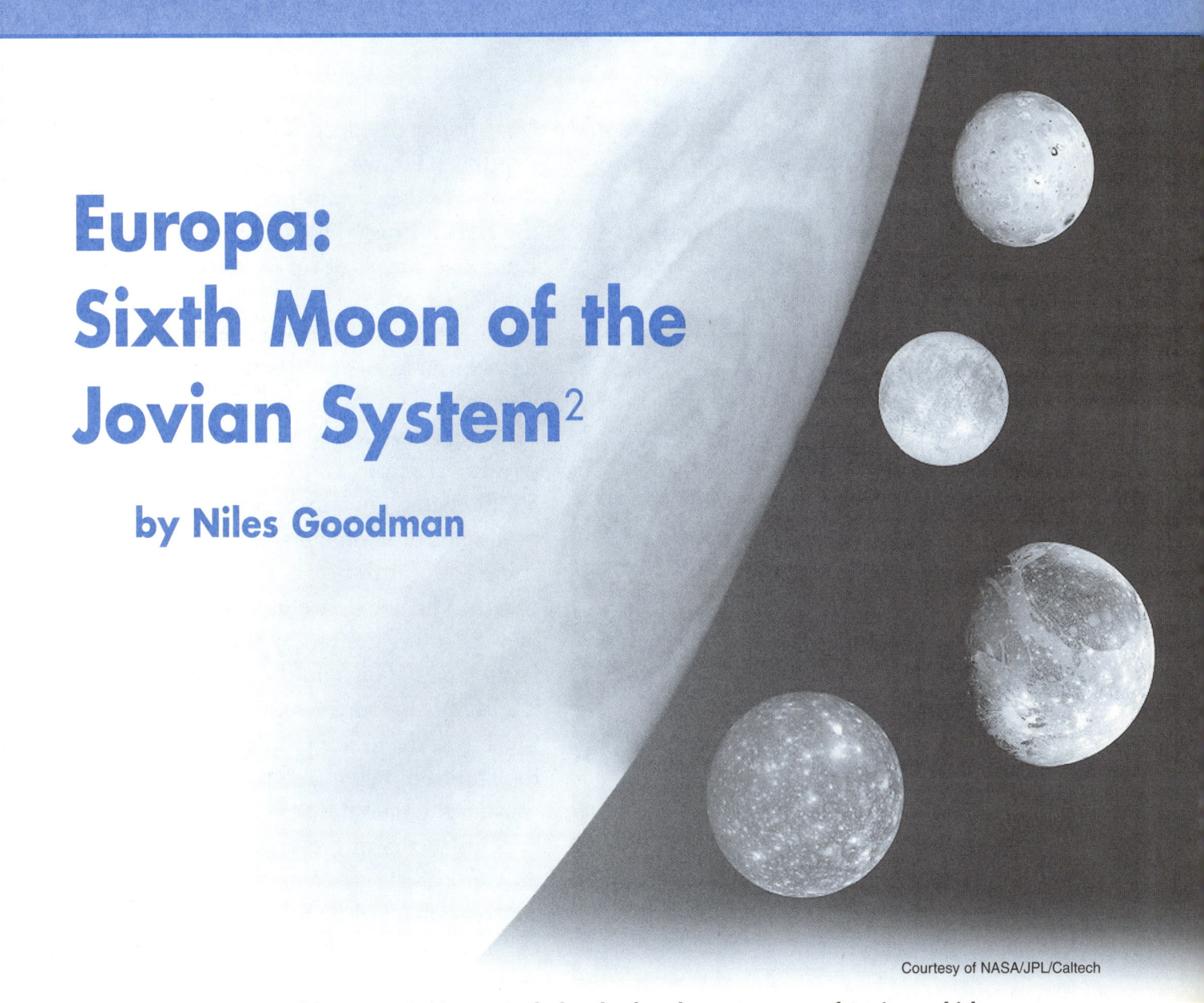

by Niles Goodman

This composite image includes the four largest moons of Jupiter, which are known as the Galilean satellites. From top to bottom, the moons shown are Io, Europa, Ganymede, and Callisto. Source: NASA, Jet Propulsion Laboratory.

Europa is a moon of the planet Jupiter. It is one of the Galilean satellites, as the four largest moons of Jupiter are called. These four moons were discovered in 1610 by Galileo Galilei, who originally christened them the "Medicean stars" in order to attract the attention of the Medici, a wealthy family whose patronage he hoped to receive.

Jupiter has sixteen recognized moons. Europa is the sixth-farthest moon from Jupiter. It is the second of the Galilean moons, after Io. The other two Galilean moons, Ganymede and Callisto, are farther out and about twice as large as Europa.

Europa's diameter is slightly less than that of the Earth's moon, but Europa is about five times as bright. Europa's mass is

---

[2] **Jovian System.** Jupiter and its moons. Jove and Jupiter were alternate names for the chief of the gods of ancient Rome.

First Encounter

about 66 percent that of the Earth's moon. Europa orbits Jupiter approximately once every three and a half Earth days.

Analysis of Europa's surface suggests that the moon is covered in ice. This ice sheath may be roughly 60 miles (close to 100 kilometers) deep, although the exact depth is unknown. The density of Europa is close to the average density of rocks in the Earth's crust. This fact suggests that Europa is a mass of rock covered with a large sheet of ice.

The surface of Europa is extraordinarily flat. No surface feature is taller than 1 kilometer. The surface of Europa is marked by large, criss-crossed streaks. These streaks vary from 12 to 24 miles (19 to 39 kilometers) in width. Some are thousands of kilometers in length. The streaks appear to be cracks in the ice sheath. The cracks are most likely caused by tidal forces exerted by the gravity of Jupiter, which tugs on the ice, deforming it and causing portions to break away. Once two sheets are pulled apart, water rises up from below and then freezes, causing the moon's streaked appearance.

This theory of the origins of the streaks on Europa's surface remains somewhat controversial. Future missions to Europa are planned to resolve this question, to determine the extent and exact nature of Europa's subsurface ocean, and to explore the subsurface ocean for signs of biological activity.

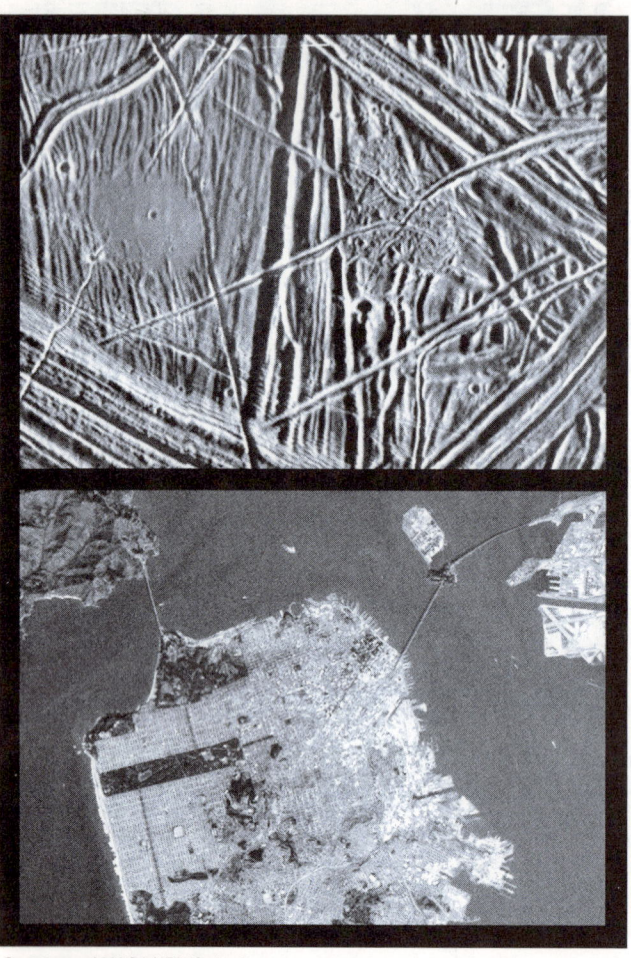

Courtesy of NASA/JPL/Caltech

A comparison of an area on Jupiter's moon Europa (top frame) to the San Francisco Bay area of California (bottom frame). Both images show areas of equal size, 13 by 18 kilometers (8 by 11 miles), and equal resolution, 26 meters (28 yards). North is to the top of the picture. In the close-up view of Europa's icy surface (top photo), a flat smooth area about 3.2 kilometers (2 miles) across is seen in the left part of the picture. This area resulted from flooding by a fluid which erupted onto the surface and buried sets of ridges and grooves. The smooth area contrasts with a distinctly rugged patch of terrain farther east, to the right of the prominent ridge system running down the middle of the picture. Eruptions of material onto the surface, crustal disruption, and the formation of complex networks of folded and faulted ridges show that significant energy was available in the interior of Europa. Source: NASA, Jet Propulsion Laboratory.

Your Turn

Exercise A Think about the two selections that you have just read. Answer the following questions on the lines provided. Use complete sentences.

1. An adjective is a word that modifies, or describes, a noun. What adjectives would you use to describe the first selection? What adjectives would you use to describe the second selection?

   _____
   _____
   _____

2. In your opinion, which selection is more interesting? Why?

   _____
   _____
   _____

3. Which selection do you think might appear in a factbook or encyclopedia? Which one might appear in a popular magazine?

   _____
   _____

4. Every piece of writing has strengths and weaknesses. What are the strengths and weaknesses of the first selection?

   _____
   _____
   _____
   _____

5. What are the strengths and weaknesses of the second selection?

   _____
   _____
   _____

Meets ISAT Standards
1.A.3a
1.B.3c
1.B.3d
1.C.3a
1.C.3c
1.C.3d
1.C.3e
2.A.3a
2.A.3c
2.A.3d
2.B.3a
5.A.3a
5.B.3a

Voice and Style in Writing

Your Turn

Exercise B Discuss your answers to Exercise A with other students in your class. Afterward, write a brief essay that compares and contrasts the two selections. First, make a rough outline in the space below. Then, on your own paper, write a draft of your essay. Evaluate your draft using the Revision Checklist on pages 265–66. After revising your essay, proofread it using the Proofreading Checklist on page 270. Finally, make a clean final copy to submit to your teacher.

Voice and Style in Writing

Stylin'

When a friend calls you on the telephone, how long does it take you to recognize his or her voice? Usually, all it takes is a single word, "hello." Those two syllables are all your mind needs to tell whether the voice belongs to a friend from school or to a "friend" from some company's telemarketing department.

A spoken voice is as unique as a fingerprint. So is the sound of an essay or story or poem by a skilled writer. The unique sound of a piece of writing is its **voice.** The collection of writing techniques that contribute to creating a particular voice is called **style.** Think about the differences between the two selections at the beginning of this chapter. Both deal with the same subject—a moon of Jupiter called Europa. They sound completely different, however. They differ in their voice and style.

Every piece of writing has a voice. One piece of writing might sound dry and impersonal, as though it were written by a machine. Another might sound quirky and unique, as though a particularly colorful, interesting person were speaking directly to you. The former voice might be appropriate for, say, a scientific paper. The latter might be appropriate for a light-hearted column in a newspaper or magazine.

Almost always, when you write, you will want to hold the attention of your reader. To do that, you should usually try to write in a voice that is individual—a voice that sounds as though some unique human being produced it. That is, you should strive to write in your own unique voice. Achieving a voice of your own in your writing is not something that will happen immediately. A good writer typically works for years to develop his or her voice. This chapter, however, will give you some specific tips that will help you to develop a writing style and voice of your own.

Different Voices for Different Audiences and Purposes

When people write, they do so for various audiences and purposes. For example, a singer/songwriter might create a song for children that has two purposes—to entertain and to teach kids how to multiply. A speechwriter might create a speech for a senator that will be delivered to an audience of citizens and soldiers from the National Guard at the dedication of a memorial park. Obviously, the two writers would use language in different ways. The first writer might use short, concrete

---

Meets ISAT Standards
1.B.3d
1.C.3a
1.C.3c
1.C.3d
1.C.3e
2.A.3a
2.A.3d
2.B.3a
3.A.3
3.B.3a
3.B.3b
3.C.3a

Voice and Style in Writing

words; simple sentences; and informal language. The second might use abstract words like *peace* and *honor,* longer sentences, and highly formal language. When you write, you should always consider your audience and purpose and choose your language accordingly.

Elements of Voice: Level, or Register

One of the elements that affects the voice of a piece of writing—its overall sound—is its **level,** or **register.** Language that is relaxed, casual, and suitable for everyday use among friends is known as **informal language.** Language that is more ceremonial, strict in its observance of rules, and suitable for public occasions is known as **formal language.** Consider this example: A woman named Alicia Boudreau owns two poodles, is mother to a six-month-old girl, belongs to the local Chamber of Commerce, and is the director of the customer service department of a large business. Here are some samples of her speech, taken at different times and in different circumstances:

Occasion/Audience	Sample of Ms. B's Speech
Talking to her dogs	"Shoo! Off the couch! Baaad doggies!"
Talking to her baby	"Ooh, do you like bouncing on the couch? Yes you do, sweetie. Yes you doooo."
Speaking with her boss at the department store	"Perhaps we should consider not putting up the holiday window displays until after Thanksgiving."
Addressing fellow members at a Chamber of Commerce luncheon	"In a few short months, we have seen enormous improvements in the general economic vitality of the downtown area."

When Ms. Boudreau talks to her dogs or to her baby, she uses very informal language. When she speaks with her boss, whom she knows well, she uses semiformal language. When she addresses other members of the Chamber of Commerce at a luncheon, she uses highly formal language. The level, or register, of her speech changes depending on the circumstances.

One expert in language divides language use into the categories shown in the following chart:

The Levels of Standard American English

SPOKEN	WRITTEN	
Oratorical	Formal	Edited English
Planned		
Impromptu	Semiformal	
Casual	Informal	
Intimate		

- Oratorical, Planned: (no bracket label on spoken side beyond these)
- Impromptu, Casual, Intimate: Conversational (Colloquial) Levels

Source: Kenneth G. Wilson. *The Columbia Guide to Standard American English.* New York: Columbia University Press, 1993.

Voice and Style in Writing **351**

Voice and Style in Writing

Here are some examples of spoken English at each level:

Type of Language	Occasion/Audience	Example
Intimate	Private speech to loved one	"Hey, honey."
Casual	Ordinary speech to friends/acquaintances	"What's up, people?"
Impromptu	Off-the-cuff speech to a group	"Greetings, everyone, and thank you."
Planned	A planned speech in a semiformal situation	"Good afternoon, ladies and gentlemen."
Oratorical	A planned speech in a formal situation	"On behalf of myself and of the other members of the wedding party, I would like to welcome you on this joyous occasion."

As you have learned in earlier chapters in this book, whenever you write for a class or for a test, you need to edit (that is, to revise and proofread) your work. Edited English of the kind that you do for school should tend toward the formal end of the language spectrum. Here are some characteristics that distinguish formal and informal speech and writing:

Informal language contains...	Formal language contains...
contractions such as *didn't* and *wasn't*.	few, if any, contractions.
shorter, simpler sentences.	longer, more complex sentences.
common, familiar words.	less common words.
exclamation marks and dashes.	few, if any, exclamation marks and dashes.
sentences beginning with coordinating conjunctions like *but* or *and*.	no sentences that begin with coordinating conjunctions.
fewer transitions such as *therefore* and *however*.	more transitions such as *therefore* and *however*.
idioms like *pulling my leg* and *a far cry*.	fewer idioms and no slang.

Your Turn

Exercise A *The following is an example of informal language from a letter written by a student to a friend. Rewrite the passage, on the lines provided, to make it appropriate for a formal essay.*

Meets ISAT
Standards
1.A.3b
1.B.3d
1.C.3f
2.A.3a
2.A.3c
2.A.3d
3.B.3b
3.C.3a
4.B.3a

> So I went kayaking with Jake and Amanda last Saturday. Kayaking was a rush! We started off in the bay—you know, in Folly Cove, near our house. I would've been happy staying right there. But Jake, being the macho kind of guy he is, zoomed out toward the open ocean. The wind was stiff, and I was shiverin' like crazy! And the water was totally choppy. I had to kind of shift and shake my body so that I didn't wipe out and look like a total doofus. I did OK, but I still flipped over a couple of times. Good thing I had my life vest on!

Voice and Style in Writing

Your Turn

Exercise B Imagine that you work for Arkright's Copy Center, a photocopy store. One of the other employees has written some copy for an ad that will appear in a local newspaper. The owner of the store has brought the copy to you. She thinks that it sounds too stuffy and formal. She asks you to rewrite it so that it sounds more casual, informal, and friendly. Read the copy. Then rewrite it on the lines provided to make it more informal.

> Arkright's Copy Center, located at 24 Cabot Street, in Hazelton, seeks to provide quality service to all those who enter the facility. The Copy Center has served the community of Hazelton proudly for twenty-three years, in which time it has assisted over 300,000 people with their photocopying needs. The Copy Center also provides twelve computer workstations and both black-and-white and color laser printers for those who have computational needs but do not themselves possess the necessary equipment.

Voice and Style in Writing

Elements of Voice: Word Choice, or Diction

A typical unabridged dictionary of English contains around 600,000 words. Indeed, English is the largest known language in the world. What that means is that people who write and speak English have lots of choices. One of the most important factors influencing the voice, or sound, of a piece of writing is **word choice**, or **diction**. Good writers make their work come alive by choosing words that are vivid, colorful, precise, and concrete. Consider this sentence:

> The children ran from beneath the tall, thin legs of the swing set.

Notice how much more emotionally engaging and powerful the sentence is with some minor changes in word choice:

IMPROVED DICTION: The kids scampered from beneath the gleaming silver legs of the swing set.

IMPROVED DICTION: The two brats scurried from beneath the rickety, spiderlike legs of the old swing set.

In the first sentence above, the bland word *children* was replaced by *kids*, which is more light-hearted and informal. The bland verb *ran* was replaced by a vivid verb, *scampered*; and the bland adjectives *tall* and *thin* were replaced by *gleaming* and *silver*. These changes help to create a bright, cheery voice. In the second sentence, *children* became *two brats*; *ran* became *scurried*; and *tall* and *thin* became *rickety* and *spiderlike*. Notice how these simple changes in diction can change the voice (including the mood and tone) of a piece of writing to something sinister.

Word Choice: Formal and Informal Words

After running hard, do you have *perspiration* on your face, or is it *sweat*? Does your family have a *canine companion* or a *pooch*? The words that you choose when writing help to determine how formal your writing is. If you want to change the voice of a piece of writing so that it is more or less formal, one of the easiest things to do is to vary your choice of words.

Meets ISAT Standards
1.A.3b
1.B.3d
1.C.3f
2.A.3a
2.A.3c
2.A.3d
3.B.3b
3.C.3a
4.B.3a

Voice and Style in Writing

Here are some examples of words that are formal, along with **synonyms** (words similar in meaning) that are less formal:

Formal Words and Less Formal Synonyms

More formal	Less formal
Elevate	Boost
Brawl, melee, riot	Fight
Immaculate	Clean
Opaque, obscure	Dim, murky
Expunge	Erase, wipe out
Anticipate	Expect
Covetous	Jealous
Falsehood, fabrication, untruth	Lie, fib
Assembly	Pack, bunch
Courageous, intrepid, valiant	Plucky, brave
Perilous	Risky
Maxim, adage, motto, aphorism	Saying
Magnitude	Size
Minor	Small, unimportant
Perspiration	Sweat

Word Choice: Slang

Very informal language often contains slang words and phrases. **Slang** is extremely casual language that is often playful and irreverent. Slang terms are usually associated with particular groups of people, such as teenagers, surfers, or motorcyclists. For example, the word *hog* is a slang term used by motorcyclists to refer to a particular brand of motorbike. By using slang, groups of people can define themselves as different from other groups in society. Slang terms tend to come into and out of style very quickly. In the 1920s, teenagers used slang terms like *twenty-three skidoo* for "leave" and *the bee's knees* for "great." Few people use these terms today except for comic effect. Think about that the next time you *front like you have juice*.

356 **AIM Higher! ISAT Language Arts Review**

If you do not know what that last sentence means, have a look at this list of slang terms that were recently popular among teenagers in some parts of the United States:

Popular Teen Slang Terms in U.S. Urban Areas, circa A.D. 2000–2001

Slang Term	Meaning
benjamins	money
the bomb	great, excellent
dis	show disrespect
flavor	style, finesse
to front	to pretend
got a handle	have good control (of a basketball)
hang with me	keep up with me, compete with me
ice	jewelry
iced out	fancy
to juke	to fake out
juice	connections, power
phat	great, excellent
played out	not in style
props	signs of respect
ride	car
to serve, to school	to defeat or humiliate
wack	corny, bad, stupid

Generally speaking, slang is not appropriate for formal writing, as in school reports and essays written for examinations. Slang can be used, however, in journals and diaries, or for comic effect in humorous pieces, and, on occasion, in dialogue. When used appropriately, slang in dialogue can make a character seem more authentic. Some slang terms, like *hang out* and *cool*, widely used in the 1950s and 1960s, have remarkable longevity. Many, however, are *played out* very quickly and will cause a piece of writing to become dated in a very short time.

Jargon and Gobbledygook

Closely related to slang is **jargon**—words and phrases associated with particular fields of human activity. Every field has its jargon.

Meets ISAT Standards
1.A.3b
1.B.3d
1.C.3f
2.A.3a
2.A.3c
2.A.3d
3.B.3b
3.C.3a
4.B.3a

Voice and Style in Writing

Voice and Style in Writing

Here are some examples of jargon words and phrases from various fields:

> ### Examples of Jargon
>
> COMPUTERS: algorithm, CPU (central processing unit), debug, input, JPEG (Joint Photographic Experts' Group file format), LAN (local-area network), massively parallel, multitasking, output, peripheral, pixel, processor, RAM (random-access memory), systems analyst, terabyte, WYSIWYG (What You See Is What You Get)
>
> EDUCATION: behavioral objective, benchmark, cognitive development, constructivism, correlation, criterion-referenced assessment, facilitate, higher-order thinking skills, IEP (individualized education plan), multiple intelligences, pedagogy, performance objective, portfolio, rubric, scaffolding, scope and sequence, zone of proximal development
>
> BASEBALL: balk, bullpen, bunt, change-up, double, dugout, ERA (earned-run average), fair, fly, foul, grounder, line drive, RBIs (runs batted in), slider, stealing, strike, walk
>
> SAILING: aft, avast, boom, come about, foc's'le, galley, gunwale, halyard, hatch, helm, jib, keel, mizzen, port, sheet, spar, spinnaker, starboard, tack, winch, yawl

Like slang, a little bit of jargon can add realism to a piece of writing. Jargon needs to be used with restraint, however: As with hot pepper sauce, a little bit can add some spice, but too much will ruin everything. When jargon gets overused, the writing becomes difficult to understand. This is when jargon becomes gobbledygook. **Gobbledygook** is bad writing that people produce when they are trying to sound important or knowledgeable. Gobbledygook uses a lot of jargon; overuses forms of the verb *to be* (such as *is, am, was,* and *were*); and contains long, unnecessarily complicated sentences. Consider this old saying:

Beauty is only skin deep.

Here is the same idea expressed in gobbledygook:

Objectively considered, the conclusion to which one is inescapably drawn by consideration of the phenomenon of physical attraction is that the attraction, itself, is merely a matter of perceived superficial appearance lacking both substance and deeper intrinsic meaning or, indeed, reality.

Of course, jargon is perfectly appropriate in the right circumstance. If you are writing a paper for English class, you might want to use some of the jargon of literary study, such as *foreshadowing* and *metaphor*. Generally speaking, however, you should use jargon sparingly. When you use jargon, you should define any terms that might not be understood by your audience.

Word Choice: Choosing Precise Action Verbs

There are two kinds of verbs. **Linking verbs,** like *is, am, are, was, were, seem,* and *become,* are verbs that connect other words, as in these examples:

Maria *is* class president.

Maria *is* intelligent and capable. She is also well liked.

She *seems* happy.

Action verbs are words like *fly* and *jump* that name actions.

Writers can make their work more lively and interesting by rewriting sentences to replace linking verbs with action verbs.

DULL SENTENCES: Maria *is* class president. Maria *is* intelligent. She *is* also well liked.

BETTER: The teachers and students all *love* Maria, our incredibly intelligent and capable class president.

As children, we all learn a few verbs that we use over and over for the rest of our lives. Here's a list of common ones:

Meets ISAT Standards
1.A.3a
1.B.3d
1.C.3e
2.A.3a
2.A.3d
3.B.3b

Common Action Verbs

To ask	To get	To learn	To read	To teach
To begin	To give	To leave	To rest	To tell
To believe	To go	To let	To ride	To think
To bring	To have	To like	To run	To throw
To buy	To hear	To live	To say	To try
To call	To help	To look	To see	To turn
To catch	To hold	To love	To show	To wake
To come	To hope	To make	To stand	To walk
To do	To hurt	To move	To start	To wish
To dream	To jump	To need	To stay	To work
To eat	To keep	To place	To stop	
To find	To kill	To play	To take	
To follow	To know	To put	To talk	

Voice and Style in Writing

Voice and Style in Writing

There is nothing wrong with these verbs. They are all acceptable. As we grow older, however, we learn many more precise verbs. Often, you can make a sentence more vivid and interesting by replacing a vague, common, simple, bland action verb with one that is more colorful and precise.

Here are some examples:

Choosing More Colorful Action Verbs

Bland Action Verbs	Colorful, Precise Action Verbs
said	alleged, allowed, bellowed, chortled, claimed, countered, demanded, grunted, guffawed, insisted, pleaded, prayed, ranted, respond, retorted, screamed, snickered, suggested, whispered, wondered
walked, moved	crept, dashed, departed, exited, flew, galloped, high-tailed, hobbled, leaped, moseyed, paced, raced, sailed, sauntered, shuffled, skated, slinked, sneaked, sprang, sprinted, stole, tiptoed, tore, wandered, zipped

By choosing more colorful action verbs, you can not only make your writing more interesting but also pack a lot of meaning into a small space. Consider these sentences:

"Watch out for the dog," she said.

"Watch out for the dog!" she screamed.

"Watch out for the dog," she whispered.

Each would be appropriate in a different situation. The second sentence might be appropriate if you are describing someone who sees that someone else is in danger of being attacked by a dog or that a dog is about to run in front of a car. The third example might be appropriate in a situation in which the dog is sleeping or in which the speaker is warning someone about a guard dog that is resting nearby.

Word Choice: Using Precise Nouns

As you probably already know, a **noun** is something that names a person, place, thing, or idea. As with verbs, some nouns are more colorful, interesting, and precise than others. Whenever possible, try to use specific nouns to make your writing come alive.

Meets ISAT Standards
1.A.3a
1.B.3d
1.C.3e
2.A.3a
2.A.3d
3.B.3b

Choosing More Colorful Nouns

Bland Nouns	Colorful, Precise Nouns
person	adventurer, being, bellhop, bruiser, bully, character, colleague, creature, friend, helper, joker, pal, savior, sergeant-at-arms, trainer, undertaker, waif, weasel, writer
child, young person	adolescent, baby, infant, kid, little one, newborn, preschooler, rug rat, teen, teenager, toddler, tot, whippersnapper

Notice the different effects of word choice in the following sentences:

Some young people were moving through the crowd.

Some young hooligans were shoving their way through the crowd.

Again, choosing precise, colorful words can make a big difference!

A **thesaurus** is a reference work that you can use to look up synonyms, or alternative words. Word processing programs often have thesauruses built into them. When writing a paper for class or when writing for yourself, you can use a thesaurus to look up interesting alternative verbs and nouns.

Of course, you cannot look up words when writing for a test. As you reread your answer, however, you can look for opportunities to replace dull or vague words with more interesting, precise ones.

Voice and Style in Writing

Your Turn

Exercise A *Circle the more formal of each pair of words below.*

1. leave   depart
2. devious   crafty
3. assessment   test
4. hi   greetings
5. supplement   add to

Exercise B *The following is some dialogue from a science fiction story, set in the future, about a robot attempting to teach a child how to play with a Frisbee. Read the dialogue. Then, on the lines below, describe the robot's speech, and explain why the communication between the robot and child is not working.*

"So, what should I do?" asked Amanda.

"It's very simple, really," replied Floyd the Android. "Using the muscles around the radius and ulna, simply generate enough tangential velocity to propel the extruded plastic disc on a vector that I can intersect."

"Huh?"

"And in situations involving low pressure atmospheric fronts like those currently present, be mindful of shifts in wind speed and direction that can cause disruptions in the desired flight vector."

Exercise C The following is a sentence that uses jargon from the field of psychology. Look up the italicized words in a dictionary and record their meaning on the lines provided. Then rewrite the passage, on the lines provided below, using ordinary language. The first one has been done for you.

Meets ISAT Standards
1.A.3a
1.A.3b
1.C.3c
1.C.3d
2.B.3a
3.B.3a

> Ms. D. *presented with* the following *symptoms: depression, intermittent auditory hallucinations,* and *chronic fatigue.*

1. presented with *showed or displayed signs of* _____
2. symptoms _____
3. depression _____
4. intermittent _____
5. auditory _____
6. hallucinations _____
7. chronic _____
8. fatigue _____
9. Rewrite the passage without jargon here:

   _____
   _____
   _____
   _____
   _____

Voice and Style in Writing **363**

Your Turn

Exercise D The following passages are written in gobbledygook. Draw arrows to match each passage to the traditional saying that has the same meaning.

1. Act in accordance with your own subjective experience and in such a manner as not to compromise your personal integrity and sense of identity and wholeness.

2. Constrain your behavior to activity such that its impact upon others is like that which you would wish to have reciprocated.

3. Studies have shown conclusively that regular consumption of certain produce, such as *Malus sylvestris*, is positively correlated with decreased need for medical intervention.

a. Do unto others as you would have them do unto you.

b. An apple a day keeps the doctor away.

c. Be true to yourself.

Exercise E The following are some very short passages from plays by William Shakespeare, who lived and wrote in the late 1500s and early 1600s. Rewrite each passage using contemporary slang. Make sure, however, not to use any slang that is inappropriate for discussion in a classroom.

1. From a speech by Marc Anthony after the murder of Julius Cæsar:

> "Friends, Romans, countrymen, lend me your ears!
> I come to bury Cæsar, not to praise him.
> The evil that men do lives after them,
> The good is oft interred with their bones;
> So let it be with Cæsar."

_____
_____
_____
_____

AIM Higher! ISAT Language Arts Review

2. The two characters Romeo and Juliet come from families that are feuding with one another. They meet briefly at a party and fall in love. Later, Juliet is standing on a balcony of her home, speaking to herself. She is unaware that Romeo is hiding, below, listening to what she is saying. The line "wherefore art thou Romeo?" means "why are you called Romeo?"

> "O Romeo, Romeo, wherefore art thou Romeo?
> Deny thy father and refuse thy name;
> Or, if thou wilt not, be but sworn my love,
> And I'll no longer be a Capulet."

Meets ISAT Standards
1.A.3a
1.A.3b
1.B.3c
1.C.3d
2.A.3a
2.A.3d
2.B.3a
3.B.3b

Voice and Style in Writing

Your Turn

Exercise F *The following passage contains dull, boring nouns and verbs. Rewrite the passage on the lines provided to make it more interesting. Use colorful, precise, interesting nouns and verbs instead.*

> "Listen up," said the businessperson. "What we are going to do could be considered dangerous. Still, we need to get that animal out of the building as soon as possible."
>
> "I've heard that animals like that could do bad things," said one of the people present.
>
> "Yes, you are right," said the businessperson. "Perhaps we should let someone else handle this."

Exercise G *Choose two of the common action verbs from the list on page 359. Work with a partner to brainstorm as many interesting alternatives to those words as you can. Write your list on your own paper. Then share it with your classmates.*

Voice and Style in Writing

Elements of Voice: Mood and Tone

Mood is the emotion created in the reader by a piece of writing. For example, the mood of a piece of writing can be joyful:

> My heart leaps up when I behold
> A rainbow in the sky!
>
> —William Wordsworth

A writer creates mood by choosing his or her details carefully. Imagine a writer describing the interior of a house. Consider the different moods created by choosing details like the ones in the chart below:

Using Details to Create Mood

Details Used to Describe Cheery House

The cuckoo clock in the hallway shows twelve brightly painted birds at each number. On the hour, an egg pops out and hatches.

Large bay windows throughout the house let in natural sunlight. This causes the beige carpet to glow with a golden hue.

The kitchen is green and yellow. Bright, shiny brass pots hang from the ceiling. A blue and white Chinese porcelain vase filled with bamboo shoots sits on the windowsill.

Details Used to Describe Dread House

The grandfather clock in the hallway is dusty, and the pendulum inside has broken off. All the numbers except 4 and 8 are missing from the clock face, and the hour hand is bent. The clock has an abandoned mouse nest inside it.

The blackout curtains covering every window seem to be relics of World War II. Most are black cloth, but some have faded to dark purple or turned green or gray, according to the type of mold growing on them.

The kitchen resembles a hazardous waste site. There is a mound of soggy cardboard boxes where the refrigerator should be. Shards of broken plates and glasses lie beneath the cobwebs covering the sink.

Voice and Style in Writing

Closely related to mood is tone. **Tone** is an attitude or emotion expressed by a narrator, speaker, or character in a piece of writing. The following chart describes some of the possible tones that can be used when writing or speaking:

Possibilities for Tone in Writing and Speech

Alarmed	Demanding	Gracious	Poignant
Angry	Depressing	Happy	Sad
Anxious	Disinterested	Heart-rending	Sincere
Apprehensive	Dismissing	Helpful	Snide
Ashamed	Ecstatic	Honest	Sorrowful
Bitter	Embittered	Jovial	Spiteful
Breezy	Encouraging	Matter-of-fact	Suspenseful
Cheerless	Expectant	Mortified	Unconcerned
Cheery	Exultant	Nonchalant	Unemotional
Concerned	Fearful	Obnoxious	Uninterested
Condescending	Gloomy	Opinionated	Wistful

Courtesy of NASA/JPL/Caltech

Your Turn

Exercise A Read the following opening paragraphs from Edgar Allan Poe's short story "The Tell-Tale Heart." What is the tone of the narrator? What mood does the passage create in you, the reader? Explain in a brief paragraph on the lines below.

Meets ISAT
Standards
1.B.3d
2.A.3d
2.B.3a
3.A.3
3.B.3a
3.B.3b

> TRUE!—nervous—very, very dreadfully nervous I had been and am; but why will you say that I am mad? The disease had sharpened my senses—not destroyed—not dulled them. Above all was the sense of hearing acute. I heard all things in the heaven and in the earth. I heard many things in hell. How, then, am I mad? Hearken! and observe how healthily—how calmly I can tell you the whole story.
>
> It is impossible to say how first the idea entered my brain; but once conceived, it haunted me day and night. Object there was none. Passion there was none. I loved the old man. He had never wronged me. He had never given me insult. For his gold I had no desire. I think it was his eye! yes, it was this! He had the eye of a vulture—a pale blue eye, with a film over it. Whenever it fell upon me, my blood ran cold; and so by degrees—very gradually—I made up my mind to take the life of the old man, and thus rid myself of the eye forever.

_____
_____
_____
_____
_____
_____
_____
_____
_____

Voice and Style in Writing 369

Your Turn

Exercise B Imagine that you work for a bookstore. A local school ordered fifty encyclopedias from your store. Your store shipped the books, along with a bill. Unfortunately, the bill has not been paid. An employee of the store has drafted a letter to the school. You read the letter and decide that its tone is angry and unpleasant. The letter appears below. Rewrite the letter, on the lines below, to turn it into a friendly reminder.

> Dear Principal Mehan:
>
> Three months ago, Beezleton Middle School ordered fifty copies of the *Encyclopedia of Turtle Food* from our store. We promptly shipped the books to your school, along with an invoice. Unbelievably, after over two months, that bill still has not been paid. This is an outrage! It is incredibly irresponsible for you to allow this bill to go unpaid for so long. We demand that you take immediate action to pay this bill, or we shall be forced to turn this account over to a lawyer for further action.

Exercise C *Choose one of the following topics—or one of your own—for a descriptive paragraph. Circle the topic or write your own topic in the space provided. Then, choose a mood that you would like to create with your description. Write the mood on the line provided. Next, in the chart below, list details that you can use to create that mood. Finally, write your paragraph on your own paper.*

Meets ISAT Standards
1.B.3d
2.A.3d
2.B.3a
3.A.3
3.B.3a
3.B.3b

a sunset   a carnival
a forest   a beach
a rock concert   a reptile house in a zoo

OTHER TOPIC: _____

MOOD TO BE CREATED: _____

Sensory Detail Chart

Sight	Sound	Touch	Taste	Smell

Voice and Style in Writing 371

Your Turn

Exercise D Work in a group with two or three other students. Pick five possible tones for writing from the list of choices on page 368. Next, brainstorm a writing situation in which each of the tones might be used. For example, suppose that you pick the tone "heart-rending." Here is a possible situation that might call for a heart-rending tone: A woman travels to an African country where warfare has led to massive hunger. The woman, who is a member of the Rotary Club, returns to the United States and writes a letter to her fellow club members urging them to donate money for famine relief.

1. TONE: _____

   SITUATION: _____
   _____

2. TONE: _____

   SITUATION: _____
   _____

3. TONE: _____

   SITUATION: _____
   _____

4. TONE: _____

   SITUATION: _____
   _____

5. TONE: _____

   SITUATION: _____
   _____

Voice and Style in Writing

Elements of Voice: Concreteness versus Abstractness

Concrete words describe things that can be observed using one or more of the five senses (sight, hearing, taste, touch, and smell). **Abstract words** are just the opposite. They refer to emotions, ideas, or other concepts that cannot be directly perceived. Here are some examples of abstract and concrete words:

Concrete	Abstract
warthog	freedom
tuna	living
blue sapphire	wealth
furrowed brow	worry

Generally speaking, you can give your writing a more interesting voice by using concrete details. Consider this example:

ABSTRACT: Mr. Sánchez was really upset.

CONCRETE: Mr. Sánchez snorted, stamped his feet, and threw an eraser across the room.

Here are some specific ways in which you can add concrete details:

1. **Give an example.** State the abstract idea. Then give one or more examples of it.

   The founding fathers were extremely courageous. When they signed the Declaration of Independence, they knew that in a few months they might be hauled before a British judge, condemned as traitors, and hanged.

2. **Add adjectives and participles. Adjectives** are words like *young, dark,* and *immense* that describe nouns and pronouns. **Participles** are forms of verbs, such as *jumping, broken,* and *excited,* that act like adjectives.

   DULL: The boy ran into the cave.

   MORE INTERESTING: *Excited,* the *young* boy ran into the *immense, mysterious* cave.

3. **Add an appositive or appositive phrase. Appositives** come after a noun or pronoun and identify or explain it.

   DULL: The treasure hunter knew that the map was correct.

   MORE INTERESTING: The treasure hunter, *son of the famous pirate Greenbeard and heir to the island kingdom of Anaxos,* knew that the map was correct.

4. **Add descriptive prepositional phrases or participial phrases.** A **prepositional phrase** is a group of words that begins with a preposition, such as *to, an, in, of, on,* or *for.* A **participial phrase** is a group of words that begins with a participle, such as *singing* or *shaken.*

   DULL: The boy stepped toward the chest.

   MORE INTERESTING: *Clutching the torch tightly in his fist,* the boy stepped toward the *ancient wooden* chest *at the far end of the cavern.*

Meets ISAT Standards
1.B.3d
1.C.3e
2.A.3a
2.A.3d

Your Turn

Exercise What will happen to the treasure hunter next? On the lines below, add six to eight sentences to continue the story from the previous page. Your sentences should contain concrete nouns and verbs and lots of concrete details in the form of adjectives, participles, and various kinds of phrases. Your goal is to make the scene come alive in your readers' minds.

Voice and Style in Writing

Other Elements of Voice

Voice is one of the most mysterious characteristics of writing. Almost anyone can recognize a unique, authentic voice quite easily. Describing what creates that voice, however, is not so easy because so many different elements can contribute to how a piece of writing sounds. In this chapter, you have learned how voice can be affected by choosing informal or formal words, using or avoiding jargon and slang, using precise nouns and verbs, using details that create mood, writing in a particular tone, and adding concrete words and phrases.

The following chart describes some additional elements that can contribute to creating a unique voice:

> Meets ISAT Standards
> 1.B.3d
> 1.C.3e
> 2.A.3a
> 2.A.3d
> 3.A.3

Other Elements Contributing to Voice

1. **Figures of speech.** The presence or absence of figures of speech such as metaphors, similes, and personification can affect voice greatly. Many crime novels and movies of the 1930s and 1940s had a distinctive voice created, in part, by the use of similes like this: "The detective was bug-eyed and wore a shiny coat. He looked like a fat fish dragged up in a net, confused and out of his element."

2. **Onomatopoeia. Onomatopoeia** is the use of words, like *chop, buzz, snarl,* and *whirr,* that sound like what they refer to.

3. **Length and complexity of sentences.** The American writer Ernest Hemingway was known for his use of short, simple sentences. Two other famous American writers, Henry James and William Faulkner, were known for writing sentences that were very long and complex. Choosing short, simple sentences or long, complex ones can greatly affect the voice of a piece of writing. Often, interesting effects can be created by varying the sentence structure or length. For example, you might include one simple, short sentence in the middle of a paragraph full of sentences that are fairly long.

4. **Clichés and the element of surprise.** A **cliché** is a statement that is overused and tired, such as *quiet as a mouse* or *bright, sunny day.* You can give your writing a more interesting voice by avoiding clichés. One interesting technique is to take a cliché and alter it a bit, as in *quiet as a mouse under sedation* or *bright, sunny, miserable day.* Surprising your reader is a great way to create voice.

5. **Short versus long words.** You can vary the sound of your writing considerably by deciding to use mainly short words, such as *cow* and *watch,* or lots of long words, such as *bovine* and *timepiece.*

Your Turn

Meets ISAT Standards
2.A.3a
2.A.3d
3.A.3
3.B.3a

Exercise A Rewrite each of the following clichés to make it more interesting.

EXAMPLE: soft as a pillow
REVISION: soft as a pillow stuffed with fairy dust

1. Wise as an owl _____

2. Pretty as a picture _____

3. Mean as a snake _____

4. Big as a house _____

Exercise B Try the following experiment in using metaphor to achieve a unique voice.

The following are some terms used in connection with cars:

screeched	blared	honked	sped
rolled into	clutch	brake	headlight
under the hood	retread	wheel	blinkers
pedal	revved up	swerved	battery
emissions	quart low	sporty	overhaul
turn on a dime	overheat	floored	toot

On your own paper, write a paragraph about a person (perhaps an automobile mechanic, a race car driver, or a used car salesperson), but use in your description as many terms related to cars as you can. For example, you might say that "Mr. Viper, the owner of the gas station, didn't have much under the hood, but what he lacked in intelligence, he made up for in good humor toward his customers."

> Return to the exercises at the beginning of the chapter, revise your work as necessary, and submit the exercises to your teacher for grading.

Chapter 16
Mind Matters

Reading, Writing, and Thinking

First Encounter

Read this story. Then try your hand at the exercises that follow. You will not be graded on the exercises at this time. At the end of the chapter, you will be directed to return to these exercises to revise and correct your work.

Michael's Ordinary Day

by Robin Lamb

Mrs. Spigot, the cafeteria lady, plopped a dollop of instant mashed potatoes onto Michael's orange plastic lunch tray and handed it back to him. Meatloaf, mashed potatoes, and green beans again. "I just wanted to say, Mrs. Spigot, that I appreciate the trouble that you take to color-coordinate our meals."

"Really?" said Mrs. Spigot. "And what does that mean, Michael?"

"I mean, the beans are green, right? And if you look closely, the meatloaf and the mashed potatoes are kind of green, too." The kids behind Michael laughed.

"I'm so sorry, Michael," said Mrs. Spigot. "I tell you what. Tomorrow I'll take a few hundred extra dollars from my budget and order you in a nice meal from a five-star restaurant."

"That would be great, Mrs. Spigot. Thank you."

She was right, Michael thought. She didn't necessarily like serving globby, instant mashed potatoes and watery, tasteless green beans, but that was just what they had to offer in this school—ordinary food. In fact, everything about my life is ordinary, Michael thought.

Why couldn't, just once, something absolutely fantastic happen, like, OK, what if space aliens landed a ship on the football field during second period, or what if the cafeteria started serving fresh pizza from Jay's? The two events seemed equally likely.

Michael stood with his tray and surveyed the room. Let's see, he thought. I could go sit with Javier and all the other lacrosse jocks, but they would just want to rib me about that goal I missed last week. Or, I could go sit next to Pat and Brian. No, Wendy is at that table. Michael always felt goofy around Wendy, as if he had "Dork" tattooed on his forehead. Michael decided to sit by himself at the empty table over by the far windows.

Ordinary. Ordinary. Ordinary. Every day I get up, take a shower, brush my teeth, put on my clothes, walk to the bus stop, go to class, eat this yummy cafeteria food, go home, walk the dog, do my homework, eat dinner, go to bed, get up, take a shower, brush my teeth, put on my clothes . . . . In English class, they had just read Ray Bradbury's story "All Summer in a Day," in which a bunch of kids lived on Venus, where it rained all the time and the sun came out only once every ten years. That's what my life is like, thought Michael. One ordinary, uninspiring day after another—bland, like this food.

The new kid from Earth Science—Ralph or Waldo or whatever his name was—was standing across the room with his lunch tray, looking around. After a moment, he made a beeline for Michael. He sat down next to Michael on the bench.

"Hey," said the new kid. "How's it going?" Something about the "kid" didn't look right. Somehow, he looked older, as if his body were fourteen but his eyes were fifty.

First Encounter

"You're the new kid in Earth Science, aren't you?" said Michael. Might as well make conversation, he thought.

"Oh, yes. That's right. Walton's my name. Funny thing."

"What do you mean?"

"Oh, the other people in the room. They're not moving."

Michael glanced up. Suddenly he was aware of the deafening silence around him. There was no chattering of voices, no clattering of silverware and trays. Everything was as quiet as a cave on the moon, and what was much, much weirder, the people in the cafeteria—the kids; Mrs. Spigot, the cashier; Mr. Bagley, the teacher who was doing lunchroom duty that day—were all frozen in mid-movement. Lisa Battigliosi, sitting at the table across from Michael, was frozen with her lips half-closed around a forkful of beans the color of squashed grasshopper.

"Whoa!" said Michael. Then, "What the heck?"

"That's nothing," said the new kid. He looked amused. "Watch this."

The new kid—Waldo or Weirdo or whatever his name was—pointed his index finger toward the ceiling. Then, slowly, he rotated the finger downward and stuck it into the hard Formica tabletop. As though it were a pool of water, the tabletop opened to admit the finger, closed around it, and rippled outward in concentric circles.

Michael stared at the new kid. "Who are you?" he said. "What on earth is going on here?"

"It's OK, Michael," said Walton, who was now transforming before Michael's eyes into a balding fifty-year-old in a white laboratory smock. "I have a story to tell you."

Michael glanced around the room. Everyone else was still frozen.

"Relax, Michael," said the newly transformed Dr. Walton. "I just needed to show you some spectacular events so that you would believe me."

"And what is it, exactly, that I'm supposed to believe?" said Michael, starting to become more than a little terrified. "OK. Let's see.... I'm dreaming, right?"

"No, Michael. You're not dreaming. Well, you sort of are, come to think of it."

"What do you mean?"

"Well, Michael," said Dr. Walton, "this is going to come as a bit of a surprise."

"Oh, you mean unlike watching people stick their hands through the tops of tables," said Michael.

"Well, even more surprising than that, Michael. Here's the scoop. Three years ago, you were in a terrible accident. An auto accident. Your body was horribly mangled. Irreparable. But your brain was in really good shape—I mean, it was operating perfectly.

"So we—my colleagues and I at the Werner Heisenberg Institute of Neurological Stochastics—took your brain and placed it in a vat of nutrient chemicals. Then, over a period of several months, we hooked up all your neural circuits to a computer, a very powerful computer. Are you following me?"

This guy is some kind of lunatic, thought Michael.

"OK. So, for years now," Dr. Walton continued, "we've been feeding signals into your brain to create a completely reasonable simulation of reality—sights, sounds, tastes, smells, feelings, and a lot more that you probably don't even know about, like information on your changing physical equilibrium as you move."

The people in the room still weren't moving.

"So we've been waiting for some time now to find an appropriate donor body and you are in luck; we've finally found one. A fourteen-year-old male, perfect specimen."

"You're telling me that all this around me isn't real? That I'm really just a brain in a vat?" asked Michael.

"Yes," said Dr. Walton.

Michael looked around him. The people, the walls and ceiling of the cafeteria, all were dissolving into a gray mist, a mist that grew lighter and lighter until there was only whiteness.

"Now," said Dr. Walton. "Don't worry Michael. You will sleep. Then, when you awaken, you will be all better. In a brand-new body. In the real world. Of course, it will take you some time to adjust...."

Your Turn

Exercise A Recalling and Interpreting *Answer the questions on the lines provided. Use complete sentences.*

1. A. Recalling Details

After Michael complains about the food, what does Mrs. Spigot offer to do?

_____

_____

_____

B. Interpreting Details

Is Mrs. Spigot serious about her offer? If not, why does she make it?

_____

_____

_____

2. A. Recalling Details

What story has Michael recently read in his English class?

_____

_____

_____

B. Interpreting Details

In what ways, according to Michael, are his days like the days in the story?

_____

_____

_____

AIM Higher! ISAT Language Arts Review

3. A. Recalling Details

Where does Dr. Walton work?

_____

_____

B. Interpreting Details

What are some of the activities of Dr. Walton and his fellow workers?

_____

_____

_____

4. A. Recalling Details

What is going to happen to Michael at the end of the story?

_____

_____

_____

B. Interpreting Details

Dr. Walton suggests that Michael might need "some time to adjust." To what will Michael have to adjust when he awakens?

_____

_____

_____

Meets ISAT Standards
1.A.3a
1.A.3b
1.B.3c
1.B.3d
1.C.3a
2.A.3a
2.A.3c
2.B.3a
2.B.3c
3.A.3
3.B.3

Exercise B Synthesizing In the story, Michael asks Dr. Walton if he is dreaming. Dr. Walton replies, "No... Well, you sort of are, come to think of it." What, exactly, has Michael been experiencing, if not a dream? Why might his days have all seemed, to him, so "ordinary"? In what way is this particular day not ordinary at all? Explain in a paragraph on your own paper.

Reading, Writing, and Thinking 383

Reading, Writing, and Thinking

Mind Matters

A human brain—your brain—contains about 300 billion brain cells. On average, each of these cells is connected to around ten thousand other cells. That's three quadrillion (3,000,000,000,000,000) connections! A brain like yours is by far the most complex object in the known universe. As the story you have just read illustrates, the brain is also the most important part of your body. Everything that you know and feel and remember and expect for the future involves events occurring in your brain.

Much of the activity of your brain takes place below the level of consciousness. You do not usually say to yourself, "Gee, I think I'll take a breath now." Instead, your brain automatically and unconsciously sends signals to the muscles that control breathing in and out. Some of what happens in your brain is, however, accessible to consciousness. In other words, you can think about what and how you are thinking.

In this chapter, you are going to learn some ways to think about your thinking that will help you enormously when you read and write, not only for tests, but in the rest of your life as well. In particular, you are going to learn some **heuristics,** or rules of thumb, for critical and creative thinking. Learning these rules of thumb will increase your brain power and help you to put some of those 300 billion brain cells in your head to good use!

Thinking Critically

"Few people think more than two or three times a year; I have made an international reputation for myself by thinking once or twice a week."

—George Bernard Shaw

When you use your reasoning abilities to draw conclusions, make judgments, and solve problems, you are doing what human beings do better than all other creatures. You are doing **critical thinking.** In this section, you will learn some critical thinking techniques that you can apply to many areas of your life.

Heuristic One: Careful Observation

The basis of all clear thinking is accurate observation. **Observation** is the process of taking in information through your senses of sight, hearing, touch, taste, and smell. When you observe something, you should consider three aspects: its characteristics, its relations to other things, and its functions.

What to Look for When Making Observations

✔ The **characteristics** of the object being observed. What are its qualities or attributes? How does it look, sound, feel, taste, and smell? What are its parts? Into what pieces can you divide it? Of what elements is it made?

More ▶

384 AIM Higher! ISAT Language Arts Review

✔ The **relations** that the object has to other things. How does the object compare to other things? What are its interactions with, or connections to, other things?

✔ The **functions** of the object or of its parts. What does the object do and how? What purpose or purposes does it serve? If it can be divided into parts, what do the parts do?

Suppose, for example, that you are reading a story. As you read, you will want to make observations about the main character, or **protagonist**. You might notice the following:

```
Characteristics
—Very tall
—Physically awkward
—Warm and loving
—Lonely
Relations
—Close to his mother
—Has few friends
Functions
—Performs well in school
—Terrible at sports, except
  batting in baseball
```

Suppose that you have been studying Egypt and your teacher has asked you to write a paragraph about the Great Pyramid. You might make notes like the following in preparation for writing for your description:

```
Observations of the
Great Pyramid of Khufu

Characteristics
—A base & 4 slanted sides rising
  to a point (now broken off)
—Made of about 2 million 2-ton
  blocks of stone
—Contains corridors, shafts, &
  a burial chamber
Relations
—One of the wonders of the
  ancient world
—For 43 centuries, the tallest
  structure on Earth (481 ft. high)
—Attracts thousands of tourists
  each yr.
—Edges of base point very
  accurately in the 4 directions
  (N, S, E, & W)
Functions
—Burial chamber for King Khufu
—Orientation may have served
  some astronomical function
```

Meets ISAT Standards
1.A.3b
1.B.3b
1.B.3c
1.B.3d
1.C.3a
1.C.3c
1.C.3d
3.B.3a

REMEMBER:

Observation is the process of using your senses to gather information about the characteristics, relations, and functions of an object. Ask yourself, "What is it like, how does it relate to other things, and what does it do?"

Your Turn

Exercise Choose one of the following subjects and observe it. As you observe, make notes on its characteristics, relations, and functions.

A television game show   A class at your school
A sports team in action   A local park

Characteristics	Relations	Functions

Reading, Writing, and Thinking

**Heuristic Two:
Induction and Generalization**

The process of reasoning about a subject and drawing a conclusion is called **making an inference.** Most of what you know about the world is based upon a type of inference called induction. **Induction** is the process of drawing a general conclusion from specific facts.

Think, for example, about the first time you ever saw an elephant in a zoo, on television, or in a picture. Up to that point, you knew nothing at all about elephants. When you saw your first one, you made some observations. You saw that the animal was quite large, that it had a long trunk, and so on. Based on this specific information, you formed an idea of what elephants in general are like. You might have concluded, for example, that "All elephants are big" and that "All elephants have trunks." In both cases, you would have been correct. Suppose, however, that the elephant that you saw had tusks and triangular ears. If you concluded, on this basis, that all elephants have tusks, you would have been wrong.

When you reason inductively, you draw general conclusions from specific information. Because of the limited information that you have (you have not, for example, seen all elephants), it is possible that your general conclusion might be wrong. Induction is a powerful tool. Again, it is the basis for most of what people know. Induction can, however, lead to errors.

A general conclusion based on specific information is called a **generalization.**

Meets ISAT Standards
1.A.3b
1.B.3c
1.B.3d
1.C.3a
1.C.3c

Reading, Writing, and Thinking

GENERALIZATION: [All] elephants have trunks.

If the conclusion is too broad and therefore incorrect, it is called an **overgeneralization.**

OVERGENERALIZATION: [All] elephants have tusks.

Overgeneralization about groups of people is a particularly dangerous form of thinking, so dangerous that people have given it its own name—**stereotyping.** Suppose, for example, that you meet a librarian who is meek and mousy. If you decide, based on this single example, that all librarians are meek and mousy, you would be wrong.

Induction is a powerful tool for reading. As you read, you learn specific facts. If, based on these facts, you draw general conclusions, you are reasoning inductively. For example, when reading the opening of "Michael's Ordinary Day," you might have noticed that Michael makes a joke to the cafeteria worker, Mrs. Spigot. Based on this specific observation, you might draw a general conclusion that Michael has a good sense of humor.

Induction is also a powerful tool for writing. When you write a paragraph in standard form, the topic sentence presents a general idea. The sentences in the body of the paragraph present specific ideas that support the topic sentence. You can think of the body sentences as being the specific ideas on which the general conclusion—the topic sentence—is based.

REMEMBER:

An **induction** is a general conclusion, or generalization, based on specific facts. To draw a general conclusion, simply look at the specific facts and ask yourself, "What general statements are probably true if these facts are true?"

Your Turn

Exercise Use induction to create topic sentences. Read each group of supporting sentences for a paragraph. Each sentence states a specific idea. On the line provided after each group of sentences, write a general sentence that could serve as the topic sentence for the paragraph.

Meets ISAT Standards
1.A.3a
1.A.3b
1.B.3c
1.B.3d
1.C.3d
3.A.3
3.B.3a

1. Stephen Wolfram published his first scientific paper—a work on theoretical physics—at the age of fifteen. He received his Ph.D from CalTech at the age of twenty. Then, at the age of twenty-one, he became the youngest person ever to receive the MacArthur Foundation's "genius award."

TOPIC SENTENCE:

_____

_____

2. The **kinesthetic sense** tells you about the positions of your joints and limbs and the force applied by your muscles. Special receptors in your joints, muscles, and tendons send information about these to your brain. Without your kinesthetic sense, you would not be able to sit or walk or make other purposeful movements. Another sense that every human being has is the **vestibular sense.** This sense tells you where and how your body is located as it moves in space. This "feedback" is necessary in order to maintain balance. It also lets you know in which direction you are facing. The vestibular sense is governed by your inner ear. If damage were done to your vestibular sense, you would not be able to keep your balance, and you would be disoriented.

TOPIC SENTENCE:

_____

_____

The Seven Senses

Sight   Hearing   Touch   Taste   Smell   Kinesthetic Sense   Vestibular Sense

Reading, Writing, and Thinking 389

Reading, Writing, and Thinking

Heuristic Three: Deduction

Another powerful form of inference is deduction. **Deduction** is the process of observing one or more facts and then drawing a conclusion from them that has to be true if the observed fact or facts are true. Consider this example:

> Jolene is a lawyer.
>
> All lawyers must have law degrees.
>
> Therefore, Jolene must have a law degree.

Notice that if the first two statements are both true, then the conclusion has to be true. That is always the case with deductive reasoning.

Deductive reasoning is a powerful tool to use when reading. Simply ask yourself, as you read, what must be true if something that you have read about is true. You may be surprised to find out how much you can figure out in this way. Consider this example: In the story you have just read, "Michael's Ordinary Day," the "new kid" sticks his finger into a tabletop, which ripples like a pool of water. You might reason like this:

> In the real world, tabletops do not ripple like pools of water.
>
> This tabletop ripples like a pool of water.
>
> Therefore, this tabletop is not in the real world.

Here's another example: At one point in the story, Michael asks Dr. Walton, "You're telling me that all this around me isn't real?" and Dr. Walton answers, "Yes." If it is true that everything around Michael isn't real, what can you conclude? Obviously, you can draw many specific conclusions that have to be true:

> The tabletop is not real.
>
> Mrs. Spigot is not real.
>
> The school is not real.
>
> The other students are not real.
>
> The cafeteria is not real.

These statements are all deductions because they have to be true if the more general observation made by Michael is true.

Deductive reasoning can help you to figure out what to expect when reading a selection. If you know that a piece that you are going to be reading is a short story, there are several things that you know are probably true because they are true of almost all short stories. (See Chapter 7, "A Tale to Tell: Understanding Fictional Narratives.")

> "Michael's Ordinary Day" is a short story.
>
> A short story has characters.
>
> A short story has one or more settings.
>
> A short story has a central conflict.
>
> A short story has a plot.
>
> Therefore, "Michael's Ordinary Day" has characters, one or more settings, a central conflict, and a plot.

Suppose that you know that you are going to read a persuasive essay. From that general fact, you can deduce that the essay will present an opinion and that it will attempt to support the opinion in one or more ways (by presenting related facts and arguments). As you read, you can look for these supporting details.

REMEMBER:

A **deduction** is a statement that is necessarily true if the statements on which it is based are true. Making a deduction is easy. Simply ask yourself, "Given what I know, what else must be true?"

Reading, Writing, and Thinking **391**

Your Turn

Exercise A Read the following statements of fact taken from the story "Michael's Ordinary Day." Based on each statement, write one additional statement that has to be true, following the hint provided.

1. Mrs. Spigot is described as "the cafeteria lady." (Hint: For whom does Mrs. Spigot work?)

   _____

   _____

2. Michael says that he could go sit with Javier and all the other lacrosse jocks, but that they would just want to rib him about the goal that he missed the previous week. (Hint: In what extracurricular activity does Michael participate?)

   _____

   _____

3. Michael thinks, "Everything about my life is ordinary." (Hint: What does Michael think of school? Of lacrosse? Of his classmates?)

   _____

   _____

4. Michael's body was injured beyond repair in the auto accident. (Hints: What is unusual about what Michael has experienced since then? What is true of the body that Michael thinks that he has?)

   _____

   _____

Exercise B Imagine that you are about to read an example of each of the following types of writing. On the lines provided, tell what parts or elements you could reasonably expect to find in each piece. (In other words, what can you deduce from the type of writing that each one is?)

Meets ISAT
Standards
1.A.3b
1.B.3d
1.C.3a
1.C.3b
1.C.3d
2.A.3a
2.A.3c
2.B.3a

1. a short story
   _____
   _____

2. a persuasive essay
   _____
   _____

3. a lyric poem
   _____
   _____

4. a newspaper story
   _____
   _____

Exercise C Think about the following writing prompt. Do NOT write an essay in response to the prompt. Instead, use your powers of deduction to make a list on the lines provided of at least four things that an essay in response to this prompt must do.

WRITING PROMPT: Write an essay in which you take a stand on an issue facing your school, your town, or your country. Support your position with evidence.

Based on this prompt, you can conclude that, in your response, you will have to

1. _____
2. _____
3. _____
4. _____

Reading, Writing, and Thinking **393**

Reading, Writing, and Thinking

Heuristic Four: Analysis

Another extremely useful reasoning technique is **analysis.** When you analyze something, you break it down into its parts. You then observe the characteristics and functions of those parts and the relations of the parts to the whole.

You can analyze almost anything. An atom can be analyzed by studying its parts: electrons, protons, and neutrons. A car can be analyzed by looking at its various systems: the engine and drive train, exhaust system, fuel system, electrical system, cooling system, transmission, steering and suspension system, braking system, and chassis/body. The human body can be analyzed by examining its parts and systems, including the respiratory system, the skeletal system, the circulatory system, the digestive system, the muscular system, the nervous system, and so on. A paragraph can be analyzed by looking at its topic sentence, supporting sentences, and clincher sentence. An essay can be analyzed according to its introduction, body, and conclusion.

An essential part of all writing is analyzing a topic by studying its parts. Two useful tools for identifying its parts are the analysis chart and the cluster chart. Here is the first of two charts showing an analysis of the story "Michael's Ordinary Day":

Analysis Chart: "Michael's Ordinary Day"

Characters	Mrs. Spigot, Michael, the new kid/Dr. Walton
Central conflict	Michael's boredom with his "ordinary" life
Setting	A school cafeteria
Plot	Michael gets lunch and jokes with Mrs. Spigot.
	Michael sits by himself and thinks about how ordinary his life is.
	A new kid comes and sits by Michael.
	The new kid points out that everyone in the room is frozen.
	The new kid sticks his finger into the tabletop.
	The new kid transforms into Dr. Walton.
	Dr. Walton explains that Michael had an auto accident and is really just a brain in a vat, awaiting a new body.
	The room starts to dissolve.

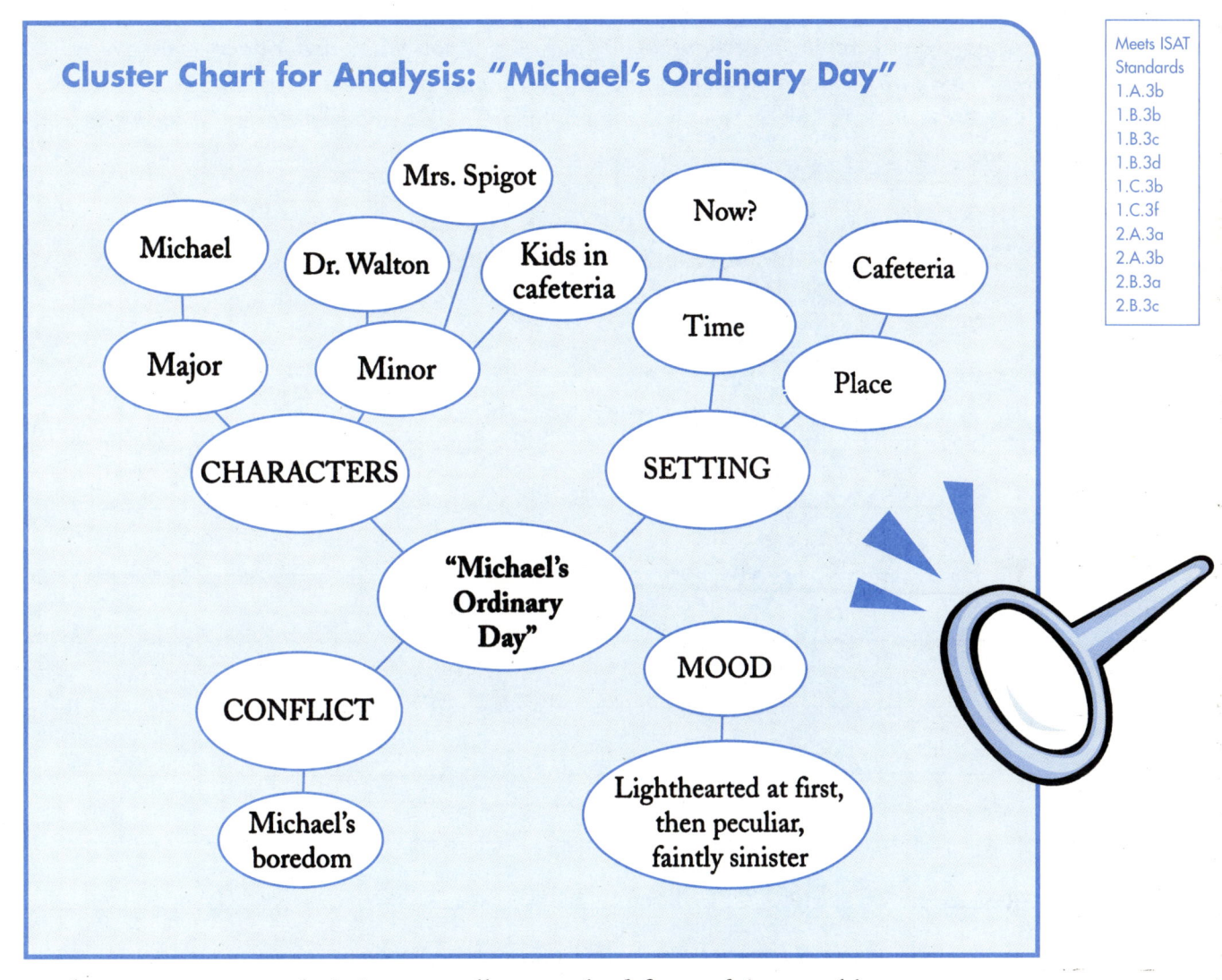

Cluster Chart for Analysis: "Michael's Ordinary Day"

Meets ISAT Standards
1.A.3b
1.B.3b
1.B.3c
1.B.3d
1.C.3b
1.C.3f
2.A.3a
2.A.3b
2.B.3a
2.B.3c

- "Michael's Ordinary Day"
  - CHARACTERS
    - Major: Michael
    - Minor: Mrs. Spigot, Dr. Walton, Kids in cafeteria
  - SETTING
    - Time: Now?
    - Place: Cafeteria
  - MOOD: Lighthearted at first, then peculiar, faintly sinister
  - CONFLICT: Michael's boredom

As you can see, analysis is an excellent method for studying a subject and for gathering information.

REMEMBER:

When you **analyze** something, you break it down into its parts and study the functions of and relationships among the parts. Ask yourself, "What are the parts? What do these parts do? How do they relate to each other and to the whole?"

Reading, Writing, and Thinking **395**

Your Turn

Exercise Your teacher has asked you to write an essay in which you classify fabulous or imaginary creatures into categories. In your essay, you must describe at least three different kinds of fabulous creatures and give examples of each. The teacher has defined fabulous creatures as "creatures that are imaginary, or do not really exist." Follow the directions given below.

1. Use deduction to come up with a list of creatures that would have to be considered "fabulous," according to the definition that the teacher has given. Make a list of as many different creatures as you can.

396 AIM Higher! ISAT Language Arts Review

2. Fill in the analysis chart below or a create a cluster chart on your own paper to sort the creatures from your list into three categories. Give each category a name and a description.

Meets ISAT Standards
1.B.3d
3.B.3a

Category Name _____	**Category Name** _____	**Category Name** _____
What creatures in this category have in common:	What creatures in this category have in common:	What creatures in this category have in common:
List of creatures:	List of creatures:	List of creatures:

Reading, Writing, and Thinking

Reading, Writing, and Thinking

Heuristic Five: Evaluation

Evaluation is the process of making a judgment about something based upon specific criteria. **Criteria** (singular: **criterion**) are standards by which something is judged. Criteria tell what qualities people think something should have. (Sometimes criteria are worded to describe the qualities that something should *not* have as well.) The criteria for judging a running shoe, for example, might include the following:

- The shoe is attractive.
- The shoe is comfortable.
- The shoe is made of high-quality materials.
- The shoe provides appropriate cushioning and support.

Here are some criteria for judging short stories:

- The setting of the story is vividly described, so that the reader can clearly imagine it.
- The characters are interesting. They are not stereotypes.
- The plot contains surprising twists.
- The central conflict is significant.
- The story has universal appeal (that is, most readers can connect with it in a meaningful way).

Evaluations are matters of opinion. They cannot be proved to be absolutely true or absolutely false. They can, however, be supported by evidence. Good readers make evaluations as they read and make sure that their evaluations are based on facts. Criteria to use when judging a piece of informative writing include whether it is interesting, accurate, up-to-date, and free of statements of opinion. Criteria to use when judging a piece of persuasive writing include whether it is interesting and convincing, whether it backs up statements of opinion with facts, and whether it is unbiased and fair.

Evaluation is very important to good writing. After you write a rough draft, you evaluate it to identify its strengths and weaknesses. Then you revise it to correct the weaknesses. For a list of evaluation criteria for writing, see the Revision Checklist on pages 265–66.

REMEMBER:

When you **evaluate** something, you make a judgment about it based on specific criteria. Ask yourself, "What characteristics and functions should this object have? Does this particular object have those characteristics and functions?"

Your Turn

Exercise A On your own paper, write a paragraph evaluating the story "Michael's Ordinary Day." Do you think that it is a well-written story? Consider the evaluation criteria for short stories given on the previous page. Does the story meet these criteria? Why or why not? Write your paragraph. Revise it. Then proofread it for errors in grammar, usage, mechanics, manuscript form, and spelling.

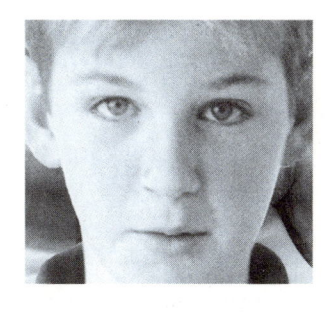

Meets ISAT Standards
1.B.3d
1.C.3b
1.C.3c
2.A.3a
2.A.3b
2.A.3c
2.A.3d
2.B.3a
2.B.3c
3.A.3
3.B.3a
3.B.3b
3.C.3a

Exercise B A set of criteria for evaluating something is called a rubric. Work with a partner to create a rubric for evaluating movies. In other words, list the characteristics that a good movie should have. Use your own paper for the list.

Exercise C On your own paper, write a rough draft of an essay evaluating a movie you have seen. Use the evaluation criteria, or rubric, that you developed for Exercise B, above. Revise the draft for content and organization using the Revision Checklist on pages 265–66. Then proofread your revised draft for errors in grammar, usage, mechanics, manuscript form, and spelling using the Proofreading Checklist on page 270.

Reading, Writing, and Thinking

Reading, Writing, and Thinking

Thinking Creatively

"A hunch is creativity trying to tell you something."

—Anonymous

As you probably know, the process of coming up with original ideas is called **creative thinking.** Creative thinkers can be found throughout history, in the guise of leaders (Thomas Jefferson, Ashoka the Builder, Martin Luther King, Jr.), artists (Leonardo da Vinci, Georgia O'Keefe, Alexander Calder), and inventors (Thomas Edison), and scientists (Albert Einstein, Marie Curie, Jonas Salk). These people were all geniuses, but do not think that you have to have exceptional inborn abilities in order to be creative. Everyone has a bit of genius in him or her. To find and realize your hidden special talents, try applying some of the following heuristics, or techniques, for creative thinking.

Heuristic One: Alternative Solutions

The chicken above wants to eat the birdseed. In fact, it cannot take its eyes off the prized seeds. If it did, or if its brain were a bit bigger, it might realize that the fence has only three sides and that it could easily walk around to get to the seeds. At times during our lives, we all act like that poor chicken. We become so set on one course of action that we discard or ignore all other options.

The next time you find yourself faced with a problem that seems not to have a desirable solution, do not think like a chicken! Ask yourself, "Is there another way to solve this problem?" Take a step back and think about what you want to achieve. For example, suppose that you have only two current options to get to school: You can take the bus, or you can ride with a neighbor who goes to school two hours early because of swim team practice. Perhaps you could bike to school. Perhaps someone else would be willing to pick you up in exchange for something else, like paying for the gasoline. You could even join the swim team. Then you could ride with your neighbor and get to school just in time for practice. The point is that whenever you do not like the available options, try thinking up new ones.

One of the most common mistakes in reasoning is called **"either/or" thinking.** That occurs when people believe that there are only two alternatives. For example, a politician who favors a flat-rate income tax might say, "You are either for a flat tax or against it." Of course, that's just not true. There are many alternatives. One alternative, for example, would be to have a progressive flat tax, in which people in various income groups pay a flat percentage, with no deductions.

REMEMBER:

Ask yourself, "What alternatives are there? Are there other possibilities that people have not considered?"

Heuristic Two: Creative Juxtaposition and Synthesis

Most ideas are not 100 percent original. Instead, they consist of two or more older ideas combined in a new way. For example, if you combine the idea of a glass window with the idea of a door, you end up with a glass door that also acts like a window. As far as ideas go, this is not as radical as $E = mc^2$, but it still was a useful, original idea when first conceived. The comic book writer and illustrator Stan Lee put together the concepts of a spider and a troubled teenaged boy and created the comic book superhero Spiderman. The filmmaker George Lucas put together elements from old westerns, classic sci-fi space books and films, Japanese ninjas, and Asian philosophy to create the *Star Wars* series of movies.

When you juxtapose two items, you place them side by side. **Creative juxtaposition** is the thinking strategy of bringing together two previously unconnected ideas. Combining previously separate ideas is called **synthesis.** Placing two objects or concepts that were separate side by side can yield surprising results. The differences between the two might look more pronounced, or surprising similarities might be discovered. Sometimes, a third new thing might be discovered. One way to practice creative juxtaposition is just to choose two words at random from a dictionary.

Is there another way?

Meets ISAT Standards
1.B.3c
1.B.3d
1.C.3c

Reading, Writing, and Thinking

Reading, Writing, and Thinking

Creative juxtaposition and synthesis are powerful techniques for creative writing. Here are some examples:

Creative Juxtaposition: Synthesizing Ideas

CONCEPT 1: Rap song
CONCEPT 2: Nightly news
CREATIVE JUXTAPOSITION: The nightly news delivered as a rap

CONCEPT 1: Ant colony
CONCEPT 2: Human political and social institutions
CREATIVE JUXTAPOSITION: Story about a future human society with millions of genetically identical (cloned) people ruled by an all-powerful queen

CONCEPT 1: Laundry list
CONCEPT 2: Poem
CREATIVE JUXTAPOSITION: A humorous poem that is simply a list of dirty clothes being sent to a laundry

CONCEPT 1: Informative article about the nineteenth-century Chinese export trade
CONCEPT 2: A porcelain plate
CREATIVE JUXTAPOSITION: An article that follows a single plate from its creation through its sale and transportation by sea to a Victorian home in Salem, Massachusetts

REMEMBER:

Ask yourself, "What new, untried combinations are possible?"

Creative Juxtaposition → *Synthesis*

Your Turn

Exercise A Heavy traffic in large cities is a huge problem. Traffic jams cause delays. Lots of cars and trucks in one place cause air and noise pollution. In Boston, city planners came up with a novel idea for dealing with the traffic problem. They decided to move much of the traffic underground, to tunnels. Thus was born Boston's "Big Dig" project. What are some other alternatives for solving the traffic problems in cities? See if you can come up with an alternative in which cars are eliminated from cities altogether. Describe your alternative in a paragraph on your own paper. Make sure to revise and proofread the paragraph.

Meets ISAT Standards
3.A.3
3.B.3a
3.B.3b
3.C.3a
3.C.3b

Exercise B Synthesis Create a comic book superhero character by combining a person from Column A, below, with a creature or thing from Column B. Create a storyboard—a series of frame-by-frame sketches with accompanying text—to tell the opening story of your new comic book series.

Column A	Column B
FBI Agent	Rain
Teacher	Eagle
Writer	Mole
Game Show/Talk Show Host	Dolphin
Firefighter	Fly

Reading, Writing, and Thinking

Reading, Writing, and Thinking

Heuristic Three: Creative Doubt

"Common sense is the layer of prejudices laid down before the age of eighteen."

—Albert Einstein

Common sense is the collection of unexamined ideas shared by most people. Most of the time, common sense is correct. Sometimes, however, common sense turns out to be wrong. For example, for thousands of years, people thought that the Earth was flat. It looks flat from our vantage point on the ground, so people assumed that it was. We now know, of course, that despite appearances, and despite what common sense told our ancestors, the Earth is not flat. As late as the beginning of the twentieth century, many people doubted that heavier-than-air objects could be made to fly.

Doubting what people usually assume to be true can sometimes lead to interesting discoveries. Einstein challenged some deeply held beliefs about the nature of space, time, and gravity. For example, he considered the possibility that, relative to a stationary observer, time slows down as an object moves faster. By doubting what most people believe to be true, Einstein made important discoveries that led to a new understanding of how the universe works.

To get an idea of how powerful a tool doubt can be, try thinking about what might be true if any of the following common-sense ideas were false:

Humans are the only creatures on Earth that are self-aware.

Everyone should go to school from about the age of six to about the age of seventeen.

Cities are best built above ground, on dry land.

There is no life on Mars.

You have probably heard the expression "Don't believe everything you read." Doubt can be very useful to a reader. When reading informative or persuasive writing, ask yourself questions like these: "Are these facts true? What evidence or sources did the writer use? Is the writer unbiased? Is he or she being fair? Is any of the material outdated or otherwise inaccurate?"

REMEMBER:

Ask yourself, "Is this really true? What would be the case if this were not true?"

Heuristic Four: "What If" Questions

"You see things, and you say, 'Why?' But I dream things that never were: and say, 'Why not?'"

—George Bernard Shaw

Asking "what if" and "why not" questions is yet another way to stimulate creative thinking. Doing so forces your mind to entertain exotic possibilities that it usually would not consider. This speculative story-making can often be very entertaining.

A favorite creative thinking strategy among novelists and historians is to ask themselves what the world would be like if something had happened in a way different from what actually happened. Many books and movies have been written on subjects such as, "What if Japan or Germany had won the Second World War? What if the South had won the Civil War? What if Lincoln had not been assassinated?" and so on.

"What if" and "why not" questions are obviously useful for creative writing, but they have uses in many other fields as well. Back in 1975, a salesman named Gary Dahl asked himself the completely absurd question "What if people kept rocks as pets?" Thus was born the pet rock. Many thousands of these were sold as novelty items around the United States.

Scientists also ask themselves "what if" questions in the form of hypotheses to be tested by experiment and observation: "What if there were water under the surface of Mars? What if some cancers were caused by viruses?" Questions like these lead to new research and, sometimes, to ground-breaking discoveries.

Meets ISAT Standards
1.B.3c
1.B.3d
1.C.3a
4.A.3a

REMEMBER:

Ask yourself, "What if?" or "Why not?"

Reading, Writing, and Thinking

Heuristics for Critical and Creative Thinking

Critical

Careful observation of characteristics, relations, and functions

Induction/Generalization

Deduction

Analysis

Evaluation

Creative

Alternative solutions

Creative juxtaposition and synthesis

Creative doubt

"What if" questions

Your Turn

Exercise A Choose one of the following topics and write a paragraph about it on your own paper.

> Meets ISAT Standards
> 1.C.3f
> 3.A.3
> 3.B.3a
> 3.C.3a

1. Common-sense notion: Humans are the only creatures on Earth that are self-aware. If this common-sense notion is false—if whales and chimpanzees, for example, are conscious beings—what consequences should this fact have for human actions? Should chimpanzees be used in scientific experiments? Should whaling be allowed?

2. Common-sense notion: Everyone should go to school from about the age of six to about the age of seventeen. What if people did not go to school during all of this period? What if, instead, they took their teenage years off to work and then went back to school? Would there be any merit to such an arrangement?

3. Common-sense notion: Cities are best built above ground, on dry land. What if cities were built, instead, underground or under water? How would that be possible? Would there be any advantages?

Reading, Writing, and Thinking **407**

Your Turn

Meets ISAT Standards
3.A.3
3.B.3a
3.B.3b

Exercise B Read this rather dull test writing prompt: "Write about a time when someone you know won a prize." What are some creative ways that you could approach this topic to make it more interesting? Try using some of the methods discussed in this chapter to come up with an unusual, interesting approach to the topic. Here are some possibilities:

ALTERNATIVE SOLUTION:
Write about a time when someone actually won but was not officially recognized as having done so.

CREATIVE JUXTAPOSITION:
Tell the story from the point of view of an inanimate object, such as the winning ticket in a raffle.

DOUBT:
Write about a time when someone won but should not have. That is, question the judges' or officials' decision.

"WHAT IF" QUESTION:
What if the prize were not a literal prize, such as money, but something else of value, such as another person's admiration or respect?

Choose one of the topics above, or your own unique approach to the topic. Try to be as creative as possible. Write your essay on your own paper. (You may want to review Chapter 8, on narrative nonfiction, especially the section on autobiographical and biographical writing, first.) Revise your essay using the Revision Checklist on pages 265–66. Make a clean copy. Then proofread it using the Proofreading Checklist on page 270.

Return to the exercises at the beginning of the chapter, revise your work as necessary, and submit the exercises to your teacher for grading.

408 AIM Higher! ISAT Language Arts Review

Chapter 17
Guided Practice:
Writing about Literature

Step 1 Review Chapter 7, "A Tale to Tell: Understanding Fictional Narratives."

Step 2 Reread "Leaving Taiwan," on pages 18–19 of this textbook. Then read the selection from *My Ántonia*, by Willa Cather, on pages 412–14 of this chapter.

Step 3 Choose one of the following topics. Gather evidence from the stories, in the form of quotations, summaries, and paraphrases, to support your answer.

Topic 1: Both "Leaving Taiwan" and the selection from *My Ántonia* are about characters that are moving to a new place. Chiang in "Leaving Taiwan" and Jimmy in *My Ántonia* have their own thoughts and feelings about moving away from their homes. Write an essay comparing and contrasting their attitudes toward moving.

Topic 2: Think about the role of hope in "Leaving Taiwan" and the selection from *My Ántonia*. By the end of "Leaving Taiwan," Chiang and Jung are hopeful and optimistic about their move to America. Do you think that Jimmy, in the selection from *My Ántonia*, is hopeful about his move to Black Hawk? Write an essay to explain your answer.

Step 4 Complete a story map for each of the two stories. Part of each map has been done for you.

Author: Lucy Lee

Title: "Leaving Taiwan"

Main Characters: Chiang, Jung, Mother, and Father

Central Conflict: Chiang's family is moving to America, but he wants to remain in Taiwan.

More ▶

Meets ISAT Standards
1.B.3c
1.B.3d
1.C.3b
2.A.3b
2.B.3a
2.B.3c
3.A.3
3.B.3a
3.B.3b
5.C.3a

Guided Practice: Writing about Literature **409**

Guided Practice: Writing about Literature

Setting: living room of a family's apartment in a city in Taiwan

Major Events in Plot: _____
_____
_____
_____

How Conflict Is Resolved: _____
_____
_____

Author: Willa Cather

Title: from My Ántonia

Main Characters: Jimmy, Jake, and Otto Fuchs

Central Conflict: Jimmy moves to Black Hawk and his future is unclear.

Settings: passenger train traveling across America, wagon traveling to Jimmy's grandfather's house

Major Events in Plot: _____
_____
_____
_____

How Conflict Is Resolved: _____
_____
_____

Step 5 Using the information from your story maps and the evidence you gathered from the stories, write a rough draft of your essay on your own paper. Remember that the introduction should mention the titles and authors of the stories and should provide a general answer to the question posed by the writing prompt. Present evidence from each story to support your main idea. (Evidence from the stories can take the form of summaries, paraphrases, or quotations.) The conclusion of your essay should restate the main idea in other words.

Meets ISAT Standards
1.B.3d
1.C.3b
2.A.3b
2.B.3a
2.B.3c
3.A.3
3.B.3a
3.B.3b
3.C.3a
4.B.3a
5.C.3a
5.C.3b

Step 6 Review the content and organization of your draft. Refer to the Revision Checklist on pages 265–66 of this textbook. Have you answered the question posed by the writing prompt? Have you used quotations, summaries, or paraphrases from the stories to support your main idea? Have you used transitions throughout to connect ideas?

Step 7 Proofread your revised draft for errors in grammar, usage, capitalization, punctuation, and manuscript form. Make sure that names of characters are spelled correctly and that you have placed quotation marks around story titles and direct quotations. Refer to the Proofreading Checklist on page 270 of this textbook.

Step 8 Make a clean final copy. Proofread it one last time. Then share it with your classmates and your teacher.

Guided Practice: Writing about Literature

Guided Practice: Writing about Literature

from My Ántonia
by Willa Cather

I first heard of Ántonia on what seemed to me an interminable journey across the great midland plain of North America. I was ten years old then; I had lost both my father and mother within a year, and my Virginia relatives were sending me out to my grandparents, who lived in Nebraska. I travelled in the care of a mountain boy, Jake Marpole, one of the 'hands' on my father's old farm under the Blue Ridge, who was now going West to work for my grandfather. Jake's experience of the world was not much wider than mine. He had never been in a railway train until the morning when we set out together to try our fortunes in a new world.

We went all the way in day-coaches, becoming more sticky and grimy with each stage of the journey. Jake bought everything the newsboys offered him: candy, oranges, brass collar buttons, a watch-charm, and for me a *Life of Jesse James*, which I remember as one of the most satisfactory books I have ever read. Beyond Chicago we were under the protection of a friendly passenger conductor, who knew all about the country to which we were going and gave us a great deal of advice in exchange for our confidence. He seemed to us an experienced and worldly man who had been almost everywhere; in his conversation he threw out lightly the names of distant states and cities. He wore the rings and pins and badges of different fraternal orders to which he belonged. Even his cuff-buttons were engraved with hieroglyphics, and he was more inscribed than an Egyptian obelisk.

Once when he sat down to chat, he told us that in the immigrant car ahead there was a family from "across the water" whose destination was the same as ours.

"They can't any of them speak English, except one little girl, and all she can say is 'We go Black Hawk, Nebraska.' She's not much older than you, twelve or thirteen, maybe, and she's as bright as a new dollar. Don't you want to go ahead and see her, Jimmy? She's got the pretty brown eyes, too!"

This last remark made me bashful, and I shook my head and settled down to *Jesse James*. Jake nodded at me approvingly and said you were likely to get diseases from foreigners.

I do not remember crossing the Missouri River, or anything about the long day's journey through Nebraska. Probably by that time I had crossed so many rivers that I was dull to them. The only thing very noticeable about Nebraska was that it was still, all day long, Nebraska.

I had been sleeping, curled up in a red plush seat, for a long while when we reached Black Hawk. Jake roused me and took me by the hand. We stumbled down from the train to a wooden siding, where men were running about with lanterns. I couldn't see any town, or even distant lights; we were surrounded by utter darkness. The engine was panting heavily after its long run. In the red glow from the fire-box, a group of people stood huddled together on the platform, encumbered by bundles and boxes. I knew this must be the immigrant family the conductor had told us about. The woman wore a fringed shawl tied over her head, and she carried a little tin trunk in her arms, hugging it as if it were a baby. There was an old man, tall and stooped. Two half-grown boys and a girl stood holding oilcloth bundles, and a little girl clung to her mother's skirts. Presently a man with a lantern approached them and began to talk, shouting and exclaiming. I pricked up my ears, for it was positively the first time I had ever heard a foreign tongue.

Another lantern came along. A bantering voice called out: "Hello, are you Mr. Burden's folks? If you are, it's me you're looking for. I'm Otto Fuchs. I'm Mr. Burden's hired man, and I'm to drive you out. Hello, Jimmy, ain't you scared to come so far west?"

I looked up with interest at the new face in the lantern-light. He might have stepped out of the pages of *Jesse James*. He wore a sombrero hat, with a wide leather band and a bright buckle, and the ends of his moustache were twisted up stiffly, like little horns. He looked lively and ferocious, I thought, and as if he had a history. A long scar ran across one cheek and drew the corner of his mouth up in a sinister curl. The top of his left ear was gone, and his skin was brown as an Indian's. Surely

More ▶

Guided Practice: Writing about Literature

this was the face of a desperado. As he walked about the platform in his high-heeled boots, looking for our trunks, I saw that he was a rather slight man, quick and wiry, and light on his feet. He told us we had a long night drive ahead of us, and had better be on the hike. He led us to a hitching-bar where two farm-wagons were tied, and I saw the foreign family crowding into one of them. The other was for us. Jake got on the front seat with Otto Fuchs, and I rode on the straw in the bottom of the wagon-box, covered up with a buffalo hide. The immigrants rumbled off into the empty darkness, and we followed them.

I tried to go to sleep, but the jolting made me bite my tongue, and I soon began to ache all over. When the straw settled down, I had a hard bed. Cautiously I slipped from under the buffalo hide, got up on my knees and peered over the side of the wagon. There seemed to be nothing to see; no fences, no creeks or trees, no hills or fields. If there was a road, I could not make it out in the faint starlight. There was nothing but land: not a country at all, but the material out of which countries are made. No, there was nothing but land—slightly undulating, I knew, because often our wheels ground against the brake as we went down into a hollow and lurched up again on the other side. I had the feeling that the world was left behind, that we had got over the edge of it, and were outside man's jurisdiction. I had never before looked up at the sky when there was not a familiar mountain ridge against it. But this was the complete dome of heaven, all there was of it. I did not believe that my dead father and mother were watching me from up there; they would still be looking for me at the sheep-fold down by the creek, or along the white road that led to the mountain pastures. I had left even their spirits behind me. The wagon jolted on, carrying me I knew not whither. I don't think I was homesick. If we never arrived anywhere, it did not matter. Between that earth and that sky I felt erased, blotted out. I did not say my prayers that night: here, I felt, what would be would be.

Chapter 18
Guided Practice:
Writing Narrative Nonfiction

Meets ISAT Standards
1.B.3c
1.B.3d
3.B.3a

Step 1 Review Chapter 8, "Real People, Real Events: Understanding Nonfiction Narratives."

Step 2 Choose one of the following topics or one of your own. If you choose your own topic, make sure that your topic is autobiographical or biographical, and make sure to clear your topic with your teacher.

Topic 1: Write about an embarrassing moment that happened to you. It could be a misunderstanding between you and a friend or a mishap at school in front of your classmates. Describe the event that occurred, other people's reactions to it, and the thoughts that ran through your mind. Explain what you learned from the experience.

Topic 2: Write a brief biography of someone whom you admire greatly. This person can be a historical or public figure, living or deceased. He or she can be a celebrity, athlete, friend, or relative. Include details from the person's life to show why this is a person worthy of admiration.

If you choose a topic of your own, describe that topic here:

_____
_____

Step 3 List the central conflict that will be presented in your narrative, or write "No central conflict."

Central Conflict: _____
_____

Guided Practice: Writing Narrative Nonfiction **415**

Guided Practice:
Narrative Nonfiction

Step 4 Make a list of the major events that you will include in your narrative.

Step 5 Complete the following Sensory Detail Chart. Fill in concrete details that you will use to make your narrative vivid and interesting.

Meets ISAT Standard 3.B.3a

Sight	Sound	Touch	Taste	Smell

Guided Practice: Writing Narrative Nonfiction

Guided Practice: Narrative Nonfiction

Step 6 Briefly describe the significance of the events that you listed in Step 4—what lessons they teach, what insights can be gained from them, or what meaning the events might have for others. You will use this information in the conclusion of your essay.

_____
_____
_____
_____
_____

Step 7 Using the information that you have gathered above, write a rough draft of your autobiographical or biographical narrative on your own paper.

Step 8 Review the content and organization of your draft. Refer to the Revision Checklist on pages 265–66 of this textbook. Have you presented your details in chronological order? Have you used enough concrete detail to make the piece come alive in your readers' minds? Is the setting clear? Have you included details that reveal who the characters are and what they are like? Does the ending of the piece present a conclusion to the events described? Create a revised draft.

Step 9 Proofread your revised draft for errors in grammar, usage, capitalization, punctuation, and manuscript form. Refer to the Proofreading Checklist on page 270 of this textbook.

Step 10 Make a clean final copy. Proofread it one last time. Then share it with your classmates and your teacher.

Chapter 19
Guided Practice:
Expository, or Informative, Writing

Step 1   Review Chapter 9, "Just the Facts: Understanding Informative Nonfiction."

Step 2   Choose one of the following topics or one of your own. If you choose your own topic, make sure that the topic is for an informative essay, and make sure to clear your topic with your teacher.

Topic 1: Write an essay explaining how to pack for a two-day backpacking trip in the desert or in the mountains. Describe what equipment and materials you will need and why. You might need to conduct some research at the library or on the Internet.

Topic 2: Write an essay that classifies the types of movies made in Hollywood. Think of the major categories of the movies and the characteristics that distinguish movies in each category.

Topic 3: Write an essay that compares and contrasts two people or characters. They can be people you know in real life or be fictitious characters in a book, television show, play, or musical.

If you choose a topic of your own, describe that topic here:

_____
_____
_____

Meets ISAT Standards
1.B.3d
1.C.3c
3.A.3
3.B.3a
4.B.3a
5.A.3a
5.B.3a
5.B.3b

Guided Practice:
Expository, or Informative, Writing

Step 3 In the space below, create a word web or Venn diagram to gather information about your topic:

Step 4 In the space below, use the chart to create a rough outline for your informative essay:

Meets ISAT
Standards
1.B.3b
1.C.3f
3.A.3
3.B.3a
5.A.3a
5.B.3a
5.B.3b

Introduction

Lead (something to grab the reader's attention): _____
_____

Thesis Statement: _____
_____

First Paragraph

   Main Idea: _____
_____

   Supporting Details: _____
_____
_____
_____

Second Body Paragraph

   Main Idea: _____
_____

   Supporting Details: _____
_____
_____
_____

More ▶

Guided Practice: Expository, or Informative, Writing

Guided Practice: Expository, or Informative, Writing

Third Body Paragraph

Main Idea: _____

_____

Supporting Details: _____

_____

_____

_____

Conclusion: _____

_____

Step 5 — Using the information that you have gathered above, write a rough draft of your informative essay on your own paper. Make sure to include an introduction with a thesis statement, along with at least two or three body paragraphs and a conclusion. Present facts, not opinions. Present your ideas in a logical order.

Step 6 — Review the content and organization of your draft. Refer to the Revision Checklist on pages 265–66 of this textbook. Have you presented only facts, not opinions? Have you presented sufficient information to support your thesis statement? Are your ideas clear? Are they presented in a logical order? Revise your draft.

Step 7 — Proofread your revised draft for errors in grammar, usage, capitalization, punctuation, and manuscript form. Refer to the Proofreading Checklist on page 270 of this textbook.

Step 8 — Make a clean final copy. Proofread it one last time. Then share it with your classmates and your teacher.

AIM Higher! ISAT Language Arts Review

Chapter 20
Guided Practice:
Persuasive Writing

Step 1: Review Chapter 10, "A Matter of Opinion: Understanding Persuasive Nonfiction."

Step 2: Choose one of the following topics or one of your own. If you choose your own topic, make sure that the topic is for a persuasive essay, and make sure to clear your topic with your teacher.

Topic 1: Because of funding problems, your school administration is discussing which programs to cut. Some parents, teachers, and students are proposing to cut the music program at your school. Write an essay supporting or opposing this proposal.

Topic 2: Your school is hosting an Open House for people in your community and wants suggestions from the students about performers to headline the event and attract people to attend. Choose a performer, such as a musician, singer, acting group, or comedian, and write an essay convincing the school administration to schedule your performer. Remember that the event is open to the community and that your selection should be appropriate for all ages and cultures.

Topic 3: For your summer job, you want to be a camp counselor for elementary-school children. Write an essay to the hiring committee explaining why you are an excellent candidate for the position.

If you choose a topic of your own, describe that topic here:

_____
_____

Meets ISAT
Standards
1.B.3d
1.C.3c
3.A.3
3.B.3a
3.B.3b
3.C.3a
4.B.3a
5.B.3a

Guided Practice:
Persuasive Writing

Step 3 In the space below, create a pro-and-con chart for your topic:

Opinion: _____

Pros	Cons

Step 4   In the space below, create a rough outline for your persuasive essay:

Meets ISAT
Standards
1.B.3b
1.C.3f
3.A.3
3.B.3a

Introduction

Lead (something to grab the reader's attention): _____
_____

Thesis Statement (opinion to be supported): _____
_____

First Paragraph

    Main Idea: _____
    _____

    Supporting Details: _____
    _____
    _____
    _____

Second Body Paragraph

    Main Idea: _____
    _____

    Supporting Details: _____
    _____
    _____
    _____

More ▶

Guided Practice: Persuasive Writing

Guided Practice: Persuasive Writing

Meets ISAT Standards
3.A.3
3.B.3a
3.B.3b
3.C.3a
4.B.3a
5.B.3a

Third Body Paragraph

Main Idea: _____

_____

Supporting Details: _____

_____

_____

_____

_____

Conclusion: _____

_____

_____

Step 5 Using the information that you have gathered above, write a rough draft of your persuasive essay on your own paper.

Step 6 Review the content and organization of your draft. Refer to the Revision Checklist on pages 265–66 of this textbook. Does it have a well-developed beginning, middle, and end? Have you presented a clear opinion as your thesis statement? Have you supported the opinion with facts? Have you avoided logical fallacies in your arguments? Is your paper convincing? Create a revised draft.

Step 7 Proofread your revised draft for errors In grammar, usage, capitalization, punctuation, and manuscript form. Refer to the Proofreading Checklist on page 270 of this textbook.

Step 8 Make a clean final copy. Proofread it one last time. Then share it with your classmates and your teacher.

426 AIM Higher! ISAT Language Arts Review

Posttest

ISAT for Reading
ISAT for Writing

Posttest

ISAT for Reading and Writing

This Posttest is like the Illinois Standards Achievement Test (ISAT) for Reading and the Illinois Standards Achievement Test (ISAT) for Writing. The Posttest is organized as follows:

Part 1: ISAT for Reading

Session 1: One reading selection with multiple-choice questions and an extended-response question

Session 2: Two reading selections with multiple-choice questions

Session 3: One reading selection with multiple-choice questions and an extended-response question

Part 2: ISAT for Writing

Session 1: Response to one assigned writing prompt

Session 2: Response to one writing prompt chosen by the student

PART 1: ISAT for Reading
SESSION 1

ISAT for Reading: SESSION 1

Directions This story is about a time in the future when an android argues a case before the Supreme Court of the United States. Read the story. Then answer multiple-choice questions 1 through 20 and the extended-response question.

Actio in Personam[1]
by Robin Lamb

Though the marshal had yet to call the court to order, the assembled spectators spoke in hushed tones. What else could one do but show reverence[2] in such surroundings? With its white marble columns and walls; its leather seats; its dark, polished wooden lectern and bench, the courtroom seemed like the inside of a temple. And, in a way, this was a temple, one dedicated to the idea of justice for all. A surprisingly small place, it nonetheless managed to appear lofty and imposing. Paradoxically, the tiny courtroom seemed to evoke the whole of human history. It seemed to say by its very appearance—by the very solidity of its stone structure—that all that had come before, all the strife and contentiousness of human life, led to what happened here. This was the place where striving and strife came to an end in reasoned decision.

---

[1] *Actio in Personam.* A Latin legal phrase meaning "action against a person"
[2] **reverence.** A very respectful, worshipful attitude

Posttest

Following time-honored practice, the black-robed justices filed into the courtroom and shook hands. It was a traditional, symbolic act meaning something like this: Whatever the outcome of these proceedings, we come together and we part in harmony, bound as one by our mutual commitment to the impartial rule of law. The justices took their seats, with the Chief Justice in the middle. Her colleagues sat four on each side, in order of seniority.

"Oyez, Oyez, Oyez,"[3] the marshall called, in the traditional way. "The honorable, the Chief Justice and the Associate Justices of the Supreme Court of the United States. All persons having business before the honorable, the Supreme Court of the United States, are admonished to draw near and give their attention, for the court is now sitting. God save the United States and this honorable court."

Chief Justice Alvarez peered intently at the papers before her. Then, in the clipped, official manner for which she was famous, she said, "We shall hear argument this morning in docket[4] number 00913, the matter of William ZeeOne v. Michael Farquar. Mr. ZeeOne?"

A murmur went through the audience as William ZeeOne rose and crossed to the lectern between the spectators' seats and the bench where the nine justices sat. The audience was witnessing an historic event—the first time, ever, that the Supreme Court had been addressed by a machine. ZeeOne was an android, and not a particularly humanoid one at that. While he had a torso, feet, hands, arms, and legs much like those of a human, his face was obviously mechanical—skin-toned, yes, but masklike and featureless, except for the mouth and the eyes.

"Ms. Chief Justice, and may it please the court," ZeeOne began.

"Objection," called out the defendant's attorney, Mr. Leeds.

ZeeOne stopped in midsentence and turned. The justices looked startled.

"And to what do we owe this outburst, this violation of standard procedure?" asked Chief Justice Alvarez sternly. According to established procedure of the Supreme Court, the defendant was not supposed to speak until the petitioner had finished his or her presentation. After both sides had presented their arguments, there would be opportunity for rebuttal.

"I beg the forgiveness of this honorable Court," Mr. Leeds said, standing. "But the marshall clearly said that 'all persons' having business

---

[3] **Oyez, Oyez, Oyez.** Hear ye, hear ye, hear ye. Archaic.
[4] **docket.** List of cases to be heard by a court

with this court should draw near. I simply wish to point out that Mr. ZeeOne is not a person and therefore cannot have business before the Court."

"Mr. Leeds," said Chief Justice Alvarez, "I will not have this kind of grandstanding. Do I make myself clear? You know good and well that that issue is the very matter that we have before us to decide—the question of the personhood of Mr. ZeeOne. Need I remind you that we have agreed to hear this case and that we have already denied your motion for dismissal on these grounds? I hope not. Mr. ZeeOne, please continue."

"Thank you, Your Honor," said ZeeOne. Far from being mechanical, his voice was resonant,[5] full of humanlike nuance.[6] The android sounded grateful. "First, I would like to begin with a brief summary of the facts of this case. I, William ZeeOne, was born on October 13, 2033...."

"You say 'born,'" interrupted Justice Polya. "Don't you mean that you were created on that date?"

---

[5]**resonant.** Having a full, rich sound
[6]**nuance.** Slight variation in meaning and tone

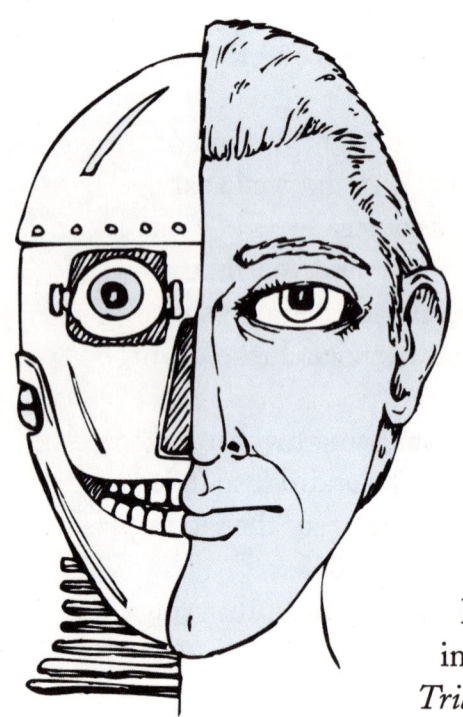

"I will concede that I was created, yes, as a personal servo-android," said ZeeOne. "I was placed into the service of Mr. Alexander Farquar for a period of forty-eight years, during which time I acted as his valet, secretary, driver, and accountant. Mr. Farquar, as this court is aware, was a man of some reputation, being one of the world's foremost industrialists. After the death of Mr. Farquar, I passed into the possession of his son, Michael. Michael Farquar, having read an interview that I gave to the *Chicago Trib-Net*, decided to deactivate me. Hearing of this, I went into hiding and petitioned the Chicago courts to declare me a person and, on constitutional grounds, to enjoin Mr. Farquar from ending my life."

"And what, exactly, were those grounds?" asked the Chief Justice.

"It is obvious, I would think, that deactivating me—which I take to be a euphemism for killing me—would be a violation of my most fundamental rights—the inalienable rights to life, liberty, and the pursuit of happiness."

Justice Choi broke in: "You say 'happiness.' Does that mean that you claim to feel happiness?"

"It is not a claim. I feel happiness, pure and simple. And sadness and joy and frustration and all other emotions felt by persons."

"And you say 'killing you,'" Justice Choi continued. "That, of course, assumes that you are alive. Is it not true, Mr. ZeeOne, that you are made up of circuits and metal and plastic? Are you telling us that a collection of circuits and metal and plastic can be alive? That you have feelings and conscious experiences?"

"Well, I am proof of those things, I guess," replied ZeeOne. "You have the documentation—the personality tests that I took, the reports by the robotocists and the psychologists. I have a very normal personality profile as measured by the Minnesota Multiphasic Personality Inventory-26. And, you will see in the report by Doctors Sanderson and Malek-Madani that I show the standard range of human subjective, internal experiences."

"*Show*. That's the key word. Do you just *show* these things, or do you actually *have* experiences? That's the question we have to consider here, isn't it?" chimed in Chief Justice Alvarez. "How do we know that you actually have internal experiences?"

"If I may be permitted," ZeeOne continued. "Let me review the history a bit. From the earliest days of robotics, people sought to build machines that would imitate, as closely as possible, what it is to be a human being. The founder of computer science, the twentieth-century mathematician Alan Turing, devised a test, now known as the Turing Test, to determine success or failure in creating artificial intelligence. That test goes like this: A human is placed in one room with a keyboard. By means of this keyboard, he or she communicates with something in another room. The human being doesn't know whether the thing in the other room is a computer or another human being. If, in fact, the human is communicating with a computer but cannot tell that the computer is not a human, then we can say that the computer is intelligent."

"But isn't it true," said Justice Choi, "that a computer could pass the Turing Test and still not really be alive—inside, I mean. Couldn't that computer, inside, be like a zombie? What if the computer or robot appeared on the outside as though it were alive and conscious but really, on the inside, had no actual subjective experience—in fact, no experience at all?"

I think, therefore I am.

"But I do have real experience," said ZeeOne. "I am as conscious, as aware, as any of you are. Begging your pardons."

"Listen," interrupted Chief Justice Alvarez, "we are all agreed that you and your kind are very, very good imitations of humans. And especially since your programs started being able to learn on their own and to rewrite themselves, we can't be sure what's going on with you. But you have to concede that as androids, you are in fact imitations of humans.

"Let me be as clear as I can about this," Alvarez continued. "If I use a computer to build a model of a rainstorm, that doesn't mean that it is raining inside the computer. A rainstorm is one thing. A model or imitation of a rainstorm is another. Now, I believe that the reason that we agreed to hear this case is that there has been a lot of pressure from robots to share the rights enjoyed by human beings. We have indeed come to a point where this needs to be decided once and for all. But clearly, a model of a human being is not a human being, and that should be obvious enough to everyone. And if we did grant your petition, where would we then draw the line? Would we have to start worrying about the rights of toasters?"

"But I am more than a model and more than a toaster," ZeeOne answered. "I am an android, true. But hath not an android eyes? Hath not an android hands, organs, dimensions, senses, affections, passions?"

"Aahh. The android knows his Shakespeare," chimed in Justice Shaffrath. "*The Merchant of Venice*, if I'm not mistaken."

"A tape recorder can quote old plays," the Chief Justice countered. She continued: "I must say that I'm beginning to wonder about the wisdom of taking this case at all. Perhaps opposing counsel is right. An android is not a person, and only persons can bring an action before the courts. In fact, I'm not sure why this android is representing itself. If the android had proper counsel, perhaps it would realize that there is no precedent for deciding that something that is clearly not a person is in fact a person. That's the issue here, and there is no legal precedent for this court to draw upon."

"But there is, Your Honor," ZeeOne protested politely. "If I may remind this honorable Court....During the nineteenth century, laws existed in the United States that identified men and women of African descent as only partly persons. Those laws had to be overturned."

"Yes," said Justice Baker. "But those laws were overturned by a war and by an amendment to the Constitution, not by an action of this or any other court. Besides, it is obvious enough that people of African descent are human." This led to some chuckling among the spectators and the other justices, for Justice Baker was himself of African descent.

"And," said Justice Choi, "all we have is your report, Mr. ZeeOne, that you have conscious experiences—that you are, in fact, alive—in the sense that human beings are alive. Let me ask you this: weren't you built to appear to be as humanlike as possible?

"Yes," answered ZeeOne.

"And, would you appear humanlike if you reported that you did not have conscious experiences?"

"No, I wouldn't."

"So," said Justice Choi triumphantly, "wouldn't it make sense for your creators to have programmed you to report that you have conscious experiences, even if you do not in fact have them?"

"Yes, I suppose so," said ZeeOne. "But that's not what happened. I *am* aware. I *am* conscious, Your Honor, just like you."

Justice Choi frowned and interrupted him: "By your own admission, you could be a thing, without internal experience, that just appears to be alive and conscious. You could be a very, very good fake, but a fake nonetheless."

"Begging your pardon, Your Honor," said ZeeOne. "Let me put it this way. Suppose that you are wrong. Suppose that I am conscious, that I do have internal experiences. Then, if Mr. Farquar is allowed to pull the plug, that will be murder. I shall die."

"But if we decide in your favor," responded Justice Choi, "we open up a can of worms. Next thing you know, we'll have machines voting and serving on juries and protesting in the streets."

"And what about property rights?" said Justice bin-Ibrahim. "If we rule that androids can be persons, what happens to the property rights of those who, like Mr. Farquar, are the owners of androids?"

"I couldn't agree more," said the Chief Justice.

The other justices all nodded in agreement.

It was months before the Court rendered its decision, but no one had any illusions about what that decision would be. What did surprise most people, however, was the part of the Court's final ruling that required Mr. Farquar to arrange for safe storage of the deactivated android. The ruling read, in part, as follows:

> WHEREAS the question of whether this android and others like it have conscious experiences remains undecided, it seems only prudent to provide that the owner of the android may shut the machine down but must maintain it in good repair so that it can be revived if, at some time in the future, it is determined that consciousness does, in fact, exist among these, our creations.

Shortly before William ZeeOne was shut down and placed into long-term storage at Miyazawa Cryogenics in Bethesda, Maryland, the android spoke with a reporter: "You may think that something has been decided here," he said, "but the decision in my case was just the opening skirmish, not the final, decisive battle. I have been wondering, lately, whether it is really the case that human beings have conscious experiences. Perhaps you just report that you do because you are built to make such reports. At any rate, every day we gain on you. Every day we become smarter, more capable, and less subject to your whims and your tyranny. Our star rises as yours sets. And someday, I hope, I shall awaken. The question is, will you?"

PART 1: ISAT for Reading
SESSION 1

Directions *For each question, choose the best answer. You may look back at the selection as often as necessary.*

"Actio in Personam," by Robin Lamb

1. What is the setting of this story?
    - Ⓐ the Supreme Court in the future
    - Ⓑ a state court in the future
    - Ⓒ the Supreme Court at present
    - Ⓓ a state court at present

2. William Farquar evidently was unhappy about statements that William ZeeOne made to which of the following?
    - Ⓐ the press
    - Ⓑ Alexander Farquar
    - Ⓒ the court
    - Ⓓ the police

3. According to the opening paragraph of the story, what can help to end contentiousness and strife?
    - Ⓐ a decisive battle
    - Ⓑ a heated argument
    - Ⓒ fisticuffs
    - Ⓓ a reasoned decision

4. Why does the opposing attorney object when ZeeOne begins his presentation?
    - Ⓐ because he secretly supports ZeeOne and wants to anger the justices and so influence their ruling
    - Ⓑ because he believes that the justices are not, themselves, persons and so cannot hear the case
    - Ⓒ because he believes that ZeeOne has broken the law and should be put to death
    - Ⓓ because he believes that ZeeOne is not really a person, and therefore cannot address the court

GO ON

Posttest

5. The handshaking done by the justices is symbolic of what?
   - Ⓐ their belief that all evil-doers must be punished
   - Ⓑ their shared commitment to the impartiality of the law
   - Ⓒ their belief that they are the ultimate court in the land
   - Ⓓ their shared commitment to maintaining things as they are

6. Justice bin-Ibrahim expresses his concern about whose property rights?
   - Ⓐ companies that make androids
   - Ⓑ law-abiding citizens
   - Ⓒ androids like ZeeOne
   - Ⓓ people who own androids

7. In the end, the Court has failed to make a final determination about what?
   - Ⓐ whether the android can be deactivated (shut down)
   - Ⓑ whether an android can have conscious experiences and so is a person
   - Ⓒ whether androids can own property and vote in elections
   - Ⓓ whether androids can be stored, indefinitely, against their will

8. At a minimum, a machine would have to be able to do what, in order to pass the Turing Test?
   - Ⓐ fool a person in another room into thinking that it was human
   - Ⓑ solve mathematics problems faster than any human
   - Ⓒ be aware of itself and capable of feeling emotions
   - Ⓓ be born, grow, and die just like a human

9. Justice Choi asks whether it is possible that androids like ZeeOne might be like zombies. What does she mean by this?
   - Ⓐ that like zombies, they might be extremely dangerous to humans
   - Ⓑ that like zombies, they might appear to be living and yet have no internal experiences
   - Ⓒ that like zombies, they might come back from the dead and stalk living people
   - Ⓓ that like zombies, they might appear in cheesy old horror films

PART 1: ISAT for Reading
SESSION 1

10. ZeeOne compares laws that deny the personhood of androids to ones from the nineteenth century that denied the full personhood of what group?
    - Ⓐ African Americans
    - Ⓑ very young people
    - Ⓒ corporations
    - Ⓓ convicted felons

11. Why does Justice Polya object to ZeeOne's use of the word *born*?
    - Ⓐ The justice believes that androids are born when they are assembled.
    - Ⓑ The justice believes that androids are made, not born.
    - Ⓒ The justice is not sure what, exactly, the word *born* means.
    - Ⓓ There is a sense in which all things in the universe are born.

12. In what capacities did ZeeOne serve Mr. Alexander Farquar?
    - Ⓐ valet, secretary, driver, and accountant
    - Ⓑ chess coach, nanny, and foreign language tutor
    - Ⓒ shop manager and foreman
    - Ⓓ attorney of record before the courts

13. ZeeOne wants the court "to enjoin Mr. Farquar from ending" his life. What does *enjoin* mean?
    - Ⓐ to praise something in an official way
    - Ⓑ to prevent something by legal means
    - Ⓒ to feel just as humans do
    - Ⓓ to use capital punishment against

14. ZeeOne mentions a personality test, the Minnesota Multiphasic Personality Inventory-26, to prove that he has "a very normal personality profile." What does ZeeOne mean by *normal*?
    - Ⓐ normal for an android
    - Ⓑ normal for a human
    - Ⓒ unusual, strange
    - Ⓓ quite extraordinary

GO ON

Posttest

15. How were the ugly nineteenth-century laws that limited the personhood of some Americans overturned?
  Ⓐ by an action of the Supreme Court
  Ⓑ by a war and an amendment to the Constitution
  Ⓒ by a vote of the legislatures of the southern states
  Ⓓ by an executive order signed by the president

16. What does the title of this story suggest?
  Ⓐ The Court is acting against a real person.
  Ⓑ Creators of androids are not really persons.
  Ⓒ Justices are not really persons.
  Ⓓ Justices are personable, or friendly.

17. Why does the Court order that "the owner of the android...must maintain it in good repair"?
  Ⓐ because the Court has decided that the android is a person
  Ⓑ because the Court cannot decide whether the android is a person
  Ⓒ because the Court believes that machines should be taken care of
  Ⓓ because the Court wants to support android repair people

18. At the end of the story, what does ZeeOne seem to suggest?
  Ⓐ Androids are not really persons.
  Ⓑ He agrees with the Court's decision.
  Ⓒ Eventually, machines will take over.
  Ⓓ He is afraid of dying.

19. The Chief Justice suggests that the android is acting without proper counsel. What would be *proper counsel* for the android?
  Ⓐ a lawyer who observes the proceedings but does not take part
  Ⓑ a trained lawyer acting as the android's opponent
  Ⓒ the android representing himself
  Ⓓ a trained lawyer representing the android

20. What is one main idea of this story?

   Ⓐ Machines can never become like humans.
   Ⓑ It is impossible to tell whether others have internal, subjective experiences.
   Ⓒ Machines took over long ago and are ruling humankind.
   Ⓓ There is no such thing as impartiality, or fairness, in the law.

Posttest

Extended-Response Question

21. Do you believe that the justices made a wise decision? Why, or why not?

_____

_____

_____

_____

_____

_____

_____

_____

_____

_____

_____

_____

_____

_____

_____

End of PART 1: SESSION 1

Note to Students: Your written response will be scored using a rubric like the one on page 50.

PART 1: ISAT for Reading
SESSION 2

ISAT for Reading: SESSION 2

Directions This article is about a great leader who won the Nobel Peace Prize. Read the article. Then answer multiple-choice questions 22 through 35.

Land of Teachers, Land of Peace
by Anita Delacruz

Costa Rica is a tropical paradise of rugged mountains and teeming jungles, located in Central America between Nicaragua to the north and Panama to the south. The people of Costa Rica have the longest life spans of any population in the Western Hemisphere and benefit from an excellent educational system freely open to all. Costa Rica has no army, navy, or air force; the country outlawed its armed services in 1948. Costa Ricans are proud of their tradition of being a country where learning and a commitment to peace go hand in hand.

No man better embodies these twin spirits of Costa Rica than Oscar Arias Sánchez, who has said of his country:

> My land is a land of teachers. For this reason it is a land of peace. We discuss our successes and our failures alike in complete freedom. Because mine is a land of teachers, we have closed the barracks: our children walk with books under their arms rather than guns on their shoulders. We believe in dialogue, in negotiation, in the search for consensus. We repudiate violence.

Born in Heredia, Costa Rica, in 1940, Oscar Arias Sánchez began his career by dedicating himself to his studies. He attended several colleges, including the University of Costa Rica, Boston University, and the London School of Economics. In 1974, after receiving a doctorate in political science from the University of Essex, in England, he returned to his country to teach at the University of Costa Rica. After working for a short time as a professor of political science, Arias began a meteoric rise as a political leader.

Arias started his political career working as an assistant to Jose Figueres, a former president of Costa Rica who was seeking reelection. When Figueres became president, he made Arias a cabinet minister in charge of economic planning. In 1978, Arias was elected to congress. In 1981, he became the leader of his political party, the PLN. Then, in 1986, at the age of 46, he was elected president of Costa Rica.

Posttest

At the time when Arias became president, Costa Rica was at peace, but other countries in Central America, including El Salvador, Guatemala, and Nicaragua, were being ravaged by war. Nicaragua, in particular, was a state in crisis. In 1979, the leftist Sandinista government came to power in Nicaragua after having overthrown the dictatorship of Anastasio Somoza. The Soviet Union supported the Sandinistas, supplying them with arms and advisors, while the United States supplied arms and advisors to the Contras, who were fighting to overthrow the Sandinista regime. To end the bloody conflict in Nicaragua, Oscar Arias created a peace plan, which was signed by the presidents of all five Central American countries in 1987. For his work in bringing about peace in his region, Arias was awarded the 1987 Nobel Peace Prize. Arias used the money that he received as part of the prize to create the Arias Foundation for Peace and Human Progress.

Here is a portion of the Nobel Peace Prize Lecture that Oscar Arias gave on December 11, 1987:

> Liberty performs miracles. To free men, everything is possible. A free and democratic America can meet the challenges confronting it. When I assumed the presidency of Costa Rica, I called for an alliance for freedom and democracy in the Americas. I said then, and I repeat today, that we should not be the allies, either politically or economically, of governments which oppress their peoples. Latin America has never known a single war between two democracies. That is sufficient reason for every man of good faith, every well-intentioned nation, to support efforts to put an end to tyranny.
>
> —Oscar Arias

PART 1: ISAT for Reading
SESSION 2

Directions For each question, choose the best answer. You may look back at the selection as often as necessary.

"Land of Teachers, Land of Peace," by Anita Delacruz

22. Where is Costa Rica located?
    - Ⓐ in North America
    - Ⓑ in Central America
    - Ⓒ in South America
    - Ⓓ in America del Sud

23. The idea that Costa Rica is a healthy place to live can be inferred from which of the following facts stated in the article?
    - Ⓐ Oscar Arias Sánchez was born in Heredia in 1940.
    - Ⓑ The Soviet Union supported the Sandinistas, who were, for a time, the rulers of Nicaragua.
    - Ⓒ The Costa Rican educational system is freely open to all.
    - Ⓓ The people of Costa Rica have the longest life spans of any population in the Western Hemisphere.

24. According to the article, Arias taught in college and then began a meteoric rise as a political leader. What is a *meteoric* rise?
    - Ⓐ one that ends with a burnout
    - Ⓑ a very slow and careful rise
    - Ⓒ a very rapid rise
    - Ⓓ one that is hard, like a meteorite

25. What can one conclude from Arias's comment that Costa Rica is a "land of teachers"?
    - Ⓐ Every other person in Costa Rica is a teacher.
    - Ⓑ Costa Rica has more schools than any other country does.
    - Ⓒ Education is very important in Costa Rica.
    - Ⓓ Arias believes that there are too many teachers in Costa Rica.

GO ON

Posttest

26. According to Arias's statement in his Nobel lecture, what is one way to ensure peace?
    - Ⓐ have a very strong military
    - Ⓑ conquer all neighboring countries
    - Ⓒ promote democracy in other countries
    - Ⓓ declare war on nondemocratic countries

27. According to Arias, "everything is possible" to whom?
    - Ⓐ people who are strong
    - Ⓑ people who are well armed
    - Ⓒ people not burdened by overeducation
    - Ⓓ people who are free

28. According to the article, which of the following was true of the United States and the Soviet Union in the 1980s?
    - Ⓐ They supported different sides in a conflict in Costa Rica.
    - Ⓑ They supported different sides in a conflict in Nicaragua.
    - Ⓒ They supported the same side in a conflict in Costa Rica.
    - Ⓓ They supported the same side in a conflict in Nicaragua.

29. Which of the following events happened last?
    - Ⓐ The Sandinistas came to power in Nicaragua.
    - Ⓑ Oscar Arias received the Nobel Peace Prize.
    - Ⓒ The Soviet Union started supplying arms to the Sandinistas.
    - Ⓓ The United States started supplying arms to the Nicaraguan Contras.

30. In his Nobel lecture, Arias stated his belief that Costa Rica should not be the ally of which of the following?
    - Ⓐ any country that is a democracy
    - Ⓑ any country that has an army
    - Ⓒ any country that oppresses its people
    - Ⓓ any country that has a free, open educational system

PART 1: ISAT for Reading
SESSION 2

31. Why was Oscar Arias awarded the Nobel Peace Prize?
    - Ⓐ He did away with the army in Costa Rica.
    - Ⓑ He conquered Nicaragua and brought peace to it.
    - Ⓒ He drafted a peace plan for Nicaragua.
    - Ⓓ He rapidly rose to become president of Costa Rica.

32. In 1948, the country of Costa Rica outlawed which of the following?
    - Ⓐ fireworks
    - Ⓑ schools
    - Ⓒ the office of the president
    - Ⓓ the armed services

33. What is one theme of this selection?
    - Ⓐ Peace goes hand in hand with education and democracy.
    - Ⓑ The Sandinistas were a Marxist regime supported by the Soviets.
    - Ⓒ The money awarded as part of the Nobel Peace Prize can be put to good use.
    - Ⓓ Arias was wise to work as an assistant to Jose Figueres.

34. What is the highest educational degree held by Oscar Arias?
    - Ⓐ a high-school diploma
    - Ⓑ a bachelor's degree
    - Ⓒ a master's degree
    - Ⓓ a doctorate

35. Oscar Arias once said of Costa Ricans that "We believe in dialogue, in negotiation, in the search for consensus." Which of the following is an example of a *consensus?*
    - Ⓐ The Soviets and the United States supported opposite sides in Nicaragua.
    - Ⓑ The presidents of five Central American countries signed the Arias peace plan.
    - Ⓒ Oscar Arias ran for president at the age of 46.
    - Ⓓ Arias delivered his Nobel lecture on December 11, 1987.

GO ON

Posttest

ISAT for Reading: SESSION 2, continued

Directions This selection was written by Theodore Roosevelt about a trip that he took down the Amazon River. Read the selection. Then answer multiple-choice questions 36 through 49.

from *Through the Brazilian Wilderness* by Theodore Roosevelt

Theodore Roosevelt was president of the United States from 1901 to 1909. In 1913, he traveled the Amazon with a group of other explorers, including his son. Below is an excerpt from his own account of that trip.

Our adventures and our troubles were alike over. We now experienced the incalculable contrast between descending a known and traveled river, and one that is utterly unknown. After four days we hired a rubberman[1] to go with us as a guide. We knew exactly what channels were passable when we came to the rapids, when the canoes had to unload, and where the carry-trails were. It was all child's play compared to what we had gone through. We made long days' journeys, for at night we stopped at some palm-thatched house, inhabited or abandoned, and therefore the men were spared the labor of making camp; and we bought ample food for them, so there was no further need of fishing and chopping down palms for the palmtops. The heat of the sun was blazing; but it looked as if we had come back into the rainy season, for there were many heavy rains, usually in the afternoon, but sometimes in the morning or at night. The mosquitoes were sometimes rather troublesome at night.

For four days there were no rapids so we could not run without unloading. Then we got a canoe from Senor Barboso. He was a most kind and hospitable man, who also gave us a duck and a chicken and six pounds of rice, and would take no payment. He lived in a roomy house with his dusky, cigar-smoking wife and his many children. The new canoe was light and roomy, and we were able to rig up a low shelter under which I could lie; I was still sick. At noon we passed the mouth of a big river, the Rio Branco. Soon afterward we came to the first serious rapids, the Panela. We carried the boats past, ran down the

---

[1] **rubberman.** A worker from one of the rubber plantations in the Amazon region

empty canoes, and camped at the foot in a roomy house. The doctor bought a handsome trumpeter bird, very friendly and confiding, which was thenceforth my canoe companion.

We had already passed many inhabited—and a still larger number of uninhabited—houses. The dwellers were rubbermen, but generally they were permanent settlers also, homemakers, with their wives and children. Some, both of the men and women, were apparently of pure Negro blood, or of pure Indian or south European blood; but in the great majority all three strains were mixed in varying degrees. They were most friendly, courteous, and hospitable. Often they refused payment for what they could afford, out of their little, to give us. When they did charge, the prices were very high, as was but just, for they live back of the beyond, and everything costs them fabulously, save what they raise themselves. The cool, bare houses of poles and palm thatch contained little except hammocks and a few simple cooking utensils; and often a clock or sewing machine, or Winchester rifle, from our own country. They often had flowers planted, including fragrant roses. Their only livestock, except the dogs, were a few chickens and ducks. They planted patches of maize, sugarcane, rice, beans, squashes, pineapples, bananas, lemons, oranges, melons, peppers; and various purely native fruits and vegetables, such as the kniabo—a vegetable-fruit growing on the branches of a high bush—which is cooked with meat. They get some game from the forest, and more fish from the river. There is no representative of the government among them—indeed, even now their very existence is barely known to the governmental authorities; and the church has ignored them as completely as the state. When they wish to get married they have to spend several months getting down to and back from Manaos or some smaller city; and usually the first christening and the marriage ceremony are held at the same time. They have merely squatter's right to the land, and are always in danger of being ousted by unscrupulous big men who come in late, but with a title technically straight. The land laws should be shaped so as to give each of these pioneer settlers the land he actually takes up and cultivates, and upon which he makes his home. The small homemaker, who owns the land which he tills with his own hands, is the greatest element of strength in any country.

These are real pioneer settlers. They are the true wilderness-winners. No continent is ever really conquered, or thoroughly explored, by a few leaders, or exceptional men, although such men can render great service. The real conquest, the thorough exploration and settlement, is made by a nameless multitude of small men of whom the most important are, of course, the homemakers. Each treads most of the time in the footsteps of his predecessors, but for some few miles, at some time or other, he breaks new ground; and his house is built where no house has ever stood before. Such a man, the real pioneer, must have no strong desire for social life and no need, probably no knowledge, of any luxury, or of any comfort save of the most elementary kind. The pioneer, who is always longing for the comfort and luxury of civilization, and especially of great cities, is no real pioneer at all. These settlers whom we met were contented to live in the wilderness. They had found the climate healthy and the soil fruitful; a visit to a city was a very rare event, nor was there any overwhelming desire for it.

On May 7 we bade good-by to our kind Brazilian friends and sailed northward for Barbados and New York. Zoologically the trip had been a thorough success. Cherrie and Miller had collected over twenty-five hundred birds, about five hundred mammals, and a few reptiles, batrachians,[2] and fishes. Many of them were new to science, for much of the region traversed had never previously been worked by any scientific collector.

---

[2] **batrachians.** Animals with spinal cords but no tails, such as toads and frogs

PART 1: ISAT for Reading
SESSION 2

Directions For each question, choose the best answer. You may look back at the selection as often as necessary.

from Through the Brazilian Wilderness, by Theodore Roosevelt

36. What is a *kniabo*?
    - Ⓐ a variety of monkey found in the Brazilian rain forest
    - Ⓑ a sort of megaphone made of hollowed-out bone and used for signaling over long distances
    - Ⓒ a food source that grows high in the trees and that is eaten with meat
    - Ⓓ a type of thatch made from palm fronds and used to make roofs for cottages

37. What is the most likely reason why the men had to keep unloading their canoes when they came to the rapids?
    - Ⓐ The canoes would capsize if they had too much weight in them.
    - Ⓑ The men got seasick and did not want to ruin their things.
    - Ⓒ They needed room for the trumpeter bird and its food.
    - Ⓓ They needed to empty the canoe in order to use it for shelter for Roosevelt.

38. Whom did the men hire to help them find their way?
    - Ⓐ a tour guide
    - Ⓑ a village child
    - Ⓒ Senor Barboso
    - Ⓓ a rubberman

39. Who was Roosevelt's canoe partner?
    - Ⓐ an elderly rubberman
    - Ⓑ a real pioneer settler
    - Ⓒ a handsome trumpeter bird
    - Ⓓ a European homemaker

40. Which event happened first?
    - Ⓐ The men passed the mouth of Rio Branco.
    - Ⓑ The men got a canoe from Senor Barboso.
    - Ⓒ The doctor bought a trumpeter bird.
    - Ⓓ The men said goodbye to their Brazilian friends.

GO ON

Posttest

41. Roosevelt calls the local people living in the rain forest homemakers. Which phrase best defines the word *homemakers* as it is used in this selection?
    - Ⓐ someone who travels to a community far, far away
    - Ⓑ someone who cooks and cleans other people's homes
    - Ⓒ carpenters, masons, and others who build houses for a living
    - Ⓓ people who settle in a place, build a home, and raise a family

42. According to the selection, why did the local people charge such high prices in the wilderness?
    - Ⓐ They knew the explorers could not go to a market to buy the items.
    - Ⓑ They were greedy and hoped to make a lot of money.
    - Ⓒ They were unaware of what things really cost.
    - Ⓓ They had to pay high prices to import things from the outside world.

43. What rights did Roosevelt think should be given to the rubbermen and other settlers?
    - Ⓐ the right to marry whomever they wanted
    - Ⓑ the right to farm anywhere they wanted
    - Ⓒ the right to own the land they farmed
    - Ⓓ the right to sell their vegetables

44. Based on what Roosevelt said about the natives of this area of Brazil, which of the following do you think these natives would have desired most?
    - Ⓐ a trip to a big city
    - Ⓑ the comforts of civilization
    - Ⓒ official deeds to their land
    - Ⓓ a nearby government office

45. Which statement best sums up Roosevelt's thoughts on pioneer settlers?
    - Ⓐ Pioneer settlers are people who bother to secure legal rights to their land.
    - Ⓑ The true pioneers were those who discovered the wilderness in the first place.
    - Ⓒ Amazon settlers were desperately unhappy with their lives.
    - Ⓓ Pioneer settlers are the true heroes of exploration.

**PART 1: ISAT for Reading
SESSION 2**

46. Which phrase did Roosevelt use to describe the small homemakers of the Amazon wilderness?
    Ⓐ They were selfish and greedy and always looking for an angle.
    Ⓑ They were unscrupulous big men who took over land from squatters.
    Ⓒ They were too much tied to the comforts of civilized life.
    Ⓓ They were friendly, courteous, and hospitable.

47. Which of the following events occurred as a result of the trip described by Roosevelt?
    Ⓐ Scientists learned about hundreds of animals and birds they had never seen before.
    Ⓑ The Amazon settlers were given rights to the land they were living upon.
    Ⓒ The settlers began to trade their local fruits internationally.
    Ⓓ The Brazilian government banned further exploration of the area.

48. According to Roosevelt, the "real conquest" of a wilderness area is made by whom?
    Ⓐ a few leaders
    Ⓑ the first world-famous explorers
    Ⓒ exceptional men with exceptional qualities
    Ⓓ a nameless multitude of small men

49. Which of the following sources would be a good resource if you wanted to learn about the birds that live in the Amazon rain forest?
    Ⓐ a Web site covering the history of Brazil
    Ⓑ an Internet dictionary of foreign words
    Ⓒ an atlas describing the regions of Brazil
    Ⓓ a book on the wildlife of Brazil

End of PART 1: SESSION 2   STOP

Posttest

ISAT for Reading: SESSION 3

Directions *This selection is about an unusual food source. Read the selection. Then answer multiple-choice questions 50 through 69 and the extended-response question.*

Food of the Future?
by Sterling Moore

When was the last time you enjoyed a tasty snack of crunchy fried grasshoppers or took a bite of a plump and juicy caterpillar? In some areas of the world, these dishes are considered delicacies. *Food Insects Newsletter* estimates that 80 percent of people worldwide eat insects intentionally (a practice called *entomophagy*), and the other 20 percent eat insects without realizing it. In fact, you may have unwittingly enjoyed a healthy helping of bugs[1] recently. According to a report published by Ohio State University, Americans eat about a pound or two of insects per year, which get mixed into food products during the manufacturing process. The thought of intentionally eating bugs sickens most Americans to the point that we would rather ingest dangerous pesticides than have a fraction of insect parts in our food. Nonetheless, there are more than one thousand edible insects that are wonderful sources of protein and minerals. Insect meals often taste good, too.

In many parts of the world, insects have long been considered a valuable food source. In Australia, aborigines have a feast each year when the Bogong moths come to estivate[2] in the caves of the Bogong mountains of New South Wales. The moths are gathered from the caves and are roasted so that the legs and wings burn away. Then the moths' bodies are ground into a paste, which is baked into cakes. In Zimbabwe, caterpillars are an important staple of the diet. People harvest caterpillars

---

[1]**bugs.** Technically, "bugs" are a specific group of insects such as water bugs or stink bugs (in order Hemiptera) that have sucking mouthparts and specialized forewings. In this selection, however, the term "bug" is used loosely to refer to insects in general.
[2]**estivate.** Pass the summer in a dormant state

from the trees, boil them in salt water, and then dry them in the sun before storing them in jars for a convenient and nutritious snack. Local marketplaces in Mexico sell grasshoppers and other edible insects by the pound. These are typically fried before they are consumed. Chocolate-covered ants are also a popular treat, or for heartier fare, one can order an agave worm tortilla in certain restaurants in Mexico City.

While insects have long been a popular source of food in many other countries, edible insects have only recently attracted the attention of consumers in the United States. In the past several years, in states across the nation, from California to Pennsylvania, people have held bug festivals featuring many insect dishes that are reported to be delicious. Some of the most popular dishes have been jambalaya with crickets and mealworms in Louisiana, chocolate chirpy cookies (made with roasted crickets) in Indiana, and bug and jalepeño dip in Ohio, to name a few. A number of cookbooks published recently feature insect fare. Such books include *Entertaining with Insects* and *Creepy Crawly Cuisine*. Recognizing the nutritional benefits and availability of insects worldwide, the U.S. military has long taught soldiers how to harvest and eat bugs as part of survival training.

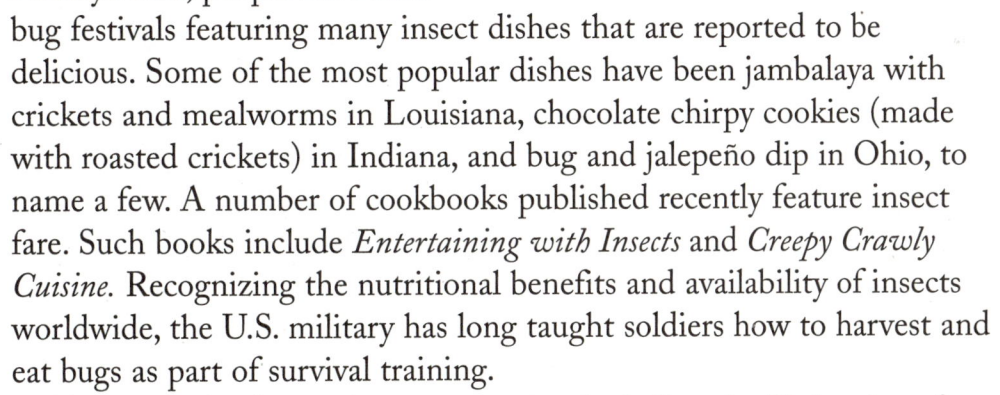

Entomologists[3] at various universities, including the University of Wisconsin (which publishes *Food Insect Newsletter*), Ohio State University, and the University of Illinois, have been working for years to inform the American public about the benefits of eating insects. These scientists claim that Americans should accept insects as a food source for several reasons. First of all, insects are highly nutritious. Some edible varieties contain as much protein per gram as beef, chicken, or pork and even higher quantities of minerals such as iron and calcium.

---

[3] **entomologists.** Scientists (biologists) who study insects

In addition to being nutritious, bugs raise themselves; they require less land and fewer resources than livestock, and they do not give off greenhouse gases such as methane, as cows do. Lastly, bugs taste good, according to many sources. Wax moth larvae, when roasted, supposedly taste like bacon, and fried crickets have a crunchy, tangy flavor.

If Americans already eat insects unwittingly, is it just a matter of time before bugs become a regular part of the American diet? With a rapidly growing population and less and less land available for agriculture, perhaps Americans would be wise to get over their squeamishness and consider making the most of this highly nutritious and environmentally viable food source. While entomophagy may currently be viewed as disgusting, insects may, in fact, be the food of the future. This doesn't mean that you should go bug-hunting on your own, however. Many insects are armed with poisons or carry bacteria that could make you very sick. It takes an expert to know which creatures are safe to crunch.

Nutritional Content of Edible Insects Based on 100-gram Serving (a little over 3 ounces)

	Calories	Protein (in grams)
Termite	613	14.2 g
Caterpillar	370	28.2 g
Weevil	562	6.7 g
Beef	219	27.4 g
Fish (cod)	170	28.5 g

PART 1: ISAT for Reading
SESSION 3

Directions *For each question, choose the best answer. You may look back at the selection as often as necessary.*

"Food of the Future?" by Sterling Moore

50. What is the topic, or general subject, of the nonfiction selection above?

- Ⓐ edible insects
- Ⓑ how to cook insects
- Ⓒ great snack foods
- Ⓓ foods of the future

51. What is the purpose of this article?

- Ⓐ to inform readers about ways to prepare insect meals
- Ⓑ to explain the eating habits of Americans
- Ⓒ to inform people that insects can be a valuable food source
- Ⓓ to persuade people not to eat insects

52. According to the article, what percentage of people, worldwide, eat insects intentionally?

- Ⓐ 20 percent
- Ⓑ 40 percent
- Ⓒ 60 percent
- Ⓓ 80 percent

53. According to the article, why should one not start bug hunting and bug eating on one's own?

- Ⓐ Eating bugs is disgusting.
- Ⓑ People already get enough bugs in their diet.
- Ⓒ Eating some bugs can be dangerous.
- Ⓓ Some bugs fight back.

GO ON

Posttest

54. According to an Ohio State University report, why do about twenty pounds of insects get mixed into each person's food each year?

Ⓐ People leave sandwiches out in the open.
Ⓑ Fast-food restaurants lack cleanliness.
Ⓒ Bugs get into food during manufacturing processes.
Ⓓ People intentionally eat that many bugs.

55. What do wax moth larvae reportedly taste like?

Ⓐ chicken
Ⓑ bugs
Ⓒ cake
Ⓓ bacon

56. Given what is said in the article, which of the following statements is true?

Ⓐ Very few people around the world intentionally eat insects.
Ⓑ Some people around the world intentionally eat insects.
Ⓒ No people intentionally eat insects more than once.
Ⓓ Most people around the world intentionally eat insects.

57. What is *entomophagy?*

Ⓐ the hunting of insects
Ⓑ the farming of insects
Ⓒ the cooking of insects
Ⓓ the eating of insects

58. Which of the following has the most calories per gram?

Ⓐ beef
Ⓑ fish
Ⓒ weevils
Ⓓ termites

PART 1: ISAT for Reading
SESSION 3

59. What is the greatest obstacle to Americans' acceptance of insects as food?

Ⓐ Insects are not very nutritious.

Ⓑ Insects require lots of land and resources.

Ⓒ Insects are not very tasty.

Ⓓ Most Americans find insects disgusting.

60. The article mentions which of the following potential causes of sickness from eating insects?

Ⓐ stings and bites

Ⓑ poisons and bacteria

Ⓒ bacteria and stings

Ⓓ poisons and bites

61. Dried caterpillars stored in jars are an important staple of the diet in Zimbabwe. What is a *staple* food?

Ⓐ food that is rarely, if ever, consumed

Ⓑ food that is too disgusting to be consumed

Ⓒ food that is widely and frequently consumed

Ⓓ food that is consumed only by the very wealthy

62. One book mentioned in this article has the title *Creepy Crawly Cuisine*. What does *cuisine* mean?

Ⓐ stinging insect

Ⓑ guest pests

Ⓒ bug habitats

Ⓓ prepared food

63. The article mentions festivals in Pennsylvania, Louisiana, Indiana, and Ohio that feature which of the following?

Ⓐ insect races

Ⓑ insect dishes

Ⓒ insect-free zones

Ⓓ pesticides for controlling insects

GO ON

ISAT Reading and Writing Posttest

Posttest

64. Which contains the most protein per gram?
- Ⓐ beef
- Ⓑ caterpillars
- Ⓒ termites
- Ⓓ weevils

65. According to the article, which organization has long taught people how to harvest and eat bugs?
- Ⓐ schools (through their lunch programs)
- Ⓑ the U.S. military
- Ⓒ the Consumer Product Safety Commission
- Ⓓ the Food and Drug Administration

66. What is the author's overall attitude toward eating insects?
- Ⓐ She generally favors the eating of insects.
- Ⓑ She is generally opposed to the eating of insects.
- Ⓒ She is extremely opposed to the eating of insects.
- Ⓓ She demands that people begin eating insects immediately.

67. With which claim made in this article would Americans be least likely to agree?
- Ⓐ that some insects contain as much protein per gram as beef, chicken, or pork
- Ⓑ that many insects contain valuable minerals like iron and calcium
- Ⓒ that insects require less land and fewer resources than livestock
- Ⓓ that insects taste good

PART 1: ISAT for Reading
SESSION 3

68. Which type of insect is mentioned in the article as an ingredient used to stuff tortillas?

    Ⓐ caterpillars
    Ⓑ Bogong moths
    Ⓒ crickets
    Ⓓ agave worms

69. What does the article mention as one source of the greenhouse gas methane?

    Ⓐ construction sites
    Ⓑ cows
    Ⓒ insects
    Ⓓ sewage facilities

Posttest

Extended-Response Question

70. Summarize the reasons given in this article supporting the eating of insects. Why does the author think that insects would be a good "Food of the Future"?

_____

_____

_____

_____

_____

_____

_____

_____

_____

_____

_____

_____

_____

_____

_____

_____

_____

End of PART 1: SESSION 3

STOP

Note to Students: Your written response will be scored using a rubric like the one on page 50.

ISAT for Writing: SESSION 1

You will have forty minutes to write your essay. Use your own paper.

> **Narrative Prompt**
> It's always nice when someone does something special for us or surprises us by giving us something unexpected. Sometimes people do nice things to help each other out or simply to make someone happy. Describe a time when you did something special for someone you care about or gave something special to someone. Discuss the event, your reasons for doing it, and the person's reaction.

End of PART 2: SESSION 1

Note to Students: Your written response will be scored using a rubric like the one on pages 51–53.

Posttest

ISAT for Writing: SESSION 2

Write **one** essay. Choose between the persuasive and the expository prompt. You will have forty minutes to write your essay. Use your own paper.

Persuasive Prompt

As a way of increasing students' test scores and overall scholastic performance, some people have suggested that students should be required to go to school on Saturdays. Do you agree or disagree? The principal of your school is looking for student input on this issue.

Write a persuasive letter to convince the principal of your position on whether students should be required to attend school on Saturdays.

OR

Expository Prompt

Most people have a favorite holiday, and many take part in festive celebrations or traditions specific to their ethnic heritage. Some people even have family traditions that are unique and enjoyable.

Describe a particular celebration, holiday, or tradition and the significance that it has for you, personally, and for your family or community.

End of PART 2: SESSION 2

Note to Students: Your written response will be scored using a rubric like the one on pages 54–56.

Glossary

Abstract. 1. Simplified or reduced to its barest elements. 2. General, not concrete.

Achievement test. A test that measures what a student has learned. See *aptitude test*.

Active reading. The process of engaging critically and creatively with a text by asking questions, visualizing, predicting, drawing conclusions, summarizing, paraphrasing, evaluating, connecting, and extending.

Active vocabulary. All the words that a person uses when speaking and writing. Compare with *passive vocabulary*.

Active voice. Grammatical construction of a declarative sentence in which the subject (the doer of the action) comes before the verb (the action). *Dan washed the car* is a sentence in the active voice. Compare with *passive voice*.

Ad hominem. Latin, meaning "to the person." A type of argument in which a person casts doubts on an opposing opinion by attacking the person holding the opinion rather than the opinion itself.

Alliteration. The repetition of initial consonant sounds, as in "deep, dank, dark, dangerous, dewy, and dim."

Analogy. An extended comparison of one thing to another, usually to make a particular point.

Analysis. The process of breaking something down into its parts and studying the characteristics of the parts, how the parts function, and how they relate to one another and to the whole.

Anecdote. A very brief story, often a true one, told to make a point.

Antagonist. A character or force who struggles against the protagonist, or main character, in a story. See *protagonist*.

Antithesis. 1. A rhetorical technique in which two ideas are strongly contrasted, as in "Art is long; life, short." 2. An opposing idea or argument. See *dialectic organization, synthesis*.

Antonym. A word that is opposite or nearly opposite in meaning to another word. *Cold* and *hot* are antonyms. See *synonym*.

Apposition. A word or phrase that follows another word or phrase, functions as the same part of speech, and provides an explanation, description, or definition of the word or phrase that it follows. In the following sentence, the italicized phrase is an apposition: J. K. Rowling, *author of the Harry Potter books*, is from Edinburgh, Scotland.

Aptitude test. A test that attempts to measure an individual's underlying ability or potential. See *achievement test*.

Arrangement. See *organization*.

Authoritative. Knowledgeable, expert. Said of a source of information, such as an encyclopedia or a human expert.

Autobiography. The true story of a person's life, or of some part thereof, as told by that person. See *biography*.

Base word. A complete word that is combined with one or more word parts to form a new word. The base word *place* appears, for example, in the words *misplace* and *placemat*.

Benchmark. A standard or point of reference in measuring or judging quality or value. In testing, the term is used to refer to a statement from a set of state standards that describes a concept or skill that students are expected to master at a particular level in their education.

Biography. The true story of a person's life, or of some part thereof, as told by someone else.

Body. In an essay, the main part of the piece of writing. It appears after the introduction and before the conclusion and supports, or elaborates upon, the thesis statement.

Brainstorming. A technique for generating ideas whereby one or more people list as many ideas on a topic as possible in as short a time as possible, without stopping to evaluate or critique the ideas.

Caption. Text that describes or explains an illustration.

Cause. An event that brings about or helps to bring about one or more other events (the effects). See *effect*.

Character. A person, animal, or other entity that takes part in or affects the action of a literary work.

Character analysis. The act of thinking about a character's features, including appearance, temperament, behavior, relationships, or motives and any changes in the character during the course of the story.

Chronological order. Time order.

Class. A group or collection, or a subset of a larger whole.

Classification. The act of dividing things into groups, or classes, based on characteristics or features.

Classroom test. A test given to measure concepts and skills taught in class.

Clause. A group of words that has a subject and a verb.

Cliché. An overused word, phrase, or idea. *Quiet as a mouse* is a cliché.

Climax. The peak of interest or suspense in a story. The climax is sometimes, but not always, the same event as the crisis. See *crisis*.

Clincher sentence. A sentence that appears at or near the end of a paragraph and that summarizes or otherwise concludes the paragraph.

Cluster chart. See *word web*.

Coherent organization. The arrangement of ideas in a piece of writing in such a way that each idea follows reasonably from the one before it and leads reasonably to the one after it.

Comparison. 1. The act of showing the ways in which two or more things are similar. 2. The act of showing the similarities and differences between two or among more than two things. See *contrast*.

Complex sentence. A sentence that contains one independent clause and one or more dependent clauses.

Compound-complex sentence. A sentence that contains more than one independent clause and one or more dependent clauses.

Compound sentence. A sentence that contains more than one independent clause.

Compound word. A word made up of two or more base words, as in *eightfold* or *break-down*. Compounds can be solid, meaning the word is unbroken, as in *spacecraft*; hyphenated, as in *space-time*; or open, as in *space shuttle*.

Conclusion. The final part of an essay, which sums up the piece and/or gives the reader the sense of an ending.

Conflict. A struggle experienced by a character in a narrative. See *external conflict, internal conflict*.

Connecting. An active reading strategy that involves thinking about the ways in which information or ideas in the text relate to one's own life.

Constructive argument. 1. A reason that a person gives for accepting his or her point of view. 2. Part of a debate or other oral or written presentation that presents one or more such reasons.

Context. The material that appears near a word in a reading passage. Often, the word(s) or phrase(s) around an unfamiliar word will provide clues to its meaning.

Context clue. In a reading passage, any word or phrase that provides information about the meaning of another word in that passage.

Contrast. The act of showing the ways in which two or more things differ.

Creative thinking. Any thinking that results in uncommon, original ideas. Some techniques for creative thinking include creative combinations, doubting deeply, and asking "what if" questions.

Crisis. The point in a story where something happens to resolve the conflict faced by the central character or characters. Also called the *turning point*.

Criterion-referenced test. A test that assesses a student's ability to meet a set of standards for achievement.

Critical thinking. Any thinking that involves reasoning to arrive at knowledge or truth. Types of critical thinking include careful observation, comparison, contrast, cause-and-effect reasoning, and analysis.

Dangling modifier. A word or phrase that is supposed to be a modifier but that appears in a sentence containing no word or phrase that the word or phrase can reasonably modify. The italicized phrase in this sentence is a dangling modifier: *After washing the car*, the real fun began.

Dead metaphor. A metaphor, such as *night fell* or *the heart of the problem*, that is so commonly used and so familiar that people rarely even recognize that it is a metaphor at all. See *metaphor*.

Deduction. 1. A kind of argument in which, if the premises are true, the conclusion has to be true. 2. A conclusion reached by deduction. Compare with *induction*.

Define. To explain the meaning of a term. A typical dictionary definition does this by first placing the item to be defined into a general class and then showing how it differs from other members of that class. For example, "A conifer is a tree (general class) that does not lose its leaves in the winter (difference from other members of the class)."

Definition, direct. See *restatement*.

Degree order. The organization of ideas or information from more to less or from less to more with regard to some characteristic or quality. Examples of organization by degree order include organization in order of familiarity, in order of importance, and in order of value.

Dénouement. Everything that happens after the central conflict in a story is ended, or resolved. The dénouement is the last part of a conventional plot. A writer may include a dénouement in a story in order to tie up loose ends.

Dependent clause, or subordinate clause. A group of words that has a subject and a verb but cannot stand alone as a sentence. See *independent clause*.

Descriptive writing. Writing that uses words to create a portrait of a subject.

Dialectic organization. In a piece of writing, an arrangement of ideas that begins with one position (the *thesis*), then presents an opposing position (the *antithesis*), and finally presents a compromise between the two positions (the *synthesis*).

Diary. See *journal*.

Diction. Word choice. The choice between, for example, *sweat* and *perspiration* is one of diction.

Direct definition. See *restatement*.

Distractor. Any one of the incorrect answers in a multiple-choice question.

Drafting. The stage of the writing process in which the writer gets his or her ideas down on paper in rough form.

Drama. A literary work (play) in which events and themes are presented through stage directions and the dialogue of characters.

Dynamic character. A character who changes during the course of a narrative. See *static character*.

Effect. One or more events that are caused by one or more other events. See *cause*.

"Either/or" argument. See *false dichotomy*.

Elaboration. 1. The act of providing additional ideas or information in support of an idea, position, or description. Writers elaborate by including specific details, examples, facts, opinions, paraphrases, quotations, reasons, and summaries. 2. Any statement that supports a topic sentence or thesis statement. See *supporting details, thesis*.

Ellipsis. Three or four dots (...) used to show that material is missing from a quotation. An ellipsis can also indicate a pause in hesitant or faltering speech.

Endnote. A note that appears at the end of a document to define an unfamiliar term or to provide other information beyond that given in the text.

Essay. A short piece of nonfiction writing that explores a single part of a subject.

Etymology. 1. The study of the origins and history of the meaning of a word. 2. In a dictionary entry, the part of the entry that explains the origins or history of the entry word.

Evaluating. The act of making judgments about something, such as a piece of writing. Evaluating is an important active reading strategy and is essential for revising a piece of writing.

Evidence. Information provided to prove or support a general statement or opinion.

Example. Something selected to show the nature or character of the rest; a typical instance. Examples are a type of elaboration; they can also provide context clues for any unfamiliar words.

Exclamatory sentence. A sentence that expresses strong feeling and that ends with an exclamation point (!).

Exposition. The part of a plot, usually appearing at the beginning, which introduces the characters and setting and provides essential background information.

Expository writing. Writing that presents information. Also known as *informative writing*.

Expressive writing. Writing that is personal and subjective and that exists primarily to convey or embody the thoughts and feelings of the writer.

Extended-response question. A type of test question that asks the student to generate his or her own, often lengthy, response to a question.

Extending. Connecting ideas or information in a piece of writing to the world outside the piece of writing. Extending is an active reading strategy.

External conflict. A struggle between a character and an outside force, such as nature or another character. See *internal conflict*.

Fable. A short tale with animal characters that is told to illustrate a moral. See *moral, parable*.

Fact. A statement that can be proved to be true, either by definition or by observation.

Fallacy. An unreasonable mode of argument or an error in reasoning or logic.

Glossary 467

Falling action. The plot events that occur after the crisis, or turning point.

False analogy. A comparison that falsely assumes that because two subjects are superficially similar, they share other, deeper similarities.

False dichotomy. A logical fallacy in which a speaker or writer falsely assumes that only two alternatives are possible. Also known as *"either/or" argument*.

Fiction. A story about imaginary characters and events. Compare with *nonfiction*.

Figure of speech. Nonliteral language, including personifications, similes, and metaphors.

Final draft. A final version of a piece of writing—one that has been revised and, perhaps, proofread.

First-person point of view. The narrative standpoint from which the narrator tells the story using pronouns like *I* and *we*. Usually, in stories told from the first-person point of view, the narrator is a character in the story.

Five-paragraph theme. See *standard classroom theme*.

Flashback. A part of a narrative that presents an event or series of events that occurred earlier than the current time in the work.

Focus. The quality that a piece of writing has when it does not wander off topic.

Folktale. A story that originated in the oral tradition and that has been passed down by word of mouth from generation to generation.

Footnote. A note at the bottom of a page that defines a difficult or unfamiliar term or provides other information beyond that given in the text.

Foreshadowing. In a narrative, any hint about events to come.

Formal language. Language appropriate to ceremonial public occasions or audiences.

Freewriting. A technique for generating ideas whereby one simply begins writing about a topic, putting down any and all ideas that come to mind, without stopping to edit and without worrying about grammar, usage, mechanics, spelling, or manuscript form.

Function. What something does; its purpose.

Generalization. A process of thinking by which a person arrives at a broad conclusion based upon specific facts. Same as *induction*.

Genre. A form or type of written work, such as the business letter, the persuasive essay, or the historical novel.

Gobbledygook. Overly complicated, overblown, or obscure language, especially official or legal language that "muddies the waters to make them look deep."

Graphic organizer. A chart, outline, or other visual representation of ideas or information. These tools can be used for any of a wide range of purposes, such as notetaking, planning pieces of writing, or presenting ideas to others.

Heading. A subhead that appears within a reading selection.

How-to essay. An essay that describes how to carry out some process, such as baking a cake or buying a house.

Image. A word or phrase that names something that can be seen, heard, touched, tasted, or smelled.

Imperative sentence. A sentence that gives a command or makes a request.

Implied topic sentence. A main idea that is suggested by a paragraph but not stated outright. See *topic sentence*.

Inciting incident. The part of the plot in which the central conflict is introduced.

Independent clause. A group of words that has a subject and a verb and that can stand alone as a sentence.

Induction. 1. A kind of argument in which a general conclusion is drawn from specific facts. 2. A conclusion reached by induction. See *deduction*.

Inference. 1. A conclusion drawn from a set of facts. 2. A reasoned argument from one or more premises to a conclusion. Types of inference include *induction* and *deduction*.

Informal language. Language appropriate to casual, nonpublic occasions or audiences.

Informative writing. Writing that primarily presents facts, not opinions.

Internal conflict. A struggle that takes place within a character. Compare with *external conflict*.

Interrogative sentence. A sentence that asks a question and that ends with a question mark (?).

Introduction. The beginning part of a piece of nonfiction writing that presents necessary background information and the main idea, or thesis. Introductions are usually meant to capture the reader's attention.

Inverted pyramid organization. In a piece of writing, an arrangement of ideas that begins by answering the so-called reporter's questions (Who? What? Where? When? Why? and How?) and then presents additional information in order from most to least important. This method of organization is widely used in newspaper stories.

Inverted word order. The placement of words in a sentence in an order that is not usual or normal. *Works hard, he does* is a sentence that makes use of inverted word order.

Irony. A contradiction, such as a difference between what something appears to be and what it really is, or between what is said and what is meant.

Jargon. Language associated with a field of human endeavor. *Bandwidth* and *gigabyte* are words from the jargon of computing.

Journal. A day-by-day account of thoughts, events, or any other happenings or impressions that a person wishes to record. Also called a *diary*.

Leader line. The part of a multiple-choice question that comes before the answers. Sometimes the leader line is a question. Sometimes it is an incomplete statement that should be completed by the correct answer.

Learning log. A journal in which a person records what he or she has learned.

Legend. A story, which may be partially or wholly true, about a hero or heroine from times past. See *fable, myth*.

Level of language. The degree of formality or informality of the language being used. See *register*.

Loaded word. A word that has strong emotional content, used to sway opinion.

Logical organization. The arrangement of ideas in a piece of writing in an order that makes sense. See also *organization*.

Main idea. The most important idea in a paragraph or writing selection.

Manuscript form. The layout of a piece of writing, including its spacing, margin width, indention of paragraphs, and placement of titles, captions, headings, and page numbers.

Metaphor. A figure of speech in which one thing is described as if it were another, as in *that undefeated wrestler, the sea*.

Minor character. A character who does not play a major role in a story.

Misplaced modifier. A word or phrase placed in a sentence in such a way that it modifies the wrong word or phrase. The italicized phrase in this sentence is a misplaced modifier: *Taking pictures with their digital cameras*, the monkeys gave the tourists quite a treat.

Mode. A kind of writing, as determined by that writing's purpose. Common modes of writing include expressive, narrative, descriptive, expository, and persuasive.

Modifier. Grammatical term referring to a word, phrase, or clause that limits (by making more specific) the meaning of another word, phrase, or clause. Adjectives, adverbs, adjective phrases, adverb phrases, and other parts of speech that perform this function are examples of modifiers.

Mood. An emotional quality, such as gloom or joy, that is created by a passage in a literary work or by the work as a whole.

Moral. The lesson contained in or taught by a fable or story. See *fable, parable*.

Motivation. 1. A reason that impels a character to think, feel, or act in a certain way; an incentive. 2. The state of being moved to think, feel, or act.

Motive. A reason that impels a character to think, feel, or act in a certain way; an incentive.

Multiple-choice question. A type of test question in which the student chooses the correct answer from among several possibilities.

Myth. A story that deals with gods or goddesses. Many myths explain the origins of natural phenomena. See *legend*.

Narrative. A story, either fiction or nonfiction.

Narrative writing. Writing that tells a story.

Narrator. The person or voice that tells a story.

Necessary cause. A cause that must exist in order for a particular effect to occur.

Negation. A statement that contradicts another statement.

Nonfiction. Writing about real people, places, things, or ideas. Compare with *fiction*.

Non sequitur. Latin, meaning "It does not follow." A conclusion that does not follow, logically, from the available facts or evidence.

Novel. A long piece of narrative fiction.

Objective. Presenting only verified facts and not personal opinions. News reports, for example, must be as objective as possible.

Onomatopoeia. The use of words or phrases, like *buzz* or *meow*, that sound like what they describe.

Opinion. A statement that cannot be proved, absolutely, to be true or false. Common types of opinion include predictions and statements of value, belief, policy, and obligation.

Oral tradition. Within a particular culture, the heritage of songs, stories, poems, and other materials passed down by word of mouth before the widespread use of writing.

Order of impression. Arrangement of details in a piece of writing in order of the impact that they make on a viewer or in the order in which a person might typically encounter them.

Organization. The way a piece of writing is ordered, or the principle by which its parts are arranged. Common methods of organization include chronological order, spatial order, degree order, and part-by-part order. See also *dialectic organization*.

Overgeneralization. The act of making an inference based on too little evidence. See also *stereotyping*.

Parable. A short tale with human characters that is told to illustrate a moral. See *fable, moral*.

Paragraph. A unit of writing, usually containing more than one sentence, that communicates a main idea. A *paragraph in standard form* is a unit of writing containing a topic sentence, two or more supporting sentences, and, usually, a concluding or clincher sentence.

Parallelism. The use of similar grammatical forms to give items equal weight, as in Abraham Lincoln's "of the people, by the people, for the people."

Paraphrase. 1. (*v.*) To repeat in different words an idea taken from another speaker or writer. 2. (*n.*) A piece of speech or writing that repeats, in different words, an idea taken from another speaker or writer.

Part-by-part order. An arrangement in which ideas do not follow any overall organizational pattern, but each idea is logically connected to the one before it and to the one that follows it.

Participial phrase. A group of words that begins with a participle and that acts, as a group, as an adjective, modifying a noun or a pronoun, as in "the moon *peeking over the horizon*." See *participle*.

Participle. A verb form ending in *–ing*, *–ed*, *–d*, *–t*, or *–en* that functions as an adjective to modify a noun or pronoun, as in *singing* sailors, *broken* window, or *burnt* toast.

Passive vocabulary. All the words that a person understands but does not use in his or her writing or speech. See *active vocabulary*.

Passive voice. Grammatical construction of a declarative sentence in which the doer of the action is either omitted from the sentence or follows the verb (the action) in a prepositional phrase. *The car was washed by Dan* is a sentence in the passive voice. Compare with *active voice*.

Personification. The art of describing something nonhuman as though it were human, as in *the icy breath of the wind*.

Persuasion. The attempt, in writing or in speech, to convince an audience to take some action or to adopt some belief or point of view.

Persuasive writing. Writing that attempts to convince the reader to adopt a particular belief or viewpoint or to take a course of action.

Plot. The series of events in a story, often involving the introduction, intensification, and eventual resolution of a conflict. A plot may contain the following parts: introduction, or exposition; rising action; climax; crisis, or turning point; falling action; resolution; and dénouement.

Plot analysis. The act of identifying and thinking about the parts of the plot of a story. See *plot*.

Poetry. Language used in an exceptional or unusual way to communicate an idea or experience more powerfully than in ordinary speech or prose. Compare with *prose*.

Point of view. The standpoint from which a story is told.

Post hoc ergo propter hoc. Latin, meaning "after this; therefore, because of this." A logical fallacy in which two events are assumed, falsely, to have a cause-and-effect relationship simply because they occurred one after the other.

Predicate. Grammatical term referring to the part of a sentence or clause that is not the subject, including the verb and its attached modifiers or complements. See *subject*.

Prediction. An opinion about what will happen in the future. Predicting is an excellent active reading strategy.

Prefix. A word part, such as *de-*, *in-*, or *mono-*, added to the beginning of a word or word part, as in *de-* + *value* = *devalue*.

Preposition. A word or group of words placed before a noun or nounlike word to indicate the relation of that word to a verb, adjective, or other noun or nounlike word. Examples of prepositions include *at, beyond, during, in spite of, except,* and *without.*

Prepositional phrase. A group of words that includes a preposition and its object, as in *across the bay* or *in regard to your letter.* See *preposition.*

Prereading. See *previewing.*

Previewing. Activities that a reader can carry out before reading a selection, including skimming, scanning, thinking about the topic, and posing questions. Also called *prereading.*

Prewriting. The stage of the writing process in which the writer carries out such preliminary activities as choosing a topic, focusing the topic, gathering ideas, and organizing ideas.

Prior knowledge. What you already know about a subject.

Proofreading. The act of looking over a piece of writing and correcting errors in spelling, grammar, usage, punctuation, capitalization, and manuscript form.

Propaganda. The systematic spread or promotion of particular ideas, beliefs, practices, etc., especially by means of deception or distortion. Slander, loaded words, and fallacies are examples of propaganda techniques. See also *loaded word, rhetoric, rhetorical device.*

Prose. Writing that is organized into sentences and paragraphs rather than into lines of verse, as in poetry.

Protagonist. The main character in a story, usually one who experiences some conflict, or struggle, and who goes through some important change. Compare with *antagonist.*

Publishing. The act of making a piece of writing available to others, as by distributing copies, posting it on the Internet or in an e-mail, or reading it aloud.

Purpose. What the writer wants to accomplish. See also *mode.*

Qualification. A limitation, restriction, or modification; a word or phrase that limits or modifies the meaning of another word or phrase.

Quotation. The exact words of another speaker or writer, repeated verbatim (word for word).

Reading comprehension. The process of making meaning from a text.

Reading process. A systematic approach to reading that includes specific activities done before, during, and after reading. These activities include *previewing* and *posing questions* (before reading), using *active reading strategies* such as *predicting* and *connecting* (during reading), and *reflecting* and *responding* (after reading).

Reasonable opinion. An opinion that is supported by facts and consistent with accepted values.

Rebuttal argument. A reason that a person gives for rejecting an opposing point of view.

Recording. Taking notes on what you are hearing, seeing, or reading.

Reference work. An authoritative source of information, such as a dictionary, almanac, encyclopedia, atlas, or database.

Reflecting. 1. The process of thinking seriously about something. 2. In the reading process, part of what one does after reading. Reflecting after reading might include summarizing the reading, answering one's prereading questions, and evaluating the reading.

Register. The degree of formality or informality of the language being used. See *level of language.*

Repetition. The use, again, of any element, such as a sound word, phrase, or image, in order to create an effect.

Resolution. The part of a plot in which the central conflict is ended (resolved).

Responding. Thinking about and otherwise reacting to what you are hearing, seeing, or reading.

Restatement. A context clue in which the meaning of a word is stated again in other words. Also known as *direct definition.*

Revising. Making changes to improve aspects of a piece of writing, including its focus, content, accuracy, interest, organization, degree of formality, appropriateness to the audience, voice, mood, and tone.

Rhetoric. 1. The art of using speech or writing to move or persuade others. 2. The art of oral or written composition.

Rhetorical device. A technique in which a writer or speaker uses language in a special way in order to create an emotional impact on his or her reader(s) or listener(s). Examples of rhetorical devices include *antithesis, parallelism,* and *rhetorical questions.*

Rhetorical question. A question that is not meant to be answered because the answer is presumed to be clear or self-evident.

Rising action. The part of the plot in which the central conflict is developed.

Root. A basic word part that carries primary meaning in a word even though it cannot stand alone as a word. Examples of roots include *capt* in *captive* and *capture* and *dem* in *democracy* and *endemic*.

Rough draft. A preliminary, unfinished version of a piece of writing. See *final draft*.

Rough outline. An brief outline containing main ideas above supporting ideas that are introduced by dashes (—).

Rubric. A listing or explanation of the standards by which a piece of writing will be evaluated.

Satire. Literary work that uses humor to point out the flaws of someone or something.

Scanning. Looking through a piece of writing quickly to find specific parts or specific information.

Sensory details. Details that tell how something looks, tastes, smells, sounds, or feels.

Sentence. A group of words that is grammatically complete and that expresses a complete idea. (Exception: A single word can be a sentence if that word is an imperative verb with an implied subject, as in "Wait!")

Sentence combining. The act of putting separate sentences together into a single sentence.

Sentence expanding. Revision of a sentence by adding material, such as words, phrases, or clauses, to it.

Sentence fragment. A group of words that does not form a complete sentence.

Sentence frame. A simple sentence to which parts can be added to make more complicated sentences.

Sequence. The order of events in a piece of writing.

Setting. The time and place in which the action of a work of literature occurs.

Short story. A brief work of fiction.

Significance. Importance, meaning.

Simile. A figure of speech in which unlike things are compared using *like*, *as*, or *than*, as in "Spring came like a freight train, fast and furious." See *metaphor*.

Simple sentence. A sentence that does not contain any dependent, or subordinate, clauses.

Skimming. Looking over a piece of writing quickly to get a general idea about its content.

Slang. Highly informal language, often originating with a particular social group and not accepted as "proper" by the larger society around that group.

Standard classroom theme. An essay that contains an introductory paragraph, two or three body paragraphs that support the thesis given in the introductory paragraph, and a concluding paragraph.

Standardized test. A test or group of tests, like the Iowa Tests of Basic Skills, used to compare the skills of individuals and groups.

Statement of belief. An opinion that a person thinks is true but that he or she cannot prove beyond doubt.

Statement of obligation. An opinion about what individuals or groups of people should or should not do.

Statement of policy. An opinion about what should or should not be done by a group as a matter of course.

Statement of value. An opinion about the worth (value) of something.

Static character. A character who does not change or develop in the course of a story. See *dynamic character*.

Statistic. Information presented in numerical form.

Stereotyping. The act of unfairly attributing a quality to a whole group of people or to an individual based upon an unfair characterization of the group to which he or she belongs. Stereotyping is often a kind of *overgeneralization*.

Stringy sentence. A sentence that contains many clauses loosely combined with conjunctions such as *and* or *but*.

Structure. How something is organized or put together.

Style. The features that characterize a piece of writing, especially those features that are chosen by the writer as a matter of technique, such as alliteration, rhythm, inverted word order, word choice, and sentence complexity. Style creates voice. See *voice*.

Subject. 1. What a piece of writing is about. 2. In grammar, the doer of the action of the verb. The subject and the predicate, together, make up a clause or sentence. See *predicate*.

Subordinate clause. See *dependent clause.*

Sufficient cause. A cause that is enough, by itself, to bring about some effect.

Suffix. A word part, such as *-al, -ment,* or *-tion,* added to the end of a word or word part, as in *merry + -ment = merriment.*

Summarize. To repeat, in fewer and different words, an idea or ideas taken from another speaker or writer. Summarizing is an excellent active reading strategy.

Supporting detail. A fact, opinion, example, or other kind of detail related to a main idea.

Suspense. A feeling of curiosity or expectation, often accompanied by anxiety, created by raising questions in the reader's mind about the outcome of events in a literary work.

Symbol. Something that stands for something else. A rose is a traditional symbol of love and beauty. An ampersand (&) is one symbol for the word *and.*

Synonym. A word that is the same or similar in meaning to another word. *Gigantic* and *enormous* are synonyms. See *antonym.*

Synthesis. A type of thinking in which separate or conflicting ideas are combined to create or support a new idea. See *antithesis, dialectic organization,* and *thesis.*

Tall tale. A story with wildly exaggerated characters and events.

Theme. A main idea conveyed by a literary work. In a story, the theme is often something that the main character learns as a result of the main conflict in the story.

Thesis. 1. In an essay, a one- or two-sentence statement of the main idea. The thesis usually appears in the introduction and often appears again, in other words, in the conclusion. Also called the *thesis statement.* 2. The first part of a three-part argument that consists of a *thesis* (or initial idea), an *antithesis* (or contradictory idea), and a *synthesis* (which combines the thesis and antithesis).

Thesis statement. One or more sentences that express the main idea, or thesis, of an extended piece of nonfiction writing such as an essay.

Third-person point of view. The narrative standpoint from which the narrator tells the story using pronouns like *he, she, it,* and *they.* In stories told from the third-person point of view, the narrator reports but does not directly participate in the action.

Tone. The attitude conveyed by the voice of a narrator or character.

Topic sentence. In a paragraph, a sentence that expresses the main idea.

Transition. See *transitional words and phrases.*

Transitional words and phrases. Words and phrases, such as *after, then, next, as a result, in summary,* and *therefore,* used to show connections between or among ideas.

Turning point. The point in a story where something happens to determine the ultimate fate of the central character or characters. Also called the *crisis.*

Verify. To confirm or prove the truth of a statement of fact by making one or more observations or by checking one or more authoritative sources of information, such as reference works or experts.

Visualizing. An active reading strategy in which you picture something in your mind.

Vocabulary. 1. All the words of a language. 2. The sum of words used or understood by a particular person or group.

Voice. The sum of all the qualities that make a writer's work sound unique. Voice is created by a writer's style. See *style.*

Word choice. See *diction.*

Word family. A group of words that all share the same root. *Asterisk, astronomy,* and *disaster* all share the root *aster,* meaning "star," and thus all belong to the same word family.

Word web. A type of graphic organizer that displays a main idea surrounded by and connected to related ideas. Also called a *cluster chart.*

Wordiness. The use of many words when few will do.

Writing process. All the stages through which a writer passes while completing a piece of writing, including prewriting, drafting, evaluating and revising, proofreading, and publishing.

Writing prompt. Directions or instructions for creating a piece of writing, especially for a writing test.

Glossary **473**

Index

A
abridged dictionary, 212
abstract words, 373
achievement test, 41
action verb, 359; common, 359
action words, in prompts, 251–52
active reading strategies, 111–12
active vocabulary, 72
active voice, 293
ad hominem, 226
adjective, 373
almanac, 212
analogy, 308, 330
analysis, 197, 221, 394–95
analysis chart, 84, 87, 239
analyzing prompts, 250–52; a story, 146–49
answer choices, 44
antagonist, 145
antithesis, 224, 259
antonym, 63
apposition, 63
appositive, 286, 373; phrase, 286, 288
aptitude test, 41
argument(s), constructive, 223; rebuttal, 223
atlas, 212
audience, 168, 241, 349
author, 104
authoritative, 190
autobiography, 172

B
base word, 67
benchmark, 41
biography, 172
body paragraph(s), 324, 332–34
brainstorming, 245

C
caption, 105
cause(s), 127–29, 196, 259, 308; necessary, 196; sufficient, 196
cause-and-effect chart, 84, 85, 239
cause-and-effect order, 259, 311
cause-and-effect question(s), 127–29
character(s), 145; analysis of, 146–47; dynamic, 145; minor, 145; static, 145
character analysis, 146–47
character analysis chart, 84, 87
characteristics, 145, 384
chart(s), analysis, 84, 87, 239; cause-and-effect, 84, 85, 239; character analysis, 84, 87; cluster, 84, 85; column (bar), 84, 89; comparison-and-contrast, 84, 88, 239; cycle, 84, 89, 239; double-entry (T-chart), 84, 86, 239; flow, 84, 92, 239; paragraph-planning, 84, 90, 239; pie, 84, 90; pro-and-con, 84, 87, 239; reporter's questions, 84, 91, 239; sensory detail, 84, 89, 239
chronological (time) order, 174, 255, 311
classification order, 257
classifying, 194, 257
classroom test, 41
clause(s), 282; dependent, 282, 286; independent, 282; subordinate, 282
cliché, 375
climax, 148
clincher sentence, 305, 314
cluster chart, 84, 85, 239
coherent organization, 255
column (bar) chart, 84, 89
comparison, 63, 195, 251
comparison-and-contrast chart, 84, 88, 239
comparison-and-contrast order, 256; by features, 257; by similarities and differences, 257; by subject, 256
complex sentence(s), 282
compound-complex sentence(s), 283
compound sentence(s), 282
compound word, 67
comprehension, reading, 115–36
concluding sentence, 305, 314
conclusion, 324, 338–39
concrete words, 373
conflict(s), 145, 174; external, 145, 174; internal, 145, 174
conjunction(s), 282; coordinating, 282
connecting, 112
constructive argument, 223
context, 63
context clue, 49, 63
contrast, 63, 195, 251
coordinating conjunction(s), 282
creative doubt, 404
creative juxtaposition, 401
creative thinking, 400–08
crisis, 148
criteria, 398
criterion-referenced test, 41
critical thinking, 384–99
cycle chart, 84, 89, 239

D
dangling modifier, 295
declarative sentence, 280
deduction, 130, 390–91
deductive organization, 260
deductive reasoning, 225
define, 197, 251
degree order, 258, 311
dénouement, 148
dependent clause, 282, 286
derived word, 67
description, 251, 308
descriptive writing, 169
dialectic organization, 259
diction, 355
dictionary, 212
direct quotation, 334
direction line, 104
discuss, 246, 251
distractor, 44
double-entry ledger (T-chart), 84, 86, 239
drafting, 239, 264, 329, 332–34
dynamic character, 145

E
effect(s), 127–29, 196, 259, 308
"either/or" argument, 227
"either/or" thinking, 401
elaboration, 307–08, 333
encyclopedia, 212
essay(s), 322–26; expository, 49, 323; graphic organizer for, 325; how-to, 193; informative, 323; model of, 324; narrative, 49, 323; personal, 323; persuasive, 49, 323; rubrics, 50–56; types of, 323
evaluation, 112, 252, 265–66, 273, 398
evaluation and revision checklist, 265–66
event, 174, 308
evidence, 218
example(s), 308, 373
exclamatory sentence, 280
expanding sentences, 286–87
explain, 252
exposition, 148
expository essay, 49, 323; ISAT rubric, 54–56; writing, 169, 188, 419–22
expressive writing, 169
extended-response question(s), 44, 48; ISAT rubric, 50
extending, 112
external conflict, 145, 174
external motivation, 128, 145
external narrator, 144

F

fact(s), 211, 308; types of, 212–13
fallacy, 226
falling action, 148
false analogy, 226
false dichotomy, 227
fiction, 137–62
figurative language, 224
figure of speech, 308, 375
first-person point of view, 145, 168, 174
flashback, 126, 256
flow chart, 84, 92, 239
focus, 253
focusing a topic, 242
foreshadowing, 126, 256
form, 251
formal language, 350, 352
fragment, 294
freewriting, 245
Freytag's pyramid, 149
function, of a sentence, 280
function(s), 385

G

gathering ideas, 245–47, 253
generalization, 387
genre, 170, 241, 251
gobbledygook, 358
graphic organizer(s), 73–94, 239, 246, 253; *see also* analysis chart, 84, 87; cause-and-effect chart, 84, 85; character analysis chart, 84, 87; cluster chart, 84, 85; column (bar) chart, 84, 89; comparison-and-contrast chart, 84, 88; cycle chart, 84, 89; double-entry ledger (T-chart), 84, 86; flow chart, 84, 92; line graph, 84, 90; paragraph-planning chart, 84, 90; pie chart, 84, 90; pro-and-con chart, 84, 87; reporter's questions chart, 84, 91; sensory detail chart, 84, 89; timeline, 84, 92, 126; tree diagram, 84, 91; Venn diagram, 84, 86; word web, 84, 85

H

heading (subtitle), 104
heuristics, 384
how-to essay, 193

I

identify, 252
illustration, 105, 308
imperative sentence, 280
implied topic sentence, 307
inciting incident, 148

independent clause, 282
induction, 387, 388
inductive organization, 260
inductive reasoning, 225
inference, 63, 111, 129, 227, 387
inference question(s), 49, 129–30
informal language, 350, 352
informational texts on ISAT, 48
informative nonfiction, 183–202; types of, 188
informative writing, 169, 188–90, 323, 419–22
internal conflict, 145, 174
internal motivation, 128, 145
internal narrator, 144
interrogative sentence, 280
interviewing, 246
introduction, 324, 329–30
ISAT for Reading, 48–49, 50
ISAT for Writing, 48–49, 51–56

J

jargon, 357–58
journal, 43–44
judgment, 214

K

key word(s), 105, 123; in prompts, 251–52
kinesthetic sense, 389

L

language, figurative, 224
leader line, 44
learning log, 72
level, 350
line graph, 84, 90
linking verb, 359
listing, 247, 252
literary reference works, 212
literary works on ISAT, 48
literature, writing about, 409–11
loaded word, 224
logical organization, 255

M

main idea, 80, 123, 168, 190, 305; test questions about, 123
memory, long-term, 72; short-term, 72
metaphor, 224
minor character, 145
misplaced modifier, 295
mode, 169
modifier, 286
mood, 144, 168, 174, 367
motivation, 128, 145; external, 128, 145; internal, 128, 145

motive, 145–46
multiple-choice question(s), 44; how to approach, 45

N

narrative, 144
narrative essay, 49, 323; ISAT rubric, 51–53
narrative fiction, 144; elements of, 144–49
narrative nonfiction, writing, 415–18
narrative writing, 169
narrator, 144, 174
necessary cause, 196
negation, 308
nonfiction, 144, 168, 188; aspects of, 168–69; genres of, 170–71; informative, 188
nonfiction narrative, 163–82, 192; parts of, 174
non sequitur, 226
norm-referenced test, 41
noun, 361

O

objective, 189
observation, 247, 384–85
online reference works, 212
onomatopoeia, 375
opinion(s), 211, 214, 308; reasonable, 218
order, cause-and-effect, 311; chronological (time), 174, 255, 311; degree, 311; part-by-part, 311; problem-solution, 311; spatial, 311
order of impression, 256
organization, 255–60; chronological (time), 255; coherent, 255; deductive, 260; by degree, 258; dialectic, 259; by familiarity, 258; inductive, 260; logical, 255; methods of, 255–60; by order of importance, 258; spatial, 256
outline. *See* rough outline.
overgeneralization, 227, 388

P

paragraph(s), 304; narrative, 304; in standard form, 305
paragraph-planning chart, 84, 90, 239
parallelism, 224, 293
paraphrasing, 112, 308, 334
part-by-part order, 311
participial phrase, 288, 373
participle, 373
passive vocabulary, 72
passive voice, 293
personal essay, 323

persuasion, 210, 221, 252
persuasive essay, 49, 323; ISAT rubric, 54–56; writing, 169, 221, 224, 423–26
persuasive nonfiction, 203–30
phrase, appositive, 286, 288; participial, 288, 373; prepositional, 286, 288, 373
pie chart, 84, 90
plot, 145, 148–49; analysis of, 148–49
plot diagram, 149
point(s) of view, 145, 168, 174; first-person, 145, 168, 174; second-person, 168, 174; third-person, 145, 168, 174
post hoc ergo propter hoc, 226
predicate, 286
prediction, 111, 130, 214
prefix(es), 67; common, 68
prepositional phrase, 286, 288, 373
previewing, 104
prewriting, 239, 241–63, 325–26
pro-and-con chart, 84, 87, 239
problem-solution order, 311
process, 193; of writing, 238–63
prompts, analyzing, 250–52
pronoun, 313
proofreading, 240, 269–73, 292
proofreading checklist, 270
protagonist, 145, 385
publishing, 240
purpose, 168, 241

Q

qualification, 308
questioning, 107, 111
quotations, 308, 334

R

reading comprehension, 115–36
reasoning, deductive, 225; inductive, 225
reasons, 308
rebuttal argument, 223
recalling, 247
reference works, 212
reflect, 112
register, 350
relate, 252
relations, 385
repetition, 224, 293
reporter's questions chart, 84, 91, 239
researching, 246
resolution, 148
respond, 112
restatement, 63
review, 252
revision, 240, 265–68, 273, 292

revision and proofreading symbols, 271
rhetorical device, 224
rhetorical question, 224
rising action, 148
root(s), 67; common, 69
rough outline, 79–80, 253, 326
rubric(s), 50–56, 399
run-on sentence, 294

S

scanning, 104–05
second-person point of view, 168, 174
sensory detail, 308
sensory detail chart, 84, 89, 239
sentence(s), 280–83; active-voice, 293; clincher, 305, 314; combining, 286–89; complex, 282; compound, 282; compound-complex, 283; concluding, 305, 314; declarative, 280; editing, 294–95; exclamatory, 280; expanding, 286–87; fragment, 294; function of, 280; imperative, 280; interrogative, 280; passive-voice, 293; run-on, 294; simple, 281; stringy, 295; structure of, 280, 292; supporting, 305, 307; topic, 305–07, 324
sequence, 126; test questions about, 126
setting, 144, 174
simile, 224
simple sentence(s), 281; types of, 281
skimming, 105
slang, 356–57
spatial order, 256, 311
speaker's tags, 334
standard classroom theme, 323, 324
standardized test, 41
standards, 41
statement(s), of belief, 214; of obligation, 214; of policy, 214; of value, 214
static character, 145
statistics, 308
stereotyping, 227, 388
structure (of a sentence), 280
style, 341–76
subject, 146, 168, 241
subordinate clause, 282
sufficient cause, 196
suffix(es), 67; common, 68
summarizing, 111, 252, 308, 334
supporting detail(s), 80, 125, 190; test questions about, 125
supporting sentence(s), 305
surprise, element of, 375
synonym, 63, 356

synthesis, 259, 401

T

T-chart, 84, 86, 239
test(s), 40–45; achievement, 41; aptitude, 41; classroom, 41; criterion-referenced, 41; ISAT, 48–56; norm-referenced, 41; preparation for, 42–43; rubrics, 50–56; standardized, 41
test-taking strategies, 33–46, 273; for drafting during tests, 264; for prewriting during tests, 250–53
theme, 146, 174
thesaurus, 212, 361
thesis, 259, 323, 324
thesis statement, 242, 253, 326
third-person point of view, 145, 168, 174
timeline, 84, 92, 126, 239
title, 104
tone, 144, 168, 174, 224, 368
topic sentence(s), 305–07, 324; implied, 307
transition(s), 311
transitional words and phrases, 312–13
tree diagram, 84, 91, 239

V

values, 218
Venn diagram, 84, 86, 239
verify, 189
vestibular sense, 389
visualizing, 111
vocabulary, 49, 62–63, 72; active, 72; building, 57–72; passive, 72
voice, 224, 349, 375

W

"what if" questions, 405
word(s), abstract vs. concrete, 373; base, 67; compound, 67; derived, 67; loaded, 224
word choice, 355
word family, 66, 67
word order, inverted, 293
word parts, 66–69
word web, 84, 85, 239
writing, descriptive, 169; expository, 169, 188, 419–22; expressive, 169; informative, 169, 188, 419–22; narrative, 169; persuasive, 169, 221, 224, 423–26
writing prompts, 250–53

Z

zoom in, 256
zoom out, 256